'HE WAS GALWAY'

'HE WAS GALWAY'

Máirtín Mór McDonogh, 1860–1934

Jackie Uí Chionna

OPEN AIR

First published in 2016 by OPEN AIR,
an imprint of FOUR COURTS PRESS
7 Malpas Street, Dublin 8
www.fourcourtspress.ie
and in North America for
Four Courts Press
c/o ISBS, 920 NE 58th Avenue, Suite 300, Portland, OR 97213

A catalogue record for this title is available from the British Library.

ISBN 978-1-84682-625-2

Printed in England
by CPI Antony Rowe, Chippenham, Wilts.

For Eibhlín Uí Chionna (née O'Malley),
a proud Galwegian, who always told a good story

The stationmaster opens a door
And clears a passage for Morty Mor,
For Morty Mor is known to own
The principal works of Galway town.
He is not one of the country set
(Though he helps them out when they lose a bet);
His sawmills hum and he sells cement,
Potash and lime to his heart's content.
The workers he sacks on Saturday night
Are back on Monday morn contrite;
In spite of his temper, deep at the core
The heart's all right in Morty Mor.

– Oliver St John Gogarty, 'πάντα ῥεῖ'
from *Rolling down the Lea*

The impression produced by his extraordinary size and by the curious INHUMAN expression of his eyes was not unpleasant. But it was terrifying. It inspired curiosity and admiration of a strange beauty; the beauty of uniqueness; the beauty of an aged oak, whose twisted massive branches and naked scarred roots are full of majesty.

– Liam O'Flaherty, *The house of gold*

Contents

Illustrations

Acknowledgments

This book could not have been written without the cooperation of a number of individuals and institutions, whose contributions I am happy to acknowledge. My first, and greatest, thanks must be to Thomas McDonogh and Tom McDonogh, (nephew and grand-nephew of Máirtín Mór McDonogh respectively), who commissioned the writing of this book, and who sponsored the research fellowship that produced it. Their enthusiasm and encouragement throughout the research process made the experience all the more enjoyable and productive. My thanks also to NUI Galway, which co-sponsored the fellowship, and to Prof. Daniel Carey and the staff of the Moore Institute for Research in the Humanities and Social Studies, NUI Galway, who provided me with such a wonderfully collegial and supportive environment in which to work.

Prof. Dáibhí Ó Cróinín and Dr John Cunningham of the History Department, NUI Galway, jointly supervised my fellowship, and I could not have asked for better mentors or colleagues. The time, care, and genuine enthusiasm they brought to the task of steering the book through its various stages went way beyond the call of duty, and I will be forever in their debt. Dáibhí's wise counsel was something I could always rely on, and I want to thank John, in particular, for generously sharing with me, as he has always done, his encyclopaedic, and insightful, knowledge of the history of Galway. My heartfelt thanks also to my colleagues at the History Department of NUI Galway, all of whom were unstinting whenever help or advice was sought. In particular, I want to thank Dr Caitriona Clear for her insights into the social history of the period during which McDonogh lived, Dr Niall Ó Ciosáin, who was most generous in helping me translate some of the Irish-language texts, and Dr Laurence Marley for his advice on the writing of biography, and his help with indexing and structure.

I owe an enormous debt of gratitude to my colleague and friend Dr Deirdre Ní Chonghaile, a native of Inis Mór, an expert in the songs of Aran, agus sár-scoláire – gan í, ní bheadh an céad caibidil ann. Mo bhuíochas ó chroí leat a Dheirdre. I also want to thank Dr Máirín Mac Carron, who was the most supportive and erudite of office mates – thank you for your insights, and for your encouragement when the research process hit the odd pothole. Many of my fellow researchers in the Moore Institute provided invaluable help and advice, and I wish to thank two in particular: Dara Folan, who was unfailingly generous in sharing numerous useful finds with me, foinsí as Gaeilge ach go háirithe, and Martin O'Donoghue.

I wish to extend my thanks to the staffs of the many archives I consulted in the course of my research, including: the National Archives in Dublin; the UCD Archives, Belfield; the Irish Jesuit Archives, Leeson Street; the University of London Archives at the Senate House Library, London; the National Archives at Kew; and the Royal Archives at Windsor Castle. I wish to thank, in particular, the special-collections staff at the Hardiman Library, NUI Galway, all of whom made the task of researching the life of Máirtín Mór such a pleasure. I also wish to thank the staff at the Civil Registration Service Galway for assistance with birth, marriage and death certificates. Others who provided great assistance were Patria McWalter, Galway county council archivist, who made available to me the photograph of McDonogh outside the Town Hall in Galway in 1899, and genealogist Cathy O'Neill, who provided much useful information on the Hernon family.

I owe a great debt of gratitude to Galway historian Peadar O'Dowd, whose previous book on the McDonogh family provided invaluable information and access to sources, and to Willie Henry, who has written extensively on Galway history. I am particularly grateful to Tom and Des Kenny, who answered numerous questions, generously read drafts of the book and provided regular doses of constructive criticism and encouragement, for all of which I am deeply in their debt. I am immensely grateful to local historian John Bhaba Jeaic Ó Confhaola, who spent an entire day walking me around the McDonogh homestead of An Crapach and environs, and introduced me to the wealth of sources held at Ionad Oidhreachta Leitir Mealláin agus Gharumna. Míle buíochais a John. I am also grateful to Guy St John Williams, grandson of Oliver St John Gogarty, for permission to use his grandfather's poem, and also for information on Count Stolberg, and McDonogh's racing interests. I am deeply indebted to historian Cormac Ó Comhraí, who first brought 'An Bodach Braon' to my attention, and who was always available to respond to queries, particularly with regard to the revolutionary period in Galway. Tá mé thar a bheith bhuíoch dhuit a Chormaic.

While I owe a great debt to all who have assisted me, in the end, any errors or omissions are mine.

Thanks are due to my editor, Sam Tranum, and all at Four Courts Press, who performed a minor miracle in getting the book out so quickly, and with such courtesy and efficiency. A first book is a major learning curve for any writer, and I was indeed fortunate in being in such safe hands.

Finally, my love and thanks go to my parents, Owen and Kathleen Callan, who always encouraged my interest in history, and to my children, Eoin and Aoife, who patiently shared their mother with 'an fear mór'. To my husband Mícheál, who was with me every step of the way – I could not have done it without you. Mo bhuíochas ó chroí leat.

Introduction

Seán Ó Faoláin, writing in 1940 about one of Galway's most famous sons, the frequently impoverished writer Pádraic Ó Conaire, said of one of Ó Conaire's cousins:

> Martin McDonagh [*sic*] is a polar contrast: the son of a poor man who got a foothold in business and left Martin with a chance to make good. Martin did so well that before he passed on he had become a TD, was chairman of various local councils, owned a saw-mill, a fishing-fleet, a flour-mill, a chemical-works, thriving shops, more or less owned the Galway Steam-Shipping Company, was a director of the gas company, a coal-importer, kept a stud of racehorses, had his own electric power years before the Shannon scheme, owned house property, including the old Claddagh, and lived on Corrib Island.[1] The business still flourishes.[2]

While the description is largely accurate, it underestimates the extent and breadth of the career of the man known to Galwegians as 'Máirtín Mór' McDonogh. In the course of his long life – he died in 1934, aged 74 – McDonogh exceeded the expectations of his father, the founder of the firm Thomas McDonogh & Sons, and in the process became the leading citizen of his native city, earning himself the soubriquet 'Mr Galway'.

What was to become an extraordinarily successful business dynasty had its origins in one of the remotest parts of Connemara, an archipelago in South Connemara known as Ceantair na nOileán. His father, Thomas McDonogh, was born in 1836 on Gorumna Island, and it was envisaged that he would eventually succeed his father in the family's business on Crappagh, which included a small shop and a number of cottages that were leased out to tenants. Thomas, however, had ambitions of his own and he married a formidable lady called Honoria Hernon from Inis Mór, the largest of the Aran Islands. Their first son, Martin,[3] was born on Gorumna in 1860, and they

1 'Corrib Island' was Inishambo, an island on Lough Corrib that McDonogh purchased in the early 1930s, located half a mile from the pier at Oughterard. 2 Ó Faoláin, S., *An Irish journey* (London, 1940), p. 179. 3 McDonogh was always referred to professionally as 'Martin McDonogh', but to his family, friends and colleagues, he was 'Máirtín', and more colloquially he was known as 'Máirtín Mór' ('big' or 'great' Máirtín), a reference not only to his stature, but to his status as an important merchant and businessman.

moved to Galway in the early 1860s, with him and their second son, Redmond.

As the eldest son of ambitious parents, much was expected of Martin McDonogh, and a good education was considered the first step in preparing the young man for the career his father envisaged for him. McDonogh was educated first at the Jesuit College, Galway and later at another Jesuit school, St Stanislaus' College, Tullabeg, Co. Offaly. He entered the Queen's College Galway in 1878 to study law, but circumstances intervened and he soon abandoned his studies and became a very able deputy to his father. By the time Martin McDonogh entered the family business full-time in 1879, it had expanded considerably, but when his father died in 1902, there were few who doubted that Martin was up to the task of taking the reins of the family's diverse retail and manufacturing enterprises. And he was certainly a man who made an impression. His friend, the MP and writer Stephen Gwynn, described him thus:

> All of the men of the family were big, but he was huge: people would come twenty miles on a Sunday to see Martin McDonogh doing feats of strength. But he burst a blood vessel in one of those weight-liftings, and the leg never healed properly, so that for fifty years his bulk could only be kept down by strict diet and exercise. Till a year before he died, nearly eighty, he was using dumb bells daily. But even in old age he gave the impression of elephantine strength – and not always of a very approachable elephant.[4]

In 1903 McDonogh entered the fertilizer business, establishing McDonogh's Fertilizers. Agriculture in Ireland was experiencing significant growth, and eleven years later, when war broke out in Europe, food exports to Britain increased, and sales of fertilizers rose accordingly. McDonogh took the various family businesses to a whole new level of success and profitability during the war years. Having harnessed the waterways of Galway for use in his sawmills and fertilizer factory, he also established a hydroelectric power station to supply his industries with power.

By this time McDonogh was a justice of the peace, an urban district councillor and a founding member of the chamber of commerce, and he held a host of other civic and public roles. He employed over 400 people, and was

4 Gwynn, S., *Memories of enjoyment* (Tralee, 1946), p. 95.

indirectly responsible for the employment of many others, but his record on labour relations was fraught, to say the least. As chairman of the Galway Employers' Federation, he approached the task of taking on the unions with all the subtlety of a sledgehammer, and frequently clashed with trade union leaders. In 1913, up to a thousand workers went on strike in Galway. Under McDonogh's unbending leadership, the Employers' Federation held out, and the strike lasted for five long weeks, resulting in great distress.

Since he was so actively involved in business and civic affairs, it is hardly surprising that politics played an important role in McDonogh's life. He had much in common with others of his generation, social status and education. He experienced much of the duality felt by the Catholic elite and rising Catholic merchant class of the time in that he saw no incongruity in arguing both for home rule and nationalism, and believed, as many nationalists did, that Ireland could only prosper economically within the British empire. Initially a committed Parnellite and home ruler, he was 22 years old when Parnell founded the Irish Parliamentary Party in 1882. Siding with Redmond following the Parnellite split in 1890, and supporting the newly formed Irish National League, he met Redmond on many occasions, and Redmond became a friend and ally. McDonogh became a member of the Irish Volunteers in 1913. He was 54 when war broke out the next year, and, unsurprisingly, given his political affiliation, he actively campaigned with Redmond for the enlistment in the British army of men from the West, with considerable success.

The Easter Rising of 1916 was to prove a seminal event in McDonogh's life. Galway was one of the few locations outside of Dublin where a significant uprising took place, and as a major businessman, employer and landowner,[5] and an enthusiastic supporter of the war, Martin McDonogh was an obvious target for local militants. The leaders of the volunteers in Galway had planned to take McDonogh hostage and, if necessary, execute him. It was only the refusal of Liam Mellowes to allow this – to the intense frustration of local Volunteers leader Tom Kenny – that saved McDonogh. When news of the Rising spread to Galway, McDonogh acted swiftly and decisively, establishing a 'committee for public safety', and having martial law declared. When the Rising ended, McDonogh was among those who declared that all but the leaders should be shown leniency. His support for the execution of the leaders, and his actions during the Rising, came back to haunt him during his Dáil

5 McDonogh owned farms in Cos. Galway, Meath, Limerick and Dublin.

career, when many of those whom he had bitterly condemned, including members of his own party, were his parliamentary colleagues, charged with running the country.

In the aftermath of the Rising, with war still raging in Europe, McDonogh was among those businessmen who lobbied the government for war contracts via the All-Ireland Munitions and Government Supplies Committee. The committee secured the establishment of four national munitions factories in the twenty-six counties in 1916, and, despite Westminster's reluctance, McDonogh managed – largely through the efforts of his friend John Redmond – to persuade the ministry of munitions to locate a fifth factory at Galway. The Galway shell factory, the smallest of the five munitions factories in Ireland, opened in 1917, and while never profitable, provided much-needed employment for over one hundred women in Galway, and was a major boon to Galway's economy during the difficult war years.

During the War of Independence, McDonogh succeeded in protecting and expanding his various businesses, and responded to the changed political landscape in the aftermath of the Treaty by sliding effortlessly into the nationalist politics of the Free State. He was 67 when he was first elected to Dáil Éireann as a Cumann na nGaedheal TD for the Galway constituency at the June 1927 general election. He was re-elected at the September 1927 election, but defeated in 1932. He was re-elected at the 1933 general election, but died during the term of the 8th Dáil, in November 1934.

In spite of his age, he was a formidable figure in the Dáil, his gruff manner marking him out as a man who would not suffer fools gladly. His Dáil career was characterized by poor attendance, accusations that he occasionally nodded off when proceedings bored him, and colourful exchanges with opposition deputies when a subject arose that interested him – usually labour relations or economic policy. As a man accustomed to taking charge and dominating every committee he was a member of, McDonogh found both the pace and the procedures of the Dáil purgatorial. In addition, his business empire was always in need of his attention, and he continued to be an active member of various civic and public bodies in Galway, as well as holding a number of directorships, with companies such as Hibernian Insurance and the Irish Tourist Association.

Outside of politics and business, if he had one great personal passion in life it was horse racing. He assembled an impressive stable. A workaholic, McDonogh appears never to have taken holidays as such, and his only form of recreation was his attendance at race meetings in Ireland and Britain. He took enormous pleasure in his horses and their successes. In one of the few descriptions of McDonogh displaying elation, we are told, again by his friend Gwynn, that:

> When Kyleclare won the Galway Hurdles on the Galway Course I ran down to congratulate his owner [McDonagh], so did others. But we might as well have spoken to a steam-roller. Brushing us all aside he bore ahead through the crowd like a tank to meet the horse coming in. There were shouts of 'Lead him in yourself Mr Martin', but he would not. It was only when the weighing was over that he relaxed enough to acknowledge the cheers. I never saw a man under such pressure of speechless excitement.[6]

For all his involvement with public bodies, and sporting and other organizations, and as a businessman, entrepreneur, employer and politician of national standing, a picture of Martin McDonogh, the man, is slow to emerge. Somewhat surprisingly, for a man who was, to put it mildly, forthright in making his views known, he failed to leave behind an archive of personal correspondence. There are precious few photographs of McDonogh, and none at all of him 'off duty' with his friends and family. He never married, and had no romantic relationships that we know of. Gwynn recalled that:

> None of those soft parts of speech which are so endearing in the West of Ireland were to be found in this huge growling man, whose very hospitality was rough spoken. But when they were carrying out his coffin (ten men staggered under it) the poor crowded round. 'The half of his charity will never be known' said a priest (and a political opponent) to me. But another put it shorter: he buried half Galway. When a sudden need for money came, people would come to him, and he would say gruffly 'It'll be all right'. If thanks were offered he swept them away with a swing of his great shoulder.[7]

Another, less flattering image of Martin McDonogh emerges in the novel *The house of gold* by Liam Ó Flatharta (more commonly known as Liam O'Flaherty). The novel charts the replacement of the old order in the

6 Gwynn, S., *Memories of enjoyment*, p. 97. 7 *Connacht Tribune*, 8 Dec. 1934.

emerging Free State by an 'oppressive native gombeen ascendancy, buttressed by the Catholic church',[8] and encompasses themes such as greed, priestly lust, alcoholism, sexual frustration and murder. The principal character of the novel, the 'fat-faced, sweaty headed swine' Ramon Mór Costello, was really Máirtín Mór McDonogh, and this biography considers, for the first time, why O'Flaherty wrote such a venomous account of the McDonogh family and the 'gombeen' culture he felt they represented. Unsurprisingly, given its content, *The house of gold* became the first book to be banned by the Irish censorship of publications board, in 1930, on the grounds that it was 'obscene'.

For all the varying – and often conflicting – opinion as to his motivations, his actions and his personality, the question remains: who was Martin McDonogh? One comment, made in reference to his brother Thomas Christopher, in many respects the playboy of the family, is particularly revealing in this regard. When his younger brother's fondness for fine clothes, entertaining and a man-about-town lifestyle was referred to by a business colleague, Martin McDonogh, somewhat ruefully, stated that 'every family is entitled to have at least one gentleman in it'.[9] While Thomas Christopher was undoubtedly the 'gentleman' of the McDonogh family, and his other brother Michael, the doctor, fulfilled the role of the eminent professional,[10] it appears that Martin McDonogh considered himself to be neither. Rather, he was, and in many ways remained throughout his life, the 'general merchant and manufacturer' he refers to himself as in the 1911 census. He was an Irish-speaking Connemara man, born in a thatched cottage in Lettermullan, who was taught the manners and given the education of a gentleman at the best schools money could buy. But scratch the surface and there was that self-same Connemara man: tough, ambitious and afraid of – and deferring to – no one.

Most of the articles written about McDonogh recognized the complexity of his personality – the gruff exterior matched by many acts of kindness and generosity attributed to him, almost always performed quietly and without expectation of recognition. One political commentator noted that 'The Galway man will tell you that Mr McDonogh owns one half of Galway, and manages the other half. Those who know him intimately say that behind a brusque and commanding manner he hides much geniality and good nature.'[11]

8 Mac Siomóin, T., 'Introduction' in Liam O'Flaherty, *The house of gold* (Galway, 2013). 9 A story recalled by Thomas McDonogh Snr, the current chairman of Thomas McDonogh & Sons Ltd. 10 Martin McDonogh's other brother, Redmond, became a successful lawyer, but died of tuberculosis in 1898. 11 *Sunday Independent*, 6 Jan. 1929.

Another noted that 'Beneath that seemingly brusque exterior was a nature that was kindliness itself when a good deed had to be done, and could be done without ostentation.'[12]

Martin McDonogh's life, career and achievements have been the subjects of vastly differing interpretations, and what he did, how he did it and what motivated him will form the greater part of this biography. Strong personalities normally elicit strong reactions, and there was no personality stronger than Máirtín Mór McDonogh's. But coupled with that strong personality were an undoubted entrepreneurship, a keen business brain and an unerring sense of civic responsibility. Whatever his faults – and he had many – he did his county and his country no small service, and in all his dealings, political and professional, he had the courage of his convictions, and never wavered in expressing them. An obituary in the *Connacht Sentinel* in 1934 declared that:

> Men like Martin McDonogh do not come our way often. Because of their very strength of character, sincerity of purpose, and large outlook they must inevitably be misunderstood. But when the history of contemporary Galway is written, the one outstanding figure in it will be the man whose body now lies in the historic cemetery of Forthill. For half a century he *was* Galway.'[13]

12 *Connacht Tribune*, 1 Dec. 1934. 13 *Connacht Sentinel*, 27 Nov. 1934.

1. Beginnings, early years and education, 1860–79

> If ever there was a unique westerner, it was Martin McDonogh. He had that astonishing quality of being Gaelic through and through, yet he was saturated with the most modern commercial thought. Also, and always, he was what our American friends call a 'go getter'.[1]

This assessment, written by T.A. Grehan of the *Irish Independent* following McDonogh's death in 1934, touches on some of his core character traits. McDonogh was the son of a Irish-speaking father, who was one of a family of twenty-one children, from one of the remotest parts of Connemara, and an Aran Islands mother. What Grehan may not have known was the degree to which the personalities, family characteristics, talents and ambitions of the McDonogh and Hernon dynasties came to define Martin McDonogh, and lay at the heart of all he was to achieve.

THE McDONOGHS OF LETTERMULLAN AND CRAPPAGH

Lettermullan is an island, now connected to the mainland by causeway, which lies at the south-western extremity of the archipelago of Ceantair na nOileáin in Connemara. Local evidence suggests that the McDonogh family were living on Lettermullan and the adjacent islands of Gorumna and An Crapach (Crappagh) from the early 1800s.[2] In 1840, Henry Comerford purchased the lands of Lettermullan (about 1,700 acres and 77 houses) from landlords Brown and Lynch of Galway for £10,300.[3] Comerford and his brother Isaac were prosperous merchants and prominent magistrates in Galway. Henry Comerford owned a very successful sawmills in Galway, and was an extremely wealthy man. Historian Pádraig Lane records that he paid over £35,000 for 4,440 acres of land in Co. Galway in the 1850s, including over a thousand acres from Sir William Gregory at Kinvara and the de Basterot property at Doorus.[4] Griffith's Valuation also records Comerford holding

1 *Connacht Tribune*, 1 Dec. 1934. 2 See Ní Chualáin, D.V., *Tús Tuile: Reilig Chuigéil*. Records of burials of McDonoghs in the local graveyard from that time are recorded. 3 Lane, P.G. 'Some Galway and Mayo landlords of the mid-nineteenth century', *Journal of the Galway Archaeological and Historical Society*, 45 (1993), 70–89. 4 Lane, P.G., 'Purchasers of land in counties Galway and Mayo in the Encumbered Estates

lands in the parishes of Drumcreehy and Kilfenora, Co. Clare. Although he owned the substantial Ballykeale House in Kilfenora, Comerford never occupied it, living instead in Merchants Road, Galway, where he could keep a closer eye on his business interests.

By the time Comerford acquired the lands in Lettermullan, Réamonn Mór McDonogh, the founder of the Lettermullan dynasty,[5] was already well established as one of the most powerful and prosperous men in Ceantair na nOileáin. The McDonoghs appear to have been a family quick to seize an opportunity. Author Tim Robinson records that Réamonn Mór, who local folklore relates was a coastguard, came upon a shipwreck, bought it for £5, found gold in it, and used the money to buy the island of Crappagh (figure 1) from the Comerfords and established a shop there.[6]

Another local legend holds that the McDonoghs came upon the wreck of a ship, salvaged the timber, sold it to a sawmills in Galway and established their shop on Crappagh with the proceeds.[7] Yet another legend has it that the signal tower at Golam Head, built *c.*1804–5 when the threat of a Napoleonic invasion was at its height, lost its roof when 'it was robbed for its lead by the Mac Donnchadha family of the nearby island of An Crapach'.[8] Questions surrounding the source of their capital aside, the McDonoghs were certainly on Crappagh by the time of Griffith's Valuation in 1855, and the ruins of the shop and the McDonogh house still survive. Though only a three-roomed structure, it was nonetheless substantial relative to the sizes of similar houses in the area. O'Dowd records that it had 'wide windows facing south, fronted by a plastered porch. To the west, high walls delineated a yard enclosed towards the harbour at the back by a two-roomed building, which was the shop and store.'[9]

Given their location on an island in one of the most inaccessible parts of Connemara, the fortunes of the McDonogh family were inextricably linked to the sea, whether by way of smuggling – to which much local folklore but no hard evidence attests – or by way of legitimate trade conducted in their

court, 1849–1858', *Journal of the Galway Archaeological and Historical Society*, 43 (1991), 111. 5 By 1898 there were 47 families of McDonoghs (using the 'o' rather than the 'a' spelling of the name) in the district of Gorumna and Lettermullan. There were also three families of Hernons (McDonogh's mother was a Hernon) still living on Gorumna in 1898. Browne, C.R., 'The ethnography of Garumna and Lettermullen in the County Galway', *Proceedings of the Royal Irish Academy*, 21:223–68 (1898). 6 Robinson, T., *Connemara: a little Gaelic kingdom* (London, 2011), p. 372. 7 The reference to a sawmills in Galway is significant, given the future association between the Comerfords, who owned the biggest one, and the McDonoghs. Robinson, T., *Stones of Aran: labyrinth* (Dublin, 1995). 8 Robinson, T., *Connemara: a little Gaelic kingdom* (London, 2011), p. 369. 9 O'Dowd, P., *In from the West: the McDonogh dynasty* (Galway, 2002), p. 5.

Figure 1 Crappagh Island (courtesy of Roger Derham)

shop. The McDonoghs were noted for their skill as sailors, and the surviving stone pier, only a short walk from the site of the original McDonogh shop, was used by Réamonn Mór and his sons to receive and despatch cargoes along the coasts of Connemara and the Aran Islands.

Consolidating Martin McDonogh's links to Aran was the fact that his grandfather Réamonn Mór had married an islander. Like his mother, whose paternal grandmother (McDonogh's maternal great-grandmother) was Ann O'Flaherty of Cill Mhuirbhigh (Kilmurvey), McDonogh's paternal grandmother, Kitty O'Flaherty, also came from Inis Mór. She may indeed have been a member of the same powerful O'Flaherty family from Cill Mhuirbhigh, although there is no evidence to support this. She married Réamonn Mór and moved to Lettermullan, where she gave birth to twenty-one children.

The remoteness of the Ceantair na nOileáin area meant that the area was ideally suited to smuggling, the objective of which was the avoidance of government revenue payments for the importation of cargoes at registered ports. Even established merchant families such as the Comerfords were not averse to the odd smuggling operation, particularly when such operations related to highly taxed cargoes such as tobacco and alcohol.[10] In the McDonoghs of Crappagh the Comerfords found ready partners. According to Joseph Mongan TD, a second cousin of Martin McDonogh's, the fortunes of the McDonogh family took a major leap forward when Réamonn Mór's son Antoine captained a smuggling ship for the Comerfords, and landed a cargo of tobacco, brandy and wine at Crappagh. Antoine's skill as a sailor enabled him to avoid the revenue cutter by sailing at night through Bealach an Dorú, a treacherous, exceptionally narrow channel, barely the width of a boat, between Crappagh and Inis Oirc.[11]

The connection between the Comerfords and the McDonoghs was later to be marked by tragedy however. Antoine was among the crew of the brig *St John,* which set out from Galway for Boston on 7 September 1849. Owned by Henry Comerford, the ship went down in sight of land during a raging storm on 7 October 1849, off Cohassett, near Boston, on the coast of Massachusetts. Antoine was among the ninety-five passengers and seven crew who drowned. He is identified on the casualty list as 'Antonio McDonough'. Two Comerfords survived: Henry Comerford, the first mate of the ship, and a nephew of the owner Henry Comerford, and Issac Comerford, an ordinary crew member.[12] The blow to the McDonogh family was enormous.

Seán Mac Giollarnáth, in his *Annála beaga ó Iorrus Aithneach,* recounts a significant piece of local folklore related to the loss of Antoine Mc Donogh. Although not referring directly to the sinking of the *St John,* he states that Antoine was drowned off the coast of America 'ag sabháil daoine eile' (saving others).[13] The account records that at the time of McDonogh's death, a local poet had a premonition of his drowning:

> San am ar cailleadh Antoine Mac Donnchadha bhí Colm Bhailís, an file, ag obair ag athair Antoine, ag Réamonn. Bhí Colm Bhailís ag

10 Mac Giollarnáth records that a Captain Comerford was 'engaged in smuggling American tobacco; the tobacco was hidden in baulks of timber that were thrown overboard and picked up by boats from Kinvara and Bell Harbour on the south side of Galway Bay'. See Robinson, T., *Connemara: a little Gaelic kingdom,* p. 372. 11 Mac Giollarnáth, S., *Annála beaga ó Iorrus Aithneach* (Dublin, 1941), p. 160. 12 Henry and Issac Comerford later became justices of the peace in Galway. 13 The *Boston Daily Bee* recorded that 'the jolly boat was hanging by the tackle, alongside, when the stern ringbolt broke and the boat fell into the water. The captain, second mate and two boys jumped in to get her clear, when about 25 passengers jumped in and swamped her. The twenty-five, together with the second mate and two boys, perished. The captain caught a rope hanging over the quarter, and was drawn on board by the first mate.' Given that Henry Comerford Jnr was the first mate, it appears the second mate referred to was Antoine McDonogh. *Boston Daily Bee,* 9 Oct. 1849.

saimhéaracht an lá seo agus i lár an lae d'eirigh sé as an obair agus siúil sé isteach sa teach. Dúirt sé le bean Réamoinn nár fhéad sé leanacht don'n obair faoi láthair. 'Céard atá ort, an bhfuil tú tinn?' a dúirt an bean leis. 'Níl', ar seisean, 'ach tá rud eicínt suas nach bhfuil ceart. Bain an chluas díom mara bhfuil Antoine caillte'. Bhí Réamonn imithe go hAcaill. Bhí sé coicís imithe nuair a thainig sé. An lá thaining sé bhí sé gruamdha brónach. Thug an bean faoi deara an brón a bhí air. 'An bhfuil tada ort?' a deir sí. 'Níl tada', ar seisean. 'Tá rud eicínt', ar sise, 'céard é?' 'Tá Antoine caillte', ar seisean. 'Seo é an páipéar a fuair mé in Achaill. Tá scéal a bháis air.'[14]

[At the time Antoine McDonogh died the poet Colm Wallace was working for Antoine's father, Réamonn. Colm Wallace was surveying one day, and in the middle of the day he left his work and walked into the house. He said to Réamonn's wife that he could not continue with his work at that point. 'What's wrong with you, are you ill?' the woman asked him. 'No,' he said, 'but something is not right. May the ear be struck off me if Antoine is not dead.' Réamonn had gone to Achill. He had been gone a fortnight when he returned. The day he came back he was very down and sad. His wife noticed the sadness in him. 'Is something wrong with you?' she asked. 'Nothing', he replied. 'There is something', she said, 'what is it?' 'Antoine has been lost', he said. 'Here is the newspaper I got in Achill. The news of his death is in it.']

The sinking of the *St John* was widely reported in the American and Irish press. An eye-witness account by the American writer Henry David Thoreau, who arrived in Cohasset two days after the loss of the ship, was published in 1855, and is among the most moving, and harrowing, accounts of the tragedy.[15] Thoreau described the bodies of drowned passengers and crew stretched out along the seashore as having 'marble feet and matted heads' and 'wide-open and staring eyes'.[16] Although many of the victims were unidentified, or unidentifiable as a result of their appalling injuries, the names of those who were identified – in some cases a parent lying alongside a child – were written in red chalk on the lids of the coffins.[17] Antoine McDonogh was one of those so identified. Thoreau encountered the first mate, Henry Comerford Jnr,

14 Mac Giollarnáth, *Annála beaga ó Iorrus Aithneach*, p. 160. 15 The account, entitled 'The shipwreck', was first published in the June 1855 edition of *Putnam's Magazine*. 16 Thoreau, H.D., *Cape Cod* (Boston, 1865), p. 16. 17 Ibid.

whom he described as 'a slim-looking youth' who seemed 'a little excited'.[18] Captain Oliver, who had survived the wreck, was nowhere to be seen, and later came in for considerable criticism due to his handling of the vessel, and his decision to try to leave the ship in the jollyboat.[19] The condition of the vessel was also severely criticized, Thoreau describing the timbers that washed ashore as being 'so rotten I could almost thrust my umbrella through them'.[20]

Like Antoine McDonogh, many of those who perished on the *St John* were from Lettermullan, and most were undocumented. Having departed from Galway docks with approximately one hundred passengers,[21] Henry notes that the ship anchored off Lettermullan for almost an entire day to take on water, and it was rumoured that Oliver used the opportunity to add passengers. These people 'were not listed on the ship's manifest and the authorities were later unable to account for all those who had lost their lives. The captain was suspected of pocketing the fares of these new passengers.'[22] Whether the stopover in Lettermullan was authorized by the Comerfords is a matter of conjecture, although given the presence onboard of two members of the Comerford family, one the first mate, it is likely that it was. Taking additional passengers on board an already crowded ship whose seaworthiness was a concern brought with it considerable risk,[23] and the inadequate numbers of both crew and lifeboats had devastating consequences. As was common practice at the time when a favoured child died, MacGiollarnáth notes that when another son was born to Réamonn Mór and his wife, they called him Antoine, in memory of the son they had lost. Sadly, that son died at the age of 8 or 9.[24] A third son was also christened Antoine, and he lived to manhood and died in America.[25]

The tragedy of the sinking of the *St John* aside, the family prospered sufficiently for their son, Redmond,[26] to be sent to Maynooth to become a priest, 'the first step on the road to affluence and importance'.[27] With the fortunes of the family on the rise, Réamonn Mór was ambitious for the futures of his other sons. Having already established links with the Comerfords in Galway, and seen first-hand their thriving sawmills enterprise, he sent his second-eldest son, Michael, to work for Henry Comerford in

18 Ibid. 19 Henry, W., *Coffin ship: the wreck of the brig St John* (Cork, 2009), p. 111. 20 Ibid. 21 A number of stowaways were subsequently discovered a few days into the voyage. 22 Henry, *Coffin ship*, p. 97. 23 *Galway Vindicator*, 3 Nov. 1849. 24 Two sons named Anthony were also born to Thomas and Honoria McDonogh, in 1867 and 1870, but both died as infants. 25 Mac Giollarnáth, *Annála beaga ó Iorrus Aithneach*, p. 160. 26 Redmond is the English version of the name 'Réamonn'. 27 Sheeran, P., *The novels of Liam O'Flaherty: a study in romantic realism* (Dublin, 1976), p. 119.

Galway. In time Michael McDonogh married Mary Comerford, one of Henry's daughters, and their first son Issac was born in 1859. Henry Comerford had no sons, so when he died in 1861, his property passed to his sons-in-law, including Michael McDonogh (known as Mícheál Réamonn Mór).[28]

Martin McDonogh's father Thomas (Tomás or Tommy Réamonn, as he was known in Connemara) was Réamonn Mór's next son. With his two surviving older brothers well established – Redmond a priest,[29] and Michael married into the Comerford family – he moved from Crappagh to Gorumna to strike out on his own, but apparently soon regretted it:

> he became discontented with life on Gorumna and downed tools. His wife, an Aran Islander, entered on a long altercation with him, the abusive terms of which are still recounted some hundred years after the event. The wrangle ended with Thomas' declaration that 'a good plan is better than all the land in Gorumna'. That plan was to move to Galway and there set up a shop to supply the peasantry of the islands and seaboard with all they might need.[30]

In another version of the story, the reason for Thomas' departure from Gorumna was frustration with the arduous process of harvesting seaweed, which was an inevitable part of life in Connemara, and supplemented many incomes, the McDonoghs' included. In his 1986 book *Stones of Aran*, Robinson notes that the family:

> owned three cartúir of land in Eoghanacht, and therefore had seaweed rights (there). One day when some ancestral Mac Donncha was wrestling with the coirleach ... his croisín broke, and he stood up in his currach and swore 'I'll never gather coirleach again, if I have to beg!' Whereupon he went off to Galway to try another mode of life, and opened a little shop, which over the course of generations has become that pillar of the business community, McDonogh's huge store on Merchants Road.[31]

While it is impossible to establish definitively whether either tale has any basis in fact, the sense of frustration evident in both, in an ambitious man

28 Henry Comerford held more than 2,000 acres in Co. Galway in 1876. *Return of names of proprietors and area and valuation of properties in counties in Ireland*, HC, 1876 (412), lxxx, 395, 148. 29 Fr Redmond McDonogh became parish priest of Oughterard, Co. Galway. 30 Sheeran, *Novels of Liam O'Flaherty*, p. 119. 31 Robinson, T., *Stones of Aran: pilgrimage* (Dublin, 1986), p. 148.

who felt that he was capable of achieving more for himself and his family, is compelling in the context of why the young couple and their two children upped sticks and moved to Galway. And Thomas' wife was a willing partner in the plan to move to Galway. Honoria had no great attachment to Lettermullan, and, as a clever and ambitious woman, she was anxious to improve the lot of her family in the place where she felt she could achieve the most.

The role his mother and her Aran family played in the formation of Martin McDonogh's character was considerable. It is no accident that as the firstborn son he was named after his maternal grandfather, Martin Hernon, rather than his paternal grandfather, or his own father. This was undoubtedly Honoria's doing, and reflects a recognition of the considerable sway she held in the marriage partnership with Thomas McDonogh. For when Thomas and Honoria married, it was Honoria, the daughter of a powerful and influential figure on Aran, bailiff to the major landowning family on the islands, and himself a major landholder and relatively wealthy man, who would have been considered the greater 'catch'. Her own considerable entrepreneurial skills, her extensive contacts on the Aran Islands, and her fierce ambition for her children formed a major part of Martin McDonogh's personality. The clannishness of the Hernons – enforced, to a large degree, by their professional association with the landowning classes – was reflected in the clannishness of McDonogh and his siblings. Of all the children of Thomas and Honoria, only one – Michael – ever married, and even he did not do so until he was middle aged. This is surprising given their significant personal wealth and position within Galway society, which would have rendered them very desirable marriage prospects, and the fact that the sons were, according to the photographic evidence, good-looking men, and the daughters, Mary Ann and Kate, were considered 'handsome' women (although no known photographs of them survive). It may have had much to do with the family penchant for keeping everything within the family, keeping the circle tight, thereby avoiding the opportunism of 'gold-diggers' or those out to undermine the family. One Galwegian went so far as to express the view that 'no-one was ever good enough for the McDonoghs'.[32] Nor, indeed, the Hernons.

32 Interview with A.K., Co. Galway, May 2013.

THE HERNONS OF ARAN

The Inis Mór poet Colm P. Ó hIarnáin (Cóilín Mhicilín) has written a narrative of the history of the Hernon family, and this unpublished work suggests that the Hernons first came to Ireland with the Spanish Armada, which was wrecked off the west coast of Ireland *c.*1588. Others have suggested that they arrived with the Cromwellians in the early 1650s, and that the name Ó hIarnáin (Hernon) derives from the term 'Ironsides' by which the Cromwellians were known, the Irish word for iron being '*iarann*'. There is no evidence to support this theory. What is clear, however, is that having settled in an area between Barna and Carna, there is much folkloric evidence that the Hernons were hard-working, enterprising people. Ó hIarnáin records that:

> they were small in stature, dark and stocky, and very quick tempered, in general appearance they resembled the Spaniards. Also they possessed other characteristics of the Spaniards, such as being excellent seamen, indeed in the early days they were often referred to as 'those bloody Spaniards'.[33]

The Hernons arrived in Aran as a result of the turf trade. As the islands were dependent on Connemara for turf, a brisk trade developed, and two of the Connemara men who serviced that trade were Bartly Hernon of An Cnoc (Knock), Lettermullan, and his brother Michael. The young men owned a *púcán*, a small traditional sailboat, which they used to ferry turf to the islands in the 1790s. They obviously became well-known, and well-liked on the island, because Ó hIarnáin records that:

> On one occasion when the brothers were in Port Murvey with a load of turf there was a wedding in progress in the village of Kilmurvey ... the brothers were invited and accepted the invitation. Aran in those days was more prosperous than Connemara and a wedding was a great social occasion, with plenty of food, drink and jollification. Whatever happened, whether it was the food, drink or romance, Bartly was reluctant to return home, and his brother had to return without him.[34]

Romance may indeed have been a factor, but it would be naive to suggest that the young Ann O'Flaherty, on whom Bartly Hernon had fixed his attentions,

33 Ó hIarnáin, C.P., *Stair na h-Iarnáin.* 34 Ibid.

was not an extremely attractive marriage prospect. The lands around Kilmurvey were owned, as was most of the island, by the Digby family, who leased the land to two families in particular: the O'Flahertys and the Dirranes. Ann O'Flaherty's father had two daughters, and no male heirs, so when Bartly – described by Ó hIarnáin as 'a very hard working and likeable young man' – made the decision to settle in Kilmurvey, and married Ann within the year, he stood to inherit a considerable holding. Bartly Hernon encouraged his brother to join him on Aran 'where the prospects of making a decent living were better than at home'. The plan worked, for, as Ó hIarnáin notes, 'Michael came to Aran and in due course married one of the Dirranes of Kilmurvey.'[35] Fortunately for Michael, the Dirranes were in a similar position to the O'Flahertys, with daughters but no male heirs, and as a result Michael eventually inherited the holding. The Hernon brothers of Lettermullan then set about consolidating their positions in Kilmurvey.

The Ó Flaithearta family, from which Honoria Hernon was descended on her mother's side, were the most powerful family on the island in the early 1800s. Pádraig Ó Flaithearta, from Kilmurvey, was the man who compiled the 1821 census of Aran, which survived the disastrous fire in the Custom House in 1921.[36] Ó Flaithearta held sway over more land than anyone else on the island, and acted, and was treated, as a man of some importance.[37] In reality, however, Ó Flaithearta was no more than a tenant, and, as Powell has pointed out, the power and influence he exerted depended to some extent on the degree to which he continued to sustain good relations with the Digby family, the owners of the islands.[38] In 1831 Ó Flaithearta was appointed the local magistrate for Inis Mór. He died in 1864.

The 1821 census of Aran provides us with an accurate picture of the Hernon families at that time. Bartly Hernon was 47, and his wife Ann Hernon, 45. Bartly gave his occupation as 'farmer, labourer', and Ann as 'flaxspinner'. In 1821 they had six children: Pat (24), listed as a 'labourer, fisherman'; Peggy Hernon (20), 'flaxspinner'; Martin Hernon (18), for whom no occupation is given; Kate (11) and Michael (9), who were at school; and Tom (3). The census noted that the family occupied ¼ cartron of land.[39] It was annotated in later years to say that Michael Hernon subsequently 'Became

35 Ibid. 36 It was being consulted by a researcher, and was out of the archive. 37 Tom O'Flaherty, referring to his maternal Ganly heritage, noted, 'I liked the emotional, soft, witty, story-telling Ganlys better than the harsh, quarrelsome, haughty, "ferocious O'Flaherties".' *Aranmen all* (Dingle, 1991), p. 163. 38 Powell, A., *Oileáin Árann: stair na n-Oileán Anuas go dtí 1922* (Dublin, 1984), p. 58. 39 A cartron is a unit of land measurement in Connacht equal to about 30 acres.

estate bailiff to the Digbys, owners of the Aran Islands', a prestigious and influential position for an islander. However, this was not the case. It was Martin Hernon, the father of Honoria Hernon, future wife of Thomas McDonogh, who assumed that role. Ó hIarnáin confirms this fact, and acknowledges the ambition of the Hernon family, when he states that:

> The Hernons were noted for being very clannish, helping one another in every way. Also they seemed to have a great interest in educating their children, an unusual ambition for the people of Aran and indeed Ireland of the day. As a direct result of this Martin … was able to take on an important job, important for the Hernons that is, that was offered on Aran at the time, agent or administrator for the landlord. Martin Hernon was known as 'The Colonel' ('An Coirnéal') thereafter.[40]

The Digbys' agent, Mr George Thompson, appointed Martin Hernon as bailiff of the Aran Islands on 7 June 1844. A letter written by Thompson set out the terms of his appointment as 'head bailiff and caretaker over the three islands of Arran [Aran], Co. Galway, at the usual salary of ten guineas per annum, which shall be increased to twelve guineas if I shall think he deserves it from his increased attention to his duties'. [41] The salary was significant, though not enormous, particularly so given the extent of the duties of the head bailiff, which were laid out clearly by Thompson:

> He is to be sober, vigilent and attentive to directions, and to keep peace and good order amongst the tenants, as far as he can do so. He is to go through the three islands at the least once a month, to see that all goes on right. He is not to permit any new cottages or houses to be built, on any pretence whatever, until leave has been first granted in writing, nor to permit any additions to existing houses, nor any new divisions of farms. And he is to make known to Mr Thompson all attempts at such doings as they shall come to his knowledge, and at the same time put a stop to them all he can. He is to attend to Mr Flaherty's directions,[42]

40 Ó hIarnáin, *Stair na hIarnáin*. 41 Letter to Martin Hernon from George Thompson, 7 June 1844, Ref: LE11 (1), Special Collections, Hardiman Library, NUI Galway. 42 This was the Pádraig Ó Flaithearta who compiled the 1821 census of Aran. He lived at Kilmurvey House, the finest house on the island. In the 1821 census he describes himself as a 'gentleman farmer', with 5 cartrons (approximately 150 acres). His household at the time comprised two house servants, a cook, a kitchen maid and a 4-year-old

> and aid him in his efforts for Mr Digby's advantage in the islands at all times. He is to collect the rents of the houses and have it ready for Mr Thompson, or such other agent as Mr Digby shall have, on his periodical arrivals on the islands. He is to protect the schools at all times, and see that they shall have every accommodation and necessary that can be had in the islands, on the masters paying for such matters at the rates others in the islands pay for the same. And in all ways he is to protect and promote Mr Digby's wishes and interests and to procure obedience to his directions from time to time, as far as in his power, writing to Mr Thompson to make report of anything which may take place not common in the islands, once a month at the least. Attention to this conduct will entitle him to the increased salary herein before mentioned.[43]

In effect, Hernon was to be Thompson's eyes and ears on the islands. In addition to rent collection, Hernon was to know all, report all, and, when called for, take on the role of Thompson's enforcer. It was an onerous responsibility, which inevitably alienated the Hernons from their neighbours, for a relatively modest salary. The real benefit of the position of bailiff was the immense power it enabled Hernon to wield over the three islands of Aran. Martin Hernon was clearly a very important man on the island, but not a popular one. Ó hIarnáin records that:

> Times were hard in those rack rent days. Poor people who could not afford to pay the rent were evicted and the land taken from them and sold, very cheap at times. There is a story told on Aran that a fourth of land, 16 ac. was sold for a spade.[44]

As bailiff, Martin Hernon was 'in a position to help his brothers and relations to buy land,[45] and as a result of this when the third generation of Hernons arrived, they had established themselves all over the island, and practically owned Kilmurvey'.[46]

Hernon's 'land grabbing', as most islanders would have perceived it, was not appreciated by his neighbours, a situation exacerbated by the fact that the

boy listed as an 'orphan'. There was also a 'piper' named John Boyle (aged 78) in residence. 43 Letter to Martin Hernon from George Thompson, 7 June 1844, NUI Galway. 44 Ó hIarnáin, *Stair na hIarnáin*. 45 Technically, as the land was owned by the Digbys, all Hernon could secure for his family were tenancies or leases. 46 Ó hIarnáin, *Stair na hIarnáin*.

Hernons had, in a very real sense, 'married in' to the island from Connemara. The islanders intense dislike of Hernon is reflected in a song that was written about him, entitled 'Amhrán na Jumpers (na Wóthers)'[47] by Mhaolra Chrochúir, a fellow Inis Mór native (see appendix). The song depicts Hernon as a land-grabbing agent of the Digbys, who had grand notions about himself, dined on fine food, drank Spanish wine, wore a powdered wig,[48] and had buckles on his shoes – a far cry from the relatively humble origins of his father, ferrying turf from Lettermullan in a *púcán*.

Martin Hernon had three sons: Tom, Bartly and Johnny. According to Ó hIarnáin, Tom settled in Kilmurvey, Bartly in Kilronan and Johnny moved to Galway city.[49] Tom, known as 'Tom an Coirnéal', married no less than four times, which 'is still considered a record for Aran'.[50] Martin also had a number of daughters, including Honoria, born in 1838, and Anne, born in 1843.

Honoria was 6 years old when her father took on the role of bailiff, so she and her siblings grew up in an environment where her family were set apart from their neighbours as a result of their relationship with the island's landlord. What effect this had on her and her siblings can only be guessed at, but it is reasonable to conclude that it engendered a clannishness, which in turn characterized her own family once the McDonoghs became established, and began to climb the social ladder in Galway. Her father's position also meant that Honoria grew up in a household where education and social ambition were prized, and unpopularity among the general populace was considered the price to be paid for any attempt to better oneself. That said, the isolation that being the child of a bailiff enforced on Honoria and her siblings must have been immense. We get a flavour of how despised bailiffs were in a letter written by Liam O'Flaherty to Edward Garnett, the English writer, critic and literary editor, in January 1925, when he describes himself as 'snowed under with debt, with a shattered constitution and as many friends as a bailiff in the west of Ireland …'[51]

Married, and living in Galway with her young family, Honoria would have been very aware of the role Martin Hernon played in the increasingly acrimonious land wars of the 1860s and 1870s, which took particularly violent form

47 Whilst the term 'Jumper' usually refers to those Catholics who converted to Protestantism in order to improve their lot, there is no evidence that Martin 'An Coirnéal' Hernon ever changed his religion. However, Ó Conchubhair appears to be using the term to describe the self-seeking actions of Hernon in ingratiating himself with his 'betters' by aping their manner and dress, whilst treating his fellow islanders with contempt. 48 Reference to a wig may relate to Hernon's role as justice of the peace on the island. 49 Ó hIarnáin, *Stair na hIarnáin*. 50 Ibid. 51 Kelly, A.A. (ed.), *The letters of Liam O'Flaherty* (Dublin, 1996), p. 111.

on the Aran Islands. Indeed it is clear that both Honoria and Thomas McDonogh were kept informed of events on the islands by way of newspaper reports, their regular trade with the islands and family correspondence. At one of his first meetings as a member of the Galway board of guardians,[52] in April 1877, McDonogh was keen to establish his own intimate knowledge of the Aran Islands when, in reference to a letter received by the board from Revd Kilbride contradicting the statements by the relieving officer regarding levels of distress on the islands,[53] he recommended that rather than involving themselves in a standoff between the islanders and the commissioners, the board of guardians should rather 'allow them settle their squabbles among themselves. I know them better than anyone here, and that is the best course to adopt.'[54] The relieving officer was Edward O'Flaherty of Kilronan, who was married to Honoria's sister, Anne Hernon.

THE MOVE TO GALWAY

Thomas and Honoria McDonogh (figure 2) made the decision to move to Galway from Gorumna sometime in the early 1860s, when their son Martin was just a few years old. A question mark, however, surrounds Máirtín Mór's precise date of birth. No birth records exist for him or his brother Redmond, who was born two years later, although the birth of their brother Thomas Christopher in 1864 is recorded in the civil records. That in itself is not unusual, for unlike England, where births were registered starting in 1837, in Ireland official birth records were only maintained from 1864. Inevitably this led to a certain ambiguity, and genuine confusion, as to age, and with the introduction of the non-contributory old-age pension in 1908, misrepresentations – both accidental, and in many cases deliberate – were made. When providing details for his matriculation examination at the University of London in June 1878, McDonogh stated that he was 18, giving him a birthdate of 1860.[55] A requirement of registration was proof of age, and McDonogh provided a baptismal certificate, signed by the Revd Martin Melleth, who served as parish priest of An Chillín, Carraroe, from 1872 to 1883.[56] It does

52 Thomas McDonogh was first elected to the Galway board of guardians in early April 1877. *Galway Express*, 7 Apr. 1877. 53 Revd William Kilbride was the Anglican minister on Inis Mór from 1855 until his death in 1899. 54 *Galway Express*, 28 Apr. 1877. 55 University of London Provincial Matriculation Register, Senate House Library, London. 56 List of 'Sagairt an Chillín', held at Ionad Oidhreachta na nOileáin, Leitir Mealláin, Co. Galway.

not survive in the university's archive, but it must have been seen by the registrar. The certificate was intended to serve as a facsimile of the entry in the parish register, which Fr Melleth would have consulted, and it confirmed McDonogh's year of baptism as 1860, and his place of baptism as 'Killeen, Galway'.[57] This indicates that McDonogh was born on Crappagh (figure 3), and baptized in Carraroe (An Cheathrú Rua).[58]

What is perplexing regarding the baptismal certificate, however, is the fact that the copy of the parish register held at the National Library of Ireland does not contain any entry for the baptism of Martin McDonogh in 1860, or indeed any other year before or after 1860. How then – and perhaps, more importantly, why – did Fr Melleth complete a baptismal certificate in 1878 based on information not contained in the parish register? It is of course entirely possible that Martin McDonogh was baptized in a parish other than An Chillín, whose records have since disappeared, or indeed that as a result of an error his baptism was never formally recorded. However, McDonogh's lifelong evasiveness and sensitivity regarding his age raises suspicion regarding the details of his birth, and, quite possibly, the marital status of his parents at the time – something that will be examined in greater detail later.[59]

In 1860, the putative year of McDonogh's birth, the city that was to be his home was considered by many to be ripe for development – and it was the sea that was identified as key to the Galway's potential resurgence. In May 1860, a public lecture in Galway on 'the industrial resources of Ireland' put forward the view that the port of Galway was 'among the very first of Irish ports'.[60] This evaluation was based on the port's strategic position and proximity to North America, and the fact that the city's extensive waterways, with the potential to generate water power, would facilitate the development of manufacturing industries. The Great Famine of the 1840s had attracted significant numbers of skilled tradesmen and artisans to take refuge in the city, and the building of the Queen's College, the Eglinton Canal, and the Galway-Clifden railway line, had kept them there. It was anticipated that the

57 'Killeen' is the English translation of the name of the parish of An Chillín, which was part of the archdiocese of Tuam, and comprised the area of Leitir Meallain, Leitir Móir and An Cheathrú Rua. 58 An Cheathrú Rua is a peninsula in Connemara located between Casla Bay and Greatman's Bay, 40 km west of Galway city. It is also known as the parish of Cillín because of the small chapel or church in Barr an Doire. 59 In the absence of any other corroborating documentary evidence, the record in the University of London register must be taken as the date for Martin McDonagh's birth in 1860, and for that of Redmond McDonagh in 1862. 60 Woodman, K., *Tribes to tigers: a history of Galway Chamber of Commerce and Industry* (Galway, 2000), p. 118.

Figures 2 and 3 Thomas and Honoria McDonogh, and Martin McDonogh's birthplace

extension of the railway westwards would bring 'enterprise, and with enterprise, jobs, wealth, and more industry'.[61]

There was plenty of opportunity then, and all that was needed were men with the necessary drive and entrepreneurial skills to take up the challenge. But the right men were thin on the ground, and that same year, 1860, saw Lord Clancarty scuttle the harbour bill, which would have instigated the building of the new pier, breakwater and dry dock that the harbour desperately needed, because the cost necessitated an additional penny on the rates, which Clancarty and his fellow landowners were unwilling to pay. It was a major setback, given that manufacturing, the development of the port and the well-being of the city in general were largely codependent. Employment in manufacturing, estimated to be worth *c.*10,000 jobs in the city for both men and women, would inevitably have meant 'a great circulation of money, and with that money would come demands for improvements, and providing them would need raw materials ... the whole of society would benefit if only gentlemen were found to initiate the cycle'.[62]

One man with the entrepreneurial skill, determination and ambition to rise to that challenge was Thomas McDonogh. Following their move to Galway, he and Honoria and their two sons initially secured temporary lodgings in Long Walk – possibly with relatives of Honoria's, as a significant number of Aran Islanders lived there in the 1860s. Originally operating as a 'fish dealer and farmer', according to the civil birth record of his son Thomas Christopher, born on Christmas Day, 1864, Thomas eventually secured a job in Gunning's sawmills in the city, and began to learn the timber trade. With a brother married into the Comerford family, before too long:

> Thomas McDonogh himself climbed into the Comerford nest when he took a position as foreman/manager in the family sawmills. Soon, he was made a partner in the firm; by the early 1870s, the business was trading as McDonogh & Comerford; before the decade was out, the name over the door was Thomas McDonogh & Sons.[63]

The store he established as part of the operation was a spectacular success, selling everything from coal to furniture, cart wheels to pre-cut timber. For much of Martin McDonogh's early childhood, the family lived above the shop in Merchants Road. Another son, Anthony Patrick, was born on 14

61 Ibid. 62 Ibid. 63 Cunningham, J., *'A town tormented by the sea': Galway, 1790–1914* (Dublin, 2004), p. 187.

Figure 4 Flood Street (St Augustine Street), Galway. The McDonogh house is the white building on the left at the end of the street.

March 1867, but died on 26 September 1868, aged 18 months.[64] By this stage the family had moved to a fine three-storey house in Flood Street, at the end of present-day St Augustine Street (figure 4). The house had been known formerly as 'the dispensary', and was the property of the poor-law guardians.

64 On the death certificate, the cause of death was listed as 'croup, 4 days, certified'.

It was rented to Thomas McDonogh in June 1867 on a thirty-one year lease.[65] The couple's first daughter, Margaret (always known as Mary Ann), was born in the house on 18 January 1869. Another son, also named Anthony, was born on 6 January 1870, but suffered the same fate as his namesake, dying on 17 January, aged just 10 days.[66] Michael Joseph McDonogh was born on 10 October 1871,[67] and the couple's last child, Kate, was born on 22 May 1873.

With so many children to care for Honoria had plenty to occupy her, but with the capacity for hard work for which she became famous, her entrepreneurial nature came to the fore. Following the move to Flood Street, Honoria acquired the lease on an adjacent vacant corner building, with wide windows at ground level facing New Dock Street. Here she established a general store, which was an immediate success. The location was ideal, close to the docks, affording easy access to the skippers of the fleet of Galway hookers that regularly plied their trade between Galway, Connemara and the Aran Islands, and Honoria was smart enough to carry stock that was in demand in the homes and smallholdings of rural Galway. With the establishment of a steam sawmills, the McDonogh empire soon expanded once more, and they began to import a variety of building materials, and, critically, guano – a natural manure originating in South America and composed chiefly of the excrement of seabirds, which was used by farmers as fertilizer. With their business enterprises now thriving, the McDonoghs had every reason to feel confident that their young family had bright futures ahead of them. And that began with a good education.

EDUCATION

Where Martin McDonogh received his primary education is a matter of conjecture. It is unlikely that he would have attended St Patrick's Monastery and School, known to generations of Galwegians as the 'Old Mon', in Market Street. This was a free school established to cater for the educational needs of the poor of Galway, and his socially conscious parents probably would not have considered sending their firstborn to such a school, given their ambitions for the social advancement of the family. A more likely choice would have

65 The owners were Mr and Mrs James Browne from Dublin, and the rent was £12 yearly. 66 On the death certificate, the cause of death was listed as 'bronchitis, uncertified, no med. attended'. Thomas McDonogh was present at the time of death. 67 The only member of the family to have married, and had issue, Michael's son, Thomas, is the current chairman of the McDonogh Group.

been St Joseph's College, known to generations of Galwegians as 'the Bish'. Founded by – and affectionately named after – the Most Revd Dr McEvilly, bishop of Galway, the Bish officially opened on 8 December 1862, and its pupils were, in the main, the sons of the emerging Catholic merchant and professional classes in Galway. However, Martin McDonogh's name does not appear on the roll books for 'the Bish', although his younger brother Redmond (born in 1862) is recorded as having attended the school sometime between 1862 and 1872.[68]

As the eldest son of an ambitious man, much was expected of young Martin, and with this in mind his secondary education followed the path of many sons of upwardly mobile Catholic merchants in the late nineteenth century, in that he was given the best education money could buy, in a Jesuit school. As historian Senia Paseta has observed, 'initially established to cater to the educational needs of the landed gentry, towards the end of the nineteenth century they began to accommodate the "rising classes", composed of merchants and professionals'. The Jesuits provided an education that 'could ensure a fluid social mobility',[69] thereby precipitating what O'Neill has described as a 'drift towards an anglo-centric ethos in the late nineteenth century'.[70] Martin McDonogh was undoubtedly a product of that system. In his poem 'The short cut', Donald Hughes describes the essential ethos of the public-school system as it existed in McDonogh's time:

> In Queen Victoria's Golden Day
> Beneath the mild and settled rule
> The grand old game[71] I used to play
> With decent chaps in a public school
> And I soon found out, as I played the game
> That you need not score a large amount
> But the shortest cut to the heights of fame
> Is to get to know the chaps who count.[72]

It appears likely, therefore, that McDonogh attended St Ignatius' College, a Jesuit school popularly known as 'the Jes', which had been in existence in

68 Patrician Brothers Past Pupils Union, *Centenary record of St Joseph's College, Galway (Patrician Brothers), 1862–1962* (Galway, 1962). 69 Paseta, S., *Before the revolution: nationalism, social change and Ireland's Catholic elite, 1879–1922* (Cork, 1999), p. 43. 70 O'Neill, C., 'Leaning towards empire: Jesuit education at Clongowes and Tullabeg (1870–1900)' (MA, NUI Galway, 2005, TH6325), p. 6. 71 The 'grand old game' in this instance can be taken to mean cricket. 72 'The short cut', quoted in Mangan, J.A., *The games ethic and imperialism: aspects of the diffusion of an ideal* (London, 1985).

Galway since 1860, when the Jesuits established their first college at Eyre Square. Three years later, in 1863, the college moved to its present location on Sea Road, where St Ignatius' church was built next door to the school. Redmond followed his brother and attended 'the Jes', but both boys subsequently completed their secondary education at another Jesuit-run school: St Stanislaus' College in Tullabeg, Co. Offaly.

Why did Thomas McDonogh send his sons away to a boarding school in the midlands, when they were already attending a perfectly good Jesuit school in Galway? First, as acknowledged even by the Jesuits themselves, 'Galway and Limerick had lesser standing in the eye of the provincial, being remote from Dublin and the establishment classes.'[73] Second, for an ambitious man, the opportunity for his sons to get to know a wide circle of 'the chaps who count' was more easily afforded at a boarding school such as Tullabeg.[74] Third, McDonogh was no doubt keen for it to be known that he could afford to send his sons away to be schooled at a prestigious public school – and the fees were indeed considerable, at £35 a year in 1870.[75] Fourth, McDonogh was not alone in his ambition for his sons to 'get on' and become a success; at Tullabeg, a new rector, Fr William Delaney, had been appointed in 1870, and was equally ambitious for his school. Finally, under Delaney's stewardship, emphasis was placed on improving scholarship for professional openings and positions in business.

Tullabeg's academic triumphs were assiduously promoted by Fr Delaney, who 'carefully built and cultivated his contacts with those whom he felt might prove useful to his project,'[76] among whom were Lord Portarlington, Lord Londonderry and the duke of Marlborough.[77] By the time Thomas McDonogh's eldest sons were ready for secondary school, the reputation of Tullabeg had spread far and wide, particularly among the rising Catholic merchant classes, of which, by now, Thomas McDonogh was a well-established member. The decision was made to send Martin and Redmond to Tullabeg, and they arrived (aged 14 and 12) in 1874 and left in 1878.

Originally conceived as a preparatory school for Clongowes, along the lines

73 Mungret College, a Jesuit boarding school located near the village of Mungret, 3 miles west of Limerick city. Costello, P., *A history of Clongowes Wood College, 1814–1989* (Dublin, 1989), p. 51. 74 O'Neill notes that 'of all the Irish schools in the 1870s, Tullabeg had perhaps most deliberately modelled itself on the fashionable English public schools. The rector prioritized cricket and boating, having first copied, word-for-word, the rules of Eton College.' O'Neill, C., 'The Irish schoolboy novel' in *Éire-Ireland*, 44: 1–2 (Spring/Summer 2009), 158. 75 College prospectus, 1870, Tullabeg Papers (Box 31), Irish Jesuit Archive, Dublin. 76 O'Neill, 'Leaning towards Empire', p. 33. 77 Fr Delaney Papers (Boxes 350–4), Irish Jesuit Archives, Dublin.

of Hodder at Stonyhurst,[78] Tullabeg had gradually evolved into a full college. From 1851 onwards, 'the school had so developed as to bring the curriculum for all classes up to the level of that of Clongowes'.[79] New buildings were erected to facilitate the increasing popularity of the school, and by 1870 'the school buildings at Tullabeg were in every way superior to those at Clongowes',[80] and the school had a student population of almost 200, helped by better teaching and enhanced rail facilities from 1859.[81] The new rail link between Dublin and Galway was significant, and may have been a factor in Thomas McDonogh's decision to send his sons there.

By the time Martin and Redmond McDonogh attended the school in the mid-1870s,[82] St Stanislaus' College had already outstripped its initial expectations, and was about to enter its golden age (the 1870s and 1880s) under Fr William Delaney. Having served as a master there from 1860 to 1865, during which time the school 'drew level in scholastic standards with Clongowes',[83] Delaney's abilities as an educationalist saw to it that scholastic standards improved significantly during his tenure. However, Delaney was aware that such standards 'could only end in frustration when they had finished their schooling, for the Catholic University could not legally confer degrees, while Trinity College Dublin and the Queen's Colleges were distrusted by Irish Catholics,[84] laity, clergy and hierarchy alike'.[85] Delaney's own alma mater, Carlow College, had already availed of the facilities afforded by the University of London for conferring extern degrees, and from 1875, Delaney embraced this model: by 1876 he had his first batch of Tullabeg boys entered for the London matriculation. For the next five years, St Stanislaus' College helped twenty-five boys pass the matriculation exam for the University of London.[86] Among the boys who matriculated at the University of London in 1878 were Martin and Redmond McDonogh. Ultimately, during Delaney's tenure, nine Tullabeg students passed the first BA exams and two boys earned a full BA from the University of London.

78 Established in 1807, Hodder Place was the original preparatory school for Stonyhurst College, the Jesuit boarding school in Lancashire, England. 79 Finegan, Revd Francis, S.J., 'Tullabeg (Rahan), 1818–1968', in *Jesuit Year Book*, 1969, p. 9. 80 Ibid. 81 In 1850 Tullamore had no rail connection, the nearest station being Portarlington. By 1854 the Great Southern and Western railway established a line from Dublin to Tullamore. By 1859 the railway connection was carried on as far as Athlone, and in 1863 the Midland Great Western Railway opened a branch line from Streamstown to Clara, Co. Offaly, 5 miles from the school. 82 Thomas Christopher McDonogh also attended Tullabeg in the late 1870s. 83 Finegan, 'Tullabeg (Rahan), 1818–1968', pp 5–24. 84 Finegan notes that Mathias Bodkin, who studied at Tullabeg from 1866–70, 'courageously declined the chance of studying for a degree in any of the then existing Irish universities for the good reason that he set high store on his Catholic heritage'. Finegan, 'Tullabeg (Rahan), 1818–1968', p. 6. 85 Ibid., p. 7. 86 The University of London is referred to in much of the official correspondence as 'London University'.

However, securing academic qualifications, for their own sake, was not the sole preoccupation of the teaching staff at Tullabeg. Writing in *The Clongowian* in 1895, Joseph McGrath,[87] who entered Tullabeg in 1875, while Martin and Redmond were pupils there, observed of his contemporaries that:

> on the threshold of manhood as they were, with high hopes and aspirations, they had seen their college suddenly springing to the front in the educational struggle, and leading the van, where yesterday she was all but unknown. The unflagging zeal, of which this success was the outcome, the untiring energy, the dauntless spirit which met and overcame all obstacles, appealing irresistibly to their youthful minds, and, happily, were to them but earnest of what they, too, would do, face to face with the world.[88]

The McDonogh boys found themselves studying at a college and under a headmaster whose names were becoming bywords for excellence, perseverance and a can-do attitude. The spirit at Tullabeg was something that already characterized the McDonogh family, and Martin, in particular, would have readily identified with it. Tullabeg boys, whatever their background, left the school with an armoury of skills with which to engage 'face to face with the world'.

Activities for students included paper chases and cricket,[89] and 'football … reigned supreme'.[90] Weather permitting, there was skating on Charleville Lake, or on the Grand Canal.[91] Cricket usually began in May. Rowing was another favourite occupation, and Delaney went to the trouble of having the Grand Canal widened at Tullabeg in order to allow it.[92] There was a debating society and a theatre where plays were regularly performed. The debating society was 'modelled on the house of commons, and had a speaker, a ministry and opposition, and each of the "members" took his title from an existing constituency'. Delaney was keen that the pupils would hone their

87 McGrath was one of those who studied for his BA (London) at Tullabeg, and he eventually became the Catholic secretary of the Royal University – the secretaryship being held jointly by a Catholic and a Protestant. When the Royal University was eventually replaced by the National University of Ireland, Sir Joseph McGrath became the university's first registrar. 88 McGrath, J., 'Recollections of Tullabeg', *The Clongownian*, 1 (Christmas 1895). 89 The first crease was laid, during Delaney's rectorship, by Father Wisthoff, a German Jesuit, and the cricketing facilities, described in detail by Pat Hone in his book *Cricket in Ireland*, were first-class, and regarded by one of the famous Lyttleton brotherhood as superior to those at Eton. Hone, W.P., *Cricket in Ireland* (Tralee, 1956). 90 Football in this context refers to rugby football, not soccer. 91 McGrath, 'Recollections of Tullabeg'. 92 Paseta, *Before the revolution*, p. 4.

debating skills in as challenging a format as possible, and, as McGrath notes, 'The masters in the college were admitted into the "house" ... [they] sat amongst us as equals we knew how to treat them as such, and in the course of many heated debates dealt them very hard knocks'.[93]

One of the outstanding teachers in Tullabeg in the 1870s, who taught McDonogh, was Fr John Conmee. He oversaw the amalgamation of Tullabeg with Clongowes in 1886, and became rector at Clongowes, serving during James Joyce's time at the school (1888–91). He is represented in Joyce's *Portrait of the artist as a young man* as the sympathetic listener, Fr Arnall, and also appears in an episode of *Ulysses*.[94]

McDonogh's path from Tullabeg to university was not altogether smooth. He sat his University of London exams twice – in 1877 and 1878 – having failed the exam first time.[95] In 1878, having left Tullabeg with his University of London matriculation secured, McDonogh was ready to begin his university education. This, however, was no ordinary undergraduate student, and remarkably, it is evident that even at the age of 18, McDonogh was clear as to precisely who and what he was. Back in Galway he enrolled as a student at Queen's College Galway, and, less than a month later, when he joined the Sodality of the Blessed Virgin Mary on 2 November 1878, he listed his occupation as 'merchant', and not student or 'scholar' as might have been expected.[96] The entry also noted that Martin McDonogh was a member of a guild, although it does not specify which one. The sodality was attached to St Ignatius' College, indicating, perhaps, a desire on the part of McDonogh to sustain the links forged with the Jesuit community during his time at Tullabeg.

UNIVERSITY CAREER

If McDonogh had been lucky in having attended Tullabeg at just the right period in the school's development, the timing of his third-level education was less fortuitous. Since its first intake of students in 1849 as one of the

93 McGrath, 'Recollections of Tullabeg'. 94 In the 'wandering rocks' episode of *Ulysses*, Joyce chronicled Fr John Conmee's altruistic efforts to gain Dignam's son entry into a Jesuit school for free. 95 McDonogh sat the matriculation exam in June 1877 and June 1878. The entry for 1878 states that the McDonogh was 'up before', indicating that although he sat the exam in June 1877, he failed, and was allowed to resit the exam in 1878. University of London Provincial Matriculation Register (Ref. D9), Special Collections, Senate House Library, University of London. 96 Jesuit archive, Dublin, SC/GALW/7/2/1, No. 333.

'godless colleges' established under the Queen's Colleges (Ireland) Act 1845, the fortunes of Queen's College Galway had fluctuated considerably. However, by 1878, the year McDonogh arrived to study law, things had begun to improve. The college experienced an upsurge – 'the largest yet known',[97] according to the local press – in entrants in 1878 as a result of the awards, exhibitions and prizes awarded to its students, in the arts and medical faculties particularly, and this was further bolstered by the admission of female students. The faculty of law however was not faring so well, and only two students graduated in law in June 1879.

Sadly, McDonogh's experience of university life appears to have reflected that of a fellow Galwegian and Tullabeg alumnus, Matthias McDonnell Bodkin from Tuam, who attended Tullabeg from 1866–70. In his novel *When youth meets youth*,[98] he was scathing about his college days at Newman's Catholic University College Dublin:[99]

> I entered the so-called Catholic University, which had neither charter or endowment, and even obtained an exhibition on matriculation, but the business was so wholly futile that I abandoned it before six months was over, sacrificing my exhibition. A smattering of Terence was the only asset derived from that wasted six months.[1]

McDonogh was to have a similarly disappointing experience at Queen's College Galway. The university's records show that he entered on 10 October 1878, having matriculated *ad eundem* from the University of London at St Stanislaus' College.[2] However, once again an anomaly in the records calls into question his precise age at the time he entered the university. Of the seventy-three students entered on the enrolment book for that year, Martin is the only one who does not give his age. His brother Redmond, who enrolled on 1 October 1878, lists his age as 16. As we have seen, the baptismal certificate presented to the University of London listed Martin's year of birth as 1860, and that of his brother Redmond as two years later, making McDonogh 18 and Redmond 16 when they began their studies. Redmond registered for an

97 *Galway Express*, 19 Oct. 1878. 98 Bodkin, M.M., *When youth meets youth* (London, 1920). The novel is an account of schooldays spent at Raglan College (in reality, Tullabeg) in the 1870s. 99 The fortunes of the Catholic University improved significantly when Fr Delaney took over in 1882. 1 Bodkin, M.M., *Recollections of an Irish judge: press, bar and parliament* (London, 1914), p. 25. 2 The Latin phrase '*ad eundem*', which means 'to, in, or of the same rank', is used in relation to the granting of academic standing, or a degree, by a university to a student whose actual work was done elsewhere, in another college, university or school.

arts degree, and Martin was one of only two students who entered to study law in 1878. He did not, however, stay long enough at his studies to take his first-year exams, and thereafter disappears from the college record.

It had all started well. At the official opening session of the academic year on 1 November 1878, at which attendance for all students was mandatory, the president, Dr Moffett, in the course of a stirring speech, remarked:

> I know not how many of you may be great; for the situations you may hereafter fill in life are beyond your control ... but the characters you make for yourselves, in human dependence on the blessing from above, are in your own power, and can never disappoint or fail you:-

The president went on to quote from Thackery's poem 'The end of the play':

> Go, lose or conquer, as you can;
> But if you fail, or if you rise,
> Be each, pray God, a gentleman.[3]

Hopes must have been high that both Martin and Redmond would graduate with respectable degrees.

Martin's abandonment of his studies was not entirely attributable to either a lack of ability or a lack of interest in academic studies. A series of events conspired against him. First, all was not well within the faculty of law – numbering only seven students in total – in the academic year 1878/9. Of the two professors, one, Professor Campion, professor of English law, was a practicing Queen's counsel, who regularly absented himself from his lecturing duties when involved in lucrative court cases, and the other, Professor Robert Donnell, professor of jurisprudence and political economy, appears to have adopted a somewhat laissez-faire attitude to his academic duties. The college president noted that 'on referring to Professor Donnell's roll book it appeared that his lectures in the first term of this session were commenced on December 7th and terminated on December 20th'.[4] After Christmas, Prof. Donnell informed the council that he would be resuming lectures on 20 March 1879 and would conclude his lectures on 5 April, thereby restricting his lectures for the entire academic year to four weeks, and not the five months prescribed by the law school.[5] It was the case then that McDonogh did not

3 *Galway Express*, 3 Nov. 1878. 4 Governing body minutes, University College Galway, 16 Jan. 1879. 5 Ibid., 3 Mar. 1879.

so much abandon his studies, but rather that the law faculty more or less abandoned him, leaving him to his own devices.

McDonogh was unlucky in his choice of faculty. His brother Redmond was more fortunate in his choice of arts, and graduated in 1882 with a second-class honours degree in English, general jurisprudence and history. He subsequently graduated with an MA in political economy, history and political philosophy in 1883. Redmond appears to have been a good student, and fully embraced college life, securing a number of prizes for composition. In addition, the *Galway Express* recorded him as having 'distinguished' himself at rugby.[6]

Thomas Christopher McDonogh matriculated at the Royal University in London in 1883, having attended St Stanislaus' College.[7] He was 19 when he eventually entered the university the following year, on 10 November 1884, to study medicine (it is unclear why he did not enter the university right after matriculation). T.C. completed his first year of study and was listed as a student for the 1884/5 term, but did not return the following year. Like his older brother, he went to work in the family business. The last of Thomas' sons, Michael Joseph, sat his matriculation exam in July 1891 at the Royal University, having been educated at Clongowes Wood College. He entered the university on 18 October 1892 and studied medicine. He stood the course: although he transferred to complete his degree at University College Dublin, he eventually graduated as a doctor.

Aside from the somewhat chaotic, not to say disappointing, nature of McDonogh's attempt at a university career, his departure from university in early 1879 had a great deal to do with the stark economic environment facing Galway that year – and an event that affected the McDonogh family profoundly. The city was in the grips of a major depression in trade, with businesses going bankrupt and factories closing (Burke's Distillery was one such casualty). The 1870s had begun in prosperity. In 1871 'business was good, jobs plentiful, debts were few, the poor rate was 60% less than what it had been the previous year, and the relief committee had been dissolved'.[8] There were a number of solid industries in Galway that were doing well: the Corrib Sawmills, Persse's Distillery, the Jute Spinning Company, the brush factory and the Salts Marine Company; others, including the paper mill, the Madeira Island Brewery and Burke's Distillery,[9] were in need of some entrepreneurial

6 *Galway Express*, 11 Oct. 1879. 7 Interestingly, in the case of Thomas Christopher, he spells his name, and that of his father, as 'McDonough' in the college register, whereas his brothers Martin and Redmond used the more common 'McDonogh'. 8 Woodman, *Tribes to tigers*, p. 125. 9 Burke's Distillery would

investment to maximize their output and profits. The *Galway Vindicator*, while optimistic about the city's many and varied advantages, was also realistic about what was needed to maximize the city's potential, proclaiming that 'With more energy on the part of our public boards, and more enterprise on the part of our monied men, there is no reason why Galway should not become one of the more progressive centres in the British Isles.'[10]

The prospects for trade at the end of 1878, however, were grim. A particularly wet and cold autumn and winter had caused widespread hardship, and agriculture in particular was adversely affected.[11] The weather had been 'the most severe witnessed for the past quarter of a century',[12] with snow and severe frosts followed by heavy rain and gusts of south/south-westerly winds. By December the *Galway Express* bemoaned the fact that the:

> very serious depression of trade ... now appears to have reached the very aphelion of intensity. With the distress, the privation, the large-increased pauperism, and the broken fortunes that we see around us, we can only hope ... that things are now at the worst, and may begin to mend with the incoming year.[13]

With widespread unemployment and poverty, civic and relief organizations in Galway were struggling to cope. The board of guardians of the Galway workhouse, of which Thomas McDonogh was by then a member, had seen the number of inhabitants rise consistently over the course of the autumn and winter months (by the end of January 1879 the number exceeded 500). The situation was not helped by the fact that in the summer of 1878, an outbreak of smallpox was notified and quarantine precautions put in place, which inevitably impacted on the commercial and trading life of the city. The outbreak began in June, and there were 78 cases in all, resulting in 23 deaths.[14]

However, at a meeting of the board of guardians held in November 1878, it was another death, that of Michael McDonogh, a member of the board, which presaged a significant change in the fortunes of the McDonogh family. Michael McDonogh, the brother of Thomas McDonogh who had married Mary Comerford, had died on 14 November 1878 at the age of 55. With his

ultimately fail. The site would become the location for McDonogh's fertiliser works. 10 *Galway Vindicator*, 29 Dec. 1878. 11 Bad harvests caused by the wet weather meant that by 1878 many farmers were unable to pay their rents in the poorer and wetter counties in the West, and the inflexible land-tenure system led to increasing calls for land reform. As a result, the Irish National Land League was founded on 21 Oct. 1879 in Mayo, with Charles Stewart Parnell as president. 12 *Galway Express*, 18 Jan. 1879. 13 Ibid., 28 Dec. 1878. 14 Ibid., 5 Oct. 1878.

brother gone, and no Comerford sons to inherit the business, the way was now clear for Thomas McDonogh to assume full ownership and management of the Comerford business enterprise. The success of his wife's provisions store in New Dock Street, and his own hard work over the course of nearly twenty years, were about to pay off. Thomas McDonogh took over the firm of Comerford & Co. effective 1 March 1879, and it seems likely that it was at this point that Martin McDonogh abandoned his studies to help his father run the newly expanded business.

In the late 1850s Sir William Gregory MP, in bemoaning the lack of industry in Galway, was dubious about the commitment to, and capacity for, the development of industry and commercial enterprise among Galway's landed gentry. He noted that 'When commercial undertakings offer to capitalists a good prospect they will be commenced in Galway, but I have little faith in such enterprises originating from and depending on country gentlemen.'[15] But the McDonoghs were no 'country gentlemen'. Rather, they were hard-working, extremely ambitious – and, in the case of Martin McDonogh, well-educated – businessmen, whose intention was not to cater to the gentry or even a middle-class clientele. They knew their market, and they had the wit, entrepreneurial flair and necessary contacts to capture that market and satisfy its needs, much as Honoria had already successfully done with her shop in New Dock Street, but at the same time to see where new opportunities lay, particularly in view of the significant changes taking place in agriculture.

From the time Martin McDonogh walked away from full-time third-level education, he became fully immersed in the family business. While his younger brothers continued with their education, as the heir, Martin set about learning his father's trade. With great ambitions for his clearly able son, Thomas McDonogh was a willing mentor. From an early age Martin had accompanied his father on business trips to Connemara and Aran, and he knew his way around the provisions store and sawmills. Now that he had left the world of academia behind him, the apprenticeship of Martin McDonogh began in earnest.

15 Melvin, P., *Estates and landed society in Galway* (Dublin, 2012), p. 251.

2. Learning the ropes: the making of a merchant, 1879–1902

In 1909, the debating society of Mungret College, Limerick, a sister college of McDonogh's alma mater, Tullabeg, considered the motion, 'Whether in the existing circumstances in Ireland the youth of the upper and middle classes ought to devote themselves to commercial and industrial pursuits rather than to the professions.' A number of strong arguments were made in favour of the motion, including that 'whilst the professions in Ireland are overcrowded, the number of capable leaders in the commercial world is so small' and that 'a successful business man can do immense service to the country by giving employment, circulating capital, and thus checking emigration'. The debaters noted that in the most prosperous countries 'the ablest and best become business men'. The motion was carried by 24 votes to 18.[1]

It is impossible to say whether these points were foremost in the mind of Martin McDonogh when he quit his university education in order to enter the family business. However, he seems to have thrown himself into his apprenticeship with determination. Even had his inclination been otherwise, as the eldest son, McDonogh could never have considered refusing his birthright and succeeding his father in the family business. This point was enunciated in an article in the *Clongownian*, in which the writer expressed the view that any young man who 'had a business of their father's to enter and succeed to' but who left it 'for any reason, except for a religious vocation, or on account of a special talent for some other work', should not be encouraged to return, as they would be:

> throwing up the happiness of home life, and the assurance of a good living, an interesting occupation, and a position of influence and usefulness. And, if he has not sense to value this, he can hardly have brains to preserve it.[2]

However, the prospects for the family business in the late 1870s and 1880s were not particularly encouraging. At the close of the nineteenth century

1 'Shall I go to business or choose a profession?', *The Irish Monthly*, 38:446 (Aug. 1910), 460–5 at 460.
2 Ibid.

Galway was, to the eyes of some observers, 'a rather down-at-heel provincial centre which had seen better days'.[3] Historian Gearóid Ó Tuathaigh has noted that 'the late nineteenth century saw Galway as a somewhat sluggish centre of manufacture', but, a lack of industry aside, still a town 'with an important role as a centre of commerce for the western region'.[4]

But to Martin McDonogh, and men like his father, it was a city that had enormous potential just waiting to be exploited. It had an excellent harbour, a railway terminus and a university. Indeed, it was an air of industry and progress that characterized McDonogh's first months working full-time in the family firm, as the summer of 1879 was dominated by the construction of the new Galway & Salthill tramway, with over a hundred men employed from early July digging up the roads and laying rails. The works, while disruptive, were also an economic boon to the town, with the workmen being paid 12 shillings a week.[5] Works were completed on 20 August, the official opening taking place on 1 October 1879.[6]

Welcome as the development of the Salthill tramway was to Galway's developing tourism industry, there were other pressing issues to be addressed. A public meeting was held on 2 November 1879 on issues such as tenant-right, the improvement of Galway Harbour and the need to develop a railway line from Galway to Clifden. All of the local MPs – and Charles Stewart Parnell – were in attendance.[7] Although not yet politically active in a public sense, the McDonogh family were unquestionably nationalist in their outlook, and committed to land reform and home rule. Parnell had, only a week earlier, been in Galway at a meeting in the Imperial Hotel to discuss the formation of the Irish National Land League;[8] Martin McDonogh's uncle Revd Redmond McDonogh, then parish priest of Oughterard, was one of those on the platform at a public meeting held at Killanin in November 1879 on the question of land agitation.[9] At the meeting, Michael Davitt had stated:

> It is the duty … of every Irishman to demand not only for the tenant the proceeds of his industry, but to demand also for Ireland the enjoyment of the wealth which God has given her, and which is now swept off to England under the pretext of imperial annexation.[10]

3 Ó Tuathaigh, G., '"The air of a place of importance": aspects of nineteenth-century Galway' in D. Ó Cearbhaill (ed.), *Galway town and gown, 1484–1984* (Dublin, 1984), p. 145. 4 Ibid., p. 142. 5 *Galway Vindicator*, 23 July 1879. 6 Ibid., 1 Oct. 1879. 7 Ibid., 29 Oct. 1879. 8 Ibid. 9 Ibid., 19 Nov. 1879. 10 Ibid.

This was a policy that Martin McDonogh, his father and his brothers fully supported, as much for practical as for ideological reasons.

By the end of 1879, the McDonoghs' interest in future harbour development was pressing. They were increasingly importing large cargoes of timber, coal and other goods, and the restrictions of the harbour were hampering the development of their business. In December 1879, the senior engineer of the Dublin docks board visited Galway and met with the harbour commissioners to advise the board as to 'the most useful way to improve the harbour'.[11] His report advocated the building of a graving dock,[12] but the harbour board rejected that option by one vote. Thomas McDonogh was one of a group of businessmen in the city who signed a hard-hitting memorial to the board, advocating the immediate commencement of works on the graving dock, which would not only 'provide much-needed employment' but would 'enhance the value and character of our port … circulate capital, and thus confer many benefits on the inhabitants'.[13] The harbour board relented and agreed to employ one hundred men at 12 shillings a week in excavating for the new floating dock. Two years later, in 1882, Thomas McDonogh was elected to the harbour board.

Elsewhere, unemployment, potato blight, and the general distress of the population were matters of such concern that in December 1879, Fr Redmond McDonogh, in an impassioned speech, declared that 'the people cannot hold out much longer; and unless aid and help can be quickly given, the death and desolation of another "46 are before us'.[14] But the bad weather of the winter of 1879 was an ill wind that would benefit the McDonoghs in the long run. The *Galway Vindicator* of 31 December reported on the wreck of a schooner, the *Fairy Fancy*,[15] which had encountered a heavy gale off the Aran Islands. The captain and crew had abandoned the vessel and taken refuge in the islands, whereupon the ship 'was boarded by Lettermullan men who took her to New Quay'.[16] The ship was towed to Galway docks by the steamer *Citie of the Tribes* and under maritime law of salvage,[17] the Lettermullan crew (who would have known the McDonoghs, and were possibly related to them)

11 Ibid., 13 Dec. 1879. 12 A graving dock is a narrow basin that can be flooded to allow a vessel to be floated in, then drained to allow the vessel to come to rest on a dry platform, and be unloaded of its cargo. They are most commonly used for the construction, maintenance and repair of vessels. 13 *Galway Vindicator*, 14 Jan. 1880. 14 Ibid., 31 Dec. 1879. 15 The ship was a three-master from Gloucester, bound for Tralee, Co. Kerry. 16 *Galway Vindicator*, 31 Dec. 1879. 17 The law of salvage acknowledges that a person (or persons) who recover another person's ship or cargo after peril or loss at sea, is entitled to a reward commensurate with the value of the property saved. Although not contractual in origin, it is still a universally recognised right.

considered the ship and its cargo of coal forfeit. A week later, McDonoghs was advertising for sale a cargo of 450 tons of 'best Scotch house coal'.[18]

Though it appears that Martin McDonogh was primarily involved in shadowing his father, he was fortunate in having another mentor to guide his progress in matters entrepreneurial. While Thomas McDonogh was making a profit dealing in salvaged coal, his wife Honoria was assiduously building up her own successful business, placing her own advertisements in the local press, and cultivating the market in her native Aran Islands. An April 1879 advertisement announced that 'Mrs McDonogh of Long Walk, Galway begs to state her lowest prices of salt, tar, etc. to her friends and numerous customers.'[19] A week later she added 'Malbay flags, at very modest rates' to the same advertisement.[20] The following year it was announced that 'Mrs McDonough has got the contract for the gas tar for 1880 and is prepared to sell same at very moderate prices.'[21]

The McDonogh enterprise, dealing as it did with a largely rural, agricultural market, was pragmatic enough to accept that its customers often preferred to pay in kind, and young beasts were often accepted in payment of a bill. Stephen Gwynn, who became one of Martin McDonogh's few close friends, recorded that McDonogh's 'special concern while his father lived was to see to the cattle and attend fairs. He acquired the connoisseurship most admired in an Irish countryside and was … the best judge in Ireland of a polly bullock'.[22] Understandably, this necessitated the acquisition of land that could be grazed and fully stocked, if it was to yield a proper profit. In the spring of 1879, the lands of Monatigue (otherwise known as St Michael's), near Craughwell, Co. Galway, were advertised for lease, in 'divisions of 30 & 50 acres'.[23] Although these were prime grazing lands, the leasing of the Monatigue estate proved problematic, as there were complex issues surrounding the treatment of tenants on the estate. Nonetheless, the McDonoghs were in need of grazing for their increasing herds, and in 1880 Martin McDonogh agreed a twenty-one-year lease for the lands. It was the

18 A heavy price had been paid for the cargo of the *Fairy Fancy*, as three Lettermullan men had been drowned in the process of salvaging the ship, including one, John Connolly, whose body was recovered, and two other unnamed men, whose bodies were never recovered. *Galway Vindicator*, 3 Jan. 1880. 19 *Galway Vindicator*, 12 Apr. 1879. 20 Ibid., 16 Apr. 1879. Malbay flags were cut stone floor flags, similar to Liscannor flags, originating in Miltown Malbay, Co. Clare. 21 The spelling of the family name in advertisements varied from week to week. *Galway Vindicator*, 24 Jan. 1880. The sale of gas tar proved to be a lucrative trade: a 40-gallon cask was selling for 9*s.* 4*d.*, while a 25-gallon cask retailed at 7*s.* 6*d.* Empties could be returned at 2*s.* each (*Galway Vindicator*, 17 Mar. 1880). 22 The term 'polly' refers to an animal that has had its horns removed. Gwynn, S., *Memories of enjoyment* (Tralee, 1946), p. 96. 23 *Galway Vindicator*, 7 June 1879.

20-year-old's first major capital investment, and a sizeable one at that: the lands at Monatigue were valued at £275.[24] The McDonoghs' livestock interests – managed by Martin – proved to be lucrative; in 1890, Martin 'sold six lots of bullocks and heifers, varying in price from £13 to 10 guineas' at the May fair in Galway.[25] The ownership of land, even if only on a long-lease basis, elevated the family to a new social standing, and in the 1901 census Thomas McDonogh listed his occupation as 'J.P., general merchant and farmer'.[26]

Learning the business for McDonogh meant travelling throughout Co. Galway, including Connemara, and doing business with farmers, often trading livestock for feedstuffs, fertilizer and other goods. His experience of interacting with farming communities led to a lifelong love of the minutiae of farming, and was one of the reasons he refused to give up his livestock, even when, commercially, it made no sense for him to maintain a herd. Indeed, the McDonogh family continued to graze livestock, including a milking herd, on the lands adjoining their home in Galway city up until the 1960s.[27] Winning the respect and trust of farmers was critical in the furtherance of the McDonoghs' business interests, and in this regard Martin McDonogh's size and strength were major factors – and he was clever enough to play them up. According to anecdotal evidence from Lettermullan, his most popular demonstration was to raise a full barrel of Guinness above his head.[28]

McDonogh got to know his customers away from the stultified atmosphere of the office in Galway, and they got to know him. He knew what they wanted, and they knew that he was not a man to be trifled with, but was nonetheless a man of his word. To the farmers he traded with, McDonogh was a city merchant, but one who spoke their language, metaphorically as well as literally, and he looked and behaved like the Connemara man he had been born. He knew his trade, recognized good stock when he saw it, and knew how farmers liked to do business. Gwynn records:

> He learnt to pick out infallibly at a glance what he wanted from among a drove of these black, hornless beasts; and he got at fairs his habit of

24 Campbell, F., *Land and revolution: nationalist politics in the West of Ireland, 1891–1921* (Oxford, 2005), p. 178. 25 *Galway Observer*, 7 June 1890. 26 1901 census, National Archives of Ireland. 27 Evidence given by Mrs Ann Gaffney (née O'Beirne), who lived in Devon Place, Galway, in the 1960s. 28 In the 1870s and 1880s, Guinness was using 36-gallon wooden barrels, a gallon of beer weighing approximately 8 lbs. McDonogh would therefore have been lifting 20 st. (130 kg), excluding the weight of the barrel. I am indebted to archivist D. McParland of the Guinness archive for this information.

> never taking a note, trusting to what he had, as naturally as the Gaelic tongue, an Irish countryman's ineffaceable memory.

An account of one encounter McDonogh had with a customer is telling in this regard:

> I saw him one day deep in talk with a frieze-coated, collarless countryman (for none of them would leave the place till they had seen 'Mr Martin' himself) … This man wanted more manure.[29] 'That will make £150 with what you paid me already. Can the holding stand it, Pat?' 'Ah now, Mr Martin, wouldn't one good litter of bonnaves nearly pay for the lot?'[30]

McDonogh agreed, and the farmer got his fertilizer.

While Martin McDonogh played an increasingly important role in the growth of the family business, his father cultivated a profile for himself – and, by association, the extended McDonogh family – through his membership of a number of public boards. In 1877, he had joined his brother Michael as a poor-law guardian, his first significant civic role. Three years later, when the position of relieving officer for the Inishmore electoral division arose, the board of guardians appointed Bartholemew Hernon, McDonogh's brother-in-law. The result was not welcomed in some quarters in Aran,[31] as the rival candidate, Walter Flaherty, was a poor-law guardian 'who resigned his seat at the board to become a candidate', only to find himself without a job and without his seat on the board of guardians.[32]

A measure of the fact that Thomas McDonogh's star was on the rise was his election to the council of the Mechanics' Institute in 1880. With his eldest son making a name for himself as a young merchant, it must have been a source of great pride to Thomas McDonogh that shortly after his election, it was announced that his second son, Redmond, described by the *Galway Vindicator* as 'a gentleman of much ability', would read a paper as part of the

29 Commercially produced fertiliser was initially known as 'artificial manure'. 30 A 'bonnave' (from the Irish '*banbh*') is the most common word used in Ireland to describe a piglet. Gwynn, S., obituary of Martin McDonogh, the *Observer*, 31 Dec. 1934. 31 The three Aran islands – Inis Mór, Inis Méain and Inis Oirr – were known collectively as the district of 'Arran' for the purposes of the poor-law commissioners. Resentment of Hernon's appointment took the form of the burning of a barn and a store of timber that he owned, for which he claimed compensation of £15 from the Arran Islands presentment sessions in Dec. 1880. He was awarded £5. *Galway Vindicator*, 15 Dec. 1880. 32 *Galway Vindicator*, 10 July 1880.

institute's 'penny readings' entitled 'The life of Milton'.[33] Redmond, 18, was clearly a busy young man, as in the same edition it was noted that he had been elected as treasurer of the Queen's College football club.[34] He was also a member of Queen's College Galway chess club,[35] and played cricket for the arts and engineering faculty.[36] McDonogh's paper to the Mechanics' Institute was favourably received, one review stating that 'a better paper could not be produced, which fact reflects much credit on the promising young gentleman'.[37]

Redmond was not the only McDonogh sibling making a name for himself, particularly with regard to sporting prowess. Both Martin and Redmond McDonogh were present when their younger brother, Thomas Christopher, 16, a student at St Joseph's College ('the Bish'), participated in the school's sports day in April 1881, where he came second in the shot-put.[38] Although Martin attended, it was his brother Redmond who was once again the star of the show, acting as a judge and speaking at the prize giving.[39]

That same year, Martin McDonogh began his career in public service the same way his father had: with his election to the Galway board of guardians. Thomas McDonogh stood once again in the North Ward, while Martin stood in the Ballintemple Ward.[40] Martin had just turned 21, the age at which men were eligible for election as poor-law guardians. Also standing, in the Islands of Aran Ward, was John Hernon, Honoria's brother, McDonogh's uncle.

The election took place in an atmosphere of high excitement in Galway, as there had been a well-attended public meeting of the Galway branch of the Land League on 21 March, addressed by T.P. O'Connor MP. In a display of their populist credentials, three members of the McDonogh family were on the platform: Revd Redmond McDonogh, Thomas Snr and Martin.[41] At a subsequent meeting, Redmond represented Galway city as one of the delegates to the Tenants' Defense Association convention in Galway, which his uncle Revd McDonogh also attended. It was a busy month for the McDonogh family, with Thomas McDonagh sworn in on the town grand jury for the first time, and Martin becoming a member of the committee of the St Patrick's temperance band. His commitment to the temperance movement was absolute, and at the first meeting he attended, he subscribed £1 for the provision of uniforms for the band.[42]

33 *Galway Vindicator*, 6 Nov. 1880. 34 Ibid., 6 Nov. 1880. 35 Ibid., 24 Nov. 1880. 36 Ibid., 19 Mar. 1881, 13 Nov. 1880. 37 Ibid., 13 Nov. 1880. 38 Ibid., 20 Apr. 1881. 39 Ibid. 40 Ibid., 5 Mar. 1881. 41 Tragically, four men were drowned in Galway Bay on their way home to Ardfry from the Land League meeting. *Galway Vindicator*, 26 Mar. 1881. 42 *Galway Vindicator*, 23 Mar. 1881.

When the election for poor-law guardians finally took place, Thomas McDonogh was the third and final candidate elected in the North Ward,[43] while Martin comfortably defeated his opponent in Ballintemple.[44] There was disappointment for John Hernon, who only secured 15 votes – further confirmation of the unpopularity of the Hernon family on the Aran Islands. The election resulted in a sea change in the composition of the board of guardians, and the seeming scramble by the more ambitious members – Thomas McDonogh and his son included – for positions was something of a surprise to long-serving guardian Lewis Ferdinand, who noted that 'he could not understand why he had been opposed' in the election, but added that now the contest was over, 'he hoped the little differences that might have arisen during the canvass would be forgotten'.[45] It was to prove a vain hope. For the naturally pugnacious Martin McDonogh, the often contentious meetings of the board of guardians would be an ideal training ground in the workings of public committees. That is, of course, when he attended, which he frequently did not; the board met once a week, and for a busy man, frequently travelling, this was quite a commitment. Membership of the board of guardians was, nonetheless, a prestigious and influential civic role, as the board commanded a considerable budget, and issued many contracts for supplies for the workhouse and infirmary, a fact of which the McDonoghs were only too aware.

By the 1880s, with Irish politics dominated by Parnell, the land question and the demand for home rule, the McDonoghs were among those in the business community determined not to let the public lose sight of the importance of promoting Irish industry, with the ultimate objective of 'returning the country to a stable economy that would allow differences about home rule to be resolved peacefully'.[46] Still, they were supporters of Parnell and the home-rule movement, and members of the Land League; Redmond, in particular, showed a strong interest in politics. The land wars of the 1880s were doubtless a burning topic of conversation in the McDonogh household, given that McDonogh's uncle, Bartly Hernon, who had succeeded his father as the bailiff on Inis Mór, found himself in the thick of it.

In May 1881 Hernon had been instrumental in the arrest of Máirtín Ó Flaithearta and Tomás Ganly, secretary of the Aran branch of the Land League, who were suspected of involvement in killing animals belonging to a

43 Ferdinand secured 203 votes, John J. Kirwan secured 195 and McDonogh secured 152. 44 McDonogh's opponent was the outgoing guardian, Denis Kelly, who secured 41 votes to McDonogh's 84. 45 *Galway Vindicator*, 2 Apr. 1881. 46 Woodman, *Tribes to tigers*, p. 128.

so-called 'land grabber', by throwing them off a cliff.[47] The men served three months in prison. In April 1882, Hernon was fired upon by an unknown assailant. That same afternoon, Seosamh Ó Flaithearta, of Gort na gCapall, was arrested on suspicion of having fired the shot. The alleged motivation for the assault was that Ó Flaithearta's father was in arrears on his rent, and since the rent book had been stolen the previous year, Hernon was the only one who could confirm this.[48] Ó Flaithearta was taken to Galway, charged and given a short prison sentence.[49] A year later, another attack on Hernon, when he was again fired upon, generated greater controversy, when Hernon identified Bryan Kilmartin as having fired the shot. Although local suspicion fell on Ganly, Kilmartin was convicted, 'on the sole and unsupported evidence of Bartly Hernon',[50] and sentenced to penal servitude for life. An intensive campaign was immediately launched by his wife and the parish priest of Aran, Fr Michael Donoghue, to overturn the conviction and have him released. Tomás Ganly, who had, upon his release from prison, 'absconded' to America,[51] confessed, on his deathbed, to two fellow islanders,[52] that it was he who had fired the shot at Hernon.[53] Ganly's brother confirmed that, in the days following the shooting, Ganly had confessed to having fired the shot. Kilmartin was released in 1884, having served two and a half years for a crime he had not committed. For the McDonoghs, this must have been an uncomfortable time, as the Kilmartin case was widely reported on, and Hernon was frequently referred to in the local press and often came before the board of guardians, reporting on acts committed against him by islanders in his role as relieving officer on the islands.

With their father and older brother fully immersed in running the family business, the younger McDonogh boys, Redmond and Thomas Christopher, occupied themselves in their studies, and in enjoying the various sporting activities the city afforded. On the few occasions when Martin could tear himself away from his work commitments, he joined them. Principal among these activities in the summer months was rowing on the Corrib, and Martin, Redmond and T.C. were all members of the Corrib Rowing Club, which was considered Galway's 'premier club'.[54] It had been established in 1864, and its

47 Powell, *Oileáin Arann*, p. 74. 48 Ibid., p. 75. 49 This family of O'Flahertys were relations of the writer Liam O'Flaherty. 50 *Freeman's Journal*, 27 Sept. 1884. 51 In a memorial addressed to the lord lieutenant, Earl Spencer, by Kilmartin's wife, she stated that Ganly had 'absconded a short time after the occurrence to America without ever acquainting his friends or relatives of his intended departure, a most unusual proceeding amongst the islanders'. 52 Peter Hernon and Bryan Flaherty. 53 As bailiff, Bartly Hernon had evicted Tomás Ganly's mother and brother from their homesteads. 54 *Galway Vindicator*, 23 July 1881.

rival, the Commercial Rowing Club, had been set up in 1875.[55] The latter, started by a group of shop assistants from the city as a less exclusive alternative to the Corrib, had taken a while to establish itself fully. As historian John Cunningham notes, 'the social background of its membership conferred advantages on the Corrib club',[56] who had better boats and facilities, at least initially. By 1880, however, the Commercial was on a much firmer footing, with new boats and an active membership, whereas the Corrib had begun to stagnate somewhat. The Corrib had been the subject of some criticism in the local press around the time the McDonoghs joined, due to the fact that 'year after year we find only the same crews coming to the scratch',[57] and this at a time when the club could select from a burgeoning new membership of 'as fine strapping young fellows as ever handled an oar'.[58]

It appears that the captain of the Corrib, Mr M. Semple, took the criticism of the press on board. The McDonogh brothers were tall and very strong, and on the next race day, 18 July 1881, Martin and Redmond were selected to crew in a coxed fours race against the Commercial.[59] Martin was stroke, and the crew put in a powerful performance. Within a few hundred yards of the off, 'the Corrib men took the lead, which they maintained to the finish, winning by several lengths', a considerable achievement given that this was their first race of the season, and they were a crew which had not previously competed together.[60] With August, and the attraction of the Galway Races fast approaching, Martin McDonogh did not compete in any further races with the Corrib, but his younger brothers became the star performers of the club that season. Redmond and T.C. competed together for the first time in a regatta in which they emerged triumphant – winning easily, 'by five or six lengths' – in the coxed pairs.[61] This success in their first race was repeated in their second, when they beat the crew of the Commercial Rowing Club in a thrilling race, which was recounted by the *Galway Vindicator*:

55 Another rowing club, St Patrick's, was established by Fr Peter Dooley in 1880, its membership drawn from his Temperance Society. The Galway Rowing Club, established in 1908, was as an offshoot of the Ancient Order of Hibernians. 56 Cunningham, J., *'A town tormented by the sea': Galway, 1790–1914* (Dublin, 2004), p. 312. 57 *Galway Vindicator*, 16 July, 1881. 58 Then aged 26, T.C. is recorded as weighing 12 st. 4 lbs. *Galway Vindicator*, 30 July 1890. 59 *Galway Vindicator*, 23 July 1881. The other members of the crew were M. Cloherty and J. Commins. A man named Hughes was cox. 60 The success of the crew is remarkable given that the Commercial crew had been 'training since May, and rowed in their splendid new boat, built specially for them this season, whereas the Corrib crew have been in training only for a few weeks, and had only their old boat to row in'. *Galway Vindicator*, 16 July 1881. 61 *Galway Vindicator*, 23 July 1881. The McDonoghs, in the *Swan*, competed against a crew comprising Charles Moon, of Moon's department store, William Binns (cox), who went on to become Galway county surveyor, and W. Barry (stroke), who rowed the *Duck*. The course 'extended from the "grid-iron" to the buoy opposite the

> After very few strokes ... they settled to their work, and, rowing well together, shot past the Commercial boat, and before they had rowed three hundred yards, were leading by about a length. The cox of the Corrib crew, seeing his men leading, headed his boat straight for the turn at the Brush Factory, and in doing so the Commercial crew got the back-water of his crew, which made her roll. Immediately, seeing this, the Commercial crew eased off, and claimed a foul, the Corrib crew holding on their course, rowed to the finish in good form. No foul occurred as the boats never collided in the least ...[62]

The tactics of the McDonogh crew attracted some negative publicity in the local press. A letter from 'An impartial observer', who appears to have been anything but, claimed that the Corrib crew had won unfairly, noting that the cox had:

> whether through stupidity or according to his instructions, I shall not venture to say, left his course and gradually closed in on the Commercial crew, who were thereby obliged to cease rowing to avoid a collision and possibly a serious accident.[63]

The disgruntled observer noted that the Corrib men, 'notwithstanding the repeated calls of the umpire to come back and start again, considered discretion the best part of valour, and "skidaddled"'.[64] Whatever the doubts of the letter writer, the result stood, and the rowing partnership of Redmond and T.C. McDonogh, and their cox Walsh, was the talk of the 1881 rowing season.

The rise of the McDonogh family was continuing apace, and may be charted in one simple manner. In 1879, Thomas McDonogh subscribed £1 to the Galway Races;[65] in 1881 he subscribed £2,[66] and by 1883 he was subscribing £3.[67] In addition, the profiles of the two eldest brothers were such that, in April 1882, when St Joseph's Seminary Athletics Club held its annual sports day, both Martin and his brother Redmond (who was still a student at Queen's College Galway) played prominent roles, Redmond acting as a judge, while 'Mr Martin McDonagh [*sic*] P.L.G. rendered valuable service at the winning post'.[68] The *Galway Observer*, in the same issue, published a poem

steamers quay'. 62 *Galway Vindicator*, 6 Aug. 1881. 63 Ibid. The implication was that Redmond McDonogh, as stroke, made the decision to change course. 64 Ibid., 6 Aug. 1881. 65 Ibid., 19 July 1879. 66 Ibid., 13 July 1881. 67 Ibid., 25 July 1883. 68 *Galway Observer*, 22 Apr. 1882. 'P.L.G.' stands

recounting the events of the sports day, but acknowledging, in the final verse, another event which had occurred that day, and which cheered those attending:

> And now 'tis all over, the work is well done,
> The hampers are empty, the prizes are won
> Now home to old Galway, and with pleasure they see,
> By the stir in the city, that Parnell is free;
> So they cheer and they shout with hearty good will,
> And the town is alight from the Square to Salthill.[69]

On 15 April, the day of the sports day, news had reached Galway that Charles Stewart Parnell had been released from Kilmainham jail, having been confined there since the previous October. The ensuing celebrations in Galway were premature, however, as Parnell had merely been allowed out on parole, and he returned to jail within a few days. However, in the interim, the Kilmainham Treaty had been agreed, and Parnell was finally released in May 1882. For the Parnellites Martin and Redmond, this was an occasion of great celebration, but the McDonoghs' attitude towards Parnell was to change quite dramatically before too long.

By 1883, Thomas McDonogh was both a harbour commissioner and a town commissioner. Martin McDonogh, meanwhile, was a poor-law guardian, a supporter of the Land League, an advocate of home rule, a prominent member of the temperance movement, and, most significantly, a well-respected merchant and dealer. And his entrepreneurial inclinations were not solely focused on the existing family businesses. In February 1883, when a group of Galway businessmen held a public meeting to discuss the establishment of a woollen mills in the city, it was sparsely attended, but the *Galway Express* reported that 'the few who occupied seats on the platform were, to use a vulgar phrase, composed of the "right stuff"'. Martin McDonogh was one of those on the platform,[70] and his subsequent involvement, as both a director and shareholder in Galway Woollen Mills, was to prove decisive in the success of the operation.

A month later, the McDonogh family were dealt a major blow. Honoria McDonogh had apparently been 'ailing for some time, but her family and friends had hoped her valuable life would have been spared for some time

for 'poor-law guardian'. 69 Ibid. 70 *Galway Express*, 24 Feb. 1883.

longer'.[71] It was not to be. The *Galway Observer* recorded that the death of 'Mrs Honoria McDonogh, the wife of our esteemed and highly respected townsman, Mr T. McDonogh … took place yesterday afternoon at her residence, Flood Street'.[72] This was the second major blow to the McDonogh family that month, and to Thomas McDonogh in particular, for in the same edition, the *Observer* noted that his brother, Patrick McDonogh, had 'died after a short illness on Tuesday 6th March, 1883, at Lettermullan, aged 38 yrs'.[73]

The death of his mother affected Martin McDonogh deeply. He was, according to those who knew him, extremely close to her. The death certificate for Honoria McDonogh notes that when she died of heart disease it was her eldest son, and not her husband, who was with her.[74] She was only 45. She had lived to see her family prosper, with her eldest sons having made it to university, and her younger sons receiving a first-class education and likely to progress to university and enter the professions. Her eldest daughter, Mary Anne, was 14, and Kate, the youngest in the family, was 10. Honoria had established a successful business of her own, and her commercial acumen more than matched that of her husband. Nonetheless, her death certificate recorded her occupation as 'wife of a merchant'.[75] The loss of his mother, which for Martin had both emotional and practical implications – as there was now the question of taking over the management of her business interests – contributed to the significant curtailment of his public life in the following year.

The standard mourning period following Honoria's death did not deter her husband and son from contesting the 1883 election for the poor-law guardians, although it was noted that neither canvassed the constituents in their wards, and they were widely praised for this.[76] Both were easily re-elected, and Martin McDonogh emerged, if anything, more forthright, even brusque, in his manner following the death of his mother. While there is no evidence to suggest that Honoria had a calming influence on her son, there is no doubt that while his father had bided his time at board of guardians meetings, at least initially, his son was far less reserved, and more impatient. Still only in his early twenties, McDonogh's blunt manner would only

71 *Galway Vindicator*, 10 Mar. 1883. 72 *Galway Observer*, 10 March 1883. 73 Ibid. 74 The death certificate, dated 12 Mar. 1883, records the cause of death as 'disease of heart, certified'. 75 Honoria would doubtless have been pleased to see her oldest daughter, Mary Ann, who died aged 85 in 1948, and never married, have her occupation recorded on her death certificate as 'independent means'. 76 *Galway Observer*, 7 Apr. 1883.

intensify as he grew older; but, it should also be noted, so did his unerring ability to cut through the mundane details, get to the point, and make a decision, traits for which he was, deservedly, recognized by his peers, even though they often found themselves on the receiving end of his sharp tongue and disdain.

One man who may not have directly felt McDonogh's disdain, but who nonetheless was the recipient of it, was Parnell. McDonogh's disenchantment with Parnell was not unusual among men of his class and political persuasion in Galway at that time. However loyal they had been to Parnell and his campaigns for land reform and home rule, two things in particular had soured relations between Parnell and many of his Galway supporters, including McDonogh. First, Parnell's decision to foist Captain O'Shea upon the Galway electorate in 1886 had angered many. Redmond McDonogh had been the campaign manager for Michael Lynch, the candidate who had originally planned to stand against O'Shea in the election, but had eventually been persuaded, as a result of intense pressure from Parnell, to withdraw his candidacy.[77] Second, Parnell's relationship with Mrs O'Shea, the subsequent divorce case, and their eventual marriage proved too much for the conservative Catholics of Galway. The local press recorded that:

> All over County Galway a decided revulsion of feeling has set in against Mr Parnell's pretensions. Among a certain class it went all very well with him till he got married … It is one of those things that countrymen cannot understand.

Although a city boy, McDonogh and his family retained, ostensibly, the moral view and code of behaviour of 'countrymen', and as a devout Catholic, there was no question of him supporting Parnell after this scandal. McDonogh's involvement with national politics waned considerably at this stage in his life, and he only really became actively involved again in 1912, with the passing of the home-rule bill. Anyway, there was hardly much time for Martin McDonogh to become involved with national politics, given the demands of the family businesses and his civic responsibilities.

Mindful that the success of their enterprise was, to a large degree,

77 O'Shea secured only 945 votes in the election, although the previous MP, fellow Irish Parliamentary Party member T.P. O'Connor, had secured 1,335 only months earlier in the general election of 1885. As the ballot papers had been printed by the time Lynch withdrew, his name was still on the paper, and he secured 65 votes, despite his withdrawal. The *Times*, 12 Feb. 1886.

dependent on the loyalty both of their own employees and of the population of Galway in general – and Martin, in particular, was mindful of this throughout his professional life – the McDonoghs often walked a thin line between protecting their business interests and displaying a philanthropic, and at times paternalistic, regard for their fellow Galwegians. In March 1890, the wreck of a ship belonging to Thomas McDonogh & Sons, which had foundered on the shore at Renmore, was set ablaze by the company, with, according to the local press, 'the view to taking out the copper and iron'. This was a pragmatic approach to salvaging what could be saved from a lost asset, but on previous occasions where vessels belonging to the company had foundered, it had been the practice of the McDonoghs to allow local people to strip the hulks for firewood. However, in this instance it appeared that 'parties were helping themselves to more of it than they were allowed',[78] and, aggrieved that their goodwill was being taken advantage of, McDonogh sent two men to guard the hulk. The watchmen were set upon by a body of men, who 'threatened them in divers moods and tenses' and the watchmen ran for their lives. The police were alerted, and Martin ordered the hulk burned. The message was clear: the McDonoghs were prepared to be generous, but they were not prepared to have their generosity, or their property rights, taken advantage of.

McDonogh was, however, famously generous and loyal to those who had proven their worth to him. Four years after the burning of the boat at Renmore, in March 1894, another boat, this time a Galway hooker belonging to the McDonoghs,[79] foundered in a strong gale, and was driven ashore at the Curragh, Renmore, Galway. The *Faugh a Ballagh* was attempting to deliver a cargo of 30 tons of flour, which it had transferred from a larger ship anchored off Galway.[80] The hooker got into difficulties, and a group of local men, observing this from the shore, boarded a four-oared rowboat and made their way to the *Faugh a Ballagh* to try to save the crew.[81] The men 'encountered heavy seas on the way out, but … held on their way till they got to the hooker which was fast sinking. There were three men on board the hooker, and two of them, at great risk, jumped into the small boat.'[82] The skipper initially refused to

78 *Galway Observer*, 8 Mar. 1890. 79 The Galway McDonoghs were not the only McDonoghs operating a fleet of Galway hookers. Thomas McDonogh's sister, Monica Mór, of Tiernee (Tír an Fhia) in Ceantar na nAileáin, owned several shops in Connemara, and one in Galway city, which she supplied with her own fleet of hookers. Cunningham, *'A town tormented by the sea'*, p. 188. 80 An anglicisation of the Irish '*fág a'bealach*', which translates as 'get out of the way'. The larger ship was the *Forfarshire*. 81 The rescue party, led by Thomas Smith, was comprised of Mark Ryan, John Molloy, Stephen Brown and Martin Brown. 82 *Galway Observer*, 3 Mar. 1894.

abandon ship, but 'another hooker came along shortly afterwards and insisted on taking him off. The men were all eventually saved, but the hooker sank shortly afterwards.'[83] Once the crew and rescuers were all safely ashore, the race began to salvage the cargo and raise the hooker, an operation that was directed by Martin McDonogh, the *Observer* reported.[84] In contrast to the contempt shown by McDonogh towards the locals of Renmore, who had abused his generosity, McDonogh's gratitude to the men who had bravely rescued both his crew and his cargo took immediate and practical form: all of the men involved in the rescue operation – and in some cases generations of their families – subsequently worked for McDonoghs.[85]

By the early 1890s, Martin McDonogh had been joined in the family business by another of Thomas McDonogh's sons, Thomas Christopher. Redmond McDonogh, meanwhile, had established his own practice as a solicitor. He had acquired a significant public profile as a result of his sporting prowess and his involvement with the Land League, and his practice was an immediate success. He was appointed as solicitor to the Galway board of guardians in 1887,[86] which proved to be a lucrative position. Three years later, when he presented his first bill for his services to the board, it amounted to £175 10*s.* 3*d.*[87] It is perhaps indicative of the overall success of McDonogh's legal practice that he could afford to wait three years before presenting his first bill. Redmond McDonogh's practice was varied. He dealt with the conveyancing and courtroom work that was the staple of most such practices. He also provided legal consultancy, much of it as a result of his carefully cultivated network of connections. In 1890, for example, Redmond was appointed as the solicitor/representative of a company established to promote the creation of a steam packet company between Galway and New York, and to win the support of the harbour commissioners for the venture. Given that Redmond's father and brothers were at that point members of the harbour board, it was a judicious appointment.[88] Redmond was also fortunate that his family's connections gave him a very broad client base to draw on. In one malicious-injury case, in which he defended six Carraroe men accused of deliberately driving the cattle of a neighbouring farmer into a boghole, five of the six were named McDonogh.[89] He also regularly defended members of his mother's family, the Hernons; in one particularly harrowing case, he

83 Ibid. 84 Ibid. 85 O'Dowd, *In from the West,* pp 116–23. 86 *Galway Observer,* 2 Nov. 1889. 87 Ibid., 8 Mar. 1890. 88 Ibid., 15 Feb. 1890. 89 Ibid., 1 Mar. 1890. The fifth defendant was a man named Faherty. The men were accused of injuring the cattle of a farmer named Carter, who had taken over the farm of an evicted tenant. Five of the nine cattle were drowned.

defended an islander, Mary Ann Hernon, who had been charged with infanticide.[90]

Redmond McDonogh 'argued with great ability,'[91] and was a robust, forthright advocate, who, in common with his older brother Martin, didn't pull any punches. In 1890, he represented a farmer in a malicious-injury case taken by a collector for the excise department. From the evidence presented, it appeared that it was the latter who was, in fact, at fault, having been drinking. However, as a public official – and therefore a gentleman in the eyes of the court – the magistrates appeared sympathetic to him. McDonogh was reprimanded by the bench for inferring as much in his questioning, and defiantly replied, 'I won't take any directions from the bench. I will take no instructions as to the questions I shall put to a witness – from your worship at all events.'[92] McDonogh upbraided members of the bench for their all-too-rare appearance at the petty sessions,[93] noting that they would, in all likelihood, not have attended in such numbers, if the plaintiff was less of a public figure, and reminded their worships that, 'on the one side is a wealthy man, and a man of influence, and on the other is a poor man, and that being so it was all the more necessary that the bench should hold the balance evenly'.[94] McDonogh's forthright manner appears to have impacted upon the magistrates, and the derisory amount of the fine imposed – *1s.* and *25d.* – signalled a significant moral victory for McDonogh and his client.[95]

Redmond was the McDonogh with the most active interest in politics, and the highest political profile. There had even been talk of his being a candidate for the Irish Parliamentary Party in the 1885 general election. However, any political aspirations he may have had came to nought, for, in May 1891, it was reported that one of Galway's 'more popular sons' had been advised to leave the country and adjourn to a warmer climate for the good of his health, and would soon be departing for Denver, Colorado.[96] The brightest star in the McDonogh family had succumbed to tuberculosis. The disease, which accounted for 45.6 per cent of all deaths in young adults aged 15–34 in Ireland in 1881–90,[97] was generally considered terminal. Only those who could afford the highest standards of medical care, and, more importantly, benefit from

90 *Galway Observer*, 24 May 1890. 91 *Galway Vindicator*, 7 Aug. 1890. 92 *Galway Observer*, 5 Apr. 1890. 93 Those sitting on the bench included the chairman, Mr R.M.S. Somerville, Mr C.E.B. Mayne, RM, Dr P.M. Rice, Sir Valentine Blake, Bt, Mr Henry S. Persse and Mr Marcus Lynch. 94 *Galway Observer*, 5 Apr. 1890. 95 Ibid. 96 Ibid., 16 May 1891. Although Colorado was Redmond McDonogh's original destination, he later moved to New Mexico, where there were a number of sanatoria for the treatment of TB. 97 Jones, G., *'Captain of all these men of death': the history of tuberculosis in nineteenth and twentieth century Ireland* (New York, 2001), p. 35.

the restorative powers of a warmer climate, had any chance of surviving. Although Redmond's diagnosis must have been a shock to the family, the move to the US gave him the best possible chance to make a full recovery, and the press reported that the prognosis appeared to be good. Redmond announced that his legal practice would continue to operate, pending his return.

With his brother away and his father's health also beginning to break, work and family pressures mounted on Martin McDonogh. As a result, he attended only two board-of-guardians meetings in 1891.[98] T.C. began to take an increasingly large role in the family business and in civic affairs, and he was elected for Aran in the poor-law elections of 1892. When it came to sitting on committees and boards, the contrast between Martin McDonogh, on one hand, and his father and brother T.C., on the other, was quite striking, particularly with regard to their *modus operandi.* This may best be seen in respect of their membership of the harbour commissioners. Thomas McDonogh was a very conscientious member from the outset (as T.C. would later be). Although a regular attender, Thomas McDonogh rarely contributed significantly to meetings. He was a solid, safe pair of hands, and slowly, over time, he won the respect and confidence of his fellow commissioners. By 9 June 1891, he chaired his first meeting. By 21 June 1892, he was signing the minutes 'chairman, pro tem'. On 1 August 1893, he officiated at the meeting that announced the results of the triennial elections to the board of the harbour commissioners; Martin was elected with a vote of 296, the highest received.

The harbour commissioners met fortnightly, but Martin McDonogh did not actually attend a meeting until 27 February 1894 – a full six months after his election.[99] Thereafter, his attendance continued to be erratic, but Thomas and Martin McDonogh appear to have had an arrangement that if one had to be absent, the other would be sure to attend, as a means of keeping abreast of proceedings and maintaining a presence. This was a strategy the McDonoghs adopted throughout their careers. T.C., in particular, who had fewer responsibilities within the family businesses, would be a very regular attender at meetings when he began to be elected to various public bodies.

By April 1892 the local press reported that Redmond McDonogh had returned to Galway, 'fully restored to health and strength. He looks much better than when he left and his countenance is a little bronzed.'[1]

98 *Galway Observer,* 5 Mar. 1892. 99 Harbour commissioners' minutes, 27 Feb. 1894. 1 *Galway*

Commenting on McDonogh's enforced sojourn in the US, the *Observer* noted that 'He speaks highly of Colorado, and considers it a great country but thinks that after all Galway has also its advantages,' and that, having returned to Galway, 'he has resumed the practice of his profession'.[2] With Redmond back, Martin resumed his public career with vigour. He first stood as a candidate, for the East Ward, in the annual election of town commissioners held on 1 September 1892, and was elected with 161 votes.[3] Martin's subsequent attendance at meetings was sporadic, but at the election of commissioners in 1894, T.C. was elected in the North Ward, and proved to be a regular attender.

Martin McDonogh's poor attendance may be somewhat explained by the relative inefficiency of the town commissioners. Meetings were often abandoned as a quorum had not been reached, and the meetings that did take place were long, with mundane matters taking a disproportionate amount of the commissioners' time. As a man with several businesses to run, and in view of his membership of other civic and public bodies, McDonogh did not like to waste time. On more than one occasion he abruptly left meetings, even those he was chairing, when he believed time was being wasted.[4] The demands on public figures such as Martin McDonogh were considerable. In one week, in April of 1894, his father Thomas chaired meetings of the Galway Gas Light Company, the Galway board of guardians, and the board of management of Galway General Hospital, in addition to attending lengthy meetings of the town commissioners and the harbour board, and serving as a justice of the peace at the Galway petty sessions.[5] Martin's obligations were similarly onerous.[6]

By this point, both Martin and his father were also involved in the establishment of the Galway Woollen Mills, an enterprise meant to make up for the loss of the bag factory some years previously.[7] From the outset, their input was critical to the operation's success. Even the *Galway Observer*, which had often criticized the lack of commercial entrepreneurship in Galway, was moved to acknowledge that 'it is quite evident that the few gentlemen who formed this committee knew what they were about and did their work well.'[8]

Observer, 9 Apr. 1892. 2 Ibid. 3 Henry Persse and Major Lynch both stood for re-election, and along with McDonogh the other candidates were L.L. Ferdinand and Michael Walsh. 4 *Galway Observer*, 21 July 1900 and 5 Oct. 1901. 5 Ibid., 14 Apr. 1894. 6 In 1895 he attended six out of the fifty meetings of the poor-law guardians, while his father attended twenty-two. Minutes of Galway poor-law guardians, 1895. 7 Established in the 1860s, the Galway Jute Spinning Company produced jute bags, mostly for the flour milling trade. It had closed in 1885, but after an appeal for investment, reopened again and operated for a few years, until finally closing in 1893. The factory employed 'two to three hundred workers in 1885 … the vast majority were women'. Cunningham, *'A town tormented by the sea'*, p. 182. 8 Aside from

The set-up costs had been considerable – £1,275 17*s*. 6*d*. in machinery (with expenditure of a further £214 planned), and £1,158 on construction costs – all of which was underwritten by the organizing committee and the share capital generated by the initial investors.[9] By May 1895, most of the machinery was in place and in working order, and the share prospectus for the new business was issued, to a generally favourable response.

Martin McDonogh's involvement in the woollen factory was instructive, not least in the sense that it highlighted the fact that entrepreneurship was not always recognized or acknowledged by members of the wider business community in Galway, who would ultimately benefit from the factory's success. The factory had been established with the best of intentions, but was not, at least initially, widely supported in the town. In a strong letter to the press, Martin Redington, one of the principal shareholders, rounded on those who were failing to support the fledgling enterprise, wondering 'when will we cease carping, censuring and condemning every effort made to improve the trade of our town?' This attitude, he argued, had led to numerous missed opportunities, and to Galway becoming 'one of the most paralized [*sic*] and decaying cities in the world'.[10] McDonogh would likely have been of a similar view. New innovations in existing industries were also subject to resistance, and in this regard the McDonogh's fleet of fishing trawlers ran into difficulties. Before an inspector of fisheries enquiry in November 1895, it was alleged that McDonogh's trawlers were among those damaging fish stocks and undermining the livelihoods of Claddagh fishermen, one fisherman alleging that 'Mr McDonagh's trawler took away his spillets and buoy'.[11] In reality, however, the days of fishing with spillets were fast coming to an end, and the McDonogh fishing fleet was equipped with the most modern equipment, maximising its catch and providing employment to many local men.

When a topic arose that mattered to him, McDonogh was a formidable advocate – or adversary. At a poor-law-guardians meeting in February 1890 at which distress on Aran was discussed,[12] McDonogh contradicted the report of the Aran medical officer, Dr Kean, who stated that all was now well and

Martin McDonogh, the others involved on the organising committee were Fr Dooley, Mr J.C. McDonnell, Mr Francis Lydon and Mr P.J. Hannon. The inaugural board of directors included Martin McDonogh and his father Thomas, Messrs Hannon and McDonnell, Charles Moon and Dr Grealy (chairman). *Galway Observer*, 25 May 1895. 9 Ibid. 10 Ibid., 9 Nov. 1895. 11 Ibid., 2 Nov. 1895. 12 The distress was due largely to a prolonged spell of bad weather that the islands had been experiencing.

that the fishermen were again able to fish, stating, 'I know myself the village of Killeany must be in a very poor way. These people have no land at all; they live by the fishing.'[13] Later that same year, McDonogh, in his capacity as chairman of the dispensary committee, was commissioned to write a report for the guardians on accusations made against Dr Kean, a report read by McDonogh to the meeting, over the course of an hour, and commended by the guardians for its balance and fairness.[14]

The quality of McDonogh's report was doubtless made possible by the fact that, unlike Dr Kean, he spoke fluent Irish, and was able, during his visit to Aran, to speak to men who knew and respected him, in their own language, and gather the full facts. All of the McDonoghs were fluent Irish speakers, and used the language when the occasion demanded.[15] But, in general, their attitude appears to have been that English was the principal language of commerce, and that while fluency in Irish could be useful, it was not a desirable, or indeed advisable, accomplishment, if one wanted to 'get on' in the world, and attain financial success and respectability. In this regard the McDonoghs were not particularly remarkable among their fellow upwardly mobile, middle-class Irishmen. The writer Liam O'Flaherty, in his novel *Skerrett,* which is set in the fictional island of Nara (an anagram of Aran) perhaps best expresses the attitude of the McDonoghs and their ilk through the words of the bailiff, Cloonan, a character based on McDonogh's uncle Bartly Hernon:

> without English ye'll remain in misery and poverty and ignorance, same as ye always were. How can ye go to America without English? How can ye get a job like I have without English? It's English gave me bacon on a Sunday morning for my breakfast and gives me tea twice a day, while ye are all living on Indian meal porridge and potatoes and salt fish.[16]

No member of the McDonogh family, although they all considered themselves nationalists, ever joined the Gaelic League, or publically supported or embraced any of the Irish-language initiatives it organized. However, Redmond McDonogh's fluency in the language was of major benefit to him

13 *Galway Observer,* 8 Feb. 1890. 14 *Galway Vindicator,* 30 July 1890. 15 Tomás Ó Broin, in an article entitled 'Sean-Ghaeilgeoirí na Gaillimhe' in St Joseph's ('the Bish') *Centenary Record* (1962), noted that 'Bhí acmhainn ag na ceannaithe móra ar fad ar labhairt na Gaeilge [all the big merchants had the capacity to speak Irish]: Tadhg Ó Neachtain, Síomón Ó Corbáin, Máirtín Mór Mac Dhonncha, Mícheál Ó Flathartaigh.' 16 O'Flaherty, L., *Skerrett* (Dublin, 1977), p. 11.

in his legal career, as he represented clients from Connemara and the Aran Islands in court. When he was defending one such client, and the judge questioned the difference it would make if one of the prosecution witnesses insisted on giving his evidence in Irish, McDonogh replied that 'it makes this difference, your worship, the man is better able to tell his lies in Irish',[17] to laughter in the courtroom. Redmond McDonogh also featured regularly in the Aran petty sessions, conducting many of his examinations of witnesses in Irish.

Redmond McDonogh's return to Galway in April 1892 proved to be short-lived, for within two years he had been forced, by reasons of ill health, to return to the United States. Once again, the respite from the cold, damp climate of the West of Ireland appears to have benefitted him, and by October 1894 he was not only practising law in the United States, but also writing articles in American journals on affairs in Ireland. The strong Catholic faith of Martin McDonogh was a feature throughout his life, and appears to have been a family trait, as his brother Redmond wrote and published on religious matters, particularly the work of the Protestant missions in Connemara. The *Galway Observer* noted that McDonogh had written an article in a journal published in New Mexico,[18] in which he argued that the level of conversions in Connemara being reported by Protestant missions was greatly exaggerated. The *Observer* concurred, noting that:

> the awful tissue of misrepresentation that circulated so brazenly is exposed by Mr McDonagh [*sic*], and laid bare in all its naked deformity of the falsehood and repulsive hideousness of its lies. Much credit is due to our talented young friend for doing such doughty service for the cause of catholicity and truth.[19]

While Martin McDonogh was the heir apparent, a hard worker, and, increasingly, raising his public profile and reputation through his involvement in a number of public bodies, it was Redmond, the second son, who was the 'golden boy' of the family – academically bright, an accomplished sportsman, popular with both his contemporaries and local establishment figures, and a young man with clear political ambitions. How his older brother Martin felt about this is impossible to say, but Liam O'Flaherty, in his novel *The house of*

17 *Galway Observer*, 28 Dec. 1889. 18 *Revista Católica* was a Catholic newspaper and printing house, directed by the Jesuit order, and established in Albuquerque, New Mexico, in 1873. The printing house moved to Las Vegas, New Mexico, in 1875. 19 *Galway Observer*, 20 Oct. 1894.

gold, hints at what McDonogh's attitude might have been. The principal character, Ramon Mór Costello, a thinly disguised caricature of Martin McDonogh, explains his social gaucheness, and his inability to forge close relationships, as being the result of the expectations and responsibilities placed on him, by his mother and others, because he was the oldest son and heir:

> It's because of the way I was brought up, struggling all the way, never any time to teach myself anything that's necessary for a man to know when he goes abroad into the world. I mean apart from work. I put my trust in the wrong people. That's the fault too of the way I was brought up. I never had time to study … There was always something. I have nobody to help me … I always had to do everything myself. I never had any time for play … I never had time to study the ways of women. Still … the intention was there, although I may be a hard man to understand.

O'Flaherty's characterization of Ramon Mór rings true for Martin McDonogh, whom O'Flaherty would have known well.

In 1898, the *Galway Vindicator* announced the death, on 30 March, of Redmond McDonogh, at the age of only 36.[20] Described as 'one of the most brilliant and popular of our young fellow citizens' the *Vindicator* recorded that:

> after a distinguished academic and university career, the young gentleman, who was second eldest son of Thos. McDonagh, Esq., J.P., one of our leading merchants, became a solicitor, and … bounded to the foremast rank of his profession, when attacked by that foul malady, which has no pity for gilted intellect, and cultured professional acumen, on the advice of medical friends he went to a more congenial climate, and equally distinguished himself professionally as was to have been anticipated. On Wednesday evening when the cablegram announcing his demise became known the whole town was in mourning, as if each family had lost a friend. We shall seldom look on his like again. We understand the remains will be brought home and interred in the family burying place.[21]

20 The McDonogh propensity for inaccuracies in dates occurs once again on Redmond McDonogh's tombstone, which states that he was 38 when he died, when in fact, having been born in 1862, he was two years younger. 21 *Galway Vindicator*, 2 Apr. 1898.

Figure 5 Redmond McDonogh's grave in Las Vegas, New Mexico

Redmond McDonogh's remains were never returned to Ireland, but were instead buried, according to his father's instructions, at Our Lady of Sorrows church cemetery, in Las Vegas,[22] San Miguel County, New Mexico (figure 5). It appears, from the various obituaries that appeared in Ireland and the United States, that McDonogh, in common with the rest of his siblings at that stage, had not married. Although Redmond was buried in New Mexico, the vote of condolence passed at a meeting of the town commissioners noted that he had died in Colorado 'where during his sojourn he had made a name for himself as a distinguished member of the American bar'.[23]

22 Las Vegas, New Mexico is not to be confused with the casino town of Las Vegas, Nevada.
23 *Galway Express*, 2 Apr. 1898.

The obituary in the *Galway Express*, a fiercely unionist paper not given to favourable comment on known nationalists such as McDonogh, was effusive:

> Death has taken away one of our most honourable and patriotic exiles, Mr Redmond McDonagh, solicitor, Colorado, son of our respected townsman Thos. McDonogh, Flood St. It is sad to think that such a hard working and clever young man just blossoming into fame and renown through the sole effect of his exceptional talents, should be torn away suddenly from this unhappy world. Much regret is felt for Mr McDonogh, who was well known to all in town, and especially his schoolmates, amongst whom he was a general favourite. He went through a brilliant course at the Queen's College, and took the degree of MA at the Royal University. He took a leading part in all the national and popular movements that went on in Galway during the most exciting periods of the agitation. In fact he threw himself heart and soul into the stirring movements of the time, and took so much interest in them that he ran the risk of imperilling his educational and prospective career.[24] However, when he took to the exercise of his profession, he soon rose to distinction, and very quickly got into a large and lucrative practice. At one time he stood a good chance of being elected member for Galway, but unfortunately his health broke down, and he had to seek the more congenial climate of Colorado. Even in Colorado he was well known as one of the rising young men of the city, till, all of a sudden, we hear he was stricken down, and after a few day's illness, breathed his last … very few have passed away of late years in Galway for which such a feeling of sympathy is felt as for Mr Redmond McDonagh.[25]

The harbour board, similarly, bemoaned the death of a young man who had 'a bright career before him'.[26]

Redmond's death impacted the McDonogh family deeply, and Martin in particular. Redmond was the brother closest in age to him; they had been sent away to school at Tullabeg together, and had started university together. They were both tough and uncompromising, but, in contrast to Martin, Redmond appears to have had a real personal charm, which he undoubtedly cultivated during his university years, when Martin was otherwise occupied, honing his business skills at their father's side. The loss of his brother must have weighed

24 Although he won prizes for his academic work in his second and third years at university, he emerged with a second-class honours MA. 25 *Galway Observer*, 2 Apr. 1898. 26 *Galway Express*, 9 Apr. 1898.

heavily on Martin McDonogh, particularly since, less than a month after Redmond's death, the *Galway Express* noted that Thomas McDonogh had been suffering from a 'severe illness'.[27] The precise nature of his illness was not revealed, but the observation that he was 'sufficiently recovered as to enable him to walk about' indicates the significant debilitative nature of his condition. The concern with which Thomas McDonogh's illness had been viewed prompted the *Galway Express* to declare its:

> great pleasure at the recovery of Mr McDonogh, who has at all times been a general favourite with the people of Galway, both town and county, and now that he is once again able to come amongst us, we can only echo the universal wish ... that he may be long spared to enjoy that popularity.

As it happened, Thomas McDonogh was spared only four more years, during which time his fluctuating health placed a significant additional strain on his eldest son.

Martin McDonogh's professional and public duties increased significantly in 1898, when his father's health began to break, and his attendance at meetings of various public bodies, in the absence of his father, became more pressing. McDonogh's somewhat brusque manner was, by that stage, very much in evidence, and, without the moderating influence of his father, was given full rein, much to delight of the Galway media, who were always happy to report on his notorious flashes of temper. One such incident occurred in July 1898, over the issue of the forthcoming Local Government Act of 1898.[28] This act represented a major rationalization and democratization of local government in Ireland, replacing the gentry-dominated system of grand juries and boards of guardians with county councils elected by all those who already had a vote in parliamentary elections, including women. Although the act was widely welcomed, in Galway it gave rise to much controversy and debate, largely over the issue of whether or not Galway city should be a county borough. Under the terms of the act, six Irish cities were to be county boroughs, but Galway was not one of them. The act specified that only a city with a population of more than 25,000 could become a county borough, and Galway's was just over 13,000.[29] Galway city, however, as the principal town in

27 Ibid., Apr. 1898. 28 The Local Government (Ireland) Act 1898, (61 & 62 Vict. C.37) was given royal assent on 12 Aug. 1898. 29 The 1901 census records that the population of the municipal borough was 13,426, down from 13,800 in the 1891 census.

Connacht, had always been a separate administrative unit. It had its own grand jury, and, from the 1860s, its own town commissioners. The significant diminution in the status of Galway city that the act would bring about was at first strongly resisted by the Galway town commissioners, and the board of guardians.

Initially, there was a consensus that the relegation of Galway to the position of a mere country town should be fought, and a resolution was passed asking Lord Morris to use his influence 'to have this ancient city included in the list of county boroughs'.[30] In time, however, 'the doubts of some of the town commissioners had grown, and those who had, at first, become a little drunk with local patriotism, were fast being sobered by considerations of economy'.[31] The board of guardians, of which most of the town commissioners were also members, were similarly exercised on the subject. One of the bones of contention was the burden of taxation on the ratepayers, should the city be designated a county borough, as distinct from an urban district. The question of the cost of appointing a mayor was particularly contentious, with one member of the board of guardians, M.A. Lynch, declaring 'A mayor indeed, with his mace – a piece of gilded stick. It was a bit of tinsel which they should not pay too much for.'[32]

A motion was put to the meeting to the effect that it would be 'much more advantageous to have Galway made an urban district rather than to have it created a county borough'.[33] E.J. Lee opposed the motion, but Martin McDonogh supported it, and a lively exchange ensued, in the course of which McDonogh implied that Lee's opposition was financially motivated. An exchange of insults began, which culminated in the following encounter, gleefully recorded by a reporter from the *Galway Express*:

> Mr McDonagh [*sic*] here rose from his seat, and putting on his hat was walking towards the door, when he made use of the expression 'I don't care a damn for you'. To this Mr Lee replied 'You're a brute Martin' to which the latter retaliated 'If I am, you are a hound. You come in here drunk, and upset the whole business of the commissioner.'[34] This set the ball rolling in earnest. Mr Lee jumped from his seat, placed himself in

30 *Galway Vindicator*, 11 June 1898. 31 Ryan, M., 'Municipal dignity? A controversy in Galway, 1898', in *Galway Archaelogical and Historical Society Journal* (1991), 146. 32 *Galway Express*, 2 July 1898. 33 Galway Poor Law Union Minute Book No. 2, 1898, pp 60a-60b. 34 McDonogh's antipathy towards drunkenness was a feature of his entire public life. He was a lifelong Pioneer, and abhorred drunkenness in all its forms, particularly when it undermined the fulfilment of professional duties.

> front of Mr McDonagh and clasping his hands behind his coat tail, demanded a repetition of the expression. Mr McDonagh, whose face now quivered with excitement, told Mr Lee that he was not afraid to repeat what he had said, but advised him to keep himself quiet, or otherwise he would adopt a means of making him do so. With the quickness of a flash of the electric fluid, Mr Lee's hands left their backward position and grasped Mr McDonagh by the throat.[35] So sudden was this change in the drama that Mr McDonagh was taken by surprise and felt incapable of acting in his defense; but this was only a momentary feeling, for in the space of two seconds he had removed his antagonists' hands from his organ of breathing, and before Mr Lee could renew his grip he was met by a sledgehammer right-hander from the Herculean arm of Mr McDonagh, which caused the claret to flow from his olfactory organ. Regardless of this concussion between McDonagh's fist and Mr Lee's nose, the latter, with true Irish pluck, made straight for Mr McDonagh's eye-glass and in order to have a fair do at the orb of sight, consequent on the difference in size and weight of his opponent, the bleeding hero made a spring, after the manner of a rooster jumping at a blackberry.[36]

The meeting then descended into something of a free-for-all, with the *Galway Observer* reporting that not only the chairman but members of the press who were in attendance became involved, and that a journalist who tried to separate McDonogh and Lee got 'a chance tip (from McDonogh) that was enough for him to get out of the way'.[37]

When the fisticuffs had abated, the meeting returned to consider its business, and the motion was deemed to have been carried. A copy was to be sent to Lord Morris, who was, unsurprisingly, confused and not a little irritated by the fact that the town commissioners, only weeks earlier, had asked him to support a diametrically opposed resolution. Lord Morris' campaign to have Galway city included as a county borough prevailed in the house of lords, to general approval in Galway, but ultimately the proposed amendment to the act did not even receive a hearing in the house of

35 The *Galway Observer*, in its 2 July 1898 account, recorded that McDonogh took Lee 'by the collar of the coat and Mr Lee made a stroke at Mr McDonagh. Mr Lee hit out as well as he could a couple of times'. 36 *Galway Observer*, 2 July 1898. McDonogh had a weakness in his left eye, and wore a monacle from his mid-30s onwards, a fact referred to in a number of descriptions, including those of Stephen Gwynn and the writer Máirtín Ó Direáin. 37 Ibid.

commons, where it was ruled out of order, and the battle for county-borough status for Galway was finally lost, much to the delight of men such as McDonogh, who had consistently opposed it.[38]

The Local Government Act of 1898 was a significant watershed in both the formulation and administration of local governance. The act, which established elected county councils, effectively ended the monopoly on local powers held by the gentry and grand juries. Although a significant element of local democracy had already been in operation via the boards of the poor-law guardians (who were partly elected by ratepayers), as Melvin has noted, 'in a gentry-saturated county like Galway, landlord and proprietorial influence dominated both the elected and ex-officio (magistrate-gentry) division of these boards'.[39] The transference of the administrative functions of the grand jury to an elected county council under the terms of the 1898 act had the effect of ending that dominance, and leaving the way clear for up-and-coming merchants, men of ambition and ability – such as the McDonoghs had been prior to their own rise to prominence – to make their mark.[40] But it was a controversial process, and one in which Martin McDonogh showed his mettle, and the tough, uncompromising manner in which he would assert his dominance for the following three decades. Under the act, the county of the town of Galway was abolished as a separate administrative area, and the town grand jury met for the last time in 1899. The town commissioners were replaced by an urban district council, elected by a much wider franchise. Such a seismic shift in the balance of power, however, was not met with any great enthusiasm by those of the gentry who now found themselves having to support a new system that significantly undermined the traditional hegemony. It was inevitable, however, that significant numbers of the old ruling elite would offer themselves for election on the new district councils, in an effort to cling on to their traditional power.

The first election to the new Galway urban district council in January 1899 very much reflected this fact, with the nominations including Sir Valentine Blake of Menlo, James O'Hara of Lenaboy and John Wilson Lynch of Renmore. But standing also in the election was Martin McDonogh, by then aged nearly 40. O'Hara, having been chairman of the town commissioners for over thirty years, appeared to be a shoo-in for the position of chairman of the new urban district council, but he was comfortably defeated by

38 It was to be thirty-nine years before the Local Government (Galway) Act of 1937 restored Galway's corporation, with a mayor at its head. 39 Melvin, *Estates and landed society in Galway*, p. 284. 40 The grand jury continued to deal with criminal matters, and to meet until it was finally abolished in 1921.

Figure 6 Martin McDonogh (centre) on the steps of the town hall, following the 1899 Galway county council election

McDonogh, by a vote of 14 to 7. A significant changing of the guard had occurred. A photograph taken at the first meeting of the new Galway urban district council (figure 6) shows Martin McDonogh on the steps of the courthouse building, a tall, well-built man, standing head and shoulders above his fellow councillors, and, significantly, standing in the front row, with his hands clasped firmly behind his back. With his election as chairman of the urban district council, Martin McDonogh's civic workload ramped up considerably. Anxious to regularize the workings of the new council (and avoid the stagnation of the previous board of commissioners), McDonogh saw to it that specific subcommittees were established on finance, lighting, roads and streets and tolls and customs, and that each had regular monthly meetings. As chairman, he sat on all of the committees, and his record of attendance was transformed, such that he rarely missed a meeting.

The dawn of the new century saw the McDonogh family in positions of power on virtually all the civic and public bodies in Galway. By January 1900 Martin McDonogh was chairman of the urban district council, while his father, also a member of the urban district council, was chairman of the

Galway rural district council. T.C. was also a town councillor, and all three of the McDonogh men were, by that time, justices of the peace, members of the harbour commissioners, and members of the board of guardians. (Thomas McDonogh, in spite of his failing health, was chairman of the latter body.) Martin McDonogh was a stickler for keeping to an agenda, and if a meeting was lasting too long, or people were rambling off the point, he would call a halt to proceedings, leading on one occasion to an accusation by James Morris that he was 'the most obstructive chairman I ever met'.[41] The local press tended to agree, and McDonogh's brusque style was described as 'bossy' and 'obdurate', and, on one occasion, when McDonogh had failed to allow a number of councillors to speak on a motion, the *Observer* noted that 'Mr McDonogh ruled the roost'.[42] McDonogh's chairmanship of the urban district council was often brought into question by the local press, but, in truth, the council was something of a dysfunctional, fractured and fractious body. Attendance was very poor, the *Galway Observer* noting that:

> a half-dozen members out of the twenty-four do all the work; about a dozen more drop in occasionally if they happen to be passing to see what is going on, and the rest – another half-dozen – forget that there is such a body as the Galway urban council at all – till the election comes round.[43]

Martin McDonogh was no stranger to the courtroom, both as plaintiff and defendant. The first significant legal proceeding he was involved with involved an advertising contract for the county council. McDonogh took a libel case against Mr Sleator, editor of the *Galway Pilot*, which, it was alleged, had published a number of articles, under the heading 'Starchambering the county contracts', which attacked the council for closing its doors to the public on the issue of the allocation of contracts, resulting in 'jobbery, rottenness and corruption'.[44] McDonogh and his fellow members of the printing committee, who were responsible for the allocation of advertising contracts, felt that the article impugned their reputations. Sparing no expense, McDonogh hired Mr Godfrey Fetherstonhaugh QC to represent him.[45] The case was considered such a contentious one that the defendant, Mr Sleator,

41 The occasion was a Galway urban district council meeting. *Galway Observer*, 27 July 1901. 42 *Galway Observer*, 5 May 1900. 43 Ibid., 26 Jan. 1901. 44 Ibid., 5 May 1900. 45 Fetherstonhaugh was one of the leading barristers of his day, and subsequently Ulster Unionist MP for North Fermanagh from 1906–16.

had requested, and been granted, a change of venue for the trial from Galway to Dublin, the judge ruling, not unreasonably, that, 'if his Lordship was being tried himself he would prefer not being tried by representatives of the very body the paper abused, and the county council must be taken substantially to represent the entire body of electors in the County Galway'. In the end, it made little difference, as Sleator, his counsel having retired from the case, and being forced to conduct his own defence, was completely overwhelmed by the enormity of what he had taken on, and the court ruled in favour of McDonogh, and awarded damages of £250.[46]

The court proceedings that revealed most about Martin McDonogh's personality occurred in July 1900. It had all begun innocently enough, when the board of guardians, of which Thomas McDonogh was at that time chairman, sanctioned the purchase of a new cooking range for the workhouse, which was installed by Robert McDonnell, a well-respected plumber in the town. McDonnell recommended that the boiler in the workhouse also needed replacing, and he was instructed to proceed. McDonnell's bill was put before a meeting of the board of guardians and amounted to a sizeable £60 6*s*. One of the guardians, E.J. Burke, considered the fee exorbitant, and in a heated discussion used the word 'jobbery' in implying that McDonnell had been given the contract owing to his good relations with the McDonogh family, and referring to the fact that the new boiler had been supplied by McDonoghs.[47] An outraged Martin McDonogh insisted that the entire board visit the workhouse and see for themselves the superior nature of the range and associated works. The visit resulted in an altercation between McDonogh and Burke, and a court case in which Burke sued McDonogh for slander (in the amount of £500) and assault and battery (in the amount of £300). The case was originally due for hearing in Dublin, but McDonogh's counsel successfully argued for the case to be moved to Galway, and it opened before the Galway assizes on 23 July 1900.

The court heard that the members of the board of guardians had adjourned to the workhouse to examine the range in situ. In the course of the visit, Burke maintained that, in the yard, McDonogh accosted him and called him a 'blackguard' for having ever raised the question of 'jobbery', and, according to Burke's testimony:

46 *Galway Observer*, 19 May 1900. 47 Ibid., 10 Mar. 1900. Thomas McDonogh was chairman of the board of guardians at the time.

> He called me a liar, and I called him a liar. He then turned round and gave me a thump on the mouth. I had my hands in the pockets of my overcoat. He hit me as hard as he was able. I was staggered and I bled profusely. I made no effort to defend myself, as I was caught from behind. I endeavoured to strike him in return. Others came between him and me.[48]

McDonogh walked off into the cookhouse, but Burke followed him and, according to his testimony:

> When I came to the cookhouse I said 'that was a bad box you gave me'; the moment I entered the door he said 'Ah E.J., you were never able to strike anyone but your wife'. I replied and said 'You have no wife'. 'You liar, you murdered your wife,' he (McDonogh) said in return.[49] I called upon those present to witness his words, and asked the nun also to witness them.[50]

McDonogh's extraordinary charge, that Burke had hit, and may in fact have murdered his wife, was not without some foundation. Burke had been arrested on suspicion that he had been involved in the death of his wife in 1882, and a charge was brought against him, but was thrown out by the grand jury. Several witnesses confirmed that McDonogh had stated that Burke had a reputation for mistreating his wife, and members of the jury would doubtless have been aware of the rumours in this regard, given the notoriety of the case. After deliberating for less than half an hour the jury concluded that the £5 lodged in court in respect of the assault charge by McDonogh, which he had submitted before formal court proceedings had commenced, was sufficient. They came to no decision on the charge of slander. It was a significant moral victory for McDonogh.

48 McDonogh gave evidence that 'Coming near the cook's door he said I did a job for McDonald. I said that's a lie. He said I was a liar; he put up his whisker to my face and I hit him with the back of my hand on the mouth. My fist was not closed.' McDonogh subsequently said that Burke 'had a grudge against the plumber; not against me, but the suggestion was that I made a profit out of the work. He is giving more trouble than all the guardians put together.' *Galway Observer*, 28 July 1900. 49 McDonogh testified that Burke had followed him into the cookhouse and started 'abusing me; he said he would beat this, that and the other out of me; I was quite cool, I said the only person I ever knew he was able to beat was his wife. I could not help it, I was irritated. I did not say he murdered his wife, didn't use the words, the reference to her was a matter of public notoriety, that he was arrested on the charge.' *Galway Observer*, 10 Mar. 1900. 50 Ibid., 28 July 1900.

Burke's comment that McDonogh 'had no wife' is interesting. In drawing attention to the fact that McDonogh's single status was considered somewhat unusual, given McDonogh's public status and wealth, Burke may have been articulating a more widely held but unspoken (in public, at least) view. Burke's comment also suggested that this was a fact McDonogh was sensitive about.

However, there were more important issues to consider as Galway entered a new century. The need for greater industrial development in the city had been a matter of debate for decades, but such development was hampered by a lack of available power to supply such industries. Water power from the fast-flowing waters of the River Corrib was the most obvious solution, but there was a conflict of interest between the needs of industry to harness the water and control its levels, and the needs of the salmon fishery, which at that time was privately owned. The fishery had existed since at least 1283,[51] but an editorial in the *Galway Observer* in 1900 hinted at frustration in Galway with regard to the rights to the water power of the Corrib, calling the legally guaranteed rights of the Galway fishery's owners to control water levels in the river 'a millstone that hangs around the neck of this town and its industries'.[52] The owners of the fishery, in addition to controlling the level of water in the river via the use of sluice gates, objected to the erection of turbines in the various waterways, as they believed they would injure salmon making their way upstream, thereby reducing stocks. Not unreasonably, it was felt that the owners of the fishery, Mr T.G.P. Hallett and his wife Lilias Sophia Ashworth-Hallett,[53] were monopolising the waters of the Corrib to their own ends in order to maximize their own profits, to the detriment of the population of Galway.

The fact that the woollen factory, which employed an increasing number of people, could not always be guaranteed the required amount of water to operate, and that a chemical company that had approached the county council with a view to establishing a factory in the city had been told they could not be guaranteed the requisite amount of water power, was enough to raise the ire of the local population, the *Observer* noting, sourly, that it was a case of 'the salmon first, and everything, and everyone else, afterwards'.[54] As the then chairman of Galway urban district council, this situation was

51 The first documented reference to the Galway fishery occurs in the pipe rolls of Edward I, dated 1283, which refers to the fishery as 'part of the property of Walter, first Earl of Ulster, in Connaught'. 52 *Galway Observer*, 2 June 1900. 53 Mrs Hallett's father, Thomas Ashworth, and his brother Edmund Ashworth, who were successful Quaker businessmen, from Bolton in Lancashire, England, had purchased the Galway fishery for £5,000 in the encumbered estates court in 1852. 54 *Galway Observer*, 2 June 1900.

anathema to McDonogh, and he frequently clashed with the owners of the Galway fishery on the issue of water rights, particularly after operations at his fertilizer plant commenced in 1910.

Pragmatism was a strong feature of McDonogh's personality, and he didn't shirk from tackling the more difficult or unpleasant aspects of Galway life. When he encountered opposition at a meeting of the harbour commissioners to the building of a new morgue on the docks, to supplement the existing morgue at the hospital, McDonogh, having personally experienced the landing of drowning victims, argued forcibly that such a facility was 'absolutely necessary. It was a shame to have persons watching dead bodies from rats.'[55] And to his credit, McDonogh was not afraid of taking on his fellow businessmen when a civic purpose was to be served. When the annual tender for the supply of coal to the Galway workhouse was being considered by the board of guardians in 1900, McDonogh stated that he believed that there was a 'price ring' operating among Galway coal merchants, who had refused to tender for the contract. McDonogh, however, outwitted the coal merchants, and invited the agent for Whitehaven Coal, based in Co. Durham, England, to submit a tender, which 'broke through any preconceived arrangements', and was 2*s.* or 3*s.* less than McDonogh stated he had expected to pay the Galway merchants, thereby providing 'a great saving to the ratepayers'.[56] How such sharp practice was perceived by his fellow businessmen is not recorded, but it can hardly have proved popular. McDonogh was also pragmatic enough to realize when money needed to spent, and was certainly not mean in doing so. On one occasion, at a board of guardians meeting, when the local parish priest asked for £60 to repair the slipway on Inis Meáin, Aran Islands, McDonogh recommended that the guardians instead spend '£100 and make a good job of it, once and for all', a recommendation endorsed by his father, who expressed his own familiarity with the slipway in question.[57]

Thomas McDonogh had come a long way from his relatively humble origins, but his meticulously calculated, hard-won rise through the echelons of Galway's business community, and his acceptance into the ranks of the merchant princes of Galway, did not mean that he was prepared to sublimate his nationalist inclinations. While many of his fellow Galway businessmen had distinctly royalist predilections, McDonogh did not, and in one instance

55 Ibid. Bodies landed at the docks were housed temporarily in unsecured sheds, used for the storing of fishing gear, and dock labourers had to protect them from attack by rats, a constant feature of quayside life. 56 *Galway Observer*, 14 July 1900. 57 Ibid., 1 Dec. 1900.

he showed a steely nationalism at a time when such a thing was neither popular nor wise. The occasion was the death of Queen Victoria on 22 January 1901, which ended the longest reign of any British monarch and signalled the end of the Victorian era. The empire was plunged into mourning, and in Galway classes were suspended in the Queen's College for a week as a token of respect. Galway urban district council adjourned their proceedings, but the Galway board of guardians, chaired by Thomas McDonogh, held their meeting as usual on the day after the queen's death, much to the annoyance of the *Galway Express,* which hissed that 'the indecency of the whole proceedings must grate terribly on everybody who has learned the alphabet of ordinary manners'.[58] The *Express* reported that the chairman had been asked to take a vote to adjourn the meeting, but had refused to do so. The fiercely unionist *Express* was outraged, stating, 'It is a pity that the chairman did not proceed with the vote (to adjourn the meeting) and thus pillory the men who refused to pay the only tribute of respect they could do to their dead queen.'[59] McDonogh's refusal to put the motion to adjourn was not, it appeared, the only instance in which the chairman had shown, at best, an ambivalence, and at worst disrespect, towards the monarchy; in the course of reporting on the heated debate on whether or not to adjourn the meeting, it was stated that 'at a previous meeting one of the members had stated "to —— with the queen"', and the chairman had not remonstrated with the guardian concerned.[60]

None of the McDonoghs were present on 21 February 1901 when a gathering 'proclaiming the king in Galway' was held in the county courthouse.[61] There was 'a flourish of trumpets by the trumpeters of the Connaught Rangers',[62] and the band of the Connaught Rangers played 'God save the king'. The McDonoghs' absence from the event was doubtless noted, particularly as, later that same day, Thomas McDonogh attended a meeting of the magistrates of Co. Galway. It appears likely that Thomas' sons inherited their father's distinct coolness towards the monarchy,[63] which may explain the fact that, in spite of his significant support for the war effort during the Great War, particularly with regard to recruitment, Martin McDonogh was never honoured in the way that his colleague Joe Young was.[64]

58 *Galway Express,* 26 Jan. 1901. 59 Ibid. 60 Ibid. 61 *Galway Express,* 23 Feb. 1901. 62 Ibid. 63 Thomas McDonogh was described as a 'nationalist' in 1889 (*Galway Observer,* 23 Nov. 1889), but by 1901 he was criticised for not being a 'thorough nationalist' at a meeting of Galway rural district council (*Galway Observer,* 8 June 1901). 64 This issue will be addressed in greater detail in chapter 4.

On the domestic front, the census of 31 March 1901 provides us with a fascinating portrait of the McDonogh family – although one aspect is puzzling. Completed by Thomas McDonogh, the census significantly underestimates the ages of his children, and possibly even his own age. McDonogh listed his age as 65, which would have given him a birthdate of 1836, and meant that he was 66 when he died the following year. He lists Martin as being 30, but if we accept the evidence in the University of London register for 1878 that he was born in 1860, he would have been 41. Similarly, Thomas Christopher is listed as being 27, when in fact he was ten years older, having been born in 1864. Mary Ann is listed as being 22, whereas, born in 1869, she was actually 32, and Kate, listed as being 20, was actually 28, having been born in 1873. Slight errors in the recording of ages, of perhaps a year or two, were common enough, but in the case of the McDonogh family the discrepancies ranged between eleven and six years, which is surely exceptional.

The census return also reflects the degree to which the social status of the McDonogh family had risen since their arrival in Galway in the 1860s: there were four servants and three other employees (a bookkeeper, a clerk and a shop assistant) living in the house in Flood Street.[65] It is also significant that Revd John Flatley was staying with the McDonoghs on the night of the census. Fr Flatley, curate at Spiddal, Co. Galway, was an ardent nationalist, a home ruler and a vocal opponent of 'gombeenism'.[66] His presence is intriguing, and may be explained by a reference in Stephen Gwynn's 1909 book *A holiday in Connemara* to 'Fr John', whom he describes as 'a friend of a friend' in Galway.[67] The description of 'Fr John' corresponds exactly to Fr John Flatley, whom Gwynn describes as 'the most original among Irish freelances', and the fact that Thomas McDonogh was dead by the time the book was written would indicate that the 'friend of a friend' was Martin McDonogh. His remarkable friendship with this priest, who was described as 'eccentric and controversial', will be examined in greater detail in chapter 3.[68]

Michael McDonogh does not appear on the 1901 census for the McDonogh household in Galway. He was by then a medical student in Dublin, and was recorded as a boarder at the home of bookkeeper Patrick

65 The servants' names are recorded as Kate McDonnell (20), Barbara Conneely (19), Walter McDonogh (22) and James Faherty (22). Maggie Mc Donogh (20) is listed as a shop assistant, Thomas Conneely (22), a clerk, and Patrick Ward (40), a bookkeeper. 66 The word 'gombeen' was used, from the late nineteenth century, as a derogatory term to describe shopkeepers and other traders who extended credit to local farmers. This led to exploitation, as the farmers were then obliged to buy their goods from, and sell their produce to, that same merchant. 67 The book documented a holiday Gwynn took in Connemara in Sept. 1907. 68 *Connaught Telegraph*, 7 June 1930.

Taylor, his wife Kate Taylor, their five young children and a domestic servant, at 7 St Vincent's Street, Dublin.[69] This house is located within sight of the Mater Misericordiae Hospital on Eccles Street, where Michael McDonogh was completing his clinical training. He lists his occupation as 'student of medicine'; he would graduate from University College Dublin later that year. Bizarrely, the age discrepancies that feature in the 1901 census return completed at his family home in Galway are replicated in his entry on the census return completed in Dublin, where he lists his age as 27. He was 30.

From mid-1901 Martin McDonogh was conspicuously absent from public life, probably because his father's increasing ill health meant he was taking on more of a managerial role in the various family businesses. His brother T.C. consequently took on a more active role in bodies such as the urban district council, the harbour commissioners and the board of guardians. In addition, Martin resigned as a director of the Galway Woollen Mills, leaving T.C. to represent the McDonogh interests.[70] He did not, however, relinquish all of his interest in the affairs of public bodies, particularly when an issue that concerned him arose. One such issue was that of the inadequate public lighting at the Galway docks. Since the harbour commissioners had dispensed with gas lighting and signed a contract with the Galway Electric Lighting Company, the lights at the docks had often failed, plunging the area into almost complete darkness. Martin McDonogh was outraged, and he attended a meeting of the commissioners in May 1901, where he complained of the impact the unreliable lighting was having on 'the poor trawling men, who come in at all hours and have to do without the light'.[71] That same month, when McDonogh chaired a meeting of the urban district council at which the need to improve the poor public lighting in the town was discussed, he showed a rare flash of humour. Living in close proximity to the docks, McDonogh would have been familiar with the less savoury aspects of Galway life, and, in reply to a councillor who stated that the lighting needed to be improved on Merchants Road, so that people could 'see what was happening in the dark corners', McDonogh replied, 'perhaps its best that they don't see what goes on!'[72]

Thomas McDonogh, although his health was failing, retained an interest in local politics. He remained chair of Galway rural district council, and continued to serve on the board of guardians. However, in 1901 he – and by extension Martin and the rest of the McDonogh family – was shaken by a

69 His named is spelled 'McDonagh' on the census return. 70 *Galway Observer*, 20 Apr. 1901. 71 Ibid., 18 May 1901. 72 Galway urban district council minutes, May 1901.

well-orchestrated coup that saw him ousted as chairman of the rural district council. In truth, Thomas McDonogh, given his ill health, had already decided to resign the chair, but in what was described in the local press as a 'terrific squabble', he was accused of not being a 'thorough nationalist', and was persuaded to stand aside to allow for the election of Michael McNeill, who was deemed to have the necessary nationalist credentials. However, once he had stepped aside and given McNeill his blessing, the nationalist members elected James W. French, who, the *Galway Observer* noted, 'was never known as a nationalist, thorough or otherwise'. The *Observer* declared that it was 'nothing short of a disgrace' that a man of McDonogh's standing, experience and integrity should be treated so shabbily. Strenuously objecting to the election of French as chairman, McNeill noted that they had come to 'elect a Nationalist and instead had elected a Tory', and Thomas McDonogh, clearly angered by the fact that he had been outmanoeuvred, noted that, had he known that French was to be his successor, 'he would have fought it out to the bitter end'.[73]

The events at the rural district council appeared to have ignited a fire in the belly of the ailing Thomas McDonogh, and he swiftly changed his mind about resigning the chairmanship of the board of guardians, offered himself for re-election, and was duly re-elected by a unanimous vote at a subsequent meeting.[74] By early 1902, his health appears to have improved somewhat, and he, Martin and T.C. all contested the municipal elections for Galway urban district council. Martin was elected for the East Ward, topping the poll, but his father and T.C. were defeated in the West and North wards, respectively.[75] Of the twenty-four councillors elected, only three, including Martin McDonogh, were not United Irish League candidates. Even though he was a UIL member, McDonogh had chosen to run as an independent nationalist, making his victory all the more remarkable.[76] His reason is unknown, but he may have felt that the McDonogh brand was more recognisable – and enduring – than any political party or affiliation.

In 1902, the McDonoghs expanded their property portfolio with the purchase of Monatigue farm, near Craughwell, Co. Galway. For this contentious and potentially problematic purchase, Thomas McDonogh drew

73 *Galway Observer*, 8 June 1901. 74 *Galway Observer*, 22 June 1901. 75 Thomas McDonogh secured only 133 votes, while T.C. secured 148. 76 Campbell has identified McDonogh as the most prominent of the UIL members in Galway, where more than 34% of the membership were businessmen and shopkeeper-graziers, and the UIL 'repeatedly campaigned on behalf of local entrepreneurs'. Campbell, *Land and revolution*, p. 234.

on the services of the bishop of Galway, F.J. McCormack, as an intermediary. The McDonoghs had leased the farm since 1880, and Thomas McDonogh had made known his interest in purchasing the estate, whereupon a number of the tenants approached the bishop, and asked him to broker a deal on their behalf. McDonogh undertook to give each of the evicted families £10 worth of the land in the event of his being successful in purchasing the estate. This gesture, with the support of the bishop, was sufficient to give him the edge when the land came up for sale in the land court. McDonogh had assured the bishop that he was 'prepared to give way to the congested districts board, should they decide upon purchasing the farm for distribution to the evicted families and other small farmers'.[77] In the event, the board were not interested in acquiring the farm, and McDonogh succeeded in purchasing it.

By this time, Martin McDonogh had, in many respects, eclipsed his father in terms of status and power as a public figure. But while Martin had the energy and drive to effect change in his various public roles, his membership of one body in particular proved an ongoing source of frustration. The harbour commissioners were a somewhat dysfunctional body. The members talked much, argued a great deal, but achieved very little. Woodman, in his history of the harbour commissioners, describes them in 1902:

> All they could do was to prevent a failure in trade rather than assist it, frustrate bad rather than advance good commercial practice. Colonel Countenay wants facilities for transporting granite. The harbour board agrees, the board of works agrees … and nothing happens. A proposal is made to repair the roads around the docks, the board of works gives its approval … and nothing happens. They gain the support of the congested districts board to build a pier at Salthill for the use of the fishermen in the bay. What happens? Nothing happens.[78]

All this was to change, once Martin McDonogh succeeded his father later that year. With a business empire to expand, he determined to make things happen.

In early August 1902, word reached Galway that Thomas McDonogh was 'seriously ill at Buxton, where he had gone for a few weeks' holiday'.[79] In reality, he had gone to the renowned spa town,[80] as part of his treatment for

77 *Galway Observer*, 18 Jan. 1902. 78 Woodman, K., *'Safe and commodious': the annals of the Galway harbour commissioners, 1830–1997* (Galway, 2000), pp 164–5. 79 *Galway Observer*, 2 Aug. 1902. 80 Thomas

the tuberculosis from which he had been suffering for years. It was to no avail. He died on 4 August 1902, five days before the coronation of Edward VII.

Unsurprisingly, Thomas McDonogh's death was covered extensively in the local newspapers. The *Galway Express,* in a lengthy editorial, described him as 'one of the leading merchants of our city', who had gone to Buxton 'for the good of his health':

> It was generally believed that with the change of air and the beneficial effects of the waters, he would overcome his illness, but Providence willed otherwise ... The deceased gentleman was one of the most popular citizens of Galway ... As a magistrate he was upright and impartial in his decisions and had the confidence and respect of the general public. He was charitable without ostentation and many poor persons in Galway will deeply deplore his loss.[81]

The *Galway Observer* echoed much the same sentiments, describing Thomas McDonogh as 'a large employer of labour, and a sound business man'.[82] Having arrived in Dublin on the mailboat from Holyhead, McDonogh's remains were conveyed to Galway on the mid-day train, where they were met by a large crowd, including his family, and the coffin was:

> borne on the shoulders of the citizens to the Pro Cathedral of St Nicholas, where it lay overnight, and after High Mass on Wednesday at ten o'clock, the remains were removed to Forthill Cemetery for internment followed by a large concourse of mourners.[83]

Unsurprisingly, those who attended McDonogh's funeral included the most prominent and the most 'influential gentlemen in the county as well as the city'.[84]

Thomas McDonogh's funeral took place on the same day as that of Alexander Moon, owner of Moon's department store, who had died only a day after McDonogh. The loss of two of Galway's most prominent businessmen cast something of a pall over the city, particularly as they occurred in the middle of Race Week. The sense of gloom that hung over the

McDonogh had, for a number of years previously, visited the spa town of Lisdoonvarna, where he had stayed at the resort's premier hotel, the Imperial, in the company of one of his daughters, who was identified only as 'Miss McDonogh'. *Galway Observer,* 19 June 1897. 81 *Galway Express,* 9 Aug. 1902. 82 *Galway Observer,* 9 Aug. 1902. 83 *Galway Express,* 9 Aug. 1902. 84 *Galway Observer,* 9 Aug. 1902.

city was intensified by the unseasonably bad weather that week. There was heavy rain falling on the day of the funerals.[85]

Remarkably, Thomas McDonogh had not made a will.[86] It therefore fell to Martin McDonogh, as the eldest son, to administer his father's estate – doubtless, as his father had directed. Given that there appears to have been no rancour within the family over the manner in which Thomas McDonogh's estate was divided among his children, it is likely that he had left clear instructions. Foremost among these was that Martin was to take on the mantle of his father in running the various McDonogh businesses. Having served a relatively long apprenticeship, lasting some twenty-three years, he was more than ready.

Thomas McDonogh had been an extraordinarily successful businessman. He had shown a keen business brain, a capacity for hard work and a level of ambition that had seen him work his way up from a foreman in a sawmills to become one of Connacht's leading merchants and employers. He had also been fortunate in his choice of wife, in his family connections and in the abilities of his sons. And it was his eldest son who was to add another crucial level of competency to the already successful McDonogh business dynasty – that of an entrepreneur. There are many definitions of what constitutes an entrepreneur, but most concur that entrepreneurs are of 'the relentless seek-and-solve breed ... they are the ones forever craning their necks, addicted to "looking around corners", and changing the world. This is the true essence of entrepreneurship: define, invest, build, repeat.'[87] In every sense, Martin McDonogh was the definitive entrepreneur: he had learned, working at his father's side, that defining one's business was the key to growing and developing it; by the time of his father's death he had the capital to invest, the energy to build and the hunger to want to repeat the process again and again. Few would have doubted that he would deliver on the faith his father had placed in him.

85 Ibid. 86 There is no record in the wills and testamentary records of the National Archives of Ireland of either Thomas McDonogh or his wife Honoria having made a will. 87 Nelson, B., 'The real definition of entrepreneur – and why it matters', *Forbes Magazine*, June 2012.

3. Taking the reins: the emergence of 'Mr Galway', 1902–13

Martin McDonogh was already 42 when his father died in 1902, but it could be argued that it was only then that he really began to live his life. His friend Stephen Gwynn suggested as much in his obituary of McDonogh, when he said that 'His gift was for doing things, and doing them himself. There was no useful thing done in Galway this thirty years past that he had not a hand in, and in many of them no one had a hand but he.'[1]

Gwynn's acknowledgment that Martin McDonogh's crowning achievements came in the last thirty years of his life – the years following the death of his father – is telling. Until that point he had done everything his father had asked of him, and had been the workhorse of the family. It had been clear from the outset that the family business, and its demands, would always take precedence in his life. In contrast, Redmond, as we have seen, had been the 'golden boy' of the family, enjoying public acclaim, popularity and a busy social life. T.C., who was a talented sportsman, bright but undisciplined when it came to academia, and popular with his contemporaries as a 'man about town', was indulged by his parents, and later his siblings, to an extraordinary degree; for all of his 72 years, he appears to have lived the life of a wealthy playboy, dabbling in business and public life only when called to do so by his father, and later his older brother. Meanwhile, the youngest McDonogh brother, Michael, managed, for most of his life, to create an entirely separate, and highly successful, career for himself in medicine.

While no personal correspondence or diaries by Martin McDonogh survive, his life prior to his father's death appears to have been focused solely on business, for which, it must be acknowledged, he had an extraordinary talent, and in which he must have taken a great deal of satisfaction when his influence enhanced the success of the various family enterprises. There is no record of his having socialized to any degree – he is never listed among the young men of the town who attended the balls or other public amusements that were a regular feature of Galway life in the 1880s and 1890s. He was active in the temperance movement, but only in an administrative capacity, and is never mentioned as having attended the frequent outings – such as day trips

1 Gwynn, S., obituary of Martin McDonogh, the *Observer*, 31 Dec. 1934.

to the Aran Islands – that other members enjoyed. And, significantly for a young man who was handsome, powerful, and wealthy, he never married. It appears, therefore, that the family business was his only means of personal expression and satisfaction, with the notable exception of his passion for horse racing. Whether he would have wished it to have been otherwise we shall probably never know, but there are some indications that such was the case, the most striking of which, as we have seen, coming from the pen of one of McDonogh's bitterest enemies, the writer Liam O'Flaherty.

FRIENDS

As O'Flaherty's characterization implies, McDonogh may indeed have been socially gauche, both as a result of his having to attend to the family business when he might otherwise have been developing the sort of social life typical of a young man of his age and status, but also as a result of having an overprotective mother. McDonogh was exceptionally close to his mother, and Honoria Hernon, the daughter of a bailiff, and as such socially isolated within her own community, may have imparted to her son the belief, which was very much a feature of her own upbringing, that others resented their success, and must be kept at arm's length. Similarly, women perceived as 'gold-diggers', who might try to snare her eminently eligible son into marriage, were kept at a safe distance.[2] But if McDonogh did not feature prominently in the ballrooms, theatres or cultural movements of Galway, that is not to say that he did not have friends. And, indeed, his choice of friends was remarkable. They were all, to one degree or another, individuals who did not conform to the norms of either their class, upbringing or occupation, and were very much their own men.

Foremost among these was Fr John Flatley, a priest of the archdiocese of Tuam, who, as we have seen, had been in residence in the McDonogh home in Galway on the night the 1901 census was taken. Martin McDonogh's long-standing friendship with Fr Flatley, a man thirteen years his senior, lasted until Flatley's death in 1929. Born in Tuam, Co. Galway, in 1847,[3] Flatley

2 O'Flaherty hints at this in his profile of Réamonn Mór's mother in *The house of gold*, a woman whose cloying manipulation of her son, and unrelenting undermining of his faith in others, ensures that his marriage to Nora, whom she did not approve of, ends disastrously. 3 Confusion exists as to his precise birthdate. When Flatley died on 8 Sept. 1929 the *Connacht Tribune* (14 Sept. 1929) recorded his age as 84, indicating that he was born in 1845. The census of 1901, completed by Thomas McDonogh, gave his age as 60, whereas if we accept the date in the *Connacht Tribune*, he would at that stage have been only 56. He,

was described as a 'broad-minded Catholic' and a 'fearless and outspoken nationalist.'[4] It is unclear when McDonogh and Flatley met, but it is most likely to have occurred as a result of their involvement in the temperance movement.[5] Described as 'quite the most remarkable priest in the archdiocese, both for his scholarly attainments and eccentric disposition', he was said to have 'many fine traits of character, and those who knew him intimately, praised him highly'.[6] Flatley's 'eccentric disposition' and his lifelong habit of voicing opinions that were unpalatable to many account for the fact that, as Gwynn noted, 'From Achill down to Galway there is hardly a parish where this quixotic fighter has not for a time been stationed.' Flatley was undoubtedly a maverick, and his transfer from one parish to the next was largely down to his penchant for taking on local establishment figures, speaking his mind and initiating projects which would benefit the local poor.[7] As Gwynn put it:

> whomever else Father John may have offended, whoever else may regard him as an enemy, he has everywhere the name of a defender of the weak against the strong, and that wherever he goes, from Clare Island to the easternmost limit of that wide and scattered arch-diocese, he will carry with him and renew about him the love and blessing of God's poor.[8]

He had much in common with McDonogh. Aside from his views on temperance, he was described as a man who 'at all times and seasons persists in speaking his extremely candid mind about persons and principles'.[9] And in expressing his opinion it was acknowledged that he had 'a sharp tongue and an even sharper pen'.[10] Like his friend McDonogh, however, it was acknowledged by those who knew him intimately that, beneath his brusque and forceful personality, Flatley had 'a most kindly disposition'.[11]

however, lists his age as 64 in the 1911 census, which would imply that he was born in 1847. 4 Gwynn, S., *A holiday in Connemara* (New York, 1909), p. 150. 5 During his time as parish priest of Aughagower in Co. Mayo, he was responsible for the building of a Temperance Hall. It was officially opened by Fr Angelus, OSFC, president of the Fr Mathew Temperance Hall, on 26 Nov. 1914. *Connaught Telegraph*, 5 Dec. 1914. 6 *Connacht Tribune*, 14 Sept. 1929. 7 In 1911, Fr Flatley announced to a meeting of the local branch of the United Irishwomen that he intended a bequest in the will of the deceased former parish priest of money to be spent 'for the use of the parish' be specifically used to 'provide a supply of good poultry, fruit trees, bees, etc., to be given to those who would be regarded as most suitable, each recipient to pay something under half cost price, the eggs of the poultry to be afterwards supplied to others, so that all in the parish might benefit by the poultry scheme'. *Irish Independent*, 20 Nov. 1911. 8 Gwynn, *A holiday in Connemara*, p. 150. 9 Gwynn, *A holiday in Connemara*, p. 147. 10 *Connacht Telegraph*, 14 Sept. 1929. 11 *Connacht Telegraph*, 14 Sept. 1929.

Fr Flatley liked to make things happen. Having been appointed as parish priest to Leenane, Co. Galway, and finding himself with a church 'so small and cramped against the hillside that fully half the congregation was habitually forced to hear Mass kneeling outside the building',[12] he immediately set to work. Two years later the archbishop of Tuam dedicated a brand-new church, with a bell tower fitted with a bell supplied by a group of Dublin businessmen.[13] Among others, Martin McDonogh and his brothers T.C. and Michael attended the event. Flatley was also, undoubtedly, unconventional. During his time in Leenane, he had welcomed the premier of Newfoundland, Sir Robert Bond, in an effort to secure his support for the selection of Killary harbour as a port of call for Canadian mails. In a presentation made to the premier on the subject of Connemara's poverty and its causes, Flatley, in an obvious reference to the system of 'gombeenism', stated that the cause was not a lack of resources, but rather 'the credit system, which he called the curse of Connemara'.[14] Bond was stunned when the Catholic priest suggested as a remedy:

> the adoption of the same course as that followed amongst Sir Robert Bond's own neighbours on the coast of Labrador, where the people had long been weighed down by a system of credit until they were organized into co-operative societies by the philanthropic efforts of a Protestant clergyman, Dr Greenfell. [15]

John C. MacDonnell, described by the local press as 'Galway's leading public man, and one of Ireland's most patriotic sons', was another of McDonogh's intimate circle of friends.[16] It says much about their close friendship that McDonogh was the first to be informed in Galway of his friend's sudden death in September 1909. The two men had much in common. Born in 1850, at Ballygar, Co. Galway, MacDonnell was the son of a merchant farmer. He had gone to Dublin to study law,[17] but was suddenly recalled

12 *Freeman's Journal*, 14 Aug. 1906. 13 Flatley's principal benefactor was a Mr James Dignan of 71 Middle Abbey Street, Dublin, and the bell, crafted by Byrne's Foundry in Dublin, was inscribed 'A gift from generous Dublin'. 14 Previously, when local shopkeepers had complained that if the cooperative movement was allowed to proceed, the businesses of small shopkeepers would be undermined, and 'that the grass would be growing in the streets of the county towns', Flatley had responded, 'If it does grow in the streets, let the grabbers eat it, it would be a good job if that kept them home from grass auctions'. *Ballinrobe Chronicle*, 23 Apr. 1898. 15 *Sunday Independent*, 26 May 1907. Flatley had been involved in the establishment of the Hollymount Co-Operative Agricultural Society Ltd in 1898, when he was serving there as curate. *Ballinrobe Chronicle*, 23 Apr. 1898. 16 *Connacht Tribune*, 4 Sept. 1909. 17 Like McDonogh, MacDonnell had also been schooled first in the local national school, and thereafter attended as a

owing to the illness of his father. Following his father's death, the management of the family business and estates occupied the remainder of his life.[18] Like McDonogh, MacDonnell had a keen interest in politics, and took an active part in the establishment of the Land League, attending meetings every week in Galway, Roscommon, Westmeath and Longford.[19] When the Land League was suppressed, and the National League sprang up in its place, he acted as regional organiser of the latter, and was one of the most active promoters of the Plan of Campaign. Having been for some years a member of the Mountbellew board of guardians, in 1891 he moved to Galway, and he became a member of the Galway board of guardians the following year.[20] He sat on various bodies and committees with McDonogh (including Galway county council, and the county hospital board) and shared with McDonogh a commitment to the promotion of technical instruction, being at one point vice chairman of the technical committee and the representative for Connacht on the standing committee of technical instruction. A wealthy man, and a significant landowner, he was also, however, a great supporter of, and investor in, Galway industry, the *Tuam Herald* noting that 'He was one of the first to take an active part in connection with the Woollen Factory, in which he [was] a considerable shareholder, and no one worked harder than he to make the Technical Congress a success.'[21] MacDonnell was also a keen horseman, and a lover of racing, a passion he shared with McDonogh. Upon his death, the terms in which the local press described MacDonnell are revealing in the context of the light they throw on the life, career and motivations of his friend, Martin McDonogh:

> The keynote of his life was patriotism. His patriotism was not of the self-seeking sort; his life was a life of self-sacrifice for the sake of the county, whose highest interests he ever sought after. It was a life moulded in integrity and practiced in honour … a pure and high-minded administrator; a man who, without murmur, gave intelligent service to his country, and a man to whom truth and honour were the vital elements of existence … He remained a stern and unswerving nationalist throughout the whole course of his career.[22]

boarder at Summerhill College. 18 In 1888 MacDonnell married Margaret Ferguson of Windfield Lodge, Mountbellew, Co. Galway, a niece of the famous Galway-born Dominican preacher, Fr Tom Burke. 19 *Tuam Herald*, 17 July 1909. 20 He remained a member of the Galway board of guardians until his death in 1909. 21 *Tuam Herald*, 17 July 1909. 22 *Connacht Tribune*, 4 Sept. 1909.

The last of McDonogh's friends to be considered here is perhaps the one who ultimately was to provide the most intimate portrait of this famously private man: Stephen Gwynn MP. Born in 1864, in Rathfarnham, Co. Dublin, into a Protestant family, his maternal grandfather was the nationalist William Smith O'Brien. Gwynn was a remarkable man, prodigiously talented and a prolific writer, who enjoyed numerous successful careers as a journalist, biographer, author, poet and politican. He served as a member of parliament for Galway city from 1906–18, and was one of five Irish MPs to serve in the British defence forces during the First World War.[23] The writer James Joyce provides a predictably unique insight into Gwynn's personality in a review of Gwynn's *Today and tomorrow in Ireland: essays on Irish subjects* :[24]

> It is hard to see into what political party Mr Gwynn should go, for he is too consistently Gaelic for the parliamentarians, and too mild for the true patriots, who are beginning to speak a little vaguely about their friends the French. Mr Gwynn, however, is at least a member of that party which seeks to establish an Irish literature and Irish industries. [...] Mr Gwynn has evidently a sense of the humorous, and it is pleasing to see this in a revivalist. He tells how, fishing one day, it was his fortune to meet with an old peasant whose thoughts ran all upon the traditional tales of his country and on the histories of great families. Mr Gwynn's instinct as a fisherman got the better of his patriotism, and he confessed to a slight disappointment when, after a good catch on an unfavourable day, he earned no word of praise from the peasant, who said, following his own train of thought, 'The Clancartys was great men, too. Is there any of them living?'[25]

Gwynn became an important member of John Redmond's inner circle as a result of his literary connections and skills, and his involvement in the Gaelic revival movement.[26] In his autobiography, published in 1926, Gwynn noted,

23 Gwynn initially enlisted in the ranks in January 1915, but later received a commission as captain, and served on the Western Front with the Connaught Rangers. At Messines Ridge, he witnessed the body of Willie Redmond, brother of John Redmond, being carried back from the front by the men of the 36th (Ulster) division. 24 Gwynn, S., *Today and tomorrow in Ireland: essays on Irish subjects* (Dublin, 1903). The review was published in the *Daily Express*, 29 Jan. 1903. 25 This is a reference to the Trench family of Co. Galway, later the Earls of Clancarty. The family's fortunes began to decline when, in 1889, the fifth Earl married an English music-hall singer, Belle Bilton, against the opposition of his father, who sold off much of the estate in retaliation. The family seat was Garbally Court, near Ballinasloe, Co. Galway. Reproduced in *Critical writings of James Joyce*, ed. E. Mason and R. Ellmann (London, [1959] 1965), pp 90–2. 26 Gwynn became Redmond's biographer after his death. Gwynn's two youngest sons, Denis

somewhat ruefully, that in spite of his lifelong commitment to Irish nationalism, the new generation of nationalists 'prefer to describe me, and the like of, as Anglo-Irish … so all my life I have been spiritually hyphenated without knowing it'.[27]

Here then were McDonogh's close friends, all of whom were distinguished by their broad thinking, their independent and often forthright (to the point of being nonconformist) natures, and their overriding sense of civic purpose and duty. If a man may be judged by the company he keeps, then McDonogh's choice of friends is a clear indicator of the strongly held personal, professional and civic philosophies that guided him throughout his life.

ASSUMING CONTROL

When Martin McDonogh inherited it, the firm of Thomas McDonogh & Sons was thriving. It was importing iron, steel, cement, Bangor slates and other building materials, and was also one of Galway's major suppliers of coal, salt and glass.[28] Following his mother's death in 1883, her successful store on the corner of Flood Street and New Dock Street was subsumed into the firm, and continued to trade as a wholesale grocers and sugar and dried-fruit importers. In 1906, McDonogh was legally assigned the house and shop from which his mother had operated her general grocery and provisions store on High Street, Galway.[29]

The Galway Steam Sawmills was importing pitch pine, deals, flooring boards and laths, and, in a logical progression from the processing of timber, began manufacturing a wide range of wooden products, including furniture, carts, wheels and timber cut to order, and dealing in provisions to supply the building industry. With increasing numbers of households moving from the open hearth to the range for cooking and heating, coal was becoming popular and profitable, and McDonoghs had been quick to capitalize on this, the importation and distribution of coal adding to the burgeoning family

Rolleston Gwynn (1893–1973) and Owen John Gwynn (1902–19), were among the pupils who attended Pearse's school, St Enda's, in Rathfarnham, Dublin. Records in the St Enda's archive, held at the Pearse Museum, Rathfarnham, Co. Dublin, confirm that Denis left the school in 1910 to attend university, while Owen entered St Enda's in September of that same year. Denis later became professor of modern Irish history at University College Cork. 27 Gwynn, S., *Experiences of a literary man* (London, 1926), p. 11. 28 O'Dowd, *In from the West*, p. 19. 29 In 1927 the adjoining sugar and general store was also purchased by the McDonogh family.

business. But as successful as the family business was when he inherited it, McDonogh was quick to institute change. Within a year of his father's death he invested in state-of-the-art machinery for the sawmills, greatly increasing its efficiency, and had a Lucas lamp installed.[30] The new lighting ensured that the sawmills could operate more efficiently and safely. Marvelling at the illuminating power of the lamp, and noting that 'the light almost resembles daylight',[31] the *Galway Express* concluded 'This is enterprise'.[32]

While the various McDonogh enterprises were thriving, the same could not be said for Galway city itself. In 1893, in a series of articles under the heading 'Ireland as it is and as it would be under home rule',[33] the *Birmingham Daily Gazette* had decried the lack of entrepreneurial skills among Galway's industrialists, noting with dismay that one of the city's few industries, the Jute Bag Company, had failed because:

> it had not capital to carry on with. Belfast men or Englishmen would have made it a big success. It stopped because it could not raise enough money to buy a ship-load of jute, and was obliged to buy from hand to mouth from retailers.[34]

While this was something of an oversimplification, there was no denying that a distinct lack of solid management skills and entrepreneurial capital limited Galway's industrial and commercial development. Historian Tomás Kenny has noted that:

> the lack of a concentrated industrial effort in Galway resulted in a waste of potential and resources. The city had a rail link, moderate infrastructure and an un-paralleled route to the Americas, but the lack of focused investment must be deemed an opportunity missed.[35]

This lack of investment, a declining population and the absence of an industrial base had seen the Galway Industrial Development Association note in 1906 that the town was characterized by 'ruined houses, empty docks and

30 *Galway Express*, 7 Feb. 1903. These powerful lamps, initially made for the automotive industry, were manufactured by the firm Joseph Lucas Ltd in London, which eventually became Lucas Industries. 31 *Galway Express*, 7 Feb. 1903. 32 Ibid. 33 Written by R.J. Buckley, the articles were published in the *Birmingham Daily Gazette* between March and August 1893, and published in book form by the Birmingham Gazette Company Ltd in 1893. 34 Buckley, R.J., *Ireland as it is, and as it would be under home rule* (Birmingham, 1893), p. 140. 35 Kenny, T., *Galway: politics and society, 1910–1923* (Dublin, 2011), p. 12.

empty streets, where there should have been ships in the harbour and factories in full swing giving work to anyone that was able to work'.[36]

Even those industries that existed and continued to operate did so in a somewhat precarious manner. In 1908, Persse's distillery closed. The traditional fishing industry of the Claddagh was also experiencing a decline, precipitated by the introduction of modern trawlers, some of which were owned and operated by the McDonoghs. The McDonogh business empire, therefore, was among the few concerns that continued to thrive, largely due to the fact that Galway was a mercantile centre, dominated by a limited number of family owned, and well-run, concerns, such as McDonoghs. Martin McDonogh, however, was not a man to rest on his laurels, and was just the man to turn this situation around. His election, in 1906, as vice president of the Galway Industrial Development Association injected much-needed vigour into the process of generating new industries and promoting local trade.

In leading the entrepreneurial charge, McDonogh was in many ways fortunate that he was, physically as well as metaphorically, a large, dominant presence on the business landscape of Galway. Although we cannot be sure of his exact size, the few photographs of him that exist are testament to his great height and build. In Liam O'Flaherty's novel, *The house of gold*, McDonogh's alter ego, the brutish Réamonn Mór Costello, is described as being '6ft 3 ins, weighing over 16 stone with large bushy eyebrows and grey eyes', a description which tallies with what we know of McDonogh. As O'Dowd has noted, 'large in stature, and abrupt by nature, Máirtín Mór looked the part of one of the West's most powerful merchants',[37] and he fulfilled that role to the hilt. Recalling the impression his friend McDonogh made on him in 1906, Gwynn noted that 'he was in all ways the biggest thing in the town; the kind of man who in America would have certainly been a millionaire'.[38] His towering presence, however, was matched by deficiencies in finesse and consensus-building, attributes that are hallmarks of effective civic figures. Even his friend Gwynn was quick to acknowledge that 'Words never came easy to this Irishman … as chairman of local boards he did much service, but had the fault that he could never suffer fools gladly – not even civilly.'[39]

36 *Freeman's Journal*, 25 May 1906. The population of Galway had fallen in every census since the Famine, and by 1901 was down to 13,426. By the time the 1911 census was taken it had fallen further, to 13,255. 37 O'Dowd, P., *In from the West*, p. 25. 38 Gwynn, *Experiences of a literary man*, p. 294. 39 Gwynn, obituary of McDonogh, the *Observer*, 31 Dec. 1934.

MANAGEMENT STYLE

As an employer, McDonogh's management style was that of an autocratic ruler, holding absolute power over hiring and firing. Potential 'troublemakers', particularly those with union affiliations, or those with known drink problems, were simply not employed.[40] But he was also a hands-on employer, who regularly visited the family's business concerns, knew most of his employees on a first-name basis and had established such good relations with his customers that there were many who, as Gwynn records, 'would [not] leave the place till they had seen "Mr Martin" himself'.[41] And whether in his professional or public life, he was always a man for plain speaking. In 1903, after an unnecessarily lengthy county council debate on the appointment of a rate collector, the *Galway Express* reported that 'Mr Martin McDonogh compared some of the speakers to the Greek orator Demosthenes'.[42] Nearly a decade later, at an urban district council meeting where a report on the construction of new houses was being considered, McDonogh, growing impatient, asked the city engineer to 'give us a report of it at the next meeting, without the big English. Very plain, simple Saxon, will do us. We don't want to carry pocket dictionaries with us.'[43] He was a tough chairman, and frequently antagonized other councillors by his dictatorial manner. In spite of this, he was repeatedly re-elected, frequently by a unanimous vote, as chairman of various bodies, one fellow councillor remarking that, although the manner of McDonogh's chairmanship was not always to everyone's taste:

> I think all of us agree that he has discharged his duty to this board with ability and courtesy, and with a business-like tact. I know there will be a couple of members who will say that some observations of theirs were dealt with rather summarily. But I think it is one of the best qualifications of a chairman to be able to put down all trivial business …[44]

The simple truth was that, like him or loathe him, civil or not, McDonogh got the job done and made things happen, a fact recognized and appreciated by even his most vocal critics.

40 McDonogh was immensely loyal to those employees he valued, and when trusted employees over-indulged on occasion, it was the case, as St John Gogarty noted, that 'The workers he sacks on Saturday night, are back on Monday morn contrite.' 41 Gwynn, obituary of McDonogh, the *Observer*, 31 Dec. 1934. 42 *Galway Express*, 23 May 1903. 43 *Connacht Tribune*, 6 Apr. 1912. 44 Ibid., 29 Jan. 1910.

THE ROYAL VISIT, 1903

Civility – or at least a pretence of it – was certainly required in 1903. The visit of Edward VII to Ireland that year elicited mixed reactions. His predecessor, Queen Victoria, was still viewed negatively by many Irish people as a result of her inaction during the Great Famine – indeed, she had been dubbed 'the famine queen'.[45] Edward VII was perceived as more of a friend to the country, and he was determined to make his visit a success. However, there was disagreement as to the appropriate response to the royal visit, with unionists understandably thrilled at the prospect of forging even stronger links with the monarchy, but republicans, radicals and some nationalists, including MPs, vehemently opposed to the visit. More moderate nationalists, including McDonogh, felt the king should be received cordially and respectfully, but that there should be no obsequious 'bowing and scraping' towards him. In his various civic roles, McDonogh found himself in the thick of the animated and often bad tempered debates that took place regarding the manner in which the king's visit should be acknowledged, if it was to be acknowledged at all. Galway county council, of which McDonogh was a member, had a Nationalist majority, and in respect of that body the decision was simple – the council decided it would ignore the visit. Galway urban council was, however, the scene of some turbulent exchanges over the event. Historian John Cunningham records that 'There were divisions, shouting, and name-calling at the meetings over the royal visit, which were reported in horrified tones by the *Galway Express*, the unionist paper.'[46] At a meeting of the urban council less than two weeks before the royal party was due to arrive, McDonogh made it clear that he favoured a dignified, though certainly not fawning, response:

> I am in favour of getting up an address to the king. He is the first king that has done anything for us here in Ireland. The introduction of the land bill shows that he has an interest in us, and therefore we should show that we appreciate his goodness. Let there be no crawling about the address. It would not suit decent men to present a crawling address, and by getting up an address of welcome there will be nothing subservient about it.[47]

45 The phrase 'famine queen' has first been used in relation to Queen Victoria in an article of that name written by Maude Gonne in 1900. The article heavily criticised the queen for her heartlessness during the Famine, and was subsequently banned. 46 Cunningham, J., quoted in 'When the king came to town', *Galway Advertiser*, 12 May 2011. 47 *Galway Express*, July 18 1903.

McDonogh's response was typical of the man, and his particular brand of civic philosophy: pragmatic, fair, but also uncompromising. It was eventually decided, by eight votes to four (McDonogh voted in favour) that the council would take part in the official welcome and the chair, James O'Donohue, would read a speech welcoming the king.

Gwynn provides us with an amusing vignette of this official welcome, which he says came about largely as a result of the efforts of solicitor Harry Murphy, who had drafted the address, and was present, 'neatly and suitably attired' on the platform to welcome the king.[48] Subsequently, 'there appeared the chairman of the council, arrayed in a top hat and dress clothes, who, taking the inscribed roll from its bearer [Murphy], thrust from him his encumbrance. "Hold my hat till I read the address to His Majesty."'[49] O'Donohue's reward (about which he was subsequently much ridiculed) was that he was knighted by the king, and became Sir James O'Donohue.

1906 ELECTION

McDonogh first came to know Stephen Gwynn when John Redmond persuaded Gwynn to stand in the 1906 by-election for the Galway city parliamentary seat.[50] Galway was avowedly nationalist in its popular politics,[51] but, as Kenny has noted, 'politically, the situation within the county was fluid. On the surface, the population was staunchly behind the Irish Parliamentary Party and the United Irish League, but people were willing to follow whoever could help solve the land issue.'[52] On this occasion the situation was complicated by the fact that the opposing candidate, and local favourite, John Shawe Taylor, was a significant landlord and chairman of the Galway Industrial Development Association, who stood as an independent and strongly

48 The king and queen arrived into Killary Harbour aboard the royal yacht on Wednesday 29 July, and having toured Connemara they boarded the train from Ballinahinch, and arrived in Galway for a grand procession and reception on Thursday 30 July 1903. 49 Gwynn, *Experiences of a literary man*, p. 296. 50 Support for Gwynn was also influenced by the fact that Fr Peter Dooley had extended the original invitation to him to stand in the election. Fr Dooley, a well-respected Galway figure, had started a popular boy's club and a loan bank, and was one of the principal instigators of the establishment of the woollen factory, of which McDonogh was a director and shareholder. Gwynn, *Experiences of a literary man*, p. 291. 51 The establishment of a new newspaper in Galway in 1909, the *Connacht Tribune*, was a major event. With its declared intention of being 'an upright national newspaper, clean and pure in sound, staunch and sound in principle'(*Connacht Tribune*, 9 May 1909), and its avowedly nationalist mindset, the new newspaper was to prove a major factor in promoting a nationalist agenda in Galway, and a significant foil to the staunchly unionist *Galway Express*. 52 Kenny, *Galway: politics and society*, p. 13.

advocated land reform. Although McDonogh was vice chairman of the same body, as a nationalist, he differed starkly from Shawe Taylor in his politics, for, as Cunningham has noted, 'although he proclaimed himself a "devolutionist", Shawe Taylor was conspicuously a unionist, and was regarded as one, not least by other unionists.'[53] McDonogh campaigned for Redmond's man and Gwynn ultimately won, garnering an impressive 64 per cent of the vote.[54] Gwynn held the seat until the 1918 election.

In a revealing insight, Gwynn noted that McDonogh had in fact supported the original nationalist candidate, Sir James O'Donohue:[55]

> because he thought Father Dooley (who supported Gwynn's candidature) had too big a say in everything. These two, priest and layman, were the chiefs of the place, and they held each other at arms' length. Though each of them was prepared to admit the other's merit, neither was enthusiastic about it.[56]

Pragmatic as always, McDonogh, deferring to Redmond's choice of candidate, switched his allegiance, and as Gwynn recalled, 'From the moment I was chosen, this man was my steady and active backer.'[57] Gwynn's election was not initially popular, as he had beaten the local favourite, but he had run a vigorous campaign, with McDonogh's imprimatur and attendance at election meetings proving critical in swinging votes in favour of him.[58]

THE FERTILIZER INDUSTRY

Politics aside, it was the development of his own business enterprises that dominated McDonogh's life in the years preceding the outbreak of the First World War. Following considerable investment, the sawmills were becoming increasingly profitable, but it was across the road that the truly significant

53 Cunningham, *'A town tormented by the sea'*, p. 224. 54 *Galway Express*, 3 Nov. 1906. 55 O'Donohue was described by Gwynn as 'a big, soft, good humoured bosthoon of a man – but shrewd. He had risen from a spade labourer, and, one way and another, had got on to the urban district council, and then into its chairmanship'. Gwynn, *Experiences of a literary man*, p. 294. 56 Ibid. 57 Ibid. 58 Gwynn records that his original election address was reviewed, with disappointment, by his election committee, which included McDonogh. The address stated that he was 'the grandson of Smith O'Brien, "who was sentenced to death in 1848". "But", said one, "we thought he was sentenced to be hanged, dhrrawn and quarrthered." "So he was," said I. "My God," said they, "and you leave out that!" So it went in duly and "grandson of William Smith O'Brien", with this appendix, figured in capitals.' Gwynn, *Experiences of a literary man*, p. 297.

investment took place, with the establishment in 1903 of what the press called 'a manure factory'.[59] Even before his father's death, at McDonogh's initiation, the company had begun importing guano, the excrement of seabirds, which is an effective fertilizer due to its high nitrogen, phosphate and potassium content. In the nineteenth century, the guano trade played a pivotal role in the development of modern input-intensive farming. The benefits of using 'artificial manures', as they were commonly called at that time, were increasingly being recognized. From the late 1850s onwards, sales of guano and other artificial manures were big business. Quality guano was selling for £7 a ton in 1862.[60] A number of Galway merchants were dealing in it, but demand often outstripped supply.

Given his strong links with – and considerable experience of – farming, McDonogh had made the shrewd decision to enter this industry, which had enormous potential for growth. McDonoghs had become an agent for W. & H.M. Goulding, one of the principal manufacturers of fertilizer in Ireland, with plants in the early 1900s in Cork and Dublin, and the Galway firm's initial foray into the distribution side of the fertilizer trade was an immediate success. Being in the right place at the right time and taking advantage of a situation was something at which McDonogh excelled, and he was fortunate to be in just the right place when an opportunity arose to enter the fertilizer business in a much bigger way. As Gwynn notes:

> the Galway agency for the big wholesalers was held by a gentleman of an old Catholic family – who was also a racing man. Where Martin McDonogh had business relations he generally had personal friends, and this friendship left him bitten with the passion for the turf. But it had other consequences, for when this old sportsman died his friend succeeded to the agency – as distributor.[61]

The gentleman referred to was Sebastian Nolan,[62] one of whose brothers, John Philip Nolan, was an MP for county Galway. Nolan's death was to provide McDonogh with a golden opportunity, and he made the most of it.

59 *Galway Express*, 19 Dec. 1903. 60 Ibid., 26 Apr. 1862. 61 Gwynn, *Memories of enjoyment*, p. 97. 62 The 1901 census records Nolan, 52, staying at the Galway County Club at 13 Eyre Square. Nolan's single status was something he had in common with McDonogh; Nolan was one of six sons, of whom only one married. Like McDonogh, Nolan was known for his generosity to his friends, and his notoriously short temper, one obituary noting 'Mr Nolan was a much misunderstood man. His wealth made him so. His friends were his friends, and his enemies – well they were legion.' *Tuam Herald*, 13 Apr. 1907.

McDonogh's success in the fertilizer business is rendered even more remarkable by the fact that, for the first few months of 1907, he appears to have experienced a period of illness, which led to his absence from meetings of all of the local authority and other civic bodies of which he was a member for approximately four months, from January until April. The precise nature of McDonogh's illness is not referred to in any of the press reports, but it must have been serious to have necessitated his absence from public life for such a long period of time.[63] It is clear that his presence was sorely missed, a fact referred to not only by the local press but also by those committees that valued the steadying influence of his chairmanship. In April 1907 a meeting of the board of guardians descended into chaos, the *Galway Observer* recording that the antics of members 'beggars description … the noise was so deafening, it was pandemonium let loose', and noting that it looked forward to the 'speedy recovery', and return, of the board's chairman, Martin McDonogh.[64]

Nolan died suddenly on 1 April 1907 on the Galway golf links at Knocknacarra, a course he had helped to found with Thomas McDonogh and other prominent businessmen in the city. Nolan's involvement in the guano trade had been significant, the *Connaught Telegraph* acknowledging him as the 'chief agent in Ireland for the sale of Peruvian guano'. Also significant was the fact that his death occurred 'at a very awkward time, just in the height of the guano season'. Nolan's company had just taken delivery of a consignment of over 2,000 tons of guano, and the ship was being unloaded at the time of Nolan's death. It was reported that 'The captain of the vessel, as soon as he heard of Mr Nolan's death, refused to allow the loading to continue unless he got security for the cost of the cargo, and Messrs Blake and Kenny (solicitors acting for Nolan's estate) stepped in and succeeded in getting the bank to provide the necessary funds.'[65] When Martin McDonogh approached Blake and Kenny with a view to taking over both the cargo and Nolan's guano business in its entirety, a sale was agreed for £10,000. It proved to be the best investment McDonogh ever made.

Not long after Nolan's death, however, the fact that there was now only one major agent for fertilizer in Galway resulted in the fertilizer manufacturers

63 One possible cause may have been problems with the leg McDonogh injured in his early twenties, which troubled him throughout his life. In 1926, McDonogh gave evidence in court proceedings that 'his ankle was sore, and he had both legs up on a chair', and it was also noted that McDonogh had a 'pallid complexion', also symptomatic of circulation problems. McDonogh's death, as a result of a 'paralytic stroke', would indicate that he had a history of blood clots and circulation problems. *Connacht Tribune*, 23 Oct. 1926. 64 *Galway Observer*, 6 Apr. 1907. 65 *Connaught Telegraph*, 4 Dec. 1909.

attempting to squeeze McDonogh. Deteriorating relations with Gouldings prompted McDonogh to embark on a venture he had long been considering. As Gwynn records:

> the combined manufacturers tightened their terms, and Martin McDonogh, looking about him, saw water power running to waste in Galway, then full of derelict mills ... He knew enough chemistry to appreciate the problem, and with one of the swift decisions that were characteristic of him (and swifter always, the greater the stake involved) he decided to manufacture and fight the ring.[66]

McDonogh's decision to enter the fertilizer-manufacturing business was made not simply as a result of his own determination not to be bullied, but rather on the basis of sound business principles. He already knew that the use of fertilizer was becoming an indispensable element of modern farming, and he was well placed to exploit such an opportunity. He had a well-established network of distribution outlets. Through the employment of commercial travellers, personal contacts, long credit, brand names and newspaper advertisements in the local press McDonogh was able to sell his products to wholesalers, retailers and general customers, while operating as a wholesaler himself. Not a man to do things by halves, he installed state-of-the-art equipment and the most advanced manufacturing processes in his new fertilizer plant. When Gwynn visited the factory, he spoke in glowing terms of what McDonogh had established, and described:

> the big modern factory established beside the river in a derelict malt store, where a turbine of the newest pattern is installed in a water-lead that for decades had run idle to the sea. Here manures are being made on the large scale for the countryside that is learning ever year the lessons of improved farming; it is the enterprise of a Galway merchant in whom lives the spirit of the old venturers – serving the town where he gives employment, serving the countryside to which he cheapens and improves the provision of a necessary.[67]

From 1910, McDonoghs were in the fertilizer manufacturing industry proper, producing sulphuric acid, superphosphate and compound fertilizers.

66 Gwynn, *Memories of enjoyment*, p. 97. 67 Gwynn, S., *The famous cities of Ireland* (London, 1915), p. 100.

In establishing the plant, Martin McDonogh had done his homework, and sought the advice of F.W. Berk, of Berk Chemicals, who had a chemical plant in Barking, just outside London.[68] As a result of Berk's advice, 'their acid plant, with a capacity of 5,000 t.p.a. [tons per annum], was a chamber-process type, using imported pyrites as a source of sulphur.[69] Their output of acid limited the production of superphosphate to about 10,000 t.p.a.'[70] Although this fell far short of the production levels of similar plants, as the only fertilizer manufacturing plant in the West of Ireland, McDonogh's Fertilizers were content to limit their operation to supplying the local market. Built on the site of the former Burke's distillery (now Jurys Inn), the plant produced fertilizer that was 'packed for sale in two-hundredweight jute sacks. The output of the factory was about 14,000 tons per annum.'[71] Because of the necessity to import raw materials by sea, a location near a major port was a prerequisite for a fertilizer plant, but what distinguished the McDonogh plant from others in Ireland was the role that water – the fast-flowing waters of the River Corrib – was to play. Harnessing the waters of the Corrib to drive all the machinery in the factory was an inspired move, in that it provided a free and infinite supply of energy, a factor that would render the plant even more profitable when restrictions on fuel, and soaring costs, came into play during the war years of 1914–18. And, as Mark Cooper and John Davis note in their history of the Irish fertiliser industry, 'the strength of the source of power was such that it was sufficient to pump circulating acid to the top of the various towers in the acid plant'.[72] The combination of Berk's chemical knowledge and McDonogh's entrepreneurial instincts created a manufacturing enterprise that would elevate the McDonogh company to new levels of profitability during and after the war. Unsurprisingly, the response of the major fertilizer manufacturers, such as Gouldings, was to try to squeeze McDonogh out of the business, and a price war ensued. But, once again, McDonogh's timing was fortunate, for, as Gwynn notes, 'There was an anxious period. Then the war came and all the manure was wanted that could be got.'[73]

68 F.W. Berk and Co. Ltd had been established by Frederick William Berk and his brother Robert Berk in 1886. Born in Crefeld, Germany, F.W. Berk received his British nationality and naturalisation papers (No. A3628) in 1882. Robert Berk's son, Arthur Douglas Berk (1884–1969), having joined the company in 1905, became chairman in 1942. 69 Over time Galwegians became familiar with, and in many cases infuriated by, the emission of sulphur fumes from the fertiliser plant. 70 Cooper, M. and J. Davis, *The Irish fertiliser industry: a history* (Dublin, 2004), p. 199. 71 Ibid., p. 85. 72 Ibid. 73 Gwynn, *Memories of enjoyment*, p. 97.

MEMBERSHIP OF THE RACE COMMITTEE

In 1907, McDonogh became chairman of the stewards at the Galway Races, and retained that position until his death in 1934, making him the longest-serving chairman in the Races' history.[74] The 'sport of kings' had always been popular among Irish people of every class and creed, but its management had, until then, been the preserve of the aristocracy and local gentry, among whom Catholics – even successful, wealthy Catholics like McDonogh – were rare. As former UCG librarian Christy Townley has stated, 'It was a big transformation from the landed gentry to the ordinary people when Máirtín Mór became chairman of the race committee. Although contributing to the running of the races, up to then, they had no say.' And now, it appeared, they had. Access to the higher echelons of Irish racing for those of a certain class or religion had been a burning issue for a number of years. Only two years after McDonogh became chairman of the Galway course, when the Irish-American politician Richard Eyre Croker's horse Orby became the first Irish-trained horse to win the Epsom Derby,[75] the horse was awarded the Freedom of Dublin, and Croker's training manager, Lt. Col. Freddie McCabe of the Curragh, was famously congratulated by a Dublin wag, who announced 'Thank God and you, sir, that we have lived to see a Catholic horse win the Derby!' [76]

McDonogh's appointment was fortuitous, for, with the appointment of the first inspector of courses in October 1907, it was clear that for the Ballybrit course to survive, considerable financial investment would be required in order to bring it up to the required standard. Conditions were primitive at the Galway course for patrons and riders.[77] McDonogh and Joe Young became a de facto two-man committee, and they took on the task of upgrading the course with energy and determination.[78] But, in an inspired move that was to prove critical to the future success of the racecourse, prior

74 Hyland, F.P., *History of Galway Races* (London, 2008), p. 441. 75 Presenting the trophy to the winning owner, King Edward VII was so appalled that an Irish-trained horse, owned by what he considered a Tammany Hall upstart, had won, that he could not bring himself to shake 'Boss' Croker's hand. 76 D'Arcy, F., *Horses, lords and racing men: the Kildare Turf Club, 1790–1990* (Kildare, 1991). Following the success of Orby in the Epsom Derby, Croker offered to fund the Irish Derby to the same value as the Epsom Derby, on condition that he be elected to the Turf Club. His offer was refused. 77 The leading English flat-race jockey in the 1910s and 1920s, Steve Donoghue (1884–1945), described the jockeys' room at the pre-war Galway Races as 'just a little tent. Still, it was shelter from the murderous rain outside.' Donoghue, S., *Donoghue up!* Quoted in Hyland, *History of Galway Races*, p. 442. 78 Young was a member of the Galway Race Committee for fifty-one years. He succeeded McDonogh as chairman in 1934, and served for twenty-three years.

to initiating investment in the course, they set about putting it on a proper legal footing. McDonogh and Young 'set down the principles that they would not receive any payment for their efforts on behalf of the Galway Races and that all the lands used for racing would be held in trust for the people of Galway', as they are to this day.[79] McDonogh and Young also convinced the owner of the Ballybrit lands, Captain Thomas Wilson Lynch, to give the race committee a 999-year lease for an annual rent of £100.[80] The lease contained a number of key concessions, negotiated by McDonogh, Young and Tom Kenny,[81] the third of the three signatories to the original lease, not the least of which was that they could 'enlarge the said enclosure without any increase in rent by taking in and enclosing further land adjoining the said enclosure to the extent of one statute acre …'[82] The potential to extend and develop a course, which, in effect, belonged to the people of Galway, and not to a group of shareholders, ensured the unique character of the Galway Races for generations to come. With the site at Ballybrit secured, McDonogh 'used all his energies, influence and business acumen towards ensuring that the quality and standard of the annual meeting in Galway was of the highest order'.[83] The transformation of the Galway Races was complete when McDonogh appointed Martin Thomas Donnellan, a shopkeeper in Shop Street and a member of Galway urban district council, as secretary/manager of the course in 1918, replacing George Mack.

'RANCH WAR' AT MONATIGUE

While McDonogh's skilful negotiations had secured a successful result at Ballybrit, negotiations in relation to his own lands were markedly less successful. Historian Fergus Campbell has observed that the 'ranch war' of 1906–9 was 'the most serious outbreak of agrarian conflict in twentieth century Ireland',[84] and McDonogh was in the thick of it. He had acquired, in controversial circumstances, ownership of prime grazing lands at Monatigue in early 1902. The tenants – who had consistently paid their rents – had sought to purchase the lands when McDonogh's lease on the property

79 Hyland, *History of Galway Races*, p. 107. 80 Ibid. 81 Tom 'Cork' Kenny was a journalist, editor and the founder of the *Connacht Tribune*. A native of Cork, he moved to Galway in the early 1900s, and established the *Tribune* in 1909. His son Desmond and his wife Maureen Canning were the founders of Kenny's Bookshop and Art Gallery. 82 Ibid. 83 Townley, C., 'History of Galway Races', in *Races centenary year of 1969*, quoted in O'Dowd, P., *In from the West*, p. 68. 84 Campbell, *Land and revolution*, p. 85.

had come up for renewal, but Thomas McDonogh's influence with the bishop had seen to it that the McDonoghs were deemed to be the most appropriate lessors, and Martin McDonogh subsequently became sole owner. The fact that Monatigue had been acquired over the heads of local tenants who had farmed the lands for generations was bitterly resented, and a series of attacks on the property, its lands and livestock ensued. In 1909, the son of a herd employed by McDonogh, a young man named Moran, was shot at from behind a wall on the public road at Ballindereen, near Gort.[85] No suspects were ever arrested, but it was generally believed that the attack was related to Moran's employment at Monatigue.

McDonogh's refusal to sell the lands at Monatigue to the tenants may be explained partly by his characteristic unwillingness to bow to the wills of others, but it was also due to the fact that as a result of his efforts, the lands at Monatigue were now greatly improved for grazing purposes, and producing prime stock. McDonogh was a great proponent of his own fertilizer product, which he used liberally on his extensive farmlands throughout the county. At Monatigue, one local man recalled that 'from his own stores (McDonogh) used much fertilizer, which enabled him to produce cattle of great weight and strength'.[86] The same employee recalled that 'one particular beast defied all efforts of the men to capture her. The big man (McDonogh) then tried, but succeeded only in catching the beast by the tail. In the ensuing tug-of-war the beast escaped, leaving Máirtín holding the tail!'[87]

Such lighter moments were rare, and in assessing McDonogh's unwillingness to give up his landholdings, Gwynn provides us with an important insight. Gwynn recalled that:

> the business of cattle-owning led to trouble over the land: it was no longer necessary to the firm, but nothing would induce him to give it up – partly because threats were used to him. But in reality, the ownership of good cattle, and the tenure of land on which they could thrive to his liking, were to him part of a man's proper life.[88]

Both of Gwynn's insights ring true. Throughout his life, McDonogh refused to be bullied or threatened by anyone; and there is no doubt that to this son of Connemara, the ownership of land and good cattle was the ultimate proof

85 *Connacht Tribune*, 12 June 1909. 86 Ibid., 4 July 1975. 87 Mr Pat Hynes, Rockfield, Athenry, Co. Galway, quoted in *Connacht Tribune*, 4 July 1975. 88 The *Observer*, 31 Dec. 1934.

that he had made a success of his life, and was a man to be respected, admired, and perhaps feared. If the tenants of Monatigue had thought to intimidate him, they had seriously misjudged their man.

Events at Monatigue continued to be a thorn in McDonogh's side for some time. Threats to employees had resulted in most locals refusing to work there, and in 1910 McDonogh was forced to employ 'two emergency men', who were the only ones prepared to work there, even for 'the high wages offered'. The provisions necessary to keep Monatigue operating were extremely costly, with much of the cost falling on the public purse, and it is doubtful whether anyone but McDonogh, with his influence and deep pockets, could have sustained the farm during the worst years of the land agitation. A sergeant and eight police kept guard over Monatigue House, where the 'emergency men' resided during the hay-saving, and all told 'about 30 police [were] kept going protecting the farm'. It was also noted that the 'police station at Monatigue is to be kept there permanently, at least until the farm has been sold'. And indeed McDonogh had, in what most considered a mere public relations exercise, agreed, in principle, to sell the land, but at what he considered a 'fair' price, and only to the congested districts board, which was something of a moot point with the tenants in question. In spite of the deference normally accorded to McDonogh in the local press, the drain on the public purse, and the tying up of police manpower as a result of the Monatigue operation, appears to have irked the Galway ratepayers, and prompted an uncharacteristic barb against McDonogh in the *Connacht Tribune*, the editor noting that 'Galway county council appear to have some sympathy with the ratepayers, and they should bear in mind that charity should begin at home.'[89]

The question of Monatigue's future was sufficiently important for it to be mentioned in the house of commons in March 1911. In a debate on land purchase in Ireland, the Galway MP William John Duffy asked the chief secretary:

> whether he is aware that Mr M. McDonagh [*sic*], of Galway, expressed a willingness, through his solicitor … to sell the interest of his farm at Monatigue, Craughwell, county Galway; have the congested districts board refused to purchase on the ground of not having money to

89 *Connacht Tribune*, 30 July 1910.

> purchase; and if so, can he say if any steps have been taken lately to open negotiations with a view to purchase?[90]

Augustine Birrell, the chief secretary, confirmed that McDonogh had offered to sell to the congested districts board, and that 'The lands will be valued and an offer made as soon as practicable having regard to the claims of other cases.'[91] But the ratepayers had to grin and bear it for some time yet, for two years later, in July 1912, there were no fewer than ten men, employed by McDonogh for harvesting at Monatigue, operating under police protection.

UNIVERSITY COLLEGE GALWAY GOVERNING BODY

In 1908, under the terms of the Irish Universities Act of that year, the Queen's College Galway, established in 1849, became University College Galway.[92] The act significantly altered the way the university was governed, the charter of 20 December 1908 replacing the corporate body, which had been comprised of the college president and six professors, with the first governing body of University College Galway, which held office for three years.[93] But crucially, the act relegated University College Galway to an inferior position, whereas previously it had been on a par with the other colleges. The government's endowment of the college – £12,000 per year, much less than the other two Queen's Colleges – was considered insufficient for the operation of a constituent college of the National University of Ireland, and the college spent decades trying to 'keep up' as a result.

The membership of the governing body numbered twenty-six, and consisted of three crown nominees, representatives from the National University senate, the academic council, the graduates, the county councils of Connacht and Clare and the urban council of Galway. Another three members were co-opted, and the president was an ex-officio member. As one of Galway's leading citizens, it was almost inevitable that Martin McDonogh would become a member of the governing body, and he did, representing Galway urban council on the governing board continuously from 1908 until his death in 1934. Although his own experience of university life had been somewhat disappointing, McDonogh doubtless began his tenure as a

90 *Hansard (Commons)*, xxii, cc1355–7W (8 Mar. 1911). 91 Ibid. 92 In 1997 University College Galway became the National University of Ireland, Galway. 93 Under the act's charter, the appointment of the governing body was to last for 'three years and three months from the appointed day'.

governor of the university with all the enthusiasm of many of his fellow governors, who believed that the Irish Universities Act represented a major opportunity to develop the Galway college in a way that would benefit the province of Connacht as a whole. The *Freeman's Journal* agreed, recognising the importance of the governing bodies in steering Queen's College in a new direction, and noting that:

> Cork and Galway should become flourishing constituent colleges … These colleges have not tapped the areas of that part of the country in which they are situate[d] for the new kind of student – the poor man – I don't believe there is so eager a student as the new kind of student. Those governing bodies have been reconstructed so that there will be upon them 20 persons of different classes and creeds who have vied with each other in expressing their willingness to work in any scheme of this kind.[94]

In identifying that there was a new class of student, that of 'the poor man', the *Freeman's Journal* was reflecting the views of many, including McDonogh, that colleges of further education, which were open to all those of sufficient academic ability, regardless of their social standing or wealth, were the way forward if industry and commerce were to develop in the West of Ireland – hence the broad spectrum (nominally, at least) of 'different classes and creeds' of the members who were to make up the governing body. For McDonogh, however, the question remained as to whether a university education was preferable to a technical education, and over time he became more and more of the view that a technical education – represented in Galway by the City of Galway Technical Institute, of which he became a governor and later chairman – was a more effective model. It had opened in January 1894, declaring that the student who attended would:

> acquire a knowledge of the sciences upon which most trades and industries depend, and of the manner in which scientific knowledge was so applied to obtain the best result with the greatest economy. His knowledge being general, it will avail him in cases where new difficulties arise, in the improvement of old methods, the extension of old industries, and even in the discovery of new ones.[95]

94 *Freeman's Journal*, 1 Apr. 1908. 95 *Galway Observer*, 20 Jan. 1894.

At the newly renamed UCG, the governing body was charged with the task of attending to 'the management and control of all the affairs of the college'. Little wonder, then, that there was such an appetite for membership of this prestigious and influential body, on which, it appeared, so much of the future of the West of Ireland depended. The governing body was concerned with such matters as the appointment of professors, the election of members to the senate, the drafting of college statutes, and the consideration and authorization of recommendations from the various standing committees. It also concerned itself with financial matters, such as estimates, tenders, bills, scholarships, refunds of fees, insurance and the purchase of equipment, and payments to lecturers, assistants and substitutes for professors, as well as such mundane matters as the supply of coal.

The membership of the first governing body included McDonogh's friend Stephen Gwynn MP, and some of Galway's other leading citizens, such as Lord Killanin.[96] But, however enthusiastic McDonogh may have been at the outset of his membership of the governing body, within the year he had established a pattern to which he would adhere for the remaining twenty-six years of his association with the college: he simply didn't attend meetings unless he had a very specific reason.[97] Governing body meetings tended to take place on a monthly basis, so the demands on McDonogh's time were not particularly onerous. But an examination of the minutes of the governing body goes some way towards explaining his lack of interest. Far from the proactive strategic planning he and some of his fellow governors had doubtless anticipated engaging in, the meetings were characterized by seemingly endless discussions regarding the salaries and pension arrangements of the professors.

When McDonogh became a member of the governing body of Queen's College Galway the representation of Catholics on the teaching staff was low. An article in the *Galway Observer* in 1895 had noted that, of the nineteen professors, only three – professors Pye, Colohan and Steinberger – were Catholics, and observed that such 'an unfair distribution … must be remedied before any satisfaction is felt with the constitution of the establishment'.[98] It is clear from the minutes that McDonogh was one of those governors who

96 Aside from a number of bishops and college professors, the membership of the governing body also included Alexander Eraut, John P. Henry, F.J. Boland, William Daly and Joseph Glynn (UCG college calendar, 1908/9). 97 On 14 Oct. 1919, having failed to attend the six previous monthly meetings, McDonogh did attend a meeting of the governing body, when the appointment of a number of new members to the university's teaching staff was being discussed. 98 *Galway Observer*, 9 Mar. 1895.

supported Catholic candidates for positions whenever possible, including, at one point, his cousin, Tomás Ó Máille, as professor of Irish.

THE McDONOGH FAMILY IN 1911

An interesting window into the McDonogh family is afforded by the 1911 census. As we have seen, the 1901 census, completed by Thomas McDonogh, was riddled with errors in the ages of all members of the family. Bizarrely, ten years later, with his father dead and Martin now 'head of family', the 1911 census repeats the errors made in the earlier census, but the discrepancies in ages vary. McDonogh lists his own age as 40, whereas he was actually 51; Thomas Christopher is listed as being 38, when he was in fact 47, Michael, now a qualified doctor and back living at home, was listed as being 34, whereas he was actually 40, Mary Anne is recorded as being 36, when she was in fact 42, and Kate's age is given as 32, whereas she was actually 38. These discrepancies are puzzling. Certainly the McDonogh family, being financially secure, had no need to exaggerate their ages in order to secure state pensions, but the tendency instead to underestimate the ages is strange. McDonogh may have been striving not to draw attention to the fact that his father had made copious factual errors in the preceding census. Or it may have been that an innate vanity, a desire to appear younger, was at play. But keeping records and accounts was a critical part of McDonogh's daily business and civic life, so the errors are surprising and perplexing.

Among the servants listed on the 1911 census was a Mary McAleenan, aged 30, whose place of birth is listed as Co. Down.[99] One intriguing aspect of the return is the fact that McDonogh appears unsure as to the precise status of McAleenan in the household. Initially he appears to have listed her as 'temporary' nurse, but the first word is then erased, such as to be almost illegible, and he then adds the word 'domestic servant' in addition to the entry 'nurse'. All of which begs the question as to why the McDonogh household required the services of a live-in nurse? McAleenan may have been employed initially, sometime after the 1901 census was taken, to care for the ailing

99 Aside from Mary McAleenan, the employees listed are Bridget Derrane (26), shop assistant, and Barbara Nee (22), Julia Grealy (24), John Moran (40) and Matt Lydon (24), general domestic servants. The name 'Gertrude' was subsequently inserted by McDonogh into the return, so that McAleenan's name is recorded as Gertrude Mary McAleenan. On the previous (1901) census, McAleenan was listed as living in Gaevaghy, Corbally, Co. Down, and working as a 'farm servant' for her aunt, Mrs Catherine McAleenan.

Thomas McDonogh, and may have been subsequently retained by Martin McDonogh, after his father's death, in a different capacity, as a domestic servant. It is also possible, however, that the tuberculosis that had already stricken the family had not been fully eradicated, and was continuing to debilitate one or more members of the family. It was certainly the case that McDonogh himself experienced another period of illness in 1911, this time lasting five months, from January to May.[1] Toward the end of May the local press recorded that his 'numerous friends' would be glad to hear that McDonogh 'who has been confined to his room for a considerable time, is up and about again. Mr McDonogh attended the meeting of the county council on Wednesday, and went for a drive yesterday'.[2] No cause for McDonogh's illness is given in any of the reports of his lengthy absence.

As head of the household, Martin McDonogh continued to provide for his two unmarried sisters, Kate and Mary Ann. Recalled as a 'robust' woman,[3] Kate took an active role in the running of the fishing trawler business, and often sailed on the trawlers herself.[4] Mary Ann appears to have spent most of her life acting as de-facto housekeeper for her older brothers at the family home in Flood Street, and later at Belmore in Salthill. Surprisingly, given the prominence of their family, the McDonogh sisters featured infrequently in Galway society press notes. Like their older brother Martin, they never appeared in the various amateur theatricals held to benefit the poor of Galway, and are never listed as having attended the charity balls that were another feature of Galway's social calendar for young people of their social class. Their sole social outlet appears to have been assisting at various charity bazaars, usually with a religious association, such as in February 1900, when they were on the organizing committee for a bazaar to benefit the Magdalen asylum in Forster Street; the 'Misses McDonogh' are not referred to again until they helped out at a stall at the Augustinian bazaar held in August 1901.[5]

Like their brothers, the McDonogh sisters appear to have been, by virtue of their family's wealth and their own social status, eminently marriageable prospects. The fact that, with the exception of Dr Michael McDonogh, who married relatively late in life, no other member of the McDonogh family married is striking. It may have been the case, as previously noted, that 'no-one was ever good enough for the McDonoghs'. However, another possibility must be considered. Both Thomas and Redmond died of tuberculosis. In

1 The 1911 census was taken on 2 Apr. 1911, during the period that McDonogh himself was recorded as being ill. 2 *Connacht Tribune*, 20 May 1911. 3 O'Dowd, *In from the West*, p. 30. 4 Ibid. 5 *Galway Observer*, 10 Aug. 1901.

addition, the deaths of two other children – the Anthonys born in 1867 and 1870 – from pulmonary-related conditions (croup and 'bronchitis, uncertified', according to their death certificates) – may have attached a stigma to the surviving siblings that proved difficult to overcome. Historian Ciara Breathnach notes that 'were it known that a member had fallen prey to TB, the marriage and employment prospects of the entire family could be jeopardized'.[6] Writing of his own experiences of the disease and its social taint the poet Seán Ó Ríordáin confirmed as much, noting that 'you and your people would hide it, lest they be put out of the area, or for fear none of your sisters would marry'.[7] The reason for this was the belief that tuberculosis could cause infertility in women,[8] and a potentially infertile wife would have been a completely unacceptable prospect in the Ireland of the early 1900s. In any event, neither Mary Ann nor Kate appears to have contracted tuberculosis: Mary Ann died at 85 of 'old age without dementia' and Kate died at 48, of breast cancer.[9]

As for the men in the family, Sir Charles A. Cameron, an eminent physician and writer of the period, noted, 'I have rarely met a poor man of mature age who was a celibate. A man's desire for matrimony appears to be inverse to his means for maintaining a family. It is rich men who remain in so-called "single blessedness".'[10] But for Martin McDonogh we must consider the possibility that the choice to remain single may not have been entirely of his making. And indeed McDonogh was sensitive on the issue of tuberculosis. When the adoption of the Tuberculosis (Prevention) Act was brought up for discussion at an urban distric council meeting, chaired by him in 1909, he was uncharacteristically silent as the members discussed the terms of the act, during the course of which Sir James O'Donoghue noted that 'any person who was found to be suffering from tuberculosis would then be hall-marked and held up for it', another councillor adding 'if you put it in force, if a man coughs in the street he is done'.[11] A committee to consider adopting the new legislation was established, with the chairman, somewhat surprisingly, not a

6 Breathnach, C. '"Heavier the interval than the consummation": bronchial disease in Seán Ó Ríordáin's diaries', in *Journal of Medical Humanities*, 40 (2014), 1–16. 7 In the original article, 'Aicme Íseal', written in Irish, Ó Riordáin wrote 'Cheilfeá féin agus do mhuintir é ar eagla go gcuirfí as a gceantar iad nó ar eagla ná pósfadh aoinne do dhriféaracha.' *Irish Times*, 13 Feb. 1971. 8 Pulmonary tuberculosis (TB) is a contagious bacterial infection that affects the lungs, but may spread to other organs. Tuberculosis can infect women's general systems via blood circulation or the lymphatic system, causing genital tuberculosis, the most common type being tubal tuberculosis, which causes infertility. 9 Civil Registration Service, Galway, Record No. 395/1948 and Record No. 405/1927. 10 Cameron, C.A., *Reminiscences of Sir Charles Cameron, CB* (Dublin, 1913), p. 168. 11 *Connacht Tribune*, 27 Nov. 1909

member. McDonogh did, however, fully support the passage of the bill, and was supportive of any measures undertaken by the council, regardless of cost, that would help to eradicate the disease. Subsequent to the act being implemented, and until the end of the First World War, better economic and social conditions, improving standards of domestic hygiene, and a wider public recognition of the factors that contributed to infection resulted in a 25 per cent reduction in the annual number of deaths from TB.[12] However, the disease continued to cast a long shadow, particularly over those families, such as the McDonoghs, who had been affected by it, and was a source of social stigma well into the 1950s and 60s.

TEMPERANCE AND ILL TEMPER

McDonogh's antipathy towards drunkenness surfaced on numerous occasions throughout his life. Most strikingly, it raised its head at an urban district council meeting in November 1909, when the returns of the town steward, a Mr Connolly, came under discussion, the secretary noting that the accounts were not 'properly made out'.[13] Connolly stated that he had not had time to complete the wages book, and McDonogh commented 'Of course not, the public houses claimed your attention.'[14] McDonogh's frustration at Connolly's appearance in the council chamber initiated a fiery discussion on the latitude extended to Connolly in dealing with what had clearly been a protracted battle with alcoholism. But McDonogh's annoyance that such an employee would be offered chance after chance to deal with his problem stemmed from his own strongly held belief that employers should lead by example. When McDonogh asked of Connolly 'Could you not come into this meeting today even half sober sir?' and Connolly curtly replied 'Amn't I sober?', McDonogh's response was sharp and to the point: 'No, you are not; and it is hard to expect that men working for 14s a week could or should do their work while a drunken man is over them.'[15] When the meeting went on to consider whether Connolly would resign or be dismissed, a case for leniency was made, and significantly, at this point McDonogh nailed his colours to the mast, declaring 'I say straight if he does not retire, I will retire. There is no use going on in this kind of way.'[16] A month later the Council

12 Jones, *Captain of all these men of death*, p. 149. 13 *Connacht Tribune*, 6 Nov. 1909. 14 Ibid. 15 *Connacht Tribune*, 6 Nov. 1909. 16 Ibid.

voted by a majority of 10 to retain Connolly's services.[17] Martin and T.C McDonogh voted against.

At that meeting, the frustration felt by the McDonogh brothers at what they perceived to be the lax management of the urban district council members boiled over. T.C. declared, 'It is no wonder that your officials should act as they do,' and Martin McDonogh added, 'It is no wonder that your *town* would be the way it is.' But the spat in the council chamber that followed said a great deal about the way in which the McDonoghs' financial success, and the power they now wielded in the business and civic community, were resented in certain quarters, and particularly so by several of their fellow councillors. McDonogh's threat to the urban district council, that he would retire if the council did not support his motion to dismiss Connolly, clearly irked some of his fellow councillors. Councillor Cunningham declared, 'you may be a wealthy man; but so far as my character goes, it stands as well as yours', and observed how McDonogh had tried to enforce his will on the council, but had not followed through on his resignation. With characteristic bullishness, McDonogh remarked that Cunningham 'should not get up to lecture me, it is not your place', and Cunningham declared, 'How dare you sir! I am as big a man as ever you were … What impudence you have … what do I care about your money?'[18]

The fact that McDonogh, a wealthy man, did not himself drink was somewhat perplexing for many of his fellow councillors, and much of Galway society in general. Even among his own social class, temperance was something of a rarity.[19] Gwynn's description of Lord Morris, for example, a man who sat on a number of committees with McDonogh, and was also a non-drinker, is striking in this regard. Gwynn recalled overhearing two Spiddal residents discussing Lord Morris' wealth. One argued that his income was £500 a year, the other claimed it was closer to £1,000, adding, 'and would you believe it, I saw that man passing my house this ten year, and he going in and out to Galway – and I never seen the colour of drink on him yet'.[20] We will never know what motivated McDonogh's aversion to alcohol. It may have been his deeply held religious beliefs, and the commitment he consequently gave to the temperance movement, or, as a man who always liked to be in complete control, it may have been down to a desire to avoid any possible

17 Galway urban district council minutes, 3 Dec. 1909. 18 *Connacht Tribune,* 4 Dec. 1909. 19 The teetotal movement, led by Father Mathew, began in 1838, and the Pioneer Total Abstinence Association was founded in 1899. McDonogh likely took the pledge to abstain from alcohol when he joined the Sodality of the Blessed Virgin Mary in 1878 at the age of 18. 20 Gwynn, *A holiday in Connemara,* p. 64.

chinks in his armour which a fondness for drink may have brought about. It appears unlikely that his decision to become teetotal came about as a result of an edict from his father or mother, as his brothers T.C. and Michael certainly drank socially. The situation with regard to his sisters is unknown. It therefore appears that McDonogh joined the temperance movement of his own volition, as a result of his abhorrence of drink and the consequences of its abuse, not only for the individual concerned, but for society as a whole.

Outside of the council chamber, it was McDonogh's increasingly significant role as a major employer and entrepreneur that was capturing the public's attention. The various divisions of the McDonogh empire had boosted direct and indirect employment, and as a by-product had bettered the lives of the small farmers of Connacht, something the local press – albeit a press that benefitted from advertising revenue from the company – readily acknowledged. A *Connacht Tribune* editorial in December 1913 said of Thomas McDonogh & Sons that, 'This firm forms one of the props and pillars of industrial Galway. It is to the city what the cotton mills are to Lancashire.'[21] But it was the fertilizer factory which was the focus of the editorial:

> The extension that has taken place in the manure factory, started during the year … was heralded with pleasure by every true Galway man. Today, that factory rears its dusky head over the ramparts of O'Brien's Bridge, a testimony alike to local enterprise and to the progressive spirit of its founders. Those who deal with McDonoghs, old clients of years standing, and new, brought there by the lure of unequalled value, all speak in the highest praise of these universal providers, who, in their sphere of activity, are the best example of practical patriots.[22]

This latter phrase would have resonated with McDonogh, and it was a theme he returned to again and again throughout his life, particularly during his years as a TD.

FISH VERSUS FERTILIZER

Not everyone was as supportive of the fertilizer plant. T.G.P. Hallett and Lilias Ashworth-Hallett,[23] the owners of the Galway fishery, suspected that

21 *Connacht Tribune*, 13 Dec. 1913. 22 Ibid. 23 Lilias Sophia Ashworth-Hallett was the daughter of

the waters of the Corrib were being poisoned, and fish and eel life destroyed as a consequence. The poisoning, they believed, related to the discharge of effluent by the McDonogh fertilizer factory,[24] which, according to an initial report by the department of agriculture, caused 'the mortality of young eels'.[25] This was of serious concern to the Halletts, as demand for eels at Billingsgate fish market in London was considerable.[26] The eel population had fallen significantly due to the pollution of rivers and overfishing, and, as a result, many eel fisheries in Ireland were on the brink of extinction. In 1909, prices were 25 per cent up on the previous year, due to the scarcity of eels,[27] and subsequent reports indicated that the numbers of eels continued to decline. Understandably, therefore, this was a highly profitable aspect of its operation which the Galway fishery could ill afford to lose.

Galway was not alone in experiencing the adverse effects of polluted water on its freshwater fish life. In the upper reaches of the Shannon, on the Brosna River, trout had been poisoned by the presence of chloride of lime in the water, the source of which was agricultural fertilizer.[28] The problems associated with pollution were exacerbated by the fact that Ireland experienced very dry weather in the early decades of the twentieth century. In 1909, the *Freeman's Journal* reported that 'salmon are literally lying in swarms on the bed of the River Corrib, with scarcely three inches of water over them. Owing to the long continued drought the river, except for a width of 8 feet, is quite dry.'[29] In such conditions, the introduction of any chemical pollutant, which could not be adequately diluted, would prove devastating to fish life.

Thomas McDonogh & Sons pleaded that the fish kill had nothing to do with them or their business. The Halletts disagreed, and monitored discharges from the fertilizer plant closely for a number of years, something that was rendered much easier in 1913, when McDonogh transferred the operation of the fertilizer plant to the former Burke's distillery site, directly across the river from the draught netting station operated by the Galway fishery at Wolfe Tone Bridge. Hallett was understandably outraged, when, on 11 July 1913, he noted 'great numbers of eel fry, dead'.[30] He was quick to assign blame to the fertilizer works, and alerted his fellow members of the fishery conservators –

Thomas Ashworth, who, along with his brother Edmund Ashworth, had purchased the Galway fishery from the encumbered estates court in 1852 for £5,000. 24 Ireland's first superphosphate and sulphuric acid plant, it remained in operation until the 1960s, when it was demolished. 25 Copy of department of agriculture report dated July 1909, Ashworth archive, western regional fishery board. 26 Jellied eels were a popular delicacy in London, and consisted of chopped eels boiled in a spiced stock that was then allowed to cool and set, forming a jelly. The dish was eaten cold. 27 *Freeman's Journal*, 18 Oct. 1909. 28 Ibid. 29 Ibid. 30 Ashworth archive, 11 July 1913.

a body of which McDonogh was a member, although he rarely attended meetings – who wrote a strongly worded letter to the department of agriculture's fishery branch. The letter stated that, since the establishment of the fertilizer works, 'a discoloration of the bed of the river from the outlet from the works for some 300 yards from the Claddagh Bridge had been noted'.[31] Corroborating photographs of the dead eel fry were enclosed with the letter.

The department was sufficiently concerned that it ordered an immediate inspection of the fertilizer factory,[32] and subsequently commissioned an eminent chemist, Richard J. Moss, of the Royal Dublin Society,[33] to examine the water emanating from the factory's condenser. Moss found hydroflus-silicic acid,[34] estimated at 18.89 grains per gallon. His report stated that,[35] when placed in a solution of the water diluted to five times its volume, a minnow 'showed signs of discomfort and in 21 minutes began to turn over on its side' – placed in fresh running water it died in 20 minutes. Also detected in the samples were iron oxide, copper oxide and a small quantity of arsenic. Moss concluded that the water discharged from the condenser at the fertilizer factory was 'injurious' to fish in the concentrations being emitted, and that the copper in the effluent would be 'fatal to algae and thus indirectly injurious to fish'.[36] Moss' report did, however, state that if the release of effluent into the river could be slowed down (and therefore diluted to a far less harmful level when it entered the river) it would be less injurious to fish life and vegetation. The department acknowledged as much in their reply, and appeared to accept McDonogh's contention that the discharge had been 'accidental'.[37] Nonetheless, the department stated that they had advised Thomas McDonogh & Sons to 'take steps to prevent its discharge in any considerable volume',[38] and would continue to take samples to monitor the situation.

The minutes of the fishery conservators indicate that they – and, it must be assumed, the Halletts – were not convinced that McDonogh would curtail

31 Letter dated 16 July 1913 from Galway fishery conservators to the secretary of the department of agriculture, fisheries branch in Ashworth archive. 32 The inspection was carried out by William Holt, fisheries inspector, who passed on the samples taken by him to Richard Moss. 33 Moss was the registrar of the Royal Dublin Society, and its chief administrator. 'Royal Dublin Society: compromise and change', in Nicholas Whyte, *Science, colonialism and Ireland* (Cork, 1999), p. 58. 34 Now known as fluorosilicic acid, this is an aqueous solution and corrosive acid, irritating to skin and having a pungent odour. Its most common application today is in the fluoridation of water to prevent dental caries. 35 The report was dated 2 Aug. 1913. 36 Ashworth archive, 2 Aug. 1913. 37 Ibid., 7 Aug. 1913. 38 Ibid.

production, when demand for fertilizer, in an Ireland where agricultural production was increasing to unprecedented levels, was driving levels of production higher and higher. And they were proved correct, as production increased significantly in 1914 following the outbreak of war that summer, and issues greater than fishery rights on the Corrib were to form the backdrop to hostilities between McDonogh and the Halletts for years to come.

The Halletts had already crossed swords with McDonogh in 1911, when the issue of two fishing platforms they had established – one off the Long Walk and the other off the Claddagh quay – was the cause of proceedings instituted by the harbour commissioners,[39] of which Martin McDonogh was a prominent member, and subsequently chairman.[40] The Halletts lost the case, and were forced to remove the fishing stations, but the most significant consequence of the court proceedings was that the Halletts' relationship with the commissioners soured significantly and irrevocably, and the fishery was now increasingly vulnerable, with a potential ally now an implacable enemy. And in McDonogh they had taken on a formidable adversary, a man whose 'resources, and his personality, made him almost impervious to challenge'.[41] In truth, the Halletts were no lightweights, either, but in the rapidly changing political landscape of Ireland during and after the Great War, the quintessentially English, staunchly unionist Halletts were unlikely to win many friends or allies in Galway in safeguarding their fishery in the face of competing and increasingly nationalistic demands, and the industrial development of the city, which was largely being spearheaded by McDonogh.[42]

McDonogh's antipathy towards the fishery owners, and indeed the board of fishery conservators, was played out publicly on a number of occasions. In 1909 he opposed the extension of the powers given to fishery inspectors to monitor, and where necessary prosecute, local fishermen taking fish from Lough Corrib. He was the only member of the board of conservators to abstain on a vote to allow unlimited and unannounced inspections, and showed himself firmly on the side of local fishermen when he stated that

39 The case eventually came before the nisi prius court in Dublin on 31 Jan. 1911, the Halletts having successfully argued for a change of venue on the grounds that they would not get a fair trial in Galway, where a number of the harbour board members were also serving justices of the peace. *Freeman's Journal*, 4 Feb. 1911. 40 McDonogh was chairman of the harbour commissioners, 1916–34. 41 Cunningham, *'A town tormented by the sea'*, p. 4. 42 Hallett became high sheriff of the county of the town of Galway in 1885, but his political ambitions lay elsewhere and he resigned in order to contest the borough of Galway 'in the Liberal and Constitutional interest'. (The *Times*, 1 Dec. 1885.) In 1891 he became vice president of the newly formed Irish Unionist Alliance, a political party established to oppose home rule in Ireland, which attracted some of the most prominent Quaker businessmen in Ireland to become members, including the Jacobs, Bewleys, Cleeves and Goodbodys.

'there were old men up the lake who felt it very hard to have men like that coming into their places, and if an arrangement could be come to whereby these old men would get back, it would be better for everybody'.[43]

AMBITIONS FOR GALWAY

That McDonogh's interests extended to the wider impression given of Galway was evidenced in 1911, when at an urban district council meeting, it was suggested that savings could be made if the size and design of proposed new council houses were scaled down. McDonogh disagreed, declaring that 'they would … have to consider the appearance of their town and he for one would be prepared for a little loss so that they could have a good class of houses'.[44] McDonogh was frequently in a minority when he advocated the building of council houses for the less well-off. Others believed that council monies would be better spent on other infrastructure schemes, which would benefit trade and industry in the town. When a medical report by his cousin, Dr Thomas McDonogh, deplored the conditions in which three families were living in tenements in Kirwan's Lane, McDonogh noted that sites for replacement housing were being looked at by the council in Kelly's Lane and Henry Street:

> We should build all up Henry Street, and I should not mind if you lost a little money on it, so long as you give those unfortunate beings, who presently live in such unsanitary dwellings, a decent house to live in. It is a scandal the way some of the people in this town are living.[45]

When the allocation of thirteen new houses erected by the urban district council at Woodquay was being considered, it was agreed that the houses would be allocated to the families who had the most children. McDonogh showed a rare flash of humour when he quipped, in the case of a man who had ten children, that a house should automatically be allocated, as 'any man who has ten children … not alone deserved the council's sympathy, but the sympathy of everyone else!' But in a statement typical of McDonogh, when the laughter had subsided, and a councillor asked what would happen if a house was allocated to a family later found to have 'hoodwinked the board'

43 *Connacht Tribune*, 23 Oct. 1909. 44 Ibid., 16 Dec. 1911. 45 Ibid., 21 Aug. 1909.

regarding the number of their children, McDonogh replied 'I will tell you what we will do, we will fire them out again.'[46]

The manner in which Galway was viewed by the outside world, and McDonogh's appreciation of the unique character of the city, was behind an extraordinary offer to purchase what many consider the jewel in the crown of Galway's archaeological heritage. The Galway Archaeological and Historical Society had been established in 1900, and over time, the society had acquired a number of artefacts of archaeological and historical importance, and was faced with the problem of where to store and curate them. In 1908 McDonogh came up with a solution: he offered to buy Lynch's Castle in Shop Street for the significant sum of £1,500, the property to be thereafter conveyed to the urban council and used as a museum for the society, and a boardroom for the council. It was a remarkable offer, but, unfortunately, not one taken up by the owners,[47] and an opportunity to bring one of Galway's finest medieval buildings into civic ownership was lost forever.[48] The building was later sold to the Munster and Leinster Bank. McDonogh appears to have been motivated by a genuine desire to preserve a significant aspect of the built heritage of Galway for future generations, and to ensure that the city was viewed as one that had respect for its antiquity. McDonogh's subsequent actions, and the considerable effort he personally invested in restoring the old graveyard at Forthill, are further proof of his belief that respect for the past, and for preceding generations, was an integral part of his duty as a public man.

GALWAY GOLF CLUB

While field sports may not have been among McDonogh's interests, he did support racing and golf, passions he acquired via his business relations with Sebastian Nolan. Thomas McDonogh and his sons Martin and T.C. began their association with Galway Golf Club when Nolan designed Galway's first golf course on lands he owned at Gentian Hill.[49] Nolan established a golf course that was, by all accounts, somewhat eccentrically operated, one commentator noting that 'the game was followed at Gentian Hill under rules

46 Ibid., 14 Sept. 1912. 47 The castle had been owned by a Mrs Kirwan, who died in February 1916. *Connacht Tribune*, 12 Feb. 1916. 48 O'Gorman, P., 'The Galway Archaeological and Historical Society', *Galway Reader*, 1:4 (1948). 49 This was Galway's first full eighteen-hole course, although a nine-hole course had been established at Renmore Barracks in 1895.

which were not exactly in accordance with those framed by the Royal and Ancient Club'.[50] By 1905 Galway Golf Club had transferred to a new course at Ballyshanduff, across the Barna Road from Gentian Hill. By 1909 Martin and T.C. were both members. Although T.C. became an avid golfer, Martin McDonogh never took to the sport, and never played. That did not, however, prevent Martin from assuming an extremely significant role in the financing and development of the club in the years following the First World War.

LABOUR UNREST

The ease with which McDonogh was able to develop and expand his various enterprises had much to do with the fact that he had a ready supply of labour to draw on. Indeed, the lack of employment options led to 10,932 people from Co. Galway emigrating in 1911–21.[51] Those who remained and worked under employers like McDonogh began increasingly to see the advantages of joining a union to press for better wages and conditions, and began to threaten the balance of power in Galway. From 1910 onwards, many workers in Galway formed branches of unions or associations, and the Galway Trades Council was formed in 1911. Those who became unionized included dockers, shop workers, those working in the building industry, the county council, the hat factory, the transport companies – and employees of the McDonogh works. The formation of the Galway Workers and General Labourers' Union (GWGLU) by a group of dock labourers in August 1911 was a significant step, for, as Cunningham has noted, the dockers 'had been neither unionised nor notably militant for twenty years'.[52] The dockers were taking their lead from their counterparts in Liverpool, who had successfully negotiated better wages and conditions as a result of strike action, and were doubtless influenced by the visit of Jim Larkin to the city in June 1911. Within months, the union came to represent most of the male labourers in the town.

The GWGLU's success in rallying workers to the union cause was viewed with horror by Martin McDonogh, and he was galvinized into action. As Cunningham has noted:

50 *Tuam Herald*, 20 Apr. 1907. 51 Report of Commission on Emigration and Other Population Problems, Statistical and Social Inquiry Society of Ireland (1955), pp 31–3. 52 Cunningham, *'A town tormented by the sea'*, p. 240.

> for the self-consciously paternalistic Máirtín Mór McDonogh, the recruitment of his employees into the union was worse than gross interference, it was a personal affront. As the leading merchant and employer in the region, therefore, he mobilised his colleagues and business clients to resist union demands, through a Galway Employers' Federation.[53]

McDonogh assumed the chairmanship of the Employers' Federation, and his bull-headed approach to negotiations with union leaders led to a stand-off. Growing increasingly impatient with union demands for wage concessions, in March 1912 McDonogh posted a 'schedule of wages' that the unions, quite rightly, perceived as a 'take it or leave it' measure, which prejudiced the ongoing negotiations. The result was a decision by dock workers not to unload a recently arrived ship until McDonogh withdrew the document. McDonogh had no intention of doing so, and, as a result, the Employers' Federation declared a lockout, which applied to all twenty-three workplaces where GWGLU members were employed, affecting five hundred labourers, and, indirectly, eighty tradesmen. Following negotiations a compromise was reached, with a wage increase across the board, and, for building workers, 'wet time'[54] and a shorter working week (five and a half days instead of six) for those who were permanently employed. The lockout of 1912 indicates the sureness of the employers' control, for, critically, the principle of the 'closed shop', an essential leverage tool for unions in organizing strike action, was not conceded. This would precipitate a move to merge the GWGLU with a larger union, thereby strengthening its hand in future negotiations and disputes. Eventually, having considered a merger with Larkin's IT & GWU, the Galway workers opted instead to forge an alliance with the National Union of Dock Labourers, which was based in Liverpool, Galway port's principal trading partner.

Galway's organized labour was determined to be in the fray for the long haul, but so was the leader of the Employers' Federation, McDonogh, whose antipathy towards unions only increased as a result of the 1912 lockout and its aftermath. And soon the next clash came, as Cunningham has noted, 'The anticipated rematch between the Employers' Federation and the former GWGLU … began in March 1913 when discussions about wages broke down.'[55] A five-week strike began, during which McDonogh was at the heart

53 Ibid., p. 241. 54 'Wet time' refers to a special payment made to employees when they are forced to cease work during inclement or severe weather. 55 Cunningham, *'A town tormented by the sea'*, p. 240.

of the some of the most riotous proceedings that Galway had seen for many years, the details of which will be considered in the next chapter.

CONCLUSION

By 1913, the business and manufacturing empire which McDonogh oversaw was considerable. He had become the biggest fish in the small pond that was Galway's business community. However, his tightly held control and management of his various enterprises was feasible because they tended to service local markets: Galway city and county, and the province of Connacht. He was not alone in limiting his ambitions to the area he knew best. Niall O'Donnellan has noted that between 1911 and 1926, trade became even more localized, with only a few businesses engaged in producing goods for export.[56] In addition, the size of Galway's manufacturing plants was small, with more than half employing fewer than fifty workers. In 1911, factory manufacturing in Galway comprised of two woollen mills, a flour mill, a mineral-water producer, two sawmills, a foundry, a stone-polishing factory, a brush factory, a glove factory and a toy factory, almost all of which had originated in the 1890s – and McDonogh's fertilizer factory, established in 1909. Thus the industries in which McDonogh became involved were those that one would have expected to find in a developing economy, where local entrepreneurs of ability tended to identify only certain types of projects that had the potential to be profitable – such as the sawmills, the flourmills, and, in particular, the fertilizer factory. O'Donnellan has observed that almost all of the owners and managers (and they were often one and the same person) of manufacturing facilities in Galway had certain characteristics in common, characteristics which were typified in the personality of Martin McDonogh. They displayed a desire 'for full control over their operation. Joint ventures between businesses were rare, and managers tended to resent the intervention of other interests such as trade unions and the state.'[57]

However, the intervention of interests such as trade unions was an inevitable part of Irish society in the years preceding the great lockout of 1913. Like it or not, McDonogh and his fellow employers were left with no option but to strive, however painfully and with whatever degree of resentment, to

56 O'Donnellan, N., 'Manufacturing industry in Galway, 1911–1957' (MA 1199, NUIG, 1979), p. 42.
57 This was certainly true of McDonogh, who described trade unions as 'trouble makers'.

reach compromises on issues related to wages and conditions. Ultimately the businessman and pragmatist in McDonogh came to realize that fact – even if he never fully accepted it. And those striving to instigate change were not just Galway's organized labour. Demands for an independent Ireland also formed part of the radical movements that were becoming more and more mainstream in Irish society at that time. Tom Kenny, the blacksmith from Craughwell, had founded one of the first Sinn Féin clubs in Co. Galway in 1907. An IRB member, extreme nationalist and advocate of radical land redistribution, Kenny and men such as Pádraic Ó Máille – a relative of McDonogh's from Kilmilkin, Co. Galway – were key to the continued rise of Sinn Féin in the county. Matters intensified with the passing of the home-rule bill in 1912, and the subsequent formation of the Ulster Volunteers, which seemed to many to presage civil war in Ireland.

The challenges that had confronted McDonogh when he had assumed control of the family businesses in the early twentieth century were considerable. Galway had long held the reputation of being a city that promised much, but delivered little – certainly in terms of commercial and industrial development. The travel writer Henry David Inglis, writing in 1838, noted that the city had, even at that stage, 'the air of a place of importance'.[58] That the fulfilment of that promise had not materialized sufficiently, even by the early 1900s, was something McDonogh had determined to change, and he was not alone. But the wider question of who would bring about that change was becoming increasingly complicated by a combination of political and economic factors. By 1903, as Ó Tuathaigh has noted, 'There were many who felt that only under native Irish government, sensitive to regional needs, could Galway, in the company of other Irish cities and towns, realise its true potential.'[59] McDonogh supported this argument, but he still saw very clearly the absolute necessity of maintaining close ties with Ireland's biggest trade partner, Great Britain, and the wider British empire. His approach to accomplishing this in the convulsive period of social, economic and political upheaval that began with the labour unrest of 1913 was to take him outside the boundaries of his native Galway, and as far as Westminster.

58 Inglis, H.D., *A journey throughout Ireland during the spring, summer and autumn of 1834* (4th ed., London, 1836), p. 23. 59 Ó Tuathaigh, 'The air of a place of importance', p. 145.

4. Labour, war and civic leadership, 1913–22

By 1913 the power that Martin McDonogh and his family wielded in Galway was considerable. As Cunningham has noted:

> As an importer and exporter, fertiliser manufacturer, livestock dealer and grazier, Máirtín Mór held many in thrall besides his workers. Small farmers within a wide radius of the town, and indeed anybody who regularly bought, sold, or needed credit in the district, sooner or later found themselves dealing with Thomas McDonogh & Sons.[1]

Dealing with Thomas McDonogh & Sons effectively meant dealing with Máirtín Mór, and he patently did not like dealing with unions. In this, of course, he was not unique among employers, but the scale of his influence in Galway was such that 'to compare his role to that of Dublin's William Martin Murphy would be to understate his local significance, although they had much in common'.[2]

LABOUR UNREST, 1913

Management-labour conflict in Galway intensified during the period 1911–23, with a general lockout in 1912, two general strikes, in 1913 and 1918, and a week of serious class riots in 1922.[3] As was most often the case in such disputes, wages were the main bone of contention, and the wages paid to some workers were undoubtedly very poor. Jack Griffin, who began work as an apprentice carpenter with McDonoghs in 1910, when he was fourteen years old, recalled that he 'worked from 6.00 a.m. to 6.00 p.m., six days a week, for four bob. Times were tough and money was scarce.'[4]

The strike of 1913, which began on 1 April, was summarized in the *Connacht Tribune*'s review of the year in the following terms:

1 Cunningham, J., *Labour in the West of Ireland* (Belfast, 1994), p. 154. 2 Ibid., p. 152. 3 O'Donnellan, 'Manufacturing industry in Galway, 1911–1957', p. 65. 4 O'Neill, M., *I remember it well: Jack Griffin's memories of Galway* (Galway, 1987), p. 25.

> The dispute circled round the position of that shifty population, known as the dock labourers. There was a baton charge of minor importance at Eyre Square, at midnight on Wednesday, April 2nd, but with the exception of one or two minor ugly incidents, the strike was conducted in the most exemplary manner by the men. The 'Tribune' exerted all its influence for peace, and largely through its efforts, and through the intervention of a representative of the board of trade, peace was brought about. The strike lasted five weeks and it was stated that thousands of pounds were lost to Galway because of it.[5]

This summary belies the impact of the strike itself, and Martin McDonogh's significant role in it. Of the 600 employees who went on strike, 130 were carters and labourers he employed.[6] McDonogh appeared to think that he could undermine the striking workers by putting his own ample shoulder to the wheel, and encouraging his fellow businessmen to do likewise, the *Irish Independent* reporting that there had been no meeting of the harbour board, 'all the members being engaged in performing the work of their absent employees'.[7] In common with their fellow employers elsewhere, Galway employers were not used to negotiating with workers' representatives and 'had to be forced into doing so'.[8] Unionized labour represented a challenge to McDonogh's hegemony; but, on a more personal level, he also revealed in his public statements a deep sense of betrayal that his workers, whom he considered he treated responsibly and with fairness, would feel the need to join unions.

Running a busy docks with skeleton crews was clearly not sustainable, and the Employers' Federation sought to bring in workers from England. With the strike escalating, and rumours rife of the impending arrival of 'scab' labour, on 15 April a large crowd gathered at the train station to meet the 2 p.m. and 9 p.m. trains, 'it having been rumoured that the Federation were importing dockers'. But the only arrivals were 60 additional police officers, brought in to swell the number already in the city to 280, under the charge of six district inspectors. Tensions ran high when forty non-union men, sent by the Shipping Federation of Great Britain, arrived in Galway on 17 April, and were brought, under heavy police escort, to the SS *Duras*, where they were safely lodged, before the majority of the city's dockers became aware of their presence. The *Duras* was anchored alongside the SS *Cape York*, whose cargo the

5 *Connacht Tribune*, 27 Dec. 1913. 6 *Irish Independent*, 1 Apr. 1913. 7 Ibid., 2 Apr. 1913. 8 Cunningham, '*A town tormented*', p. 241.

men were tasked with unloading. The docks were heavily guarded by police and picketed by the striking dockers. In spite of the tensions, only one incident came before the courts, and it was not one of the strikers but a woman named Murray who was brought up on a charge – of having struck one of the imported workers who had entered McDonoghs' yard on the head with a frying pan. When released, she was escorted home 'by a cheering crowd of strikers and sympathisers'.[9] The unloading of the cargo completed, four days later the blackleg workers left Galway, having been 'escorted to the station by a force of about 180 police'.[10]

Low wages and short time prevented those who were lucky enough to have employment from accruing any great savings, and a strike resulted in great hardship for the strikers. McDonogh acknowledged this fact, noting that 'When our people strike it means ruin to the industry and ruin to the people themselves.'[11] Strike pay was slow in coming, and, as a consequence, the distress of strikers' families was severe and widespread.[12] With families becoming increasingly desperate, one local pawnbroker declared that, 'if the strike continued, he could not stand the strain that would be put upon him'.[13] There is anecdotal evidence that McDonogh personally intervened to ensure that the families of strikers did not suffer excessive hardship, by providing money to local priests for distribution to the hardest-hit families, on the strict understanding that the money was given directly to the wives of workers,[14] and that its source was never revealed.[15] But this was only a temporary solution to an acute problem, and McDonogh was fully cognizant of the fact that conditions for workers must improve, particularly with regard to the question of 'fair wages'. At the AGM of Galway county council in June 1915, McDonogh spoke in favour of establishing a minimum rate of pay for contractors, arguing that 'There was no question … that wages would go up, and the sooner that was recognized the better.'[16] In an earlier Galway county council debate over increasing the salaries of country surveyors, however, he had been somewhat more cynical, stating 'my experience is that the more salary a man gets, the more time you must give him to spend it'.[17]

The main issue for McDonogh, therefore, appears not to have been the

9 *Galway Observer*, 19 Apr. 1913. 10 *Irish Independent*, 22 Apr. 1913. 11 O'Donnellan, 'Manufacturing industry in Galway, 1911–1957', p. 66. 12 It was noted that the first strike pay had been paid on Saturday 5 Apr. 1913. *Irish Independent*, 7 Apr. 1913. 13 *Connacht Tribune*, 19 Apr. 1913. 14 McDonogh presumably feared, not without justification, that if given to the striking men much of the relief money would end up in the tills of local publicans. 15 Local NUDL leader William O'Flaherty confirmed as much at a Galway urban district council meeting in 1920, which will be examined in greater detail in chapter 4. 16 *Connacht Tribune*, 19 June 1915. 17 Ibid., 14 June 1913.

question of wages, but his resentment of union interference in the running of his various businesses. In a broader sense, class solidarity across nations, in the form of syndicalism, was anathema to McDonogh, and served to intensify the dislike of 'foreigners', bordering on xenophobia, that was a feature of McDonogh's personality all his life. The growth of syndicalism throughout Europe and in Ireland had largely bypassed Galway, where, it must be said, the labouring class were conservative and hesitant to embrace the militancy of Larkinism.

The resolution of the 1913 general strike saw the employers, including McDonogh, giving more than they had originally offered, but far less than the workers had looked for. The labourers had wanted an extra 3*s.*, and were offered 1*s.*, although they also obtained the concession of being paid by the week instead of by the hour.[18] In spite of his animosity towards unions in general, McDonogh's attitutude to one union leader in particular, William O'Flaherty, the president of the NUDL, is interesting. At an urban district council meeting in April 1913, when the previously belligerent actions of O'Flaherty at a meeting of the Employers' Federation were referred to, it was suggested that the federation agree to meet with the unions again, but without O'Flaherty. McDonogh objected, stating that 'There are two sides to every question, and there is no use adopting a bullying tone. It is far better to do such business in an amicable and fair spirit,'[19] subsequently adding that it was 'a matter for the workers' union, and if they want to bring this man with them, let them'.[20] O'Flaherty was to repay McDonogh's respect for his position some years later, in a way neither of them could have imagined in 1913.

OIREACHTAS 1913

With the strike concluded and normal trade resumed, a major event was looming on Galway's social calendar that was expected to bring an influx of visitors and much needed revenue to the city. McDonogh would not have fully appreciated the illustrious company he was keeping when he attended the opening of the Oireachtas in Galway in July 1913. Apart from the Gaelic League president, Douglas Hyde, and Eoin McNeill, among the delegates were Pádraig Pearse, Séan Mac Diarmada, Éamonn Ceannt, Thomas

18 O'Donnellan, 'Manufacturing industry in Galway, 1911–1957', p. 66. 19 *Connacht Tribune*, 19 Apr. 1913. 20 Ibid.

MacDonagh, Éamon de Valera, Cathal Brugha, Piaras Beaslaí, Séan T. O'Kelly, Bulmer Hobson, Liam de Róiste, and local League activists such as Colm Ó Gaora, Seoirse Mac Niocaill (George Nicholls), Tom Kenny, Alf Monahan (Ailbhe Ó Monachain), James Carter, Mícheál Ó Droighneáin and two cousins of McDonogh's, Pádraic Ó Maille and Pádraic Ó Conaire. Indeed, as historian Dara Folan has noted, 'the photograph of the gathering of the ard fheis delegates outside of the town hall is arguably tantamount to a who's who of the "coming revolution", including as well the first three presidents of independent Ireland'.[21]

However, at the opening of the first Oireachtas to take place outside of Dublin, something of a faux pas occurred: the urban district council was not treated with the requisite degree of respect. A breakdown in communication meant that the local Oireachtas committee were 'unaware of the presence of the urban council in their official capacity' (in the person of McDonogh, as chairman), and McDonogh was not initially invited to appear on the platform, nor referred to in the formal speech of welcome.[22] The secretary of the Oireachtas committee, Séamus Mac Artuir, was forced to write to the press, expressing the committee's 'regret ... irrespective of whose fault it was, that the urban council should have been inconvenienced. Had we known of their intention of being present, we would have gladly made suitable arrangements.'[23] As the man at the centre of the breach of protocol, McDonogh, somewhat uncharacteristically, appears to have kept his temper in check and brushed off the unintended slight, subsequently speaking, in fluent Irish, to the most senior members of the Gaelic League's executive committee.

It was during the Oireachtas in Galway that George Nicholls (Seoirse Mac Niocaill), a young solicitor in the city,[24] and a prominent local Gaelic Leaguer and member of Sinn Féin, was appointed 'head centre' of the Galway branch of the IRB, an appointment that was to have significant repercussions for McDonogh during the 1916 Rising.[25]

21 Folan, D., 'The 1913 Galway Oireachtas', in *Journal of the Galway Archaeological and Historical Society*, 65 (2013), 98–114 at 107. 22 *Connacht Tribune*, 26 July 1913. 23 Ibid. 24 Pádraig Pearse and Nicholls were connected, in that there is a suggestion that Pearse became romantically involved with Nicholls' only sister, Eveleen Nicholls, around the time she was elected to the Coiste Gnótha of the Gaelic League. Eveleen Nicholls died while swimming in the seas off the Blasket Islands, trying to save the life of a young island girl. The girl was rescued but Nicholls drowned. George Nicholls maintained that Pearse had in fact proposed to her, but that Eveleen had declined as 'she did not want to abandon her mother to the problems ... in her home'. Pearse later wrote a lament for Nicholls, entitled 'A Chinn Áluinn' (O Lovely Head) that began 'O lovely head of the woman that I loved'. 25 Hosty, J., Bureau of Military History (BMH) Witness Statement (WS) 373, pp 2, 3.

SALTHILL BAZAAR

The successful hosting of the Oireachtas in Galway created a much-needed optimism in the city, which McDonogh swiftly capitalized upon. His 'can do, will do' approach was very much in evidence in a major initiative he spearheaded in 1913: the development of Salthill as a community and tourism resource. McDonogh initiated, and was chair of, the Galway Citizens' Bazaar Committee.[26] The objectives of the committee were 'the making in Salthill of a public park for the citizens in general, but especially for the poor of the slums', and the construction of 'a pier or jetty', which would be used by fishing boats, pleasure craft, and the Galway Bay Steamboat Company.[27] The committee envisaged that 'The pier would also be a grand promenade,'[28] along which shelters would be erected at intervals to provide cover from the rain. The mission statement of the committee was pure McDonogh:

> For well nigh 100 years the people of Galway have been living in expectation of the stranger coming along with great trans-Atlantic schemes, and all these unrealized hopes have had the baneful effect, on nearly three generations, of preventing any initiative on the part of the people themselves. Now, at last, we propose to change the programme, and see what we can do for ourselves … we ask every citizen for his encouragement and subscription. A shilling subscription from the workingman will be as thankfully received as the larger contribution from those who can afford it.[29]

In the week following the initial appeal, a total of £97 6*s.* was donated, and the fundraising efforts of McDonogh and his committee eventually raised £521 6*s.* 1*d.*[30] At the opening of the bazaar, Fr Travers, of the organizing committee, noted that 'There is a new spirit arising. Men have been found who are honest, energetic and earnest and … they are worthy of the public support.'[31] Fr Travers acknowledged in particular McDonogh's contribution, noting that he 'had always cheerfully given his time and his valuable advice to every undertaking for the good of the town'.[32] McDonogh's reply was typical:

26 The other members of the committee were Stephen Faller and Joe Young (treasurers), and James Redington (secretary). 27 *Galway Observer*, 21 May 1913. 28 Ibid. 29 McDonogh himself subscribed £5, and Lord Killanin £10. *Connacht Tribune*, 19 July 1913. 30 *Connacht Tribune*, 27 Sept. 1913. 31 Ibid. 32 Ibid., 27 Sept. 1913.

> there was nothing for the betterment of the people of Galway, or for the good of the town, that he would not help to push on. If they all went together and tried to do what was right and helped each other, they could do a good many things and effect great improvements at very little cost to the community.[33]

It was a measure of the trust placed in McDonogh that the profits of the bazaar were lodged in a bank account in his name.[34]

While McDonogh was clearly committed to expenditure on civic projects for the good of the city, he was uncompromising when it came to what he considered the unnecessary expenditure of public monies. In January 1913 McDonogh 'threatened to resign membership of the harbour board because of an honorarium voted to Pilot Walsh, since elected harbour master'.[35] At issue was the amount paid to Walsh, who had been a pilot in the employ of the harbour commissioners for some thirty years, and had resigned as pilot prior to taking up his appointment as harbour master in 1913. McDonogh felt that the amount of the honorarium paid to Walsh – £376 – was excessive, and set a dangerous precedent, particularly given that Walsh was still in their employ, and that the limited funds of the commissioners were urgently needed for essential improvement works on the harbour. At a harbour board meeting the following month, in 'a curt letter' amounting to one sentence – 'I beg to resign my position upon the harbour board' – McDonogh did just that, or rather attempted to. The harbour commissioners were as one in their view that he should not be allowed to resign, as he was, in the words of the chairman, 'a useful man'. The secretary's assessment was somewhat more blunt: if McDonogh resigned it would be 'a pity: he is one of the biggest payers of dues'.[36] McDonogh was persuaded to remain a member of the board, and the honorarium to Walsh was significantly reduced.

IRISH VOLUNTEERS

The home-rule crisis continued to dominate Irish politics in 1913. Although Connemara and the west of the county were predominantly nationalist-leaning, most of east Galway, and Galway city itself, in common with McDonogh, was resolutely pro-Redmond and anti-Sinn Féin. As a response

33 Ibid., 27 Sept. 1913. 34 Ibid., 27 Sept. 1913. 35 Ibid., 27 Dec. 1913. 36 Ibid., 8 Feb. 1913.

to the formation of the Ulster Volunteers in 1913, several Galway branches of the Irish Volunteers were established around the county, with the city branch established at a meeting chaired by George Nicholls in the town hall in Galway on 3 December 1913. The meeting was addressed by Eoin Mac Neill, Pádraig Pearse and Sir Roger Casement, among others.[37] Surprisingly, McDonogh did not attend,[38] but the meeting was nonetheless a great success, with 600 men enrolling as Volunteers – within a week over a thousand men had signed up throughout the county.[39] However, as Kenny has pointed out, 'few who enrolled on the initial night became active volunteers'.[40] McDonogh assumed a dominant role in Volunteers activities in Galway, meeting with John Redmond frequently when he visited the city on Volunteers business. Subsequently, there were those who believed that McDonogh's motives in assuming such a prominent role in the Volunteers were less to do with a desire to protect Galway, and more to do with ensuring that the more radical members did not come to dominate, and by their actions undermine the social and economic security of Galway, in which he, and his fellow employers, had a significant interest.

By June 1914, when McDonogh chaired a meeting of the Volunteers in Eyre Squre, an additional 150 men had enrolled, the press noting that the 'strength of the Galway Corps is now close to 500'.[41] It was noted that the Craughwell volunteers, who came to the meeting on bicycles, 'were much admired for their splendid discipline'.[42] The discipline of the Craughwell men, under their leader Tom Kenny, was to play a critical role in the Rising two years later.

At the time, McDonogh appears to have been more directly occupied with the promotion of a major expansion plan for the port of Galway, but his involvement with the Volunteers ramped up considerably once war broke out in July 1914, and Redmond issued the call to arms. Quickly, McDonogh chaired a meeting at the town hall, at which he introduced Padraig Pearse, who was the principal speaker, to raise funds to enable the Irish Volunteers to buy weapons. Typical of McDonogh was the bluntness with which he explained Pearse's objective, noting that 'Mr Pearce [*sic*] had come from Dublin to explain to them the best manner of procedure, and it would not be so much a question of speaking as putting their hands in their pockets.'[43] McDonogh was appointed as one of a triumvirate of treasurers, the others

37 Ibid., 6 Dec. 1913. 38 It was noted that 'for unforeseen reasons the chairman they expected to preside could not do so'. This may have been McDonogh. *Connacht Tribune*, 6 Dec. 1913. 39 *Tuam Herald*, 20 Dec. 1913. 40 Kenny, *Galway: politics and society, 1910–1923*, p. 14. 41 *Freeman's Journal*, 22 June 1914. 42 Ibid. 43 *Connacht Tribune*, 25 July 1914.

being P.S. McDonnell and R. Carter, who immediately began seeking subscriptions to arm the local Volunteers.[44] McDonogh subscribed £20.[45] Interestingly, the Volunteers movement on the Aran Islands was as strong as that in Galway, with Fr Farragher succeeding in recruiting a company of over 100 islanders in August 1914. Among the local committee of the Volunteers were Thomas and Bartly Hernon (of Curough and Onaght, respectively), both cousins of McDonogh's.[46]

THE FIRST WORLD WAR

McDonogh was 54 when war broke out in 1914, and, as a committed home ruler, as he saw it, his duty was clear. His commitment to the war was absolute. And he was not alone, for, as one Volunteer observed, when war broke out 'the town of Galway went recruiting mad'.[47] McDonogh supported the lord lieutenant's recruiting drive from the outset of the war to its end. He frequently addressed recruitment meetings with Redmond, who was a personal friend, with significant success.[48] When the split occurred in the Volunteers in August 1914, a meeting was called in the town hall in Galway, presided over by McDonogh, who was, unsurprisingly, avowedly Redmondite in his sympathies. Galway Volunteers treasurer Frank Hardiman noted that:

> Drills and parades went on in the usual way until a requisition was sent to the secretary,[49] and signed by Martin McDonagh … requesting that a meeting of the Volunteers be called … for the purpose of considering the advisability of placing the Volunteers under the authority of John Redmond. This meeting had disastrous results, ending with the breaking up of the Volunteers in Galway – the larger following going over to Redmond, to assist him in his recruiting campaign for the British army.[50]

The actual vote, when taken, had resulted in a tie, but McDonogh declared the motion, 'that the Irish Volunteers deserve the support of the meeting' to

44 Pearse stated at the meeting that 'Guns will be got in, no doubt about it. A few cargoes will be seized, but we must risk that. Guns will be got in elsewhere, and they will be got in here,' to applause from the audience. *Connacht Tribune*, 25 July 1914. 45 Ibid. 46 *Connacht Tribune*, 22 Aug. 1914. 47 Courtney, T., BMH WS 447. 48 Chairing a meeting of Galway urban council, McDonogh adjourned it on hearing of the death of his old friend John Redmond in March 1918, declaring that 'a greater Irishman we shall not see in our time'. Kenny, *Galway: politics and society, 1910–1923*, p. 13. 49 The secretary of the Volunteers in Galway was Seamus Carter. George Nicholls was president. 50 Hardiman, F., BMH WS 406.

be lost.[51] John Hosty of Shantalla, Galway, a Volunteer who sided with McNeill when the split came, declared that 'The Irish Volunteers had both press and people against them. The finest body of fifth columnists in Ireland were in Galway town'.[52] The result was that most of the Galway Volunteers supported Redmond, joined the National Volunteers, and marched away to war.

As the war continued into the winter of 1914, Martin and T.C. took an active and often decisive part in swelling the ranks of the Galway men enlisting. At a recruitment meeting held in Tuam, '100 men with band and banner' from Galway were led by Martin McDonogh, who afterwards dined with Redmond and his wife, who had attended the rally.[53] The motivations of those who enlisted were many and varied, and included the belief that in so doing they were enhancing the prospects of home rule being introduced. Others enlisted for adventure, or 'for no other reason than to see what war was like, to get a gun, to see new countries and to feel like a grown man', in the fiery words of the future IRA leader, Tom Barry.[54] The journalist Michael MacDonagh's book, *The Irish at the front*, published in 1916, and designed to boost recruitment figures in the south of Ireland, characterized the Irish troops as 'ever gallant and dutiful, buoyed as much by lashings of holy water as they are by warrior esprit'.[55]

Not everyone was as enamoured of the war, and in one instance a 'dastardly outrage' interrupted a recruitment meeting,[56] and was characteristically dealt with by McDonogh. In attendance was the UCG president, Alexander Anderson, and three Galway MPs, Stephen Gwynn, William O'Malley and W.J. Duffy.[57] In the lead-up to the meeting a group described as 'some minor Sinn Féiners',[58] had been hanging about, threatening to disrupt it. Gwynn was in full flight, endorsing Redmond's call for the formation of an Irish Brigade,[59] when suddenly the hall was plunged into darkness:

> five of the main cables had been cut at the riverside, near the convent, and at a given signal the sixth was severed.[60] Almost at the same moment little glass globes containing sulphuric acid and carbide of calcium were

51 Hosty, J., BMH WS 373. 52 Ibid., p. 4. 53 *Freeman's Journal*, 7 Dec. 1914. 54 Barry, T., *Guerilla days in Ireland* (Tralee, 1955), p. 2. 55 Haughey, J., *The First World War in Irish poetry* (Plainsboro, NJ, 2002), p. 18. 56 *Galway Observer*, 3 Oct. 1914. 57 William O'Malley was MP for Galway Connemara from 1895 to 1918. William John Duffy was MP for South Galway from 1900 to 1918. 58 *Galway Observer*, 3 Oct. 1914. 59 Gwynn was shortly to enlist himself, at the age of 50, in January 1915. 60 John Hosty, of Shantalla Road, Galway, gave evidence that it was Tom Hynes, Michael Kavanagh and himself who had been detailed to 'cut the wires at a certain time'. BMH WS 373, p. 6.

> flung towards the platform and into the body of the hall.[61] Immediately these came into contact with any object they burst, emitting a foul smelling liquid that created a disgusting stench throughout the hall.[62]

The actions of the saboteurs had been anticipated. Candles were lit, and Gwynn announced, 'We will hold our meeting outside, if they will not allow us to hold it here.'[63] McDonogh, as chairman, took charge and announced that the meeting would be held on the steps of the courthouse, which was directly across the square from the town hall, and a table was hastily set up there as those attending the meeting filed out. But McDonogh was seething, and one further interruption, this time by O'Halloran, a former secretary of the Labourers' Union, who mounted an improvised platform of his own close to Gwynn, caused him to lose his temper. As O'Halloran engaged in an 'incoherent interruption', McDonogh shouted 'Order!' When O'Halloran ignored him, McDonogh caught O'Halloran up and promptly hurled him from his self-appointed pedestal. He came hurtling down the Courthouse steps without mishap, but he had yet some "eloquence" left, and when he sought to deliver himself of this, he was driven towards the river by indignant spectators' where,[64] as Cunningham notes, 'other furious Redmondites threw the hapless trade unionist into the nearby river'.[65]

When a teacher named Madden, from St Ignatius' College, enquired of the men on the platform 'Who gave the Irish Party authority to act as recruiting sergeants?'[66] he was rounded on, and received some 'rough handling', the police having to intervene to protect him. Gwynn made a powerful speech, and the meeting concluded with a chorus of 'God save the king', a voice in the crowd adding 'and God save Ireland'. St Patrick's Brass and Reed Band struck up the 'Marseillaise', and Gwynn was carried 'through the streets to the square, where he was cheered repeatedly'.[67] The young men who carried Gwynn aloft were Volunteers from Castlegar, and it appears they had an ulterior motive. John Hosty stated that Gwynn was carried:

> shoulder high until they reached the Abbey church, when the poor man kicked to be let down. The "ruffians" had cut his braces, and the pants

61 Hosty confirmed that the so-called 'stink bombs' 'were manufactured in a UCG laboratory, and distributed amongst a few reliables who got into the hall', ibid. 62 *Galway Observer*, 3 Oct. 1914. 63 Ibid. 64 Ibid. 65 Cunningham, J., 'A great believer in the *Internationale*': A British trade union in Galway, 1911–36' in Ó Ciosáin, N. and J. Cunningham (eds), *Culture and society in Ireland since 1750: essays in honour of Gearóid Ó Tuathaigh* (Dublin, 2015), pp 197–218. 66 Ibid. 67 Ibid.

> were nearly off. It was a standing joke for years how Mr Gwynn nearly lost his pants.[68]

The public and business lives of McDonogh frequently overlapped, and while Gwynn was in Galway for the recruitment meeting, McDonogh prevailed upon him to head a delegation from the harbour commissioners to Galway county council in support of a loan of £60,000, for which the harbour board were applying. Galway's harbour had, for decades, experienced stunted development, and what Kieran Woodman describes as 'a despairing inertia'.[69] In June 1914, McDonogh, his patience at an end, had come up with a plan. He proposed that an application be made to His Majesty's treasury 'for a loan of £60,000, repayable without interest within a period of 50 years, for the purpose of carrying out the necessary improvements …'[70] In presenting his plan to the harbour commissioners, 'McDonogh, "in no uncertain language" reminded his fellow commissioners how often he had pointed out that local ports were "done" when even medium-sized vessels up to 3,000 tons could not enter in safety and berth in security.'[71]

The outbreak of the war was to prove decisive, and it is easy to see why Gwynn was a valued friend of McDonogh's. In his presentation to the council, Gwynn argued convincingly that the harbour was too small, and its depth too shallow, to accommodate the bigger ships of 5,000 tons burden that were by then the norm for commercial business – an argument McDonogh had been articulating for decades. Gwynn had been well primed by McDonogh, and argued that the commercial futures of the county and city were at stake. While the county councillors prevaricated over whether they should commit council monies in guaranteeing the £60,000 loan, the secretary of the council handed McDonogh a trump card when he suggested that 'if the Galway urban council go guarantee for £200 of every £470 paid by the county council it would relieve the matter greatly'. McDonogh, the chairman of the urban district council, replied, 'You may take it you will get that,' promising that the council would raise a rate of *1d.* in the £ to cover the guarantee.[72] The motion was carried, and McDonogh proved to be as good as his word in securing the approval of the council.

68 Hosty, J., BMH WS 373, p. 7. 69 Woodman, *Safe and commodious*, p. 177. 70 Ibid., p. 178. 71 Minutes of harbour commissioners, June 1914. 72 Galway county council minutes, October 1914.

RACEHORSES AND THE GALWAY RACES IN THE WAR YEARS

From the early 1900s, McDonogh had begun to buy a few blood horses to race. The outbreak of the war provided him with an opportunity to add significantly to his string of horses, as Gwynn explained:

> A German noble had a racing stable in Ireland and Martin McDonogh had found accommodation for his string. Things moved fast in August 1914, but before the property of alien enemies was declared confiscate, Martin McDonogh, acting on his own initiative, had registered the horses in his own name. They were paid for at leisure, whether legally or illegally I do not know, but knowing the man, I know it was a fair price. All his breeding was done from what he acquired then, and was done, not inland on the rich grass of Meath or Limerick, but on the rough pasture, fertilised for generations with sea-weed, in air charged with ozone from Galway Bay. And the horses throve and were the passion of his life.[73]

This 'German noble' was Count Stolberg, a well-known breeder and trainer of racehorses, who often rode his own horses at race meetings. Frederick Leopold Stolberg, a Catholic, was a native of Saxony in Germany, and he had moved to Ireland sometime in 1891 or 1892, when he was in his early twenties, and settled near Dunshaughlin, Co. Meath.[74] The move had come about largely, it would appear, because of his interest in horse breeding and hunting. Count Stolberg's racing colours were chocolate and white hoops, blue sleeves and cap,[75] and since McDonogh's chosen racing colours were yellow, red sleeves and black cap, the colours of the German flag, it is interesting to speculate on whether they may have been selected by McDonogh as subtle homage to Stolberg, the German from whom his breeding stock came.[76]

The opening day of the Galway Races of 1914, which took place on 5

73 Gwynn, obituary of Martin McDonogh, the *Observer*, 31 Dec. 1934. 74 Count Stolberg appears on the 1911 census, aged 42, living in Navan and giving his place of birth as 'Saxony, Germany'. He was a popular figure in both racing circles and with the general public, the *Kildare Observer* in 1932 noting 'it was a pity the war took him from amongst us, for he was very popular, and always rode his own animals when possible'. *Kildare Observer*, 14 May 1932. 75 *Freeman's Journal*, 22 Apr. 1914. 76 The end of war did not result in an easing of restrictions on German-owned horses. In May 1919, the registry officials were instructed that no race entries were to be accepted 'for horses the property of any persons being German, Austrian, Hungarian, Bulgarian or Turkish subjects or in which such persons have any interest whatsoever'. TCA, Minutes, 21 May 1919. This prohibition lasted until 1926.

August, only days after the outbreak of war in Europe, 'was favoured with glorious weather and a crowd of splendid proportions',[77] and proceeded without incident; but the prospects for future meetings were a lot less promising. One side-effect of the war was the establishment of a ministry to ensure that valuable resources were not wasted. As a result, horse-racing was centralized, and it was proposed that the only race meets that could take place were those at the Curragh, Baldoyle, Leopardstown, Fairyhouse and Punchestown, which were close to the main training centres of the Curragh and Clonsilla. Galway was not to be allowed hold its race meeting for the duration of the war.

Understandably, Galway racing enthusiasts and traders were outraged, and McDonogh, as Galway's leading citizen and chairman of the Race Committee, led the campaign to change the mind of the ministry. McDonogh informed the ministry that the town of Galway depended on Race Week, and the cancellation of the races would have a devastating effect on the local economy. His influence, along with that of Joe Young, both of whom were actively involved in recruitment drives, clearly bore fruit. Having used their contacts in the military, and after several trips to England and meetings with the ministry, McDonogh got his exemption, and the Galway Races continued throughout the war years.[78] It was McDonogh's first coup of the war, and it not only proved fortuitous in the short term, but secured the future of the races for some time to come. For, as Fergus D'Arcy has noted, 'the war, which brought conscription to Britain, brought a British racing invasion to Ireland … as British racing was disrupted to a vastly greater degree than it was in Ireland'.[79]

THE FERTILIZER BUSINESS

The outbreak of war impacted negatively on the Irish economy, at least initially. With competing pressures on supply markets, agriculture in Ireland suffered, and prices fluctuated. But very quickly this situation was dramatically reversed. With British agriculture suffering as a result of the large numbers of farm workers enlisting, Ireland once again became Britain's larder. Demand for Irish agricultural products boomed as a consequence, and accelerated from February 1917 onwards, when Germany adopted a policy of

77 *Connacht Tribune*, 8 Aug. 1914. 78 Hyland, *History of the Galway Races*, p. 83. 79 D'Arcy, *Horses, lords and racing men*, p. 244.

unrestricted U-boat warfare. The result was 'a period of high demand and higher profits for Irish farmers and industrialists'.[80] The financial return on McDonogh's foresight and investment in establishing the fertilizer factory was enormous, and elevated the McDonogh business empire to an entirely new level of profitability.

Although 'artificial manures' had been available commercially since the 1860s, demand continued to rise as the press extolled the virtues of using fertilizers to boost yield. A number of field demonstrations with artificial fertilisers were widely reported on. In the case of a 15-acre farm near Inniscarra, Co. Cork, it was noted that when the land was divided into equal plots, the untreated land yielded a harvest of 30 cwt of hay per acre, which, valued at 50*s.* a ton, yielded an income of £3 15*s.*; the land treated with 2 cwt of nitrate of soda, however, yielded 63 cwt per acre, adding an additional value of £4, which, even when the cost of the fertilizer – £1 3*s.* – was taken into account, still meant an additional profit of £2 17*s.*[81] For the farmers of Ireland, it was not difficult to appreciate just how profitable the judicious use of good fertilizer could render their crops. Any increase in demand served to enhance that profitability, and the outbreak of war in Europe precipitated a boom in Irish agriculture.

It was a company formed by two German brothers, Frederick and Robert Berk, which had provided much of the technical know-how McDonogh had needed to establish his fertilizer plant, and that continued to advise him during the war years. F.W. Berk and Co. Ltd had been established in London in 1886. A warm relationship appears to have developed between McDonogh and the Berk family, to the extent that there was a belief in the McDonogh family that, during the First World War, McDonogh had interceded and secured the release of Frederick Berk, who was a German national born in Crefeld,[82] when he was interned as an enemy alien. While it would be interesting if McDonogh, a man in the forefront of the recruitment movement, who had been largely responsible for the establishment of a munitions factory in Galway, intervened on behalf of a German national, such a scenario does not stand up to scrutiny. Frederick Berk had received his nationalization papers in Britain in 1882, and therefore would have been immune from internment. In addition, Robert Berk was classified by the

80 Hill, M. and J. Lynch, 'Ireland: society and economy, 1912–49': multitext.ucc.ie/d/Ireland_society_economy_1912–49, accessed 12 Feb. 2014. 81 *Nenagh Guardian*, 31 Jan. 1914. 82 Krefeld, also known as Crefeld until 1929, is a city in North Rhine-Westphalia, Germany. It is located northwest of Düsseldorf, its centre lying just a few kilometres to the west of the River Rhine.

Alien Advisory Committee as 'Class 7': 'German men in London who have been in the country 35 years, and have English wives still living, and whose characters and records are satisfactory.'[83] The company's unimpeachable loyalty to the British war effort was further consolidated when, at the end of the war, F.W. Berk & Co. were among those companies that agreed to participate in a scheme to employ disabled veterans to work in their factories.[84] Regardless of the precise nature of it, the depth of the relationship is reflected in the fact that when McDonogh died, a wreath sent by the Berk Chemical Company offered condolences on the death of 'an old, sincere, and trusted friend'.[85]

The benefits of the fertilizer business extended far beyond the McDonogh family, for, as Gwynn observed, 'the manure factory was a good thing for McDonogh and Sons; but it was a better thing for hundreds of small farmers'.[86] Cooper and Davis have noted that, before 1921, the Irish fertilizer industry was 'based almost entirely on imported fertiliser materials (with the exception of an unquantified amount of indigenous bones and similar organic materials of animal origin)'.[87] Demand was such, however, that even with the difficulties of importing raw materials during wartime, by the end of the First World War, there were about twenty factories, of various sizes, producing fertilizer in Ireland. But McDonogh's foresight had seen to it that the McDonogh fertilizer plant was ideally placed to capitalize on a golden opportunity. Pragmatic as ever, McDonogh knew his market, and as a result 'business was transacted on a credit, or barter, basis as hundreds of small farms relied on the company for essential agricultural supplies and McDonoghs were quite willing to accept payment in cash, livestock, or other property'.[88] As a result, McDonogh significantly added to his livestock herds, which he continued to graze on his various lands in Co. Galway and elsewhere.

But McDonogh frequently had to deal with more pressing and practical concerns in the management of his businesses, such as in November 1914, when a ship from Canada, laden with 2,000 tons of timber, bound for McDonoghs, ran aground in a gale on Mutton Island.[89] After a significant salvage operation, damage to the bow of the ship, where she had been holed,

83 Home Office Registered Papers, HO 45/11522/287235, 70/49, National Archive, Kew, London. 84 The *Times*, 20 Sept. 1919. 85 *Connacht Tribune*, 1 Dec. 1934. 86 Gwynn, obituary of Martin McDonogh, the *Observer*, 31 Dec. 1934. 87 Cooper and Davis, *The Irish fertiliser industry*, p. 76. 88 Spellissey, S., *The history of Galway* (Limerick, 1999), p. 114. 89 The ship, the *Nordlyset*, had an Aran pilot named Hernon aboard, who is likely to have been a relative of McDonogh's, although no details other than the man's surname are given.

was repaired, and the boat eventually unloaded its cargo at Galway docks, McDonogh personally overseeing operations throughout.[90]

CONFLICT WITH THE FISHERY

While the increased productivity at the McDonogh fertilizer works to meet wartime demand was a major boon to the local economy and local agriculture, it was greeted with far less enthusiasm by the owners of the Galway fishery. Following the eel kill in the summer of 1913, the department of agriculture had continued to monitor water samples from the river adjacent to the fertilizer factory, and even before production had ramped up considerably following the outbreak of war, a report in February 1914 indicated that hydrofluosilicic acid was present in a concentration of 147.58 grains per gallon, almost eight times the level detected the previous August. The report concluded that 'the present sample would be rapidly fatal to fish, even when diluted with fifty times its volume of water',[91] and the company was warned that it would be 'in a serious position' if it did not immediately take sufficient steps to implement the report's recommendations.[92] If McDonogh had been at all rattled by the letter from the department, he certainly did not show it. In a terse reply, he stated that the high levels of acidity detected were due to the manner in which the sample was taken, noting that 'our man tells us that the bottle was rinsed four times in the concrete trough, and stirred up a lot of sediment'.[93] Hallett, the owner of the Galway fishery, remained unconvinced and tried to enlist the support of the fishery conservators. But the chairman, Scrope Doig, was not anxious to take on Martin McDonogh in a war of words that might ultimately end up in the courts, unless there was sufficient evidence that the chemical effluent being discharged from the manure works was injurious to fish life. Hallett organized a visit to the fertilizer works with both Doig and another member of the fishery conservators executive committee, McNeill, where they met McDonogh and his plant manager, Mr Coy.[94] Hallett recorded that, having been shown the condenser and sludge tank, the visitors were emphatically assured by McDonogh that there was 'no acidity' in the water then standing there. Hallett promptly produced a strip of blue litmus paper, dipped it in

90 *Connacht Tribune*, 14 Nov. 1914. 91 Ashworth archive, letter from R.J. Moss, FIC, FCI, to the secretary of the department of agriculture, dated 11 Feb. 1914. 92 Ashworth archive, 14 Feb. 1914. 93 Ibid., 18 Feb. 1914. 94 The visit took place on 28 Feb. 1914.

the tank, and found that it immediately turned red.[95] Clearly unhappy to have been so publicly wrong-footed, McDonogh reluctantly agreed to measures to address the problem, including raising the height of the sludge tank and introducing a filtration area at its base, which, when filled with lime, would serve to neutralize any acid in the water. McDonogh ensured that these works were instituted, but, once war broke out, the more pressing priorities of production took precedence over environmental concerns, and there was little sympathy for the Halletts – and virtually no appetite for taking on McDonogh, no matter what the consequences for the fishery. The result was that, for the duration of the war, and throughout the tumultuous years that followed, the Halletts were more or less on their own in their efforts to halt the discharge of excessive amounts of effluent into the River Corrib from McDonogh's fertilizer plant.

In addition to his commitment to the war effort, the breadth of McDonogh's vision, and his ambitions not only for his own businesses, but for Galway, were remarkable. As early as 1915 he was hosting a familiarization trip to Galway for travel journalists, believing that tourism had the potential to become a major industry in the West. In March 1915 the *Connacht Tribune* reported on yet another business coup, resulting from the 'enterprise' of McDonogh.[96] A ship, the SS *Celtic Queen,* had arrived in Galway from the Macabi Islands with a cargo of 2,500 tons of raw Peruvian Guano, a cargo originally destined for Belgium.[97] In response to the British declaration in November 1914 that the North Sea was now a war zone, on 4 February 1915 Admiral von Pohl, commander of the German High Seas Fleet, had countered by declaring the waters around Great Britain and Ireland a war zone. Every enemy merchant vessel encountered in that zone could legitimately be destroyed.[98] McDonogh was fortunate that the German U-boat fleet was based at Ostend in Belgium, the intended destination for the cargo of guano, and seeing his chance, he 'secured the cargo on the high seas'.[99] McDonogh's astute move in taking advantage of the volatile shipping situation had significant implications not only for his fertilizer works, but for agriculture in the West of Ireland, at a critical time when food supplies were in desperately short supply in Great Britain.

95 Blue litmus paper turns red under acidic conditions. 96 *Connacht Tribune,* 27 Mar. 1915. 97 The Macabi Islands are located off the coast of Peru, and were a major source of guano. 98 The submarine blockade was extremely effective. In January 1915, 43,550 tons of shipping had been sunk by U-boats. The number of sinkings steadily increased, an average of 1.9 ships being sunk daily, amounting to an average loss of 100,000 gross registered tons per month. 99 *Connacht Tribune,* 27 Mar. 1915.

McDonogh's business philosophy was highly individualistic. He could not – and would not – allow anyone to take advantage of him, or his businesses. But he also had an inherent decency, which occasionally surfaced. In 1915 a young man named Butler was up in court on a charge of having stolen a plank of larch, valued at 9*d.*, from McDonogh's yard. The man insisted to the arresting officer that McDonogh had told him he could take the plank, but McDonogh denied ever having done so. McDonogh, himself a justice of the peace, was in the courtroom, and, without having been summoned, proceeded to address the court. He stated that 'this was not the first, nor the hundred and first time timber was taken. Yet he was for letting the accused go, and he did not desire to press the case.'[1] The prosecuting solicitor remonstrated with McDonogh, advising him not to 'bully' the court and declaring, 'You are not on the bench now.' McDonogh replied, 'I can go on the bench any time I like.'[2] Significantly, none of the sitting magistrates intervened at any point in this exchange, and the chairman eventually acknowledging McDonogh's generosity in seeking to have charges against the young man dropped. McDonogh stated, 'I don't want to do this youngster any harm, but it may be a caution to him,'[3] and the accused was bound over in the sum of £5 and two sureties of £2 10*s.* each. It is striking that McDonogh would take time out of his busy working day to attend court and speak up for a young man who had stolen from his business.

On another occasion, McDonogh became chairman of a bazaar to raise funds for restoration work on Forthill Cemetry. At the opening, he acknowledged that, with war raging, there were 'other causes more intimately connected with the everyday life and the material well-being of the people of Galway than that which the committee had this year selected'.[4] However, in a comment revealing of his own deeply held beliefs, McDonogh went on to observe that:

> In any country, or in any place, people who had no regard for the memory of those who had gone before them showed a lack of manhood and Christian feelings, and the man or woman who had no pride or regard for their forbears, would do very little for themselves or the community.[5]

It was clearly a cause close to McDonogh's heart, as both his parents were buried there, and he would ultimately join them in 1934, but as a Galwegian

1 Ibid., 17 Apr. 1915. 2 Ibid. 3 Ibid. 4 *Connacht Tribune*, 7 Aug. 1915. 5 Ibid.

he also recognized the significance to Galway people of this ancient cemetery, and was prepared to do his bit to ensure its survival, even at a time of great turmoil in the city.

Alongside his business and civic dealings, McDonogh was determined to make whatever contribution he could towards the war effort. He and T.C. continued to attend recruitment meetings, but with less success, as enlistment rates dropped sharply after 1915,[6] influenced in part by Sinn Féin, which began a campaign of intimidation against those directly involved in the recruitment drive. Following an attack on Joe Young's business, McDonogh expressed his anger at what he saw as the mindless adherence to the Sinn Féin 'cause' among the perpetrators, whom he described as 'more like rabbits than men; fellows who look around and see what other fellows are thinking about before they give an opinion of their own'.[7]

RECRUITMENT AND COLLEGE POLITICS

By 1916, McDonogh's civic responsibilities were considerable. He became chairman of the Galway harbour commissioners, a position he retained for the next eighteen years until his death in 1934,[8] and also assumed the chairmanship of the urban district council. His commitment to the war effort remained undiminished, and when the lord lieutenant visited Galway to attend a recruitment rally, McDonogh placed his carriage at his disposal, and later dined with him at the Railway Hotel in Eyre Square.[9] At the rally McDonogh was in more lyrical form than usual, stating that he was 'in sympathy with those who were fighting the people's fight and the fight of civilization and freedom of the world'.[10]

That same month McDonogh was requested to take on another 'fight' when the students of University College Galway submitted a resolution to Galway county council asking for representation on the university's governing body. The chairman considered it 'a very proper demand', but McDonogh, going one further, could not resist adding, 'There are professors up there who are not able to educate students at all, and are making pious sneaks of them.'[11]

6 Kenny, *Galway: politics and society, 1910–1923*, p. 16. 7 *Connacht Tribune*, 12 Feb. 1916. 8 McDonogh's long tenure as chairman was second only to that of Col. James O'Hara, who had held the position 1865–95. He was succeeded as chairman by his brother, T.C., who served until his own death in 1936. 9 *Connacht Tribune*, 4 Mar. 1916. 10 Ibid. 11 Minutes of Galway county council meeting held 10 Feb. 1916, and *Galway Express*, 19 Feb. 1916.

This was an extraordinary statement, particularly from a man who was a member of that self-same governing body; but the fact that his comments elicited shouts of 'Hear! Hear!' and applause, indicates the degree to which McDonogh was echoing the opinion of many of his fellow councillors. The county council passed, unanimously, a resolution that the students of UCG should be represented on the governing body, and further resolved 'that copies of this resolution be sent to the other county councils of Connaught', with the intention that such a resolution would be similarly adopted by them, which it duly was. McDonogh's suggestion that all of the Connacht councils be brought on board in support of the students' call for representation was astute, and had the potential to bring extreme pressure to bear on the university, as each voted yearly subventions to the college, which made a significant contribution towards the salaries of the lecturers and professors.[12]

If McDonogh's comments had prompted a positive response from his colleagues on the county council, the reaction among his fellow members of the university's governing body was far less sanguine. Prior to the governing body meeting at which the question of student representation was due to be discussed,[13] McDonogh was 'enthusiastically cheered by the students as he entered the boardroom'.[14] His comments at the county council meeting, however, were greeted with consternation and fury by both the president and the governing body, and the meeting had to be adjourned as a result. McDonogh was unrepentant and unruffled by the indignation of his governing-body colleagues, but his actions were the subject of an item on the agenda for the next governing-body meeting of 9 March 1916. Professor Seaghan Mac Énrí went so far as to propose that a motion be put before the meeting, that 'legal opinion be obtained as to whether the College has grounds for an action for damages on account of the above statement, and, if their opinion be in the affirmative, that such action be immediately taken'.[15]

Outraged and insulted as the impugned professors of the college may have felt, the course of action advocated by Mac Énrí was somewhat radical – and risky. The college was, at that time, struggling financially, and by the end of the year was carrying a deficit of £113 16*s.* 11*d.*[16] Costly legal proceedings,

12 Aside from Co. Galway, these included the county councils of Clare and Mayo. 13 The candidate who had been put forward by the student body to represent them was Conor O'Malley, who, as Dr Conor O'Malley, later became professor of opthalmology and otology at the college in 1931, and served on the governing body alongside his brother, Dr Michael O'Malley, who was professor of surgery, from 1924–56. Both were cousins of McDonogh's, from Kilmilkin, Co. Galway. 14 *Connacht Tribune*, 26 Feb. 1916. 15 Agenda, dated 3 Mar. 1916, governing body papers, NUI Galway archive. Mac Énrí was appointed professor of ophthalmology and otology at UCG in 1916. 16 Balance sheet, dated 30 Sept.

conducted in the glare of both the local and national press, were something the college needed to avoid at all cost. Consequently McDonogh, wisely, did not attend the meeting at which his comments at the county council meeting were being discussed, and, a number of professors having vented their fury and castigated McDonogh for his lack of respect for his colleagues on the governing body, the matter was quietly allowed to drop.

In practical terms, the college had, potentially, a great deal more than its dignity to lose if it took on Martin McDonogh, who was in a position to observe both the inner workings of the university, as a member of the governing body, and those of the urban district council, and influence the decisions made by both bodies. This was never more obvious than in March 1916, when the question of the registrarship of the college came before the county council and the urban district council. At issue was a memorial, signed by 145 graduate and undergraduate students, protesting an attempt to oust Prof. J.P. Pye from the position of registrar of the college.[17] The urban district council and the county council supported Dr Pye, the latter noting that he was:

> a staunch and unsupported upholder of Catholic claims at Queen's College during a period of years when such a course was neither fashionable nor profitable. That Dr Pye would many years ago have been president of the college but for the fact that he was then, and is now, an Irish nationalist home ruler … Dr Pye is at least as an Irishman and a Galwayman entitled to equal consideration with foreign-born professors of enemy nationality.[18]

The county council were so incensed at the threat to Pye's registrarship that it warned 'if Dr Pye is removed from the office of registrar the council will cease to send a representative to the governing body and will discontinue the grant made from Co. Galway rates for college purposes'. The latter point particularly exercised the minds of the professors and lecturers, whose salaries were dependent on the endowment of the college by the local authorities. In spite of the best efforts of the urban district council, the county council and

1916, presented at governing body meeting held 21 Nov. 1916, NUI Galway archive. **17** Pye matriculated 1866 QCG, MD 1871, MCh 1871 (Queen's University Calendar, 1880). **18** This comment likely relates to Prof. Valentine Steinberger, a German national and professor of modern languages at the university. A dislike of foreigners, bordering on xenophobia, was a feature of McDonogh's personality that reared its head frequently throughout his life.

McDonogh, who fully supported Pye continuing as registrar, the governing body refused to yield to pressure and the college secretary, Fr Hynes, was appointed as registrar instead of Pye.[19]

Unbowed, McDonogh was soon back to his usual phlegmatic self. While chairing a meeting of Galway urban district council, he became extremely agitated in a debate with a fellow councillor over the burning of bedclothes of tenants who had contracted tuberculosis. The councillor claimed this was costly and unwarranted, as the disease was not infectious. McDonogh, whose own family had been blighted by the disease, replied, 'Not infectious! It is the most infectious disease in the country,' adding that the Tuberculosis Act was 'one of the best acts ever passed in this country. What does it matter about the cost of replacing clothes burned, if we can help to save life thereby?'[20]

EASTER RISING

The saving of lives was not foremost in the minds of the men who were preparing to risk their own in pursuit of Irish independence, and for those who believed that the time was right to strike for an independent Ireland, McDonogh and the wealthy merchant class he represented were obstacles that had to be overcome at whatever cost, just as much as the might of the British empire. When the Rising was being planned in 1916, McDonogh was fortunate that there were clear divisions among the Volunteers leaders in Galway. While on the one hand the man sent by the Dublin leadership to mobilise the Galway Volunteers, Liam Mellowes, believed the Rising would constitute an attack on British rule in Ireland, the local leader, Tom Kenny, was not alone among his fellow Galwaymen in holding a different, more radical view. Kenny envisaged 'a radical transformation of Irish society and the creation of a more egalitarian Ireland that was fairer to small farmers and labourers'.[21] With this in mind, Kenny had members of the old home-rule guard, including McDonogh, very much in his sights. He planned to strike a

19 UCG governing body minutes, 6 Apr. 1916. 20 *Connacht Tribune*, 4 Mar. 1916. There were two Tuberculosis Prevention (Ireland) Acts – in 1908 and 1913. The 1913 act differed from the previous act in that while the 1908 act increased the powers of local authorities and public health officials to deal with tuberculosis, the 1913 act, as Jones has noted, 'shifted the responsibility for management of TB schemes onto county councils, replacing the joint hospital boards and boards of guardians, which, under previous health acts, had been entrusted with sanatorium-building,' Jones, G., 'The campaign against tuberculosis, 1899–1914' in G. Jones. and E. Malcolm (eds), *Medicine, disease and the state in Ireland, 1650–1940* (Cork, 1999), p. 166.

blow for the labouring classes by seizing both land and cattle from wealthy landowners, merchants and strong farmers (and McDonogh ticked all three boxes), in addition to the planned attacks on the local police and army.

It is doubtful that McDonogh ever fully appreciated just how close he came to being assassinated in 1916. Thomas Hynes' testimony that 'it was our intention to take a few prominent men – Martin McDonagh (Máirtín Mór), Joe Young, etc., and occupy the post office' told only half the story.[22] For the Volunteers, taking Galway was absolutely essential if the Rising was to succeed in Connacht, but this was no easy proposition. As historian Conor McNamara has observed, while the Irish Volunteers:

> remained committed to the separatist cause and flourished in rural parts of Galway such as Athenry, Clarinbridge and Kinvara, nationalists in the towns of the east of the county remained resolutely pro-Redmond, and antipathy towards Sinn Féin, particularly amongst the urban poor, remained profound.[23]

An essential element of the plan was the port of Galway, which would have to be taken or at least neutralized. There was, in addition, the large RIC barracks in Eglinton Street, in the city centre, and the army camp at Renmore, a few miles outside the city, and the military training centre for West Connacht. Taking control of all these important locations was a big task for a relatively small, ill-equipped group of men, especially given that Galway city was considered to be a 'loyalist' city – one rebel even referred to it as 'the most shoneen town in Ireland'.[24] Furthermore, the antipathy towards Sinn Féin among both the urban poor and the wealthier and more powerful members of Galway society ensured that there was likely to be limited public support for the Rising. The military council in Dublin, in considering this reality, had instructed George Nicholls, the Irish Volunteers leader in Galway, to strengthen his hand by arresting the city's two most prominent businessmen: McDonogh and Young. But the threat to the men was more serious, for as historian F.X. Martin recorded:

> The R.I.C. were to be called upon to surrender and warned that MacDonagh [*sic*] and Young would be hanged if resistance were offered.

21 Campbell, F., 'The Easter Rising in Galway', *History Ireland*, 2:14 (2006), p. 25. 22 Ironically, Nicholls later became the election agent for McDonogh and his fellow Cumann na nGaedheal TDs. 23 McNamara, C., '"The most shoneen town in Ireland": Galway in 1916', *History Ireland*, 19:1 (2011), p. 34. 24 Courtney, T., BMH WS 447.

> Should the police not surrender, the two men were to be summarily executed and the barracks then stormed.[25]

The military council believed so strongly that taking such prominent men hostage would be effective that they relied on it to underpin their plan for Galway. The plan was that when the RIC had surrendered or been overcome the rebels were to march on Renmore Barracks. Whatever hope there was of storming the police barracks:

> it was realized that Renmore Camp could not be taken through direct attack by the small ill-equipped group of men under Nicholls. For this reason it was desirable that MacDonagh [*sic*] and Young be still alive so that they could be produced for the second time as hostages under threat of execution. The two prisoners were to pay the price if the British commanding officer at Renmore refused to surrender.[26]

It was an audacious plan, and might well have worked had not time and breaches in both security and the chain of command intervened. As Thomas Kyne recalled, 'There was great confusion. We did not know what to do, and as far as Galway city was concerned, it was too late to do anything as RIC and military were already alerted.'[27] The fact that on Easter Tuesday a force of a hundred volunteers was unable to take the RIC barracks at Clarenbridge, Co. Galway, even though it was defended by only five RIC officers,[28] shows how strategically important McDonogh and Young's capture might have been. It could be argued that hostages such as McDonogh might have been enough to persuade the police to surrender. The simple fact was, however, that in spite of their number, the Volunteers in Galway were severely lacking in arms and ammunition. Pearse, in an official report on the Galway brigade in 1915, had reported that 'practically all the men are armed',[29] but this was more wishful thinking on his part than actuality, and when the fighting commenced the Galway Volunteers were hampered by their lack of arms.

News that rebels were active in Oranmore, Clarinbridge and Athenry was greeted in Galway by anxiety, rumour and hysteria. Telegraph lines had been cut, trains were not running, shops and factories were closed and all roads out of the town were considered too dangerous to travel. With Galway virtually

25 Martin, F.X., 'The 1916 Rising – a coup d'etat or a "bloody protest"?' *Studia Hibernica*, 8 (1968), 115. 26 Ibid., 116. 27 BMH WS 714, p. 4. 28 Martin, 'The 1916 Rising – a coup d'etat or a "bloody protest"?', 115 29 *The Irish Volunteer*, 25 Dec. 1915, p. 5.

cut off from news of developments elsewhere, there were fears that the rebels were approaching the town. A special edition of the *Connacht Tribune* carried on its front page the ominous banner headline 'Is it insurrection?'[30] The news that had reached Galway was that the 'rising', consisting of about 600 men led by Mellowes, was creating mayhem in the county, and that Galway was the next target. McDonogh immediately sprang into action, and an emergency meeting of the urban district council was called at the town hall on the Wednesday of Easter Week. Aside from the urban district council members themselves, more than a hundred of the town's citizens crowded into the building and heard McDonogh, who took the chair, dramatically declaring that the meeting was now a 'committee of public safety'.[31] A resolution was passed, calling on 'the authorities and people of Galway to co-operate to crush by every possible means the efforts of disaffected fanatics and mischief-makers'. Prof. Pye proposed that the citizens of Galway be invited to 'offer themselves for enrolment as special constables or in any way the authorities consider they may be useful in the present crisis'.[32]

A citizens' militia known as the National Volunteers was established under the direction of Captain J.P. O'Neill. The army agreed to provide the militia with rifles and bayonets, and they were tasked with the job of patrolling the streets. The post office was placed under armed guard, and notices of martial law were posted stating that 'all licensed premises in the urban district of Galway were to remain closed forthwith, and all persons were to remain indoors between the hours of 5pm and 8am'.[33] Shopkeepers put up their shutters and brought money and valuables to the banks. Parties of police then began to search for prominent Sinn Féiners and Volunteers. George Nicholls was the first to be arrested, followed by Frank Hardiman, and they were taken to a naval vessel in Galway Bay. They were later joined by professors Steinberger and Walsh, Jim Carter and John Faller. In his position as chairman, McDonogh deplored the fact that:

> they had been plunged into civil war … A whole lot of men had, according to rumour, tried to hold up the public offices, the post office

30 *Connacht Tribune*, special edition, 27 Apr. 1916. 31 In assigning this name to the committee, McDonogh was echoing events that occurred in the course of the French Revolution, when the original Committee of Public Safety (Comité de Salut Public) was established in March 1793 by the National Convention, and later restructured by the National Convention in July 1793, during the so-called Reign of Terror, which lasted from 1793 to 1794. The Comité formed the de facto executive government of France during this time of major unrest and upheaval. 32 *Connacht Tribune*, special edition, 27 Apr. 1916. 33 Ibid.

> and places like that in Dublin. What on earth effect could that have in ten or twenty years as regards the government of this country?[34]

But however appalled McDonogh was, he was focused enough to arrange that meetings of the 'committee of public safety' would be held every day during the week to review the evolving situation.

Further panic ensued when, on Tuesday, a British warship, the HMS *Gloucester*, steamed into Galway Bay and indiscriminately opened fire along the coastline, and further inland. The shelling provoked terror in the small fishing villages around the bay. People abandoned their homes and headed for the perceived safety of Galway, the *Galway Express* reporting that 'streams of peasant refugees are fleeing … to seek the shelter denied to them by the folly of their own friends and neighbours'.[35] As the week progressed, more British naval ships arrived. The sound of shelling was audible to Mellowes and his army of about 600 men 12 miles away in east Galway. Hearing a rumour that a large force of British troops were on their way to confront them, on Thursday morning Mellowes and his men retreated south to Moyode Castle, to consider their next move. The swiftness and decisiveness of the British authorities' response to the outbreak of hostilities, the rebels' lack of proper weaponry and the absence of any real support for the Rising from the people of Galway, had all but put paid to any chance the rebels had for success. In common with the people of Galway, Craughwell, Turloughmore and Loughrea locals had come out to aid their local RIC in suppressing the rebels. Undeterred, Mellowes was for carrying on, linking up with the Clare Volunteers, and continuing the fight in the south, but the more pragmatic Tom Kenny and Martin Finnerty overruled him. The men were addressed by Fr Tom Fahy at Limepark and informed that the Rising was over in Dublin, and that the full force of the British military was now likely to descend on Galway. The force was disbanded and the men were advised to find their way home as best they could in order to 'preserve their lives for the next fight'.[36] By Saturday 29 April, five days after it had begun, the Rising was effectively over in Galway. Scores of rebels were arrested and imprisoned, prior to their deportation to English jails, and as prisoners were being escorted to ships in the docks they were booed and heckled,[37] for McDonogh and his fellow civic

34 McNamara, 'The most shoneen town in Ireland', p. 36. 35 *Galway Express*, 3 May 1916. 36 Campbell, F., *Land and revolution*, p. 217. 37 Four hundred rebels were picked up and interned in Galway Jail before being transported to Richmond Barracks in Dublin. Eventually, 328 Galway prisoners were deported to Frongoch, the majority of whom were released at Christmas 1916.

figures were not the only ones to consider the actions of the rebels traitorous. Sinn Féin's disruption of recruitment meetings in the town had irked those Galwegians – and there were many of them – who had relatives serving in the armed forces, and provoked the pro-Redmond *Connacht Tribune* to exclaim, 'Sinn Féin has hitherto been treated with generous tolerance in the city … that tolerance has reached its limit. The puny plotters have only themselves to blame.'[38] Public opinion was at one with the urban and county councils in their condemnation of the Rising, the *Tuam Herald* describing it as 'a melancholy exhibition of midsummer madness', and the rebels as 'degenerate sons'.[39]

The upheaval caused by the Easter Rising meant that the quarterly meeting of Galway county council, scheduled for Wednesday 3 May, was 'delayed for more than three quarters of an hour owing to the insufficiency of the members attending to form a quorum'.[40] Nonetheless, both of the McDonogh brothers were in attendance, and, notwithstanding the events of Easter Week, it was very much business as usual for the councillors. In fact, the focus of the meeting was not the Rising itself or its consequences, but rather the recent death of the county surveyor, and the now vacant position.[41] The only reference to the happenings of the previous week was mention of the destruction of Messrs A. Thom's in Dublin, which had been burnt out in the course of the Rising,[42] meaning that the council's printing would now have to be 'done locally, or it would not be done at all'.[43]

McDonogh's response to the execution of the leaders of the Rising echoed that of Redmond, who had 'accepted their doom as just',[44] and in the house of commons had acknowledged that 'this outbreak … has been dealt with with firmness, which was not only right, but it was the duty of the government so to deal with it'.[45] Redmond had, however, pleaded for leniency for those duped into following the lead of others, and urged the government 'to take only such action as will leave the least rankling bitterness in the minds of the Irish people, both in Ireland and elsewhere throughout the world'.[46] McDonogh followed Redmond's lead in condemning the Rising, and

38 *Connacht Tribune*, 3 Oct. 1914. 39 *Tuam Herald*, 13 May 1916. 40 *Connacht Tribune*, 6 May 1916. 41 Ibid. 42 Considered at the meeting of the governing body of UCG held in May 1916 was a letter to the secretary, Fr Hynes, which began, 'Dear Father Hynes, Any hope of an advertisement? We have been hard hit by the recent fires in Dublin. The works of our printers are now a wilderness of ruins. Some of our best advertisers have been burned out.' UCG governing body minutes, May 1916 (paper archives). 43 *Connacht Tribune*, 6 May 1916. 44 Gwynn, S., *John Redmond's last years* (New York, 1919), p. 224. 45 HC Deb., 3 May 1916, Vol. 82 cc30–9. 46 Ibid.

appealing for clemency for all but the ringleaders, whose indiscriminate attacks on public and private property he considered to be both criminal acts, and treasonous. The *Tuam Herald* agreed that 'the ringleaders have properly been executed'.[47] The Galway urban district council's passage of a resolution condemning the Rising, therefore, was not unusual. Sean Lemass, in an exchange with McDonogh in the Dáil in 1928, observed that 'those of us who had the honour to participate in the Rising of 1916 will remember the flood of resolutions that were passed by Deputy McDonagh … and others throughout the country denouncing the traitors and denouncing their disloyalty', but went on to acknowledge that 'practically every board in Ireland was solemnly passing these resolutions about treason and disloyalty and a few years later every one of these boards was passing resolutions to erase from their minutes the resolutions passed a few years previously. Loyalty is a relative term … ,'[48] as indeed proved to be the case in Galway.

McDonogh's public stance on the execution of the leaders of the Rising, which carried much weight locally, would dog him for the rest of his life. Of the meeting presided over by McDonogh, John Hosty noted:

> Here in Galway the 'big citizens' meeting of Easter Week, the resolutions passed and the special Constables who did their stuff to a man, should prove, and will show, what the quislings of the period were prepared to do for king and country.[49]

Hosty's use of the term 'quisling' is significant in light of another document relating to McDonogh that has recently come to light.[50] This poem (or it may have been a ballad for which no music survives) is entitled 'An bodach bréan', which translates as 'The stinking lout':

> Cé hé an bodach breilleach bréan
> D'inis bréag fá [faoi] lucht tír-ghrádha
> Nuair a hiarradh cuing na nGall[51]
> [a] Réabadh thall ar pháirc an áir?
>
> An Fealltóir 'sé Máirtín Mór
> Árd a ghlór i n-aghaidh Gaedheal

47 *Tuam Herald*, 13 May 1916. 48 Minutes of Dáil debate, 28 June 1928. 49 Hosty, BMH WS 373, p. 15. 50 I am indebted to historian Cormac Ó Comhraí, who came across this document in the papers of George Nicholls, and brought it to public attention. 51 '*Cuing*' means *adhastar* or yoke.

Má mhaireann aon fhear díobh beo
Is leis is ró-mhór an sgéul!

Nuair [a] tosuigheadh ar an ngleo
Rinne mór leis an arm dubh
An dream a cuireadh i mbruid
Máirtín a thug leid 'ghá luadh!

'Sé a ghríos an Pílear Heard[52]
Chleacht ceird an fhealltóir chruaidhe
Chuir sé iomhdha coir 'n-a leith
Mian leis a mbeith san uaigh

Cá rachaidh an Bodach Bréan
Chun an Ifrinn féin is teo
Beidh diabhal ghá chur i gcóir
Ar a thóin beidh lasair bheo!

Seághan na Sagart freisin ann![53]
Clann Carey dá mbruith fá réir[54]
Scríbhinn Pigott dá ndógh mhall [go mall?][55]
Diarmaid na nGall leo go léir![56]

52 This refers to the much-hated (among republicans at least) District Inspector G.B. Heard. 53 Sean na Sagart, real name John Mullowney, was a notorious priest catcher, who informed on priests and Catholic teachers in the eighteenth century. From Ballyheane, Co. Mayo, he began to spy on priests during penal times for financial gain. His reward was £20 for knowledge leading to the arrest of a priest and £10 for the arrest of a teacher teaching illegally. A deeply unpopular figure, he was eventually murdered, and his body thrown in a lake, by local Catholics. 54 This is a reference to James Carey, leader of 'the Invincibles', the secret society responsible for the Phoenix Park murders of Thomas Burke, undersecretary to the lord lieutenant, and Lord Frederick Cavendish, the chief secretary of Ireland in 1882. Carey turned queen's evidence, and betrayed his co-conspirators, his evidence resulting in the execution of five of his associates. His life in danger as a result of his betrayal, Carey was given a new identity and safe passage to South Africa, but was murdered on board when his identity was discovered by a fellow passenger, Patrick O'Donnell. 55 Richard Pigott was a journalist and former nationalist who turned to vilifying and betraying his former associates by selling information about them to their political opponents. To destroy Parnell's career, Pigott produced fake letters, which purported that Parnell had supported one of the Phoenix Park murders. Parnell was vindicated when the letters were revealed as forgeries, and Pigott fled to Spain, where he shot himself in a Madrid hotel room. 56 Diarmuid Mac Murchadha, later known as Diarmuid na nGall (Diarmuid 'of the foreigners'), was the king of Leinster responsible for bringing the Anglo-Normans to Ireland, having solicited help from King Henry II of England in order to retrieve his kingdom, which he had lost to Ruaidri Ua Conchobair, the high king of Ireland.

Bácfar Máirtín go bheith in am
Cruadhlaoch, Tom, gus Coisdla saoghlach[57]
Beidh diabhail ag béastáil Young[58]
Ag clann Donna fágfar aoileach[59]

The identity of the author of the poem is unknown, but the original was found in papers seized in a raid on the home of George Nicholls, who may or may not have been responsible for writing it.[60] Regardless of its author's identity, the poem is a scathing indictment of McDonogh and his actions during the Easter Rising, and the placing of McDonogh in a veritable 'rogue's gallery' of the most despised and vilified traitors in Irish history is indeed striking. What is perhaps most striking about the poem is the fact that the author was in any way surprised at McDonogh's response to the Rising, for he was a nationalist who subscribed to the ideal of an independent Ireland, which nonetheless would be in a position to fully exploit its privileged commercial relationship with the British empire. In this regard McDonogh had much in common with Arthur Griffith, of whom it has been said:

> he had a large-minded conception of nationality and wished to create an Irish civilization that would be as acceptable ultimately to the old unionists as to the nationalists. Politically, he preached hatred of England, but he looked forward to peace with England as the ideal. 'I want peace with England' he declared in one of his speeches, 'but first let England take her one hand off Ireland's throat and her other hand out of Ireland's pocket.'[61]

This was a sentiment with which McDonogh would have readily concurred.

57 This likely refers to McDonogh's brother Thomas (T.C.), who played a major role in the recruitment drive, and otherwise supported the war effort. 58 Joe Young, the Galway businessman, civic figure and friend of McDonogh's, who was responsible for the recruitment effort in Galway during the First World War. Young was later awarded an OBE for services to the war effort. 59 I am indebted to Dr Niall Ó Ciosáin, of the History Department, NUI Galway, for this transcription of the original Irish script. 60 As a keen Gaelic Leaguer, Nicholls' Irish would certainly have been good enough for him to have written it. 61 Lynd, R., 'Arthur Griffith: the patriot' in *Galway of the races: selected essays* (Dublin, 1990), pp 109–10.

MUNITIONS FACTORY

With the Rising effectively dealt with, it was the prospect of putting his own hand into England's pocket – or more specifically her considerable war chest – that occupied McDonogh's energies in the spring and summer of 1916. His biggest coup during the Great War was his successful lobbying, at the highest political levels, for the establishment of a shell factory in Galway. He and a number of his fellow businessmen and councillors had been pressing the government hard for the establishment of a munitions factory in their city,[62] citing the abundant water power and skilled workforce available – and now they could make no little play on the fact that, during the Easter Rising, Galway had stood firm and loyal to the crown. It is hardly surprising then that one of the items discussed during the first urban district council meeting to be held in the aftermath of the Rising was the establishment of a munitions factory in Galway. In March 1916, at the request of the urban district council, 'and a number of Galway citizens who have guaranteed to finance such a factory in the event of securing government contracts', including McDonogh, the Midland Great Western Railway Company (of which McDonogh was a director) had sent its chief locomotive engineer, a Mr Morton, to Galway.[63] A munitions expert, Morton was shown around a number of prospective sites for a factory,[64] and identified the former Persse's Bonded Warehouse on Earl's Island as the most suitable.[65]

Securing a munitions factory for Galway was remarkable, as there was little or no appetite at government level for the location of a munitions factory on the west coast of Ireland. From the war's outset, Irish businessmen had strongly lobbied the imperial government for war contracts through their All-Ireland Munitions and Government Supplies committee. They secured approval for four national munitions factories in 1916, despite Westminster's reluctance.[66] A group of Galway businessmen, however, led by McDonogh, with strong support from Redmond, persuaded the committee to lobby the

62 Not all councillors were as committed to the munitions factory as McDonogh. In April 1916 he chaired a public meeting to discuss it, and only four of the twenty-four urban district council councillors attended. McDonogh commented, 'I am afraid you could not get some of the urban councillors to do more than talk.' *Connacht Tribune*, 22 Apr. 1916. 63 Ibid., 25 Mar. 1916. 64 Ibid. 65 Two buildings were constructed for the factory on the site of the old distillery. Part of the complex survives and now serves as the theatre and student union bar at NUIG. 66 Two munitions factories were established in Dublin – the Dublin shell factory and the Dublin fuse factory – a shell factory was established in Cork and a cartridge factory established in Waterford. When the armistice came into effect, the Dublin shell factory employed 809 people, the Dublin fuse factory employed 557, the Waterford cartridge factory employed 519, the Cork shell factory employed 148 and Galway employed 115.

ministry of munitions to locate a fifth factory at Galway.[67] By the following July, McDonogh's persistence appeared to have paid off, and he headed a delegation to meet the minister for munitions, Hon. Edwin Samuel Montagu,[68] who had succeeded David Lloyd George to the position in July 1916. In a letter to Redmond following his meeting with the Galway delegation,[69] Montagu referred to the problem of sourcing the right sort of machinery, particularly in light of the fact that the Galway delegation (and specifically McDonogh) had requested 'that the machinery should be of a nature capable of adaptation to marine repairing work after the war'.[70] It is clear that the ever pragmatic McDonogh was planning ahead for a time that the war would be over and the port of Galway would be in need of the services of the best marine-repair machinery – which, conveniently, would be found right on its doorstep, courtesy of the ministry for munitions. In the end it proved impossible to source such machinery, but in October 1916 McDonogh received a telegram from Redmond:

> Martin McDonogh, Galway – Happy to say we have just received promise of munition factory for Galway – Redmond.

Formal confirmation arrived a month later,[71] and plans to make the factory operational were immediately taken in hand by McDonogh personally. The Galway shell factory opened in February 1917, and the first shell was manufactured on 17 February, under the supervision of Captain Downie, chief expert of the munitions industry in Ireland.[72] It was a mark of McDonogh's pivotal role in securing the factory for the city that this first shell was presented to him with the following inscription:

> Galway National Shell Factory
> The first shell manufactured
> 17–2–1917
> Presented to
> Martin McDonagh Esq.[73]

67 A cabinet report on the winding down of the munitions factories after the war – dated 18 Oct. 1918 – noted that Ireland had accounted for a mere 0.22% of the ministry of munitions' expenditure. 68 The meeting took place in the offices of the ministry for munitions at Whitehall. 69 The letter was dated 21 Oct. 1916. 70 *Connacht Tribune*, 28 Oct. 1916. 71 Ibid., 4 Nov. 1916. 72 Gregory, A. and S. Paseta (eds), *Ireland and the Great War: 'a war to unite us all'?* (Manchester, 2002), p. 79. 73 This misspelling of McDonogh's name is surprising given the significance of the presentation. The shell was

The capital to establish the munitions factory was £5,000, of which £2,000 was put up locally. At least some of this capital – and likely a considerable proportion of it – came from McDonogh, who was chair of the local munitions committee. McDonogh's continued involvement in the munitions factory, and his relationship with both the directorate and the ministry, were critical to its success. Captain Downie, who visited the factory frequently, was full of praise for the local munitions committee, but 'especially Mr Martin McDonogh and his brother', noting, 'I have been a perfect stranger to these gentlemen … but I cannot speak in too high terms of the manner in which I have been treated every time I came down here.'[74]

The shell factory was to provide much needed employment for some 115 women, government regulations stipulating that only 5 per cent of the workforce could be male. Women recruited to these factories were unionized by the Britain-based National Federation of Women Workers, which compelled Irish employers to adhere to the minimum wage of £1 per week for women in government-controlled employment. Workers from the Galway munitions factory were sent to Dublin or London to be trained.[75] Make-up parts were imported from England, and the munitions ministry undertook to buy as many eighteen-pound shells as the factory could produce. It was the smallest of the five munitions factories in Ireland and, as a business proposition, was never profitable. By November 1918 it was producing only 800 shells a week, far fewer than projections had allowed for, at a production cost of 12*s.* 7*d.* per unit, for a contract price of 12*s.*. Plans were afoot in 1918 to increase production to 2,000 shells a week, which would have yielded a profit, but the ending of the war in November 1918 put a halt to these, although the factory continued to produce shells to meet its contract until March 1919.

GALWAY JAIL

In January 1917, as the munitions factory prepared to open, McDonogh headed to London to champion yet another cause on Galway's behalf. He was a member of a delegation, which included Lord Killanin and two MPs, to

apparently used as a doorstop in the offices of Thomas McDonogh & Sons for many years prior to its donation to the Galway City Museum. 74 *Connacht Tribune*, 3 Feb. 1917. Captain Downie was described as having 'a solid capacity for work … a hustler. The description may be true enough but he is not the type that mistakes hustling for action. He is of the type that gets things done.' 75 O'Donnellan, 'Manufacturing industry in Galway', p. 64.

lobby the chief secretary for Ireland, Henry Duke, to reverse a decision to downgrade Galway Jail from a county prison to a minor prison. They made the point that the prison had served a crucial role in the detention of those involved in the Rising of 1916,[76] and the chief secretary assured the delegation that the matter 'would be subject to reconsideration after the war'.[77] Duke was as good as his word, and Galway Jail remained in operation as the county jail of Galway until 1 May 1939.[78]

In March 1917 McDonogh's work in support of the war effort intensified when the urban district council took steps to acquire lands compulsorily for the purpose of letting as allotments. McDonogh was chairman of the tillage subcommittee, and, acting promptly, was soon reporting that 'lands at College Road had been allotted to 108 plot holders at 17/6 each'. The allotments proved so popular that the urban district council considered acquiring additional lands to meet the demand. The council went so far as to pass a resolution that the road sweepings of manure collected by the council's carts 'be stored and sold to allotment holders in spring'. At the same meeting at which the allotments were discussed, McDonogh also reported that the council had arranged with the National Bank Ltd to take £5,000 worth of the new war loan bonds. [79]

By August 1917 it was clear that a significant shift had occurred in public opinion regarding the Rising, and Galway county council attempted to rescind its previous unanimous resolution condemning the rebellion. The motion did not pass – the vote being 11 to 11 – but the result was nonetheless significant, given that the membership of the council had not changed since the original vote.[80]

Even as war was being waged in Europe, and the occasional trade-union dispute disrupted trade, for the firm of Thomas McDonogh & Sons, it was very much business as usual. One of McDonogh's most famous customers from that period was W.B. Yeats. In 1917–18, Yeats set about renovating his newly acquired Norman tower at Ballylee, near Gort, Co. Galway, thereafter known as Thoor Ballylee. The poet had very firm ideas about what he wanted, and writing to Maud Gonne declared, 'I dream of making a house that may encourage people to avoid ugly manufactured things – an ideal poor man's

76 The number of committals in Galway Jail was 496 in 1914, 379 in 1915 and between 800 and 900 in 1916. *Freeman's Journal*, 12 Jan. 1917. 77 Ibid. 78 The jail thereafter was demolished and became the site of Galway Cathedral, the buildings and grounds having been sold by Galway county council to the bishop of Galway for the nominal sum of £10 in April 1940. *Galway Observer*, 20 Apr. 1940. 79 Galway urban district council minutes, 8 Mar. 1917. 80 *Connacht Tribune*, 4 Aug. 1917.

house. Except a very few things imported as models we should get all made in Galway or Limerick.'[81]

Supporting local suppliers was a very laudable objective, but, after Yeats ordered most of the building materials from a firm in Gort, it became common knowledge that the firm were experiencing 'considerable difficulty in securing payment'.[82] Yeats' pleading of poverty, and a crippling overdraft, cut little ice with other local suppliers, and he was eventually forced to embark on a lecture tour of America to earn enough to clear his debts, and allow restoration works at Ballylee to continue. So passionate was Yeats about the project that he wrote the following poem:

I, the poet William Yeats,
With old mill boards and sea-green slates,
And smithy work from the Gort forge,
Restored this tower for my wife George.
And may these characters remain
When all is ruin once again.

The 'sea-green slates' of which Yeats writes so vividly were acquired from McDonoghs of Galway – but not without some difficulty. McDonogh was unwilling to supply customers who had a reputation for not paying promptly, regardless of who they were, and Yeats was informed that advance payment would be necessary. The *Connacht Tribune* records that 'Ever a great contact man, he used his friendship with ... Stephen Gwynn, to have the slates sent out. Gwynn was also a close friend of Mr McDonagh [*sic*], and through this network the slates were delivered.'[83] Yeats wrote to Gwynn from Oxford on 5 October 1917, asking him to exert his influence on McDonogh, a strategy which evidently worked.[84]

'WAR FLOUR'

Rebel uprisings aside, the war continued to afford McDonogh considerable business opportunities, which he was not slow to exploit. He spotted the potential of the former Regan's flour mill at Nun's Island, which was taken

81 Letter dated 13 May 1918 from W.B. Yeats to Maud Gonne MacBride in White, A., and A. Norman Jeffares (eds), *The Gonne-Yeats letters, 1893–1938* (Syracuse, 1991), p. 393. 82 *Connacht Tribune*, 13 June 1975. 83 Ibid. 84 Ibid.

over by McDonogh Milling and Trading Company in 1917, having been idle for twenty years.[85] With wartime demand for flour soaring, and import and transport costs becoming increasingly problematic, McDonogh acquired Cloran's (originally Regan's) flour mill, and a major investment programme in the building and its machinery was undertaken.

The acquisition of the flour mill proved to be very astute. But McDonogh's involvement in the flour industry was not confined to production – it extended to the sourcing of wheat. As early as 1907 the Galway Industrial Association, of which McDonogh was a member, had waged a campaign against foreign flour, and for Irish flour. At that time it was estimated that £1 million a year was being spent in Galway on foreign flour, which, the *Galway Observer* tartly noted, 'wasn't even as good as the local stuff'.[86] Indeed, a report commissioned by the Irish Flour Millers Association noted that only 10 per cent of flour used by Galway bakeries was Irish, one importer alone spending £6,000 to £7,000 per month on 'foreign flour'.[87] McDonogh soon changed that when he acquired Regan's mills, and set out to source wheat from solely Irish sources. As Greville observed, McDonogh, 'seeing the need for saving transport and realizing that it was a commercial proposition, decided to purchase the mill and run it on war flour'.[88] Henry Greville's reference to 'war flour' relates to the fact that wheat was in short supply for the duration of the war, and flour producers were required, under strict government controls, to maximize their output by producing whole-wheat flour instead of the more finely milled and sifted white flour.[89] McDonogh had enough contacts within the farming community to secure the necessary supplies of wheat needed to operate his flour mill, and, as was the case with the company's fertilizer, had the distribution network to ensure that his product got to his customers on a regular basis, and under terms that were workable for both small and larger-scale farmers, and the bakers and shopkeepers he did business with. While the McDonoghs were able to run the mill profitably during the war years, by the mid-1920s, when competition

85 The mill had been operated by Mrs Ann Regan, who leased it from Thomas Joyce. Griffith's Valuation of 1855 gave it a rateable valuation of £100. In the mid-1850s, the area was a hive of activity, with a corn mill directly adjacent, beside the entrance to the Poor Clare Convent, and known as Rushe and Palmer's mill. Eventually Regan's flour mill was taken over by Michael Cloran & Sons, but the business floundered and the mill was abandoned in 1897. 86 *Galway Observer*, 11 May 1907. 87 Ibid. 88 Henry Greville, 'Milling in Ireland', *Milling Magazine*, 14 June 1924. 89 Anecdotal accounts from the period record that some housewives were so reluctant to use the flour for their finer baking that they resorted to sieving the wholewheat flour through silk stockings to produce a finer, higher grade flour with a whiter colour.

became keen, McDonogh realized the necessity of bringing the mill up to date, and another major investment programme was undertaken.[90] The flour mill was still employing twenty people in the 1950s.[91]

BELMORE

Sometime in 1917, Martin, T.C., Mary Ann and Kate moved from the old family home in Flood Street to one of Galway's 'big houses' – the property known as Belmore, adjacent to the promenade in Salthill. The house had become available following the death of its previous occupant, Prof. Steinberger. He had been arrested and treated with excessive and unwarranted harshness during the 1916 Rising in Galway, and subsequently died as a result of his ill treatment.[92] The McDonoghs were doing exceptionally well financially during the war as a result of their various business enterprises, and could well afford to transfer to this much grander house, situated on its own lands. But the principal attraction for McDonogh of moving to Salthill was more practical. Belmore offered him the chance to keep some of his livestock, including some racehorses, on the lands adjacent to the house, thereby providing him with an opportunity to indulge his twin passions of raising livestock and breeding racehorses literally in his own backyard.

While Mary Ann and Kate appear primarily to have served as housekeepers for their brothers, Kate was also involved in the family business during the war years. The McDonoghs already owned and operated a fleet of Galway hookers, which traded between Galway, the Aran Islands and Connemara.[93] In 1917, with demand rising for food supplies, including fish, Kate, the youngest of the McDonogh siblings, took charge of a new venture established by the company: the operation of a deep-sea trawler fleet. It is an indicator of how well the McDonogh business empire was faring during the war years that the company purchased four of these trawlers, the most successful of which was the *John Summers.* Very little is known about Kate McDonogh, but from

90 Greville, 'Milling in Ireland'. 91 *Galway Advertiser,* 19 Dec. 2002. 92 On 27 April, Steinberger had been taken from his home and imprisoned on board an overcrowded and insanitary ship in Galway Bay, which then transported him and other prisoners to Cobh. Steinberger was by then over 70, and 'the harsh treatment he endured during the weeks of his internment cannot but have contributed to his subsequent illness. He died of pneumonia on 3 Nov. 1916.' O'Neill, R., 'On modern languages', in Foley, T. (ed.), *From Queen's College to National University: essays on the academic history of QCG/UCG/NUI, Galway* (Dublin, 1999), p. 374. 93 The *Fág a'Bealach,* the *Mary Anne* and the *Successful* (which had an engine) were among the Galway hookers owned by the McDonoghs.

anecdotal evidence she appears to have shared some of the physical traits of her brothers, being a tall and robust woman, who 'is remembered as having often sailed on the trawlers'.[94] Her presence on the trawlers distinguished her from other women involved in the fishing industry in Galway – apart of course from her aunt, Monica McDonogh, who operated her own fleet of Galway hookers and established a trade network servicing her shops in High Street, Galway, Tír an Fhia (Tiernee) and Casla (Costello).[95] Kate McDonogh also served as a director of Thomas McDonogh & Sons, and had a small shareholding in the company, but appears never to have been allowed any real power to influence decisions; her death, in 1927, is not referred to in the minutes of the company's AGM that year – she simply disappears from the records.

There was much to occupy Martin McDonogh in 1917. He was one of two public representatives selected to represent Connacht at the Irish Convention in 1917 (Ballina Union chairman J. Flanagan was the other), and his brief was to 'press for special parliamentary representation for Galway'.[96] McDonogh's participation likely came about because of his pre-eminence as Connacht's largest employer, and Galway's premier civic figure. In addition, his friend Stephen Gwynn had been among those who had first suggested the convening of such a group of delegates to address the Irish question and other issues related to the enactment of self-government for Ireland, including its economic future both within and outside the British empire. Comprising 101 members from throughout the thirty-two counties, the Irish Convention sat in Dublin from July 1917 to March 1918, and McDonogh was a regular attender, if not a regular contributor.

McDonogh was also busy in Galway. In addition to his other successful operations – the fertilizer plant, sawmills, flour mill and store – he was also involved in the supply aspect of the war effort. The Galway Woollen Mills, in which all three McDonogh brothers were shareholders, was booming, and at the company's AGM in May 1917, it was noted that the previous year had seen 'the most successful year's trading in the history of the company', with a turnover of £50,828 having generated net profits of £3,439 4*s.* 4*d.*[97] This was

94 Formal obituaries refer to her as 'Catherine McDonogh', and less formal references refer to the fact that she was known as 'Katie'. *Connacht Tribune*, 23 Apr. 1927. 95 Monica McDonogh died on 29 Jan. 1933, and her obituary described her as 'a woman of great intellect, quiet and reserved and very fond of her home and family'. Remarkably, no mention is made to her extensive business interests, although it was acknowledged that 'She never took any part in public life but in her heart she had a great desire of seeing the city of her adoption flourish and progress.' *Connacht Sentinel*, 31 Jan. 1933. 96 *Freeman's Journal*, 10 July 1917. 97 The profits in the previous year had been £2,118 14*s.* 5*d.* (*Connacht Tribune*, 12 May 1917).

largely attributable to the fact that the mills were producing cloth used in the manufacture of uniforms for the British armed forces.

In August of that year, the MP for Galway (Connemara division), William O'Malley, visited McDonogh in the company of another MP, William Kennedy Jones, and Bernard Alfieri,[98] all of whom were greatly impressed with the extent of McDonogh's various operations, as O'Malley noted:

> In the early part of the day I took K.J., and our mutual friend, Alfieri, to see Mr Martine McDonagh and his huge works.[99] Jones was glad to meet Mr McDonagh, a man interested in horses and horse racing. Mr McDonagh, like Jones, kept some racers. Mr McDonagh showed us round his works, the extent of which astonished Jones.[1]

There was a price to be paid for McDonogh's prominent involvement in the war effort. On the 31 August 1917, the Galway Steam Sawmills, owned by McDonoghs, was completely gutted by fire. The outbreak was detected about 1 a.m., and immediately reported to the police and military authorities. By the time the local fire brigade arrived the fire had taken hold and:

> efforts were directed to confining the area of the flame. A detachment of military from Renmore Depot with several lines of hose, arrived about 3 o'clock, and, assisted by a number of naval men,[2] set to work immediately with great effect.[3]

The urgency of containing the fire was paramount, due to the danger of it spreading to adjacent stores and residences, and the gas works only 80 yards away. McDonogh, as might have been expected, led from the front and directed the entire operation throughout the night, according to a first-hand account written by O'Malley, who had visited the various McDonogh enterprises only the previous day, and was present at the scene of the fire:

98 Alfieri was a noted British photographer, and keen angler, who co-authored (with W.J.M. Menzies) the book *Where to catch salmon and trout* (London, 1937). 99 It is interesting to note that, even in the company of Englishmen, McDonogh was referred to by the Irish form of his name, i.e 'Máirtín' – although in this case the name is spelled phonetically, as it might be when pronounced in French. 1 O'Malley, W., *Glancing back: 70 years experiences and reminiscences of press man, sportsman and member of parliament* (London, 1933), pp 68–9. 2 McDonogh did not forget the actions of the 'naval men' and at a subsequent meeting of the urban district council, it was agreed that 'the men who had helped to put out the recent fire at the McDonoghs premises be paid 5*s.* each', with McDonogh himself recommending that 'P. McClough and his son, who rendered particularly good service, to be paid 10*s.* each'. Galway urban district council minutes, 13 Sept. 1917. 3 *Freeman's Journal*, 3 Sept. 1917.

> A big crowd gathered, while Mr McDonagh [*sic*] directed the fire brigade. Twenty-five extinguishers would have no effect on that fire. Mr McDonagh's great fear was that one building that was stored with timber might catch fire. 'If that catches fire,' he said to me, 'the whole town will be burned down.' Fortunately that building escaped. In a few hours the enterprise of three generations of McDonaghs was brought to nought.[4]

The blaze appeared to have been started deliberately, most likely because, as the *Freeman's Journal* noted, 'Messrs McDonogh were contractors for the manufacture of munition boxes, a large number of which were destroyed.' Indeed the article was headed 'Fire in Galway: saw mills on government work destroyed'.[5] Whatever the motivation for the blaze, it had severe consequences. Almost a hundred employees lost their jobs. Getting the operation up and running again was 'out of the question given the impossibility of replacing the machinery until after the war'.[6] The *Freeman's Journal*, in lamenting the loss of the jobs and the destruction of the mill, noted that Martin McDonogh was 'very popular locally'.[7] In spite of the devastation wrought by the destruction of the sawmills, 'the McDonaghs were not disheartened', O'Malley wrote. 'They set to work to erect a bigger and more up-to-date establishment. They employ more men in their various undertakings than any firm in the West of Ireland.'[8]

POWER GENERATION AND COMMEMORATION

In 1918, McDonogh was presented with an opportunity to diversify his interests yet again, and, in what was a logical extension to his other water-powered enterprises, enter the power-generation business. A premises was purchased by McDonogh in Bowling Green, which formerly had been operated as a tuck and flour mill by the Gunning family. It had been sold by the commissioners of public works in June 1883 to Bartholomew Connolly of Mainguard Street, who operated a woollen mill on the site. He subsequently

4 McDonagh was fortunate that, as O'Malley noted, 'During our inspection the rain came down in torrents and we all got "drowned".' This downpour, after a prolonged dry spell, may have served to dampen down the timber store and adjoining buildings sufficiently so that they did not catch fire. O'Malley, *Glancing back*, pp 68–9. 5 *Freeman's Journal*, 3 Sept. 1917. 6 Ibid. 7 Ibid. 8 O'Malley, W., *Glancing back*, pp 68–9.

mortgaged the premises to the Bank of Ireland but defaulted on the payments, and the mill ceased operation in 1910. It was then sold to Martin and T.C. McDonogh by the bank in November 1918.[9] Having made significant modifications to the premises, Martin McDonogh installed a hydroelectric turbine, which was driven using water power from the Middle River, the waterway that also supplied power to the fertilizer factory downstream at Quay Street. The electricity generated was distributed to the various McDonogh enterprises around the city, making McDonoghs self-sufficient from the point of view of power supply. In addition to saving the company money, the hydroelectric turbine also generated income, as there was sufficient surplus power to charge plate batteries for a number of other businesses, including the Clifden Electric Light Company. Batteries were brought in by truck to the Bowling Green premises, where they were charged and then despatched by truck.

In the changing Ireland of 1918, McDonogh remained uncompromising and unapologetic regarding his support of the war, a fact recognised at the highest levels. He was elected to the executive committee charged with erecting in Dublin a permanent memorial to 'The Irish officers and men of His Majesty's forces who fell in the Great War', which was to take the form of 'a war memorial home to provide board, lodging and recreation for those who fought in the war, and those serving in the imperial forces of the crown'.[10] Founded in the summer of 1919, the Irish National War Memorial Committee's first president was the lord lieutenant of Ireland, Field Marshal Viscount French of Ypres (who gave the first donation to the committee: £100). Stephen Gwynn was one of the committee's treasurers. After much debate about the form the memorial would take, the original plan was judged unwieldy and unsustainable and abandoned. The committee eventually contracted Sir Edward Lutyens to design the war memorial gardens at Longmeadows, Islandbridge, Dublin, which now stands as 'one of the finest such memorials in Europe'.[11] His support for such national causes aside, McDonogh was also conscious of the cost of the war closer to home, and in June 1918 Thomas McDonogh & Sons contributed £5 towards the fund for the relief of the dependents of the Carna U-boat disaster.[12]

9 *Galway Advertiser*, 15 Apr. 1993. 10 *Freeman's Journal*, 18 July 1919. 11 Royal Dublin Fusiliers Association, RDFA/020, Irish National War Memorial Committee archive, correspondence. 12 *Freeman's Journal*, 1 July 1918. The fund was established to provide support for the families of seven fishermen from Carna who were drowned when their fishing boat, the *Pretty Polly*, was sunk without warning by a German U-boat on 31 May 1918 off the coast of Carna.

The end of the war, when it finally came in November 1918, did not signal an end to Galway's labour troubles. On 14 December a general strike took place affecting the harbour commissioners, Galway Steamship Company, the urban district council, Galway Gas Company and McDonoghs. One hundred of the 200 workers who went on strike were employees of McDonoghs. The National Union of Dock Labourers was demanding an increase of *12s. 6d.* per week, which, the *Connacht Tribune* noted, would cost Martin McDonogh, '£6,000 per annum'.[13] The first day of the strike coincided with the general election, and with the strikers firmly allied to the Sinn Féin cause, 'when Máirtín Mór appeared with the Redmondite candidate, a chant went up: "We will win the strike."'[14] The dispute was settled after five weeks, following the intervention of a Franciscan priest.[15]

THE 1918 GENERAL ELECTION

The general election of December 1918 marked a turning point in Irish electoral history, and Anglo-Irish relations in general. The political environment at the time was certainly conducive to change, as two-thirds of the electorate were eligible to vote for the first time.[16] At the same time, frustration with the perceived failures and outmoded policies of the Irish Parliamentary Party presaged a swing to Sinn Féin, which was viewed as a younger, more vibrant and much more radical political force. By the time of the election, Sinn Féin had garnered significant support, and not only from among the new electorate, and the result was the virtual annihilation of the Irish Parliamentary Party, which retained only 6 of the 74 seats it had won in the previous election, and a landslide victory for Sinn Féin, which won 73 of the 105 seats. Out of 40,496 votes cast in Co. Galway, 31,271 (77 per cent) were cast for Sinn Féin.

WAR OF INDEPENDENCE

Politically speaking, the War of Independence, which is conventionally held to have begun on 21 January 1919, had only a minimal impact on Galway. As

13 *Connacht Tribune*, 21 Dec. 1918. 14 Cunningham, 'A great believer in the *Internationale*'. 15 Ibid. 16 The Representation of the People Act 1918 provided for the granting of voting rights, for the first time, to women over 30, and to all men over 21 (military servicemen had to be over 19). This meant a

Kenny has noted, 'scattered RIC raids and arrests aside, 1919 was uneventful. The Volunteers were busy organizing, drilling and raiding for arms. There were some agrarian incidents, but they were relatively isolated.'[17] Economically, while the situation on the whole remained serious, McDonogh's various businesses were continuing to reap the benefits of their virtual monopoly on aspects of the agricultural and mercantile trade in Galway and its environs. But given the evolving and increasingly volatile political situation, there were clear challenges ahead.

In May 1919 the annual conference of the Britain-based National Union of Dock Labourers was held in Galway, and it was acknowledged by Galway urban district council that 'the whole economic future of Ireland is bound up in the manner in which capital and labour co-operates in the common advancement'.[18] Significantly, at this meeting of the NUDL, McDonogh had:

> stated in a nutshell an economic truth that ought to be realized by all, when he pointed out that high wages were not the difficulty, but the real difficulty lay in increased production, and unfortunately there was not the power or the facility for increased production in Ireland.[19]

This represented something of a shift in McDonogh's thinking, but his relations with trade unions remained fraught. During the inaugural meeting of the Galway branch of the Irish Transport and General Workers' Union, Cathal O'Shannon asked the audience: 'in the famine days who starved? Was it the merchants and Martin McDonoghs of Galway who starved?'[20]

Although he was the bête noir of some Galway trade unionists, ever the pragmatist, McDonogh's views with regard to unions had certainly matured, if not softened, by this point in his life. In May 1919, following a representation from the Galway Branch of the NUDL to the governing body of UCG,[21] McDonogh seconded a motion to increase the wages of a college porter and a gardener by *2s. 6d.* a week each.[22] Even more significantly, at a meeting of the governing body in October 1919, McDonogh tabled a resolution that proposed 'that the ordinary college fee of every man-student for the session 1920–1, and subsequent sessions, be £2, and that £1 of this fee be paid to the College Union'.[23] The resolution was passed.

broader and younger electorate, and the Irish electorate increased from 700,000 to almost 2 million as a result. **17** Kenny, *Galway: politics and society, 1910–1923*, pp 26–7. **18** *Connacht Tribune*, 31 May 1919. **19** Ibid. **20** *Connacht Tribune*, 22 Nov. 1919. **21** McDonogh appears to have preferred the NUDL to the newly formed ITGWU, which was more radical. **22** UCG governing body minutes, 6 May 1919 ('Papers').

ALCOCK AND BROWN

McDonogh missed perhaps the most exciting event to happen in Galway in the bleak post-war year of 1919: the arrival of John Alcock and Arthur Whitten Brown, following the first successful transatlantic flight, which landed near Clifden on 15 June 1919.[24] Capt. Alcock and Lt. Brown arrived in Galway later that same day, and thousands waited in the rain outside the Railway Hotel in Eyre Square to welcome the two pilots. A civic reception was held at 1 p.m. by the urban district council, with T.C. McDonogh presiding, his brother being 'indisposed'.[25] T.C. had the honour of welcoming the men he called, 'Those two intrepid and brave airmen who were the first to fly from the shores of America to the shores of Ireland, and wished them long life and happiness.'[26] Messrs T. Dillon & Sons presented each man with a Claddagh ring, Capt. Alcock stating that he would 'always keep it, and always wear it as a lucky charm'.[27] As chairman of the urban district council it would have fallen to Martin McDonogh to officially host the formal dinner for the celebrated airmen that evening, but, as the *Freeman's Journal* reported, he was 'unable to be present through illness',[28] and it again fell to T.C. to stand in. There is some confusion regarding the reason for McDonogh's absence, the *Connacht Tribune* recording that McDonogh was 'unable to be present as he was away in Dublin at the time'.[29] But whatever the reason, it is clear that the much more sociable T.C. McDonogh revelled in his role as host of this momentous day in Galway – and aviation – history.

THE HARBOUR

Martin McDonogh remained focused on the main challenge facing Galway's economy and its economic future: the development of the harbour. The subject of a ship-building and ship-repair facility becoming established in Galway had, as we have seen, been on McDonogh's mind during the war, and he raised it again at a meeting of the harbour commissioners in December

23 Ibid., 14 Oct. 1919 ('Papers'). 24 Alcock and Brown flew a modified First World War Vickers Vimy bomber from St John's, Newfoundland to Clifden, Co. Galway. They made landfall in Galway at 8:40 a.m. on 15 June 1919, not far from their intended landing place, after less than sixteen hours of flying time. The aircraft was damaged upon arrival because of an attempt to land in what appeared from the air to be a suitable green field but turned out to be a bog at Derrygimla, near Clifden. Neither of the airmen was hurt. 25 *Connacht Tribune*, 21 June 1919. 26 Ibid. 27 Ibid. 28 *Freeman's Journal*, 17 June 1919. 29 *Connacht Tribune*, 21 June 1919.

1919, bemoaning the lack of activity in the harbor, and stating that 'unless we got more ships, or some trading for the port, I don't think we'll have any business here next year'. However, McDonogh did hold out some hope for the future, and revealed that he had been:

> written to privately by a Belfast man. I told him we would be very glad to see him here and that we would give them all the help we could and any ground in our possession that they wanted. I have not heard anything since.[30]

It may well have been the case that the mystery 'Belfast man' had been in contact with McDonogh previously, at around the time he was lobbying the government for the munitions factory, but even if he had not, the very fact that, even as far away as Belfast, McDonogh was the perceived 'go-to' man in Galway with regard to the development of the harbor, and the industrial development of the city in general, is a measure of how significant a figure, in national terms, he had by that stage become.

If 1919 had been a relatively quiet year for Martin McDonogh, 1920 was to prove much less so. From a business perspective, he was intensely frustrated by the mismanagement of the government of the 1st Dáil following its establishment on 21 January 1919. He complained at an urban district council meeting that 'trading at Galway port had almost become a thing of the past', citing, in particular, the difficulty of having coal delivered to the harbour. Referring to his own company's operation, Martin McDonogh claimed that 'if they were allowed to get coal from Glasgow, the freight would be only 2*s.* a ton, but the coal controller would not permit them to get their coal there'.[31] Describing government officials as 'a lot of fellows who never were able to – and never did – any business for themselves', he added, 'They know nothing about business, and they upset everything.' An instance of what he called 'the vagaries of government officials' was outlined by T.C. McDonogh. McDonoghs had chartered a vessel to transport a cargo of coal from Glasgow, when they received a telegram from the coal controller stating that 'they would not be allowed to get coal at Glasgow'. With obvious frustration, he added, 'Then, after the vessel had gone elsewhere, they got a letter saying they would be allowed to get a cargo of coal in Glasgow.'[32] There was laughter in the council chamber, but for Thomas McDonogh & Sons it was no

30 *Connacht Tribune*, 27 Dec. 1919. 31 At the same meeting McDonogh described the coal controller as 'like a small god; you cannot go near him'. *Connacht Tribune*, 3 Jan. 1920. 32 Ibid.

laughing matter, and the implications not just for their own company, but for those who worked on the Galway docks, were extremely serious.

More significant, however, was the arrival of the Black and Tans in Galway in the spring of 1920. By the summer the war between the Black and Tans and the IRA had reached its peak, with the result that a number of public events were cancelled, and others, including the Galway Races, were called into question. The weeks leading up to the races of 1920 were particularly fraught. The shooting of two police officers in an attack on a police convoy in Tuam had resulted in what the archbishop of Tuam described as the 'vengeful and ruthless' sacking of the town by the Black and Tans. The *Freeman's Journal* reported that the men, who were fully armed:

> marched into the streets, smashed public houses, and it is alleged looted their contents freely, dragged young men out of bed, and threatened to shoot them then and there, set fire to some of the most valuable properties in the township, and only retired to their quarters after they had become satisfied with a regular orgy of destruction.[33]

With the races set for 4–5 August, Galway city became the next target, when, on 30 July, the premises of a Mr O'Connor, a known Sinn Féin sympathizer, who ran a newsagents and tea shop on Shop Street, was bombed with a hand grenade and fired upon by a group of 'intoxicated soldiers'. In spite of this, McDonogh was determined that the races would go ahead, the press noting that he was 'working like a Trojan to secure special passenger trains for Galway races ... while special horse trains have been secured, no definite promise has, so far, been given that anything beyond the auxiliary passenger trains to Athenry can be run'. McDonogh spent the week leading up to the races in Dublin with the course manager, Mr Kerins, and continued to personally lobby the railway management. With less than a week to go, he informed the press 'at any rate, we shall get the horses there, and the crowd will follow'.[34]

Due to the coordinated efforts of Galway's public figures and its general populace, the Galway Races of August 1920 proved to be a major turning point in the city's fortunes – proving that the city could manage its own affairs under the new regime. In addition, the manner in which the races were managed reflected a continuity between the old regime and the new in the fraught years of the War of Independence, and serves to highlight

33 *Freeman's Journal*, 22 July 1920. 34 *Connacht Tribune*, 31 July 1920.

McDonogh's role as a stabilising influence in that process. In an editorial headed 'Pleasure, profit and peace', the *Tribune* noted that 'the prophets of evil have been confounded. We have an infinite belief in the capacity of Irishmen in comporting themselves with dignity and restraint and in governing and controlling their own household. This week has justified the belief.' It was acknowledged that the races had passed off without a hitch, and had 'proved that if Ireland were governed by the people who alone can understand Ireland, it would be one of the happiest and best-ordered countries in the world'. The police had been absent from the races, and in their absence the crowds and traffic were regulated by the Volunteers, who had shown 'a commendable desire to do their best'. The crucial role played by McDonogh in ensuring that the races went ahead was acknowledged, the *Tribune* noting that McDonogh, 'under the most difficult and discouraging circumstances, worked unceasingly that the meeting might be brought off'. The *Tribune* was also at pains to point out the significant financial benefit to the town of the races, noting that 'Ballybrit brings money to a town where that useful commodity is all too scarce. It enables hundreds to provide against the barren months.'[35] For Galway, there were to be many such barren – and increasingly fractious – months ahead.

1920 LOCAL ELECTIONS

In the aftermath of the 1918 general election, which saw Sinn Féin make significant gains in all constituencies, the outcome of the council elections of 1920 might have been predicted. The elections were held in two stages, the urban-area local elections in January and the rural-area elections in June. In Galway Sinn Féin won control of both local councils, a feat it replicated throughout the country, gaining control of 72 out of 127 town councils.[36] Martin McDonogh topped the poll in the urban elections for the East Ward, securing 198 first preference votes. T.C. only secured 9 first preferences, but benefitted from 128 transfers from Martin.[37]

At the urban district council's first meeting, the burning question was the election of the chairman, with the ousting of Martin McDonogh from his long-held position of power virtually certain. McDonogh added to the drama of the occasion by arriving late, and having 'a conversation with the

35 *Connacht Tribune*, 7 Aug. 1920. 36 Irish Office, 'Monthly commentary', 4 Aug. 1920, CO 906 19. 37 *Connacht Tribune*, 24 Jan. 1920.

secretary relative to who would take the chair ... Mr M. Redington said that right belonged to the outgoing chairman, and Mr McDonogh took the chair.' Cllr Moloney proposed McDonogh as chairman, and Cllr Coogan proposed the Sinn Féin candidate, Dr Tom Walsh. Among the three candidates elected for Labour was the NUDL's William O'Flaherty. To the surprise of many, not least McDonogh himself, O'Flaherty chose to support McDonogh over Walsh, who had been a past treasurer of the GWGLU. But it was the manner in which he articulated his reasons for doing so that left the meeting stunned:

> 'I want to convey to the members around here that the man who does the most for Galway is the man we want as chairman.' He referred to the fact that Mr McDonogh was his strongest opponent on the vital matters between them. But then when these matters in dispute were settled he [Mr Flaherty] was finished with Mr McDonogh. Mr Flaherty then spoke of Mr McDonogh's work for Galway. Thousands of pounds had been earned through his energy, and especially as far as the racecourse business was concerned. 'I give him credit for that. I am not speaking in his favour as a capitalist or employer. I am speaking of the man as I find him. Even tomorrow I may be fighting him.' 'That is your job man – that is your job' commented the chairman, and there was a ripple of laughter. 'This is my profession' assented Mr Flaherty, 'but I am seconding the election of Mr McDonogh, and I intend to vote for him because he is the best man, and the man that has something at his back; and I go further and say that he is the man that has relieved the poor of Galway for years – relief that many do not know anything about – relief that has been given through societies and sodalities, and I have it from the clergymen who work among these poor people that Mr McDonogh would not allow his name to be mentioned.'[38] Mr Flaherty sat down and a silence fell upon the meeting.[39]

O'Flaherty was to pay a heavy price for his magnanimous support of McDonogh. As Cunningham has noted, 'If Máirtín Mór seemed surprised at the encomium, O'Flaherty's members were also. Days later, at a meeting attended by national organizer [of the NUDL], Ted Harte, his resignation was demanded in a unanimous vote.'[40]

38 Coming from a staunch union man, this statement would appear to confirm the anecdotal evidence that McDonogh had indeed provided relief, quietly, to the families of striking workers, many of whom were his own. 39 *Connacht Tribune*, 31 Jan. 1920. 40 Cunningham, J., 'A great believer in the *Internationale*',

There was more drama to come in the inaugural meeting of the reconstituted urban district council. When one of McDonogh's supporters opined that, 'Mr McDonogh does not give a snap who is elected,' it is clear that O'Flaherty's support, and the significance of the change that was taking place in the replacement of the old guard with the new, had affected McDonogh, and even as he laughed and responded that indeed he did not 'care a pin':

> a trace of emotion was noticeable in his voice, although his features bore the same, set look. 'You may imagine that I had everything arranged, as to who would propose and who would second me and all that. I did not speak to any member, either Mr Maloney, or Mr Flaherty, or anybody else.'

Emotions were further heightened when Cllr Redington stated that he supported McDonogh's election as chairman, and 'recalled the latter's action when the council was £5,000 in debt, when he (McDonogh) and Mr Donnellan had to pay the cheques for a few weeks. That debt was wiped out two years ago.'[41] The acknowledgment that McDonogh (and Donnellan) had effectively bankrolled Galway urban district council during a time of financial crisis had a sobering effect on all those present. However, the vote ultimately went in Walsh's favour, 14 to 9, and McDonogh's tenure as chairman of the urban district council came to an end.[42] When McDonogh declared the election of Walsh, and vacated the chair, the *Tribune* noted 'there wasn't a murmur in the room, but a slight cheer was raised by a group congregated on the landing outside'.[43] Clearly conscious of the momentous nature of the occasion, even the new chairman had words of consolation for McDonogh, Walsh stating 'There is a certain amount of sadness connected with every change … Perhaps Mr McDonogh and myself have not always seen eye to eye. Still, I feel rather uncomfortable in replacing him.'[44] As for McDonogh himself, whatever emotion had overcome him earlier in the proceedings soon evaporated, and the old confident and uncompromising Máirtín Mór was once more in evidence. When he expressed the hope that the new members would do as good a job as their predecessors had done, and the new chairman

p. 8. **41** *Connacht Tribune*, 31 Jan. 1920. **42** Those who voted for McDonogh were Cllrs Redington, Curran, O'Flaherty, Griffin, Donnellan, Moloney and Young, as well as T.C. and Martin McDonogh. Walsh secured the votes of Cllrs Naughton, Bailey, Coogan, Cooke, Grehan, Lee, Connolly, Walsh, O'Dea, O'Flaherty, Coolahan and the two female councillors, Mrs Nicholls and Mrs Hardiman, as well as his own. **43** *Connacht Tribune*, 31 Jan. 1920. **44** Ibid.

responded 'it is a good thing you have as good an opinion of yourself Mr McDonogh', McDonogh replied, 'Yes, I have a fair opinion of myself,'[45] and he, T.C. and some of the older councillors promptly left the meeting.

Remarkably, when the question of who would become vice chair was raised and Mrs Nicholls was nominated, O'Flaherty opposed her nomination on the grounds that 'No lady could do the business as well as a man.'[46]

In the subsequent months, as the new council set about its business, the *Connacht Tribune* acknowledged that there was much to be regretted in McDonogh's removal from the helm, noting that:

> whatever failings might be charged against him, [he] had never shown lack of courage and steadfastness of purpose when once assured of the justice of his cause, and had never quailed before mob law when the interests of the citizens had to be safeguarded.[47]

Moreover, in purely financial terms, it was clear that the balance of power had swung away from those who had traditionally contributed the most to the development of the city, like McDonogh, and towards those who contributed far less, and:

> when the old members, who had been reduced to a considerable minority, and who in rate-paying capacity were infinitely stronger than the majority, were swept from the most important committee without mercy and without apology … representative government was scarcely permitted to function.[48]

McDonogh, though no longer in control, still exerted significant power and influence as a councillor. However, having been ousted as chairman in January, he resorted to his old habit of non-attendance, and failed to attend any further meetings until May 1920.[49]

If the Sinn Féin victory in the urban election had been emphatic, the party's showing in the rural election was even more so. The die-hard republicans clearly differentiated themselves from everyone else, one Sinn Féin election poster proclaiming: 'Vote for us as you vote for the Irish Republic. Vote for Martin McDonogh, Thomas [T.C.] McDonogh and Lord Killanin and you vote for the English connection, and the continuance of the present

45 Ibid. 46 Ibid., 31 Jan. 1920. 47 Ibid., 17 Apr. 1920. 48 Ibid. 49 Ibid., 15 May 1920.

regime of Prussianism, militarism and slavery.'[50] It was signed by the Sinn Féin candidates Michael McDonagh,[51] George Nicholls, Thomas Ruane and Thomas Walsh.[52] With such rhetoric abounding, it is surprising that the *Tribune* described the county, rural and district elections of June 1920 as 'the most spiritless election ever held in the county'.[53] Even as only half the electorate (and in some areas only one-third) chose to exercise their mandate, the scale of the Sinn Féin victory saw many 'prominent men disappear'.[54] This did not include Martin McDonogh, who once again drew on his considerable family connections and business associations, and, as an independent candidate for the Aran Islands, was easily re-elected to the county council. The first meeting of the new Galway county council, which took place in June 1920, was marked by what the *Tribune* described as 'the most important and most unique step yet taken by any public board in Ireland – the decision to conduct the proceedings in the Irish language'.[55] George Nicholls was elected chairman, a position he held until 1925. One of his first acts was to move the recision of the resolution passed by Galway county council, under McDonogh's stewardship, condemning the Easter Rising. The resolution having been unanimously carried, Nicholls 'formally crossed out the resolution with red ink and marked it "rescinded, but preserved as a document of historical importance"'.[56] A significant changing of the guard had occurred, and for men of the old guard, like McDonogh, the only choice to be made was whether to adapt to the changed political climate, or follow the path to political irrelevancy exemplified by the Irish Parliamentary Party. Unsurprisingly, McDonogh was not yet ready to be put out to political pasture.

MONATIGUE

Pastures of another kind preoccupied McDonogh in the latter half of 1920. McDonogh's purchase in 1901 of the Monatigue lands, 'over the heads of the evicted tenants, who live on small and uneconomic holdings adjoining', had been bitterly resented by locals.[57] An attempt to burn Monatigue House had occurred in June 1907, and in the following months, shots had been fired at one of McDonogh's farm employees, a threatening letter had been sent to one

50 Ibid., 29 May 1920. 51 No relation to Martin and T.C. 52 *Connacht Tribune*, 29 May 1920. 53 *Connacht Tribune*, 5 June 1920. 54 Ibid. 55 *Connacht Tribune*, 19 June 1920. 56 Ibid., 16 May 1942. 57 *Connacht Tribune*, 12 May 1923.

of his herds, and eighteen head of cattle had been driven off the land.[58] Ten armed men had also fired shots into Monatigue House, terrifying six labourers engaged in saving hay on the farm.[59] None of this had intimidated McDonogh into selling Monatigue.

In 1919 another attempt was made by locals, who approached McDonogh with a view to purchasing the lands. McDonogh finally agreed to sell in April 1920, but only once the lands had been appropriately valued, and his stock there sold off. McDonogh and the local committee were to nominate their own valuers, and there was to be a compromise price, suggested by an umpire, which would be binding on both sides.[60] The committee appointed a valuer but McDonogh did not, and he ignored the committee's correspondence. When, as a result, agitation resumed, McDonogh complained to the two local TDs – Padraic Ó Máille and George Nicholls – and asked them to intervene.[61] Ó Máille and Nicholls called on the services of local councillors John Broderick and Stephen Jordan, and further arbitration was agreed, but to no end – McDonogh persistently chose to ignore requests to provide his own valuation, and appeared in no rush to sell.

In the summer of 1920, the IRA attempted to force McDonogh's hand. Gilbert Morrissey, O/C of the Athenry battalion, confirmed that, on 30 August 1920, he and his men had burned down Monatigue House, on the grounds that the house, among others, 'had been examined by the British forces with a view to their occupation'.[62] Campbell notes that 'the IRA's intervention may have complemented the agrarian agitation'.[63] Although Martin McDonogh was the owner of the lands of Monatigue, it was his brother T.C. who, according to the deeds, was the owner of the substantial house that stood on the property.[64] T.C. was paid £4,725 in compensation for the burning of his property.[65] The Monatigue lands did not pass into local hands until June 1930, via the land commission.

58 Ibid., p. 178. 59 Confidential Print, 1907–8, PRO CO 903/14/55. 60 *Connacht Tribune*, 1 May 1920. 61 Ibid., 12 May 1923. 62 Morrissey, G., BMH WS 1138. Morrissey wrongly dates the burning of Monatigue House to 'the early months of 1921', whereas newspaper accounts confirm that the events occurred in August 1920. 63 Campbell, *Land and revolution*, p. 267. 64 The *Freeman's Journal* stated that the house was the property of Martin McDonogh, and noted that although the 'large residence and out offices were totally destroyed by fire … hay stored nearby was not interfered with'. 65 *Connacht Tribune*, 9 July 1921.

NUNS, TERROR AND ATROCITIES

While McDonogh was unwilling to take the advice of anyone when it came to his own property, in one instance at least, his advice was sought – and ignored. Thomas McDonogh, Martin McDonogh's nephew and current chairman of the company, records that Martin McDonogh was consulted by the Benedictine order of nuns, who had fled their convent at Ypres when it was destroyed in the early days of the First World War. The contact with McDonogh is likely to have come about through John Redmond MP, who was aware of the nuns' plight, and was asked, in 1915, to write an introduction to an account of their community at Ypres, and its destruction at the hands of the invading German army.[66] 'This little community is now in exile in England', he wrote. 'Their abbey and beautiful church are in ruins ... what is their future to be?'[67] Having moved to England and then to Co. Wexford, the nuns were considering the purchase of Kylemore Castle in Connemara. McDonogh apparently advised the nuns against purchasing the estate, as he believed the title was compromised, particularly so since the property as offered for sale did not include the valuable fishing rights in the vicinity of the castle. The nuns, however, chose to ignore his advice, and purchased the former home of Mitchell Henry, which thereafter became known as Kylemore Abbey, and took up residence there in December 1920.[68]

The Benedictine nuns had chosen a rather unfortunate time to move to Ireland. Attacks on individuals and property, perpetrated by the IRA and the Black and Tans and Auxiliaries, had become increasingly common throughout the country. Business and social life was severely disrupted, and in some cases rendered impossible. In Galway tensions escalated on 8 September with a gun battle at Galway railway station, during which a notorious RIC officer, Edward Krumm, and two Volunteers, Seamus Quirke and Seán Mulvoy, were shot dead. The city was placed under curfew, but the funeral of the two Volunteers became an occasion for a public display of defiance by an outraged Galway populace, with no fewer than forty clergy officiating at the Mass. The response of the Black and Tans was to go on a rampage. Houses of suspected republican sympathizers were raided. The Sinn Féin Hall was

66 Barry O'Brien, R. (ed.), *The Irish nuns at Ypres: an episode of the war* (London, 1915). Written by Dame M. Columban, whose account is authenticated by the mother prioress of the community at Ypres, Mother Maura, OSB, the book details the attack on the nunnery at Ypres, which began on 7 Oct. 1914. 67 Barry O'Brien, *The Irish nuns at Ypres*, p. 4. 68 The estate, which included Kylemore Castle and 10,000 acres, was purchased by the nuns for a little over £45,000.

burnt, and so were the offices of the previously unionist, but by now strongly republican, *Galway Express* newspaper.

Two months later the kidnap and murder of the popular young priest, Fr Michael Griffin, who was known to be a republican sympathizer, created an outcry, not just locally but nationally and in Britain, where Lloyd George was forced to assure the house of commons that no crown forces were implicated. In a letter to the chief secretary, Dr O'Dea, bishop of Galway, was unequivocal: 'It is the belief of all in Galway that Fr Griffin was shot by government forces. The people of Ireland do not shoot their priests.'[69] An estimated 12,000 people attended the funeral, which was by far the biggest Galway had ever seen, and Martin McDonogh was among those civic figures who, on account of the crowds, took their seats an hour before the funeral Mass was due to begin.[70] Elected councillors now became targets for arrests and searches or worse. On 19 October, McDonogh's fellow urban councillor Michael Walsh (Míchéal Breathnach), a prominent member of Sinn Féin, was taken out of his home at High Street,[71] pushed down to Long Walk and shot dead.[72] This understandably shocked and terrified the Sinn Féin councillors, and was bitterly condemned by McDonogh. It appears that McDonogh was never in any danger of attack by crown forces, such was his prominence in the town and his perceived 'loyalty' to crown administration. He chose, therefore, to focus on consolidating and protecting his businesses, and on the various civic causes that were dear to him.

INVOLVEMENT WITH NSPCC

One of those causes was the National Society for the Prevention of Cruelty to Children (NSPCC).[73] Both Martin and T.C. were members of the Galway branch, and served as chairmen.[74] The Galway branch had been established in 1911, and its remit extended to both the city and the county. During the war,

69 *Connacht Tribune*, 27 Nov. 1920. 70 Ibid. 71 Walsh was proprietor of The Old Malt public house, which had previously been owned by McDonogh's uncle, the father of writer Pádraic Ó Conaire, and Ó Conaire had frequently stayed in the house following his return to Galway in 1914. 72 Walsh, 39, was shot through the head. He left a wife and eight children. 73 The NSPCC operated in Ireland from 1889 to 1956, when it was succeeded by the Irish Society for the Prevention of Cruelty to Children (ISPCC). The first Irish branch of the NSPCC was founded in Dublin in May 1889, and branches were founded in Cork and Belfast in 1891. 74 T.C. was elected chairman in July 1923. One of the McDonogh sisters also became a member of the committee in July 1921, although she is only called 'Miss McDonogh' so it is unclear whether it was Mary Ann or Kate. *Connacht Tribune*, 2 July 1921.

at the suggestion of Martin McDonogh, the Galway branch 'placed its premises and its experience at the disposal of the committee for the administration of the Soldiers' and Sailors' Families' Association', whose funds were distributed throughout the city and county by the society and its officers. The strain placed on the society and its fundraising efforts during the war years was considerable, and by May 1915 its funds were 'completely exhausted'.[75]

There is no doubt that McDonogh's commitment to the work of the society was considerable. The sympathetic interest he took in it was acknowledged by those involved in child welfare in Galway. Brother Frisby, supervisor of the Salthill Industrial School, stated that:

> it was largely due to his assistance, and that of his brother, that it had proved such a success in Galway … those who knew Mr McDonogh would be aware that whatever assistance he gave would be very substantial, for he was as large in heart as he was in mind and body.[76]

And there was certainly much for the society to do, with appalling cases of child neglect and extreme poverty being reported on regularly in the local press. At the AGM of the society in 1921, one particularly harrowing case was described: 'In a single room cabin at Lettermore, a family of ten motherless children, ranging in age from a girl of fourteen to a baby of three months' were living in abject poverty, 'with nothing but potatoes to eat, and sometimes there were not enough of these … the girl of fourteen was compelled to act as mother. None of them knew English and none had been attending school.' The society congratulated itself on the fact that the children 'were taken in hand by Mr Owen Dockery, our inspector, and brought to industrial schools, where they will be educated and equipped for the battle of life'. A pantomime was presented at the town hall each year to raise funds for the NSPCC, which had its office at 8 Eyre Square.[77]

POST-TREATY GALWAY

Much of the poverty and destitution that required the intervention of the NSPCC came about as a result of the high levels of unemployment in Galway during the War of Independence and the Civil War. In 1922 there were 900

75 As a result, the society organised a 'Children's Day' street collection on 6 May 1915. *Connacht Tribune*, 1 May 1915. 76 Ibid., 2 July 1921. 77 Ibid.

men unemployed in Galway town,[78] and a job in any of the various McDonogh enterprises was considered 'a godsend'.[79] And although 'conditions, when viewed through modern eyes, were rather harsh, especially in the flour mill, fertilizer and timber works, where smells, as well as endless dust often made breathing difficult', there is no doubting the fact that a job with McDonoghs was considered a job for life, and as a result McDonoghs 'employed half of Galway, and the other half looked on in envy'.[80]

When Dáil Éireann narrowly passed the Anglo-Irish Treaty by 64 votes to 57 on 7 January 1922, the provisional government of Southern Ireland was established and Ireland entered what was to be a formative and convulsive stage in its history. The authority of the provisional government under the Treaty was to provide a 'provisional arrangement for the administration of Southern Ireland during the interval' before the establishment of the Irish Free State. The British government transferred 'the powers and machinery requisite for the discharge of its duties'.[81] McDonogh and his fellow businessmen and public figures had to once again recalibrate and deal with yet another manifestation of state and civic authority, and, as might have been expected, the experience was not always as efficient or satisfactory as men such as McDonogh might have wished. Within months of its establishment, the fledgling Free State was threatening to tear itself apart, with pro- and anti-Treaty forces engaging in a bitter and bloody civil war.

McDonogh's primary objective during this time was to protect his business interests, and in this regard he was largely successful. However, on occasion he drew fire by taking a stand that was neither wise nor politic. For example, at a meeting of Galway urban council in April 1922, he was one of only two councillors to object to the passing of an order that the families of Black and Tans, Auxiliaries and RIC men must be given two months' notice to quit the council's cottages. On this occasion, unsurprisingly, his will did not prevail.[82]

TALBOT CLIFTON

In April 1922 McDonogh became involved in one of the most extraordinary events of those troubled times. It was not politics but a mutual interest in horse racing that prompted the assistance he gave to Talbot Clifton of Kylemore House.[83] Clifton was an English landowner and traveller. Educated

78 *Connacht Tribune*, 6 Jan. 1923. 79 O'Dowd, P., *In from the West*, p. 104. 80 Ibid. 81 Article 17, Anglo-Irish Treaty, 1921. 82 *Irish Times*, 15 Apr. 1922. 83 Christened John Talbot Clifton, he was

at Eton College and Magdalene College, Cambridge, he succeeded to the family estate at Lytham, Lancashire, at the age of 14. A colourful and eccentric character, with a taste for adventure, from an early age he was a compulsive traveller who explored Canada, Siberia, Burma, Malaya, Indonesia, Africa and South America. Unsettled in the aftermath of the First World War, during which he had served as a dispatch driver, and bored with life on the Lytham estate, he and his wife Violet moved to Kylemore House in Connemara,[84] which he had purchased in 1917. There Clifton indulged his passions for hunting and shooting, and driving his collection of cars along the remote roads of Connemara at breakneck speed. He also formed a number of friendships, including with his nearest neighbour, Oliver St John Gogarty at Renvyle House,[85] and, at some point, with Martin McDonogh. The two men had much in common. Clifton was described as 'a giant of a man',[86] the same height as McDonogh – 6 feet 4 inches – and he was a racing man. He had a fearsome temper, and, a keen golfer, one caddie remarked of him that he was 'a hell of a big fellow and a bad bugger … if he drove into the rough, in his rage, he grabbed you and shook you like a rabbit'.[87] In his youth Clifton was something of a womanizer, at one point engaging in a passionate affair with the actress and famous beauty Lily Langtry, a former mistress of the then Prince of Wales, later King Edward VII.[88]

On 1 April 1922, a group of IRA men arrived at Kylemore House, and attempted to commandeer one of Clifton's cars. Clifton offered them his Ford, but the men wanted the more glamorous Lanchester sports car.[89] Clifton defiantly locked the gears on the car to prevent them from taking it, but under pressure from the armed men, his mechanic released the gears, and the men drove away with the car. Infuriated when word reached him that his car had become something of a trophy, and was to be seen 'at every market,

always known as Talbot Clifton (1868–1928). **84** Violet Clifton (née Beauclerk) was as keen a traveller as her husband. They married in 1907, having met while both were travelling in Peru. Talbot subsequently revealed that he had fallen in love with her after hearing that she had shot the horse she had ridden during her time in Peru, because she couldn't bear the thought of anyone else riding it. Her biography of her husband, entitled *The book of Talbot*, won the 1933 James Tait Black Prize, and in 1935 she was nominated for the Nobel Prize in Literature, but the prize was ultimately not awarded that year. The couple had two sons and three daughters. **85** Gogarty had purchased Renvyle House in 1917. When Renvyle House was burned by anti-Treaty forces on 29 Feb. 1923, the Gogarty family moved to Kylemore House, and this remained the Gogarty holiday home thereafter. Renvyle House was rebuilt and opened as a hotel in 1930. **86** *Irish Independent*, 20 Jan. 2008. **87** Kennedy, J. *The Clifton chronicle* (New York, 1992), p. 28. **88** From the correspondence between the two, the affair appears to have occurred in early 1890. **89** Clifton's biographer, John Kennedy, records that the car was green, and, its chassis pitted with bullet marks, was retained and driven by Clifton, with some degree of pride, for a number of years after its return to him by the IRA. Kennedy, *Clifton Cronicle*.

at every meeting; they drove the young women about in her',[90] Clifton determined to retrieve it, and, with his usual reckless impetuosity, organized an ambush. On the night of 13 April, Clifton, fully armed, blocked the road on which the Lanchester was passing, containing six IRA men. The men were forced out of the car, and when one, Captain Eugene Gilan, made a run for it, Clifton shot him. Eventually Coneely, the man who led the group that had confiscated the car, persuaded Clifton that he had a prisoner in the car whom he had to deliver to Westport, but promised that he would return the car the following day. The car was eventually allowed to leave, but Clifton's mechanic, a man named Conboy, persuaded him that once the wounded Gilan was found, his comrades would return to arrest Clifton, and he was advised to leave the country without delay.

Fortunately for him, Clifton heeded the advice, and the following day 'he made a rapid night ride to Dublin, entrained to Belfast, and crossed to England'.[91] Not long after his departure, a party of armed men arrived at Kylemore House to arrest him, and, not finding him there, proceeded to seize the house and other property. Clifton's wife and children had stayed behind in Kylemore, and seeking advice on the best course of action open to her in her somewhat precarious position – the IRA had already raided the house, and threatened to 'shoot him here and now' if they found her husband – she travelled to Galway by train and sought out 'the one she called her mother and her father – that was Martin McDonagh [*sic*], a merchant of Galway'.[92] Quite how Violet Clifton came to have such a level of intimacy with McDonogh after having known him for only five years is unclear. However, McDonogh proved to be a tower of strength and practical support to Violet Clifton. In her colourful account of the events, she noted that:

> His brother Thomas (T.C.), more cautious than Martin, thought that the McDonaghs [*sic*] would be wiser to stand clear of this trouble, but Martin asked if Violet had telegraphed to her husband to advise him not to return. Martin said 'I'll strengthen your counsel by also telegraphing to him. I'll send you home in this motor car; it will be followed by a lorry for your goods – clear the house of everything.'[93]

McDonogh was as good as his word, and shortly after Mrs Clifton's return to Kylemore, the lorry arrived and was packed with the silver and other

90 Clifton, V., *The book of Talbot* (New York, 1933), p. 333. 91 *Irish Independent*, 10 June 1922. 92 Clifton, *The book of Talbot*, p. 337. 93 Clifton, *The book of Talbot*, p. 338.

valuables. On the following day with the aid of the nuns at Kylemore Abbey, Violet Clifton returned to England.[94] Clifton's friends in Ireland had been making efforts to secure the release of his house, lands and other property from IRA hands, but:

> from a letter written by the deputy divisional commanding officer, IRA it appears they refuse to recognise any intermediaries … neither house, land nor anything else will be returned until such time as he stands his trial before a civil court in Ireland on a charge of shooting at officers of the IRA with intent, and of seriously wounding an officer of the IRA while in the discharge of his duty.[95]

Clifton required police protection for a year, but eventually made his peace with the republicans, to the extent that his Lanchester was returned to him. Talbot Clifton died in Tenerife in March 1928.[96]

CUMANN NA NGAEDHEAL

When the Irish Free State (Saorstát Éireann) came into being on 6 December 1922 as a result of the Anglo-Irish Treaty signed exactly twelve months previously, the challenges facing the Free State government were enormous. Politically, socially and economically, Ireland needed strong leadership, clear direction, and a willingness to make the newly established state work. By the end of 1922 McDonogh and his fellow Galwegians had survived ten long years of labour unrest, war, insurrection and civil war. McDonogh, 62, had already proven that he had the staying power to survive, and, more importantly, the will to carry on and consolidate what he had achieved in his long and frequently controversial career. He had enough on his hands, with his various business and civic interests, without wishing to become involved in national politics. However, the conduct of Dáil proceedings, and as a result the management of the country's economy and political affairs, was such that he was not alone in becoming frustrated, which would eventually lead him to enter national politics. The *Galway Observer* reflected the views of many in 1922 when it noted of the Dáil that 'some of the business it went through was more like that of a parish council'.[97] The TDs came in for sharp criticism, the

94 Kennedy, *The Clifton chronicle*, p. 29. 95 *Freeman's Journal*, 12 June 1922. 96 *Connacht Tribune*, 31 Mar. 1928. 97 *Galway Observer*, 10 June 1922.

Observer noting, 'It is remarkable what a tendency some of the members have to rake up personalities ... it is so much of this miserable squabbling that has lots of people actually ashamed of them.'[98]

As a man experienced in the ineffectual 'squabbling' of local councils, McDonogh realized only too well that what the country needed was strong, effective leadership, which could rise above the pettiness of local politics, and the politics of personality. And, as an experienced businessman, he realized that a stable country was essential for a stable economy. He had been infuriated when the Galway race meeting [Galway Races] of August 1922 had to be abandoned, due to 'the condition of the country',[99] and had made every effort to ensure that the races went ahead, using all his influence with the railway company to put arrangements in place such that race-goers could get to Galway – but to no avail.[1] The consequences to the economy of Galway were immense. As the *Connacht Tribune* noted bleakly:

> Ireland has lost by this fratricidal strife morally as well as materially, and the tragedy is that the loss has yet to be fully accounted and that it comes upon a nation that has just secured its freedom after a struggle of centuries and at a time when we need all the wealth and work we can secure for national reconstruction.[2]

Given his own political pedigree and philosophy, the natural home for McDonogh was in Cumann na nGaedheal, whose centre-right outlook very much chimed with his own. It is unclear when precisely McDonogh joined Cumann na nGaedheal, but in affiliating himself with the party, he was, ironically, allying himself with men such as George Nicholls, his would-be assassin in 1916, and his own cousin, the prominent former Sinn Féin politician, Pádraic Ó Máille, with whom he had been bitterly and publicly at odds for many years. But the end of the Civil War signaled a period when, as historian Cormac Ó Comhraí has observed, 'Loyalty was fluid and both sides struggled to ensure that personal loyalty wouldn't prove stronger than political loyalty.'[3] In a prime example of such 'fluid' loyalty, Monsignor McAlpine, parish priest of Clifden, who had been a bitter opponent of Sinn Féin, became 'an enthusiastic supporter' of Pádraic Ó Máille TD,[4] describing him as 'a sterling

98 Ibid. 99 *Irish Independent*, 22 July 1922. 1 *Connacht Tribune*, 15 July 1922. 2 Ibid., 12 Aug. 1922. 3 Ó Comhraí, C., *Revolution in Connacht* (Dublin, 2014), p. 151. 4 A founder member of Sinn Féin, Ó Máille was first elected as a Sinn Féin MP for Galway Connemara at the 1918 general election, but, in line with the party's election manifesto, refused to recognise the parliament of the United Kingdom and

Irishman, a practicing Catholic and a wise statesman'.[5] McDonogh was, it could be argued, all those things, in addition to being a man who had dealt with the British administration, in a business context, at the very highest levels in relation to his involvement with the munitions factory, and in relation to the war contracts allocated to woollen mills and his own sawmills. He was a significant businessman and employer, and a man who, in spite of his aversion to trade unions, appeared to have come to an accommodation with them, albeit a grudging one, to the degree that he was prepared to acknowledge that their claims for better wages and conditions were justified, and negotiate with them. In December 1922, Ó Maille had been wounded in an assassination attempt in which his fellow TD, Sean Hales, was killed. Ó Máille, however, appreciating the need for reconciliation following the Civil War, some months later at a public meeting stated 'Tá mé sásta lámh an té a chuir na piléar ionam a chroitheadh' ('I am willing to shake the hand of the person who put the bullets in me').[6] From 1923 onwards, Martin McDonogh found himself confronted with a similar challenge. Would he – could he – for the good of the emerging Irish Free State, bring himself to engage politically with men who resented his power and wealth, considered him a 'quisling' of the former administration, and would happily have seen him dead only a few years previously?

instead took his seat in the 1st Dáil at the Mansion House, Dublin, in January 1919. He was re-elected as a Sinn Féin TD for the Galway constituency at the 1921 elections. He supported the Anglo-Irish Treaty and was re-elected as a pro-Treaty Sinn Féin TD for Galway at the 1922 general election, and subsequently elected as a Cumann na nGaedheal TD for Galway at the 1923 general election. 5 Ó Comhraí, *Revolution in Connacht*, p. 158, and *Connacht Tribune*, 18 Aug. 1923. 6 Bairéad, T., *Gan Baisteadh*, (Dublin, 1972), p. 114, quoted in Ó Comhraí, *Revolution in Connacht*, p. 160.

5. Business and politics in the Free State, 1923–34

The commercial, economic and political challenges facing the fledgling Free State at the beginning of 1923 were considerable, and the immediate priority for the government was to forge alliances with those in the commercial world who were considered 'safe hands' and could contribute to the building up of the new state. It is testament to the regard in which McDonogh was held that he was one of those appointed by the ministry of industry and commerce to the commission on reconstruction and development in February 1923. McDonogh was in illustrious company: his fellow commission members were Senator Sir J.P. Griffith,[1] Sean Milroy TD, Prof. C.F. Bastable,[2] Frank Daly, Thomas Johnson TD,[3] Richard Kelly KC, Senator T. McPartlin, Sir Walter Nugent and Prof. Pierce F. Purcell.[4] The brief of the commission was to 'inquire into and report on the prospects of trade and industry in the immediate future, to make suggestions as to the stimulating of commerce and manufactures, and to advise as to the relief of unemployment.'[5]

In Galway too, safe hands, strategic planning and entrepreneurial flair were similarly required. The Royal Galway Institution, established in 1839 to promote 'arts, agriculture and manufactures', became the Galway chamber of commerce in 1923. Significant problems faced the new organization. The lack of a meaningful industrial base (aside from the McDonogh enterprises) was perceived as the city's greatest problem, in addition to a falling population and the decline of the Claddagh fishing industry. When the establishment of the Chamber of Commerce was first mooted, and a provisional committee appointed, McDonogh's name was top of the list.[6] McDonogh subsequently played an active role in the chamber's activities, and assumed the role of president twice, in 1929 and 1933.

1 Griffith was chief engineer to the Dublin port and docks board (1898–1913), and regarded as one of the greatest authorities on port engineering. The originator of the Liffey hydroelectric scheme, he served as chairman of both the Irish water power committee and the Irish peat inquiry committee. 2 Bastable was professor of political economy at TCD, 1881–1926. 3 Johnson, a trade unionist and politician, was leader of the Irish Labour Party from 1917–27. He served as TD for Dublin County from 1922–7. 4 *Cork Examiner*, 10 Feb. 1923. Purcell was professor of civil engineering in UCD from 1909–53, and a member of the industrial research council. 5 Ibid. 6 Ibid., 21 Mar. 1923.

MONATIGUE

In 1923 the changed political climate in Ireland saw the reconstitution of the land commission in the Irish Free State by section 2 of the Land Law (Commission) Act, 1923,[7] which made provision for the compulsory purchase of land owned by non-Irish citizens. In light of the fact that untenanted land could now be compulsorily purchased and divided out among local families, demands for land distribution resulted in yet more disturbances on McDonogh's lands at Monatigue. A number of tenants renewed their agitation for the division of the land, placed their stock on the lands to graze and were arrested and had their stock seized.[8] The *Tribune* reported that McDonogh 'had promised the tenants that he would take the case into the republican courts so that the whole matter might be thrashed out, and a settlement arrived at. The question never, however, came before these courts.'[9] There was significant local sympathy for the men arrested, and when they gave an undertaking that they would not interfere further with Monatigue until the matter was fully dealt with by the land commission, they were released and their stock was returned to them, the military handling the matter 'with promptitude, courtesy and tact'. Whatever Martin McDonogh's intentions were regarding the lands, his brother T.C. appears at one point to have harboured notions of living the life of a country squire, as it was reported that 'it was at one time believed that Mr Thomas McDonogh had intended to convert Monatigue into a residential farm'. Those plans had ended when the house was destroyed by the IRA in 1920.

While Martin McDonogh's various businesses and civic responsibilities – the latter of which were increasingly taking on a national dimension – dominated his life, there were occasional opportunities to combine business with pleasure. He visited London sometime in July or August 1923 for what appears to have been a mixture of business, attendance at horse-racing meets and visiting friends. He visited Gwynn at the house of commons, and Gwynn records that during McDonogh's time in London he went to see a play entitled 'Send for Dr O'Grady', based on a novel written by George A. Birmingham.[10] The play featured a character named Dr Lucius O'Grady, and

7 The act also dissolved the congested districts board. 8 The tenants arrested were John Kennedy (Lydon), Martin Kennedy, Tom Rooney, and Dominick Broderick, all of Cahercrin, Athenry. *Connacht Tribune*, 5 May 1923. 9 Ibid. 10 The play ran at the Criterion Theatre, Westminster, London, from 4 July to 11 Aug. 1923. Wearing, J.P., *The London stage, 1920–1929: a calendar of productions, performers and personnel* (London, 2014), p. 239.

Gwynn noted that McDonogh was apparently struck by the similarities between the character and the Galway solicitor Harry Murphy, who had been election agent for Gwynn. He asked Gwynn, 'Did you see that play about Harry Murphy? Where did the fellow hear of him? Who told him about the ruffian?' Gwynn clarified that '"Ruffian", in Martin McDonogh's mouth, was a term of endearment.'[11]

Opportunities to enjoy such leisure activities were rare for McDonogh, however, as the various McDonogh enterprises continued to thrive and absorbed much of his time. McDonogh's wartime flour-milling operation had succeeded in positioning itself so strongly in the domestic flour market that by 1924 its signature product, Corrib Cream flour, was the dominant brand in the western market, and the mill was operating on a twenty-four hour basis to keep up with demand. By 1929, the milling division of McDonoghs became a limited company – the McDonogh Milling and Trading Company – with a share capital of £20,000. The company continued to thrive throughout the 1930s, and employed over thirty people, having added to its range of products by introducing other brand names, such as Home Glory and West Cream.[12] Another commercial venture in which he was a major shareholder, the Galway Bay Steam Boat Company, was also thriving, and McDonogh was elected chairman in January 1925.[13]

IRISH TOURIST ASSOCIATION

January 1925 also saw McDonogh become involved in an area that he had long championed, and for which he had great ambitions for the West: the tourism industry. The Irish Tourist Association (ITA), which promoted 400 hotels in its first brochure in 1925, marketed the fledgling Irish Free State as a destination.[14] Formed at the initiative of the then minister for industry and commerce, Patrick McGilligan TD, the ITA had its genesis in a number of existing provincial tourism organizations, collectively calling themselves the Tourist Organisation Society of Ireland, and comprising two main tourism representative bodies, the Irish Tourist Association, Cork and the West of Ireland Tourist Association, of which McDonogh was a founding member.

11 Gwynn, *Experiences of a literary man*, p. 294. 12 Greville, 'Milling in Ireland'. 13 *Connacht Tribune*, 7 Jan 1925. 14 In 1939, Bord Cuartaoíchta na hÉireann was established by an act of the Dáil. This organisation took over from the ITA, with statutory powers to register and grade hotels, and was the forerunner of Bord Fáilte, which was established in 1955.

Both organizations had been promoting tourism in their respective regions, but, by 1925 the society appeared to be 'within sight of a movement on a national basis, allied with the government and the big foreign railways and shipping companies'.[15] The two organizations had agreed a strategy of 'pooling their resources and initiating a great campaign' to secure publicity for the attractions of their districts.[16] It was an eminently sensible strategy, particularly given that the practicalities of funding such an organization could be easily taken care of by the simple device of local authorities striking a rate. The minister had already suggested that county boroughs 'strike a rate not exceeding *1d.* in the £; urban councils a rate not exceeding *3d.* in the £, together with the penny rate raised by the county authority'.[17]

Raising the necessary funding to market Ireland as a tourism destination was one thing: actually attracting tourists was another. The *Irish Times* expressed the view that 'Ireland can offer the world not only beef, but beauty.'[18] In an economic context, however, the simple truth was that Ireland's 'world' was effectively Britain: 90 per cent of Irish exports were to Britain in 1925, and 90 per cent of tourists to Ireland were British.[19] Ireland, as a tourism destination, was no easy sell, for, as Thompson has noted, 'cajoling English tourists into visiting the country that their army had recently ransacked expresses exactly, even epitomises, the general attitude of the Irish post-colony's new bourgeoisie towards the British bourgeoisie.'[20] However, the reference to one of Ireland's most important industries, the beef trade, was quite deliberate: the editorial was unequivocal in its view that tourism needed to be elevated to the status of an industry, as worthwhile and potentially profitable as agriculture. And it was for this reason that men such as Martin McDonogh, with not only a background in industrial development, but also an intimate knowledge of the tourism potential of the West of Ireland, were specifically targeted as potential board members of the newly established Irish Tourist Association when it was founded in January 1925. McDonogh's response was immediate, and positive, and he became one of three vice presidents of the organization.[21]

McDonogh's determination to play an active role in the association was such that he initially travelled to meetings in Dublin on a regular basis, but,

15 *Irish Independent*, 3 Mar. 1925. 16 Ibid. 17 Ibid. 18 *Irish Times*, 23 Mar. 1925. 19 Thompson, S., '"Not only Beef, but Beauty ... ": tourism, dependency, and the post-colonial Irish State, 1925–1930' in Cronin, M. and B. O'Connor (eds), *Irish tourism: image, culture and identity* (Clevedon, 2003), p. 264. 20 Ibid., p. 263. 21 Howard Harrington, a wealthy Irish-American lawyer who lived at Dunloe Castle, Killarney was the first president of the assocation, and the three vice presidents were Dr W. Lombard Murphy (son of William Martin Murphy) from Dublin, Mr J.J. Foley of Cork, and McDonogh.

as had always been the McDonogh modus operandi, he swiftly ensured the election of his second cousin Josie Mongan, a hotelier from Carna in Connemara, to the association's committee. Thereafter it was Mongan who most frequently, and very ably, represented the interests of the West at association meetings.[22] There appeared to be widespread support for the idea of a national tourism development and promotion authority, with the major industry stakeholders coming on board in whatever practical way they could. The Great Southern Railways had already offered the new ITA a premises at Westland Row,[23] and it was anticipated that 'the good offices of the minister for external affairs may enable the headquarters of the Free State in London, Paris and New York ... [to] be available as centres for the Irish Tourist Association'.[24]

The government, in offering the services of its embassies abroad,[25] showed that it was ready to lend significant moral support to the new tourism organization – if not its full financial backing, which was to become an issue in the years to come. In one of the ITA's first initiatives, at McDonogh's suggestion, Stephen Gwynn was commissioned to write an illustrated guidebook on Ireland to help promote the country to visitors. To its credit, the fledgling tourism organization was determined that standard pricing protocols be put in place, and no excessive pricing for specific events, such as the Galway Races, which McDonogh had complained of for decades, would put tourists off and give Irish tourism a bad name. The work of the ITA produced results, and in August 1926 J.J. O'Brien, the secretary of the association, stated that 4,000 tourists had landed at Dún Laoghaire and Rosslare 'on one day last week', further noting that 'they would be worth £10 per head, and it would be no exaggeration to say that they would spend £50,000'.[26]

POWER GENERATION

The mid-1920s saw McDonogh in particularly vigorous form when it came to the harnessing of any and every opportunity that would underpin the success of the new Irish state, and it was clear that the generation of power

22 Mongan was the grandson of his aunt, Mary Ann Lydon (née McDonogh). Mary Ann Lydon's daughter Honor had married Martin Mongan of Carna, and Joseph Mongan was Honor's son. 23 The ITA subsequently moved its office from Westland Row to 14 Lower O'Connell Street in 1927. 24 *Connacht Tribune*, 28 Feb. 1925. 25 Patrick McGilligan, minister for industry and commerce 1924–32, also assumed the role of minister for external affairs in 1927, following the assassination of Kevin O'Higgins, until 1932. 26 *Irish Independent*, 10 Aug. 1926.

was to be critical to that success. Here at least Galway was very much ahead of the game, as the city had been the first in the country to generate its own electricity. The Galway Electric Company was the first electricity undertaking to be established in the country, in 1888, and by the time the ESB was established in 1927, the Galway Electric Company had been in operation for almost forty years.[27] This station operated until 1929, when, on completion of the Ardnacrusha scheme, the ESB acquired the premises.

The breadth of McDonogh's knowledge of technical matters relating to hydrology, and the generation of hydroelectric power, was certainly impressive, given that he never had any formal training in engineering. In 1925 McDonogh was called to give evidence before Coimisiún na Gaeltachta, mostly relating to the development of the harbour and the potential for the fishing industry. However, he was recalled to give additional testimony, the commission members enquiring of him whether there was 'anything [he had] to say in general about the development of Galway'. McDonogh identified power generation as a major advantage Galway had, noting that there was 'practically no use made of Galway water as compared with the amount of power that could be made available'.[28] He noted that there was more power in the waterways of Galway in the summer than the winter, something he attributed to the course of the river, which he believed was:

> all wrong to get greatest fall power. The fall you get from any turbine in the town is from 9 feet to 9 feet 6 inches. There is no reason why you could not get 18 to 20 feet fall. The great bulk of water that at present runs away under the bridge could be made available, and plenty of water would be left for the fishing etc. You could get many a thousand horse power.[29]

McDonogh proposed a radical change to the course of the river in the city, the implications of which would have proved controversial, but which were based on solid evidence from his various watermill operations in the city. He gave evidence that at one time there were thirty-two separate turbines drawing power from the Corrib and its ancillary waterways, but that by 1925 there were only four enterprises generating hydroelectric power: the Perry-operated Galway Electric Company, the woollen factory, the ice factory and

27 The Galway Electric Company was established and run by the Perry family. Ireland's first municipal power plant was established at Fleet Street, Dublin, by Dublin Corporation in 1892. 28 Minutes of evidence, Coimisiún na Gaeltachta, Aug. 31 1925, p. 9. 29 Ibid.

McDonogh's own station, which mostly supplied McDonogh's fertilizer factory. He was adamant (if a little disingenuous) when he stated that he did not think there 'would be a lot of complicated questions and interests involved' in diverting the river, and was of the view that it would 'be easy to give them all the same amount of power'. It was McDonogh's view that harnessing virtually free water power in order to further develop Galway industry represented an enormous opportunity, and could be accomplished with relatively little investment: 'the power is there; the only thing that you want is development', he observed.[30] What he did not allow for, however, was the Galway fishery, whose owners he had already clashed with on more than one occasion, but this was much less likely now because, in the changed climate of postcolonial Galway, the English owner of the fishery, Col. Cross, was in a far weaker position to challenge Galway's biggest employer than had been the case previously, and McDonogh knew it.

DEATH OF KATE McDONOGH

Martin McDonogh was present when his youngest sister, Kate, died on 22 April 1927 at Belmore, Upper Salthill. Her death certificate, which, bizarrely, was signed by her brother, Dr Michael McDonough,[31] in his capacity as assistant registrar, states that she died of 'cancer of breast, recurrent' and 'internal cancer', from which she had been suffering for four months. Aged 48, she was three years older than her mother Honoria had been when she died, and, similarly, her 'rank, profession or occupation' was defined by her position within the McDonogh family; she was described as a 'merchant's daughter'. Kate McDonogh's obituary made no mention of her significant business acumen, merely stating that 'The deceased lady had many estimable qualities of character', [32]and that, as we have seen, she was 'remembered as having often sailed on the trawlers'.[33] The premises of Thomas McDonogh & Sons closed as a mark of respect on the following day, 23 April, but it was business as usual on Monday 25 April.[34] It was praise for their chairman and not regrets on the loss of Kate McDonogh that dominated the sentiments of

30 Ibid. 31 For reasons unclear, Dr Michael McDonough chose to spell his name in a manner different to his siblings. 32 There are references to Kate McDonogh having been a 'tall, striking looking' woman. A photograph of the other McDonogh sister, Mary Ann, taken when she attended a wedding of one of her Hernon cousins on Inis Mór in 1938, when she would have been 69, reveals an equally tall woman with distinctive features, wearing a beret and trenchcoat. O'Donnell, E.E. (ed.), *Images of Aran: photographs by Father Browne, 1925 & 1938* (Dublin, 1998), p. 72. 33 *Connacht Tribune*, 23 Apr. 1927. 34 Ibid.

the urban district council; in passing a vote of condolence to McDonogh, the councillors noting that 'they had great admiration for Mr McDonogh … he was a man whom they all respected, and he wished they had three or four more like him'.[35]

THE FISHING INDUSTRY

The McDonogh family had entered the fishing industry – specifically steam trawling – during the war years, the war having greatly reduced Britain's fishing fleet and created enormous export opportunities for the Irish fishing industry. Entrepreneurs like McDonogh brought significant private investment to the fishing industry, which created not only employment in catching and processing fish, but also in increased boatbuilding. But in spite of government support for such initiatives – Sinn Féin had, for example, established groups in 1919 to investigate the development of Ireland's natural resources, including mineral deposits, forestry and fisheries – the boom for the fishing industry was not to last. A report on fisheries commissioned in 1921 recommended the creation of a ministry of fisheries, and the development of cooperatives, but, as Sylvester Ó Muirí has noted, 'in the years of independence after 1922, increased landings of fish in Britain and the collapse of the Continental herring market seriously affected Ireland. The fishing industry declined and many fishermen emigrated.'[36] Some years later, in 1927, when McDonogh was a TD, he spoke on his suggested strategy for the development of the fishing industry, which was effectively that the Dáil would 'appoint a committee of men who know something about the industry, and let them suggest, in collaboration with the minister, what should be done.'[37] McDonogh's plan was eventually adopted, and an advisory committee established, of which, inevitably, he became a member.

The haemorrhaging of fishermen from the industry was something McDonogh was familiar with. In a Dáil debate in 1930, he acknowledged that:

> during the Great War a number of men along the coast went into the navy and were lost,[38] and a number have gone to America … in certain

35 Ibid. 36 Ó Muirí, S., 'Sea fisheries in Ireland, 1890–1952', presented at the conference 'Irish fisheries, food products and exports: a historical perspective', 9 Nov. 2013. 37 Dáil Debate, Committee on Finance, Vote 61, Office of the Minister for Fisheries (Resumed), 8 July 1927. 38 The problem was particularly marked in Galway, as the Claddagh fishing village had 'given more men in proportion to its

areas men will have to be imported to teach the people how to fish again.[39]

In his evidence to the commission, McDonogh revealed much about his attitude to women in business. Asked whether his aunt, Monica McDonogh, was still involved in the fishing industry, he stated, 'No, she gave up the boats. Being a woman she could not deal with it direct as a man would.'[40] He made no remarks with regard to his sister, Kate, who, prior to her death four months previously, had, by all accounts, been very ably running the McDonogh family's fleet of steam trawlers.[41]

FORESTRY

Although McDonogh's evidence to Coimisiún na Gaeltachta concentrated on power generation and the fishing industry, evidence given on forestry management by one of his most trusted employees provides a fascinating insight into the way McDonogh was calibrating his various companies in respect of the future needs of the emerging state. Frederick Coy,[42] then manager of the Galway fertilizer factory, was among those selected to give evidence before the commission delegation on the question of 're-afforestation and timber'.[43] Coy stated that he had been working in Galway for nineteen years, and had spent most of that time 'buying timber … and looking for timber'. He had previously held the position of manager of the McDonogh sawmills.[44] Coy presented a well-researched written statement to the commission, which advocated the afforestation of certain parts of Connemara on the grounds that it would:

population than any other community of similar size in Great Britain or Ireland … by June 1919 there were over 400 demobilised sailors in Galway, the vast majority of these men being from the Claddagh. Most were former fishermen whose boats had become un-seaworthy during the war years and many more fishing boats had been sold off to support the needs of the families.' Henry, W., *Galway and the Great War* (Cork, 2006), p. 133. 39 Dáil Debate, Committee on Finance, Vote 54, Fisheries and Gaeltacht Services (Resumed), 5 June 1931. 40 Minutes of evidence taken before Coimisiún na Gaeltachta, Galway, 31 Aug. 1925, p. 6. 41 O'Dowd, *In from the West*, p. 31. 42 Coy was born in 1883 in England. His son Leslie H. Coy was born in Galway in 1910, and went on to become manager of the McDonogh fertiliser plant. 43 The delegation consisted of General Richard Mulcahy (chairman), TDs Pádraig Baxter and Patrick Hogan, Pádraig Ó Siocfhradha ('An Seabhac'), Séamus Ó hEochadha ('An Fear Mór'), L.C. Moriarty, secretary of the deptartment of fisheries, and Dr Tomás Breathnach of UCG. Minutes of evidence, Coimisiún na Gaeltachta, 31 Aug. 1925, p. 4. 44 Coy gives his occupation as 'foreman, sawmills' on the 1911 census, but had been promoted to manager shortly thereafter, as he was certainly manager of the plant during the war years.

> provide employment, improve the climate, add to the appearance of the scenery, give shelter, and if properly cared for will ultimately be of great commercial value; it would be a source of supply, of material which is constantly in demand, and should thus prove a good paying proposition.[45]

Although signed by Coy and a Mr Alex McInnes,[46] the report was undoubtedly prompted by McDonogh,[47] the evidence presented based substantially on the McDonogh family's experience of the timber industry, and the recommendations designed to ensure that future supplies of timber would be assured. Forestry was undoubtedly an area ripe for investment in Ireland. As Eoin Neeson has noted:

> in 1908, the departmental committee on Irish forestry estimated the area under forest in Ireland to be in the region of 1.5 per cent of the total land area of the island (i.e. *c.*310,000 acres or 125,200 hectares), much of it being forest planted by estate landlords during the late 1700s and early 1800s.[48]

Demands due to fuel and timber shortages during the First World War had significantly reduced the forest estate, and, following independence, a modest afforestation programme was established by the Free State government. Coy's evidence reflected government policy, in that it recommended confining the afforestation programme to poor-quality marginal land, while land that was 'fit for agricultural purposes' was excluded,[49] thereby ensuring that the emerging state could produce sufficient food to feed its population. In 1928 a new Forestry Act was introduced 'to make further and better provision for promoting afforestation'.[50] Thereafter, any new forest planting that occurred was undertaken almost exclusively by the state.

In the years leading up to and immediately following 1926, Galway's

45 Minutes of evidence, Coimisiún na Gaeltachta, 31 Aug. 1925, p. 4. 46 McInnes (1877–1944) was managing director of Messrs McAinsh and Co. Ltd timber and manufacturing company of Westport. The company later moved to Tourmakeady, where McInnes planted extensive forests of hybrid larch. He became president of the Home Grown Timber Merchants Association of Éire. 47 Giving evidence on the same day as McDonogh was Prof. Tommy Dillon, professor of chemistry at UCG. He had already given evidence to the commission in Dublin, but had 'been asked by the secretary of the chamber of commerce to make a statement regarding … industries in Galway and Connemara'. The chairman of the chamber at that time was Martin McDonogh. 48 Neeson, E., *A history of Irish forestry* (Dublin, 1991), p. 97. 49 Ibid., p. 134. 50 Annual Report of the Department of Agriculture 1925/26.

economic prospects continued to fluctuate, with signs of positive growth pitted against grinding, unrelenting poverty. One of the more positive signs of Galway's recovery emerged in the 1926 census, the first taken since 1911, which revealed a slight reversal in the long-term decline of Galway's population: it increased by about a thousand.[51] Unemployment, however, remained high, and the levels of poverty in Connemara, in particular, were extreme, with near-famine conditions in evidence in many areas, exacerbated by a series of poor harvests in the preceding years. McDonogh had advocated in his evidence to Coimisiún na Gaeltachta that the key to overcoming the poverty and unemployment endemic in parts of Co. Galway was an increased focus on the natural resources with which the local population were already familiar, through fishing and kelp-making, and the development of new industries such as forestry that were suited to the West of Ireland. Never a man to wait for others to take action when he could do so himself, McDonogh continued to lobby at both government and local level for the reform and expansion of the fishing industry, urging fishermen to join the fisherman's association and adopt a more professional approach to the landing and marketing of their fish.

ASSAULT CHARGES

McDonogh's increasing involvement in the fishing industry saw him elected to the general council of the fisherman's association at a meeting held in Howth, Co. Dublin, in August 1926.[52] Two months later, however, his name was in the papers for an entirely different reason, when in October 1926 he was the defendant in an assault case brought by a Spiddal publican and grocer, William Kelly. The altercation occurred when Kelly called to McDonoghs hardware shop on Merchants Road to order some paint, but when he returned to collect the paint later that evening he was told that, as his account was £40 in arrears, McDonogh had given instructions that 'he could not get any more goods'.[53] Kelly asked to see McDonogh, and gave evidence that on knocking on the door of McDonogh's office he was told to come in, and he told McDonogh 'it would be shame for him to go home without the paint, and that he was prepared to pay the account due'.[54]

51 The 1926 census recorded that the population of Galway city had increased by 7.3%, from 13,255 in 1911 to 14,233 in 1926. *Connacht Tribune,* 28 Aug. 1926. 52 *Cork Examiner,* 24 Aug. 1926. 53 *Connacht Tribune,* 23 Oct. 1926. 54 Ibid.

McDonogh, 66, stated that he was suffering from a sore ankle at the time,[55] and was sitting with both legs up on a chair reading his paper, and stated that he replied 'What shame is it?' and then rose and 'struck him a blow on the jaw'.[56] Kelly stated that 'only that he caught the jamb of the door he would have fallen downstairs',[57] and that McDonogh had 'addressed him as a b______d and used other strong language'. McDonogh maintained that Kelly had rushed in suddenly, and not knowing who he was, 'in order to save his ankle he hit him and then caught him by the back of the neck and put him outside the door. He then finished reading his paper'.[58] McDonogh contended that Kelly's manner – his bursting into the office unannounced, and his subsequent attempt, fifteen minutes later, to exit the building through a small window – indicated that Kelly was, in fact, intoxicated. McDonogh had recommended that Kelly send for the civic guards, which Kelly did not deny. It also emerged that on that same day, Kelly had ordered furniture in McDonoghs, which was subsequently delivered, and which Kelly paid for, but that Kelly could not recall the purchase, even though it was clearly recorded in the company's accounts.

A number of things are striking about McDonogh's testimony. First, he at no point denied having hit the man. Indeed when Kelly stated that he had invited McDonogh to 'go out and fight in the street', McDonogh replied that 'only for his sore ankle he would have obliged him'. In addition, when Kelly's solicitor stated that Kelly had 'received a very severe blow', McDonogh replied, 'He did not. I think if I got a proper blow at him he would have more than a swollen jaw.'

Crucially, his refusal to apologize to Kelly and keep the matter out of court was founded on the fact that McDonogh:

> did not think there was any apology needed. He looked upon the whole thing as a trumped-up case to get money. Before the solicitor's letter came a man had come to him suggesting that he should hush the thing up and pay some money to the plaintiff.

McDonogh refused. Subsequently, McDonogh's solicitors received a letter from Kelly's solicitors asking for a written apology and for legal and medical

55 This may be related to the leg injury McDonogh sustained in the twenties, which never healed fully, and continued to trouble him for the rest of his life. 56 *Connacht Tribune*, 23 Oct. 1926. 57 According to the floor plan of the building, there were only two steps on the stairs in question. 58 *Connacht Tribune*, 23 Oct. 1926.

costs to be covered, or Kelly would take a civil case. Again, McDonogh refused. The prosecuting counsel, Mr MacDermott, noted that although:

> Mr McDonogh holds an honourable place in Galway, a position well-earned and well-won (he) seemed to think, however, that he was a law unto himself … Even taking the defendant's own evidence, he was guilty of an unprovoked assault on a customer of his.

This was indeed the case. Whatever the provocation, McDonogh's actions had been excessive, when there had been no direct assault on his person. In announcing his judgment, however, the judge stated that:

> he was driven to take Mr McDonogh's explanation on the broad facts of the case. He had done what 99.999 percent of men would have done: put the intruder out of his room by the back of the neck. The law, however, did not allow for human frailty and there must be a decree for damages.

The judge awarded the derisory sum of 20*s.* to Kelly, and expenses of £3 13*s.*[59] Kelly can hardly have been pleased with the outcome, given that his original claim had been for £100 damages. The verdict aside, it is significant that McDonogh chose to face the charge of assault rather than pay off Kelly, have his dominance over Galway business life called into question or give rise to any future vexatious suits. And McDonogh's belief that he could rely on the goodwill of the local judiciary was not without good cause.

ENTERING NATIONAL POLITICS

The assault case of late 1926 had gripped Galway, and provided proof, if proof were needed, that McDonogh was still a man able and willing to take on a fight. In addition, his robust testimony to Coimisiún na Gaeltachta indicated a willingness, even enthusiasm, to take a more active role in the development of national policy. The next logical step was for McDonogh to become actively involved as a member of a political party, and in joining Cumann na nGaedheal, he was joining a party whose policies very much agreed with his own. On the land question, however, in his own county at

59 Ibid.

least, the party's policies had polarized the population. By January 1924 there were 276 Cumann na nGaedhal *cumainn* in Ireland, and, as Ó Fathartaigh notes, 'the main stimulus for joining was the 1923 Land Act, but, barring the city, there were none in west Galway'.[60] Moreover, there was a perceptible split in the county, such that, 'if west Galway wanted radicalism, east Galway wanted a conservative measure that would transfer 24,084 acres there locally, and it had twenty *cumainn*'.[61] As a significant landowner, whose ownership of the lands of Monatigue had placed him in the thick of the increasingly fractious debate surrounding land redistribution, McDonogh was well aware of the issues involved, but, crucially, he was also a major stakeholder, who could potentially turn the situation around.

The invitation to McDonogh to join Cumann na nGaedheal came from his friend Patrick Hogan TD, from Kilrickle in east Galway.[62] As minister for agriculture, Hogan believed that market forces – particularly cattle exports – should shape Irish agricultural development.[63] McDonogh was a significant cattle exporter, whose crucial role in the development of agriculture in the West, as a result of his fertilizer factory, and his significant client base in Britain, put him in the forefront of those who had a role to play in agricultural development. Politically speaking, however, McDonogh had a somewhat problematic CV for the post-independence party: a former Parnellite and Redmondite, he had enthusiastically supported the war and vehemently opposed Sinn Féin, the party from which Cumann na nGaedheal had sprung. McDonogh, however, was not unique in the evolution of his political credo, and it was significant that, since independence, he had shown a willingness, in both his business and civic roles, to work constructively with the new political regime. McDonogh's introduction into the party, however, was not universally popular. Revd Malachy Brennan PP,[64] a member of the standing committee of Cumann na nGaedheal and president of the north

60 Ó Fathartaigh, M., 'Cumann na nGaedheal, the land issue and West Galway, 1923–1932', in *Journal of the Galway Archaeological and Historical Society*, 60 (2008), 157. 61 Ibid. 62 Hogan was one of three younger members of the Cumann na nGaedheal government – the others being Home Affairs Minister Kevin O'Higgins and Patrick Gilligan, minister for industry and commerce – who, 'had all sat in the same economics class in University College Dublin'. Daly, M.E., *Industrial development and Irish national identity, 1922–1939* (Syracuse, 1992), p. 14. 63 Politically and personally, Hogan and McDonogh spoke the same language. At an election rally in June 1927 Hogan, then minister for lands and agriculture, declared that 'The shower of rain that fell this morning is of much more importance to the farmers of County Galway than any discussion about the Oath or the Treaty.' *Connacht Tribune*, 11 June 1927. 64 Brennan (1877–1967) was a priest and republican. A member of the Gaelic League, and of the national executive of Sinn Féin, he served as a judge in the republican courts. Following the Treaty, he was a staunch supporter of the Free State government.

Roscommon executive of the party, resigned from the standing committee because of his objection to the targeting of men like McDonogh by the party, stating that the party was prepared to 'join any coalition or to accept the support of any individuals who would keep them in office'.[65] Fr Brennan, however, was very much in the minority, and for many in Galway the recruitment of Máirtín Mór McDonogh into the party was a major coup, which would pay dividends in the forthcoming general election.

The selection of McDonogh on the Cumann na nGaedheal ticket for the June 1927 election was based not only on his extensive experience of local politics, but also because of his influential role as Galway's major employer.[66] The belief was that he could – and would – deliver the seat for Cumann na nGaedheal in Galway. The choice of McDonogh as a candidate was perhaps also influenced by the fact that at a meeting of the Coiste Gnótha in March 1927, it was agreed that each constituency 'should bear the entire expenses of the election; including the candidates' fees'.[67] Having a wealthy man as a candidate was therefore a distinct advantage. McDonogh's candidature was proposed at the Galway constituency convention on 7 May 1927 and ratified at a meeting of the Coiste Gnótha on 20 May 1927.[68]

On the campaign trail, McDonogh presented himself as a candidate in the same way he had always presented himself as a businessman and civic leader – as a straight talker who didn't stand on ceremony. At his first election meeting, in Clonbur, Co. Galway, the *Connacht Tribune* observed that 'Mr McDonogh's common-sense speech evidently impressed his audience.'[69] His no-nonsense approach was also in evidence the following month, when, addressing delegates attending the Irish Technical Instruction Association congress in Galway, he stated that:

> it was time something practical should be done, and technical education was the only means he saw for that purpose. When he was a boy, he knew more about Latin grammar than he did about English,[70] and he knew nothing about mathematics. It was all practically useless, and the sooner something practicable in the way of education was done in this country the better.[71]

65 *Connacht Tribune,* 10 Sept. 1927. 66 Galway was a nine-seater from 1923–37, having previously been a seven-seater from 1921–2. 67 Minutes of meeting of Coiste Gnótha, 14 Mar. 1927, Cumann na nGaedheal archive, UCD. 68 Ibid. 69 *Connacht Tribune,* 28 May 1927. 70 McDonogh certainly knew his Shakespeare. During an urban district council debate on travelling salesmen selling goods at street markets, to the detriment of rate-paying shopkeepers, he remarked, 'There is something rotten in the state of Denmark if they cannot be removed.' *Connacht Tribune,* 6 Nov. 1926. 71 *Connacht Tribune,* 25

Figure 7 Martin McDonogh canvassing in Clifden during the June 1927 election.

McDonogh concluded by stating, 'I will not detain you any longer, because I have an unfortunate habit of saying what I think and what I say might not sometimes agree with some of my hearers.'[72] This was the Martin McDonogh that the people of Galway were familiar with, and, whether they agreed with his politics or not, they knew at least that he was unlikely to be subsumed into any party machine. At an election meeting in Clifden, McDonogh was photographed in what was called 'characteristic attitude', and declared, 'The time has come for every man to take his side'[73] (figure 7). On 9 June 1927 McDonogh proved his worth and was elected, polling an impressive 4,570 first preferences.[74]

McDonogh's constituency colleagues following the June 1927 election were an eclectic bunch, reflecting just how wide the chasm was between himself and even his own party colleagues. Seán Broderick, from Prospect Hill in Galway city, had been Officer Commanding, 4th Battalion, Galway Brigade of the IRA during the War of Independence. In 1919 he had been arrested by the Black and Tans, put against a wall and shot. Assumed dead, he was only wounded and managed to escape. Supporting the Treaty in 1922, Broderick led the IRA into Renmore Barracks on the day the British left in June of that

June 1927. **72** Ibid. **73** *Connacht Tribune*, 11 June 1927. **74** After transfers were taken into account, McDonogh was elected on a poll of 5,983 votes. *Connacht Tribune*, 18 June 1927.

year. He was elected to Dáil Éireann as a Cumann na nGaedheal TD for the Galway constituency at the 1923 general election. Patrick Hogan, 36, was first elected at the 1921 general election as a Sinn Féin candidate for Galway. A supporter of the Treaty, he later joined Cumann na nGaedheal, and in 1922 he was appointed to the cabinet of W.T. Cosgrave as minister for lands and agriculture. In spite of the disparity in their ages, Hogan became one of McDonogh's very few personal friends, and they held each other in high regard. McDonogh's Fianna Fáil colleagues were Frank Fahy, 47, a teacher and barrister from Kilchreest in Co. Galway. Fahy had been first elected at the 1918 general election as a Sinn Féin MP for South Galway, but took his seat in the 1st Dáil. He was re-elected as TD for Galway in the 1921 general election, but having sided with the anti-Treaty forces, did not take his seat in either the 3rd Dáil or the 4th Dáil. He joined Fianna Fáil when the party was founded in 1926. Mark Killilea Snr, 31, was a farmer, shopkeeper and founder member of Fianna Fáil. He was elected to Dáil Éireann on his first attempt, at the June 1927 election. Thomas P. Powell, 35, was a national schoolteacher, and was also elected to the Dáil on his first attempt in 1927. The constituency colleague with whom McDonogh most frequently locked horns, both inside and outside the Dáil, was Dr (John) Seán Tubridy, 31, a dispensary doctor from Lettermore in Connemara, not far from the old McDonogh homestead on Crappagh. Dr Tubridy was a popular and highly respected medical officer for Connemara, who had frequently risked his own life in tackling epidemics of cholera, typhus and Spanish flu – and clashed with Galway county council officials and the Galway board of guardians as a result. He took the anti-Treaty side in the Civil War, and the Free State government, in what can only be regarded as an act of spite, removed him from his job and advertised his position. Following a sustained campaign of protest by his loyal patients and fellow doctors, the department of health was forced to do a U-turn, and Tubridy retained his position.

The other Galway deputies elected in 1927 were William Duffy of the National League Party and the Labour Party's Gilbert Lynch,[75] who took the final seat. Duffy, born in 1865, and only five years younger than McDonogh, had the practical experience of being one of the few people to have served both in the British parliament and in Dáil Éireann. First elected at the 1900

75 The Galway branch of the Labour Party had been established in 1926, the formal proposer being McDonogh's cousin, the writer Pádraic Ó Conaire. *Connacht Tribune*, 26 June 1926. Ó Conaire canvassed for Lynch in the June 1927 election. Lynch was only the second Labour TD to be elected for Galway, the first being T.J. O'Connell, who had been elected in 1922, and re-elected in 1923.

general election as IPP MP for South Galway, he had held the seat until his defeat at the 1918 general election by the Sinn Féin candidate Frank Fahy. Unlike McDonogh, Duffy soon realized that the politics of independent Ireland did not suit him, or perhaps his advanced age meant that he found the rigors of travelling to Dáil sessions too gruelling. Either way, he did not contest the September 1927 election, and retired from politics. Gilbert Lynch, on the other hand, was a young, dynamic and ambitious candidate, with whom McDonogh had already clashed on account of his trade-union activities in Galway.[76] Lynch was to serve only three months as a TD, and it was thanks to McDonogh that he made one of the most impassioned and admired maiden speeches in the Dáil's history.

McDonogh was 67 years old when he entered the Dáil for the first time on 23 June 1927, making him one of its oldest members.[77] He made his maiden speech on 29 June, in a debate on a labour-related topic: the Unemployment Insurance Acts. His opening salvo, 'As an unfortunate employer I think I should contribute something to this debate',[78] set the tone of what was to come. As a maiden speech it was typically forthright, unequivocal and not lacking in arrogance. McDonogh castigated those on the Labour and Fianna Fáil benches who 'will not get their feet wet and who take care not to work too long' and went on to note that the country was 'paying wages which it cannot afford'.[79] He expressed the view that 'no one … except a lunatic, would start a new industry here, except under protection'. Warming to his task, McDonogh went on to state that his 'experience of labour representatives is not very pleasant, and I am sure that their experience of me has not been very pleasant either'.[80] There was more robust talk of trade-union leaders (or 'trouble-makers' as he referred to them), McDonogh noting that 'I am not afraid of any of them, and I never was'. And, not content with antagonising the Labour deputies present, he went one step further and not only personalized his comments, but did so in a manner that revealed, once more, his deep-seated xenophobic tendencies. Referring to one trade-union organizer who had come to Galway, McDonogh stated:

76 Lynch (1892–1969) was third-generation Irish, born in Stockport, near Manchester. Sworn into the IRB in 1913, he used his role as a labour activist and member of the Independent Labour Party to smuggle ammunition into Ireland during his visits. At Easter 1916, having again smuggled guns into the country, he found himself in the GPO. He was injured climbing over a barricade, but, as a result of his Lancashire accent, escaped arrest and made his way back to England. 77 Aside from Duffy, McDonogh's other constituency colleagues had an average age of 36. He was two years older than Sir James Craig, his closest contemporary in the Dáil. 78 Dáil Debate, Private Deputies' Business – Unemployment Insurance Acts, 29 June 1927. 79 Ibid. 80 Ibid.

> A gentleman was imported from Manchester. He says he is of Irish parentage and Irish descent. The gentleman who was imported proceeded to make new regulations and new rules … It is a pity that there is a feeling that the labour world at present does not want to give a fair return for wages. It is frankly and openly Bolshevik. We imported that from England and other places. The ordinary Irishman in this country is all right. Any trouble we had politically or any other way is generally due to some importee, or to someone with foreign blood. I do not think I can contribute anything more to the debate but, as an initial effort, I have not done so badly.[81]

Clearly pleased with himself, McDonogh might have expected the 'gentleman … imported from Manchester', in the person of Gilbert Lynch, the trade unionist and Labour deputy for Galway, to respond, as indeed he did. Lynch later recorded that, although he had resolved to speak in the debate, he wouldn't have spoken so early, 'but for the fact that Mr Martin McDonogh … spoke, and in his speech he blamed the trade union officials and attacked me, saying these included men from Manchester. I got up to reply to him immediately.'[82] Lynch stated:

> I happen to be an importation from Manchester, that terrible Bolshevist referred to by Deputy McDonogh. One thing I wish to make clear is, that though I am an importation from Manchester I happened to be an importation in 1916,[83] and in spite of what deputies on the other side have said I have no regrets. We Irish in Manchester have no apologies to make for doing our duty to our country, and we have nothing to be ashamed of.[84]

The subsequent verbal jousting between McDonogh and Lynch prompted one deputy to jokingly query 'whether the fight between Deputy McDonogh and Deputy Lynch was a private fight or if I might join in?'[85]

With the demands of his new parliamentary career pressing on him, McDonogh was forced to cut back on his participation in most of his civic committees. In July 1927 he presided at a meeting of the harbour commis-

81 Ibid. 82 Lynch, G., *The life and times of Gilbert Lynch*, Studies in Irish Labour History 13 (Dublin, 2011), pp 57–8. 83 Lynch had been an active participant in the Rising, serving in both the GPO and Liberty Hall. 84 Dáil Debate, Private Deputies' Business – Uunemployment Insurance Acts, 29 June 1927. 85 The deputy was Bryan Cooper, an independent, who represented Dublin County.

sioners, but noted that 'he would not have come to the meeting were it not in connection with arrangements about the *Muenchen*'. This was a cruise ship owned by the North German Lloyd line that was due to dock in Galway later that month, the first such vessel to visit in many years.[86] The development of Galway as a transatlantic port was a long-standing ambition of McDonogh's, and he pulled out all the stops to ensure that the first visit went smoothly. Under his direction, Galway rolled out the red carpet for the *Muenchen*. The streets were festooned with decorations, and a fly-past was organized with three planes of the Irish Air Force. A formal ceremony of welcome took place on board the ship when it arrived on 27 May 1927, and the ship's passengers and crew were welcomed by enormous crowds at Galway docks.[87] Although there had for many years been reservations expressed about how easy the port of Galway was for larger ships to access, McDonogh, in typical fashion, assured Herr Klose, the North German Lloyd line's agency inspector, that the line need have no fears with regard to entering Galway Bay:

> No trouble could occur in Galway Bay unless a man went looking for it. As long as they came in the south channel, and keep clear of the margurita anyone in that room could guide the ship up to where she was.[88]

The proceedings concluded with a ceremonial 'wedding' of the Lloyd line to the Port of Galway, complete with a Claddagh ring.[89] The success of the inaugural Lloyd line cruise-ship visit, and the increasing numbers of German and American cruise ships, along with passenger vessels bringing emigrants to the United States,[90] heralded the beginning of a major new phase in the development of Galway's port. From May 1927 to December 1928, there were fourteen sailings of transatlantic liners to and from Galway.[91]

86 The *Muenchen* carried 170 first-class passengers, 344 second-class and 602 third-class, and it had a crew of 360. Woodman, *Safe and commodious*, p. 192. 87 Keen to be associated with the new initiative, Clare county council was represented by its chairman, Mr O'Loughlin, who presented an address to Mr Klose 'welcoming the Muenchen to Galway Bay, which washes the shores of Clare'. *Connacht Tribune*, 28 May 1927. 88 *Connacht Tribune*, 28 May 1927. McDonogh was referring to the Margarita Rock, or Margaretta Shoal, a navigational hazard in Galway Bay, near Blackrock. The rock was so named because a sailing ship, the *Santa Margarita*, ran aground there in September 1807. *Freeman's Journal*, 25 Sept. 1807. I am indebted to Dr Deirdre Ní Chonghaile for this reference. 89 *Connacht Tribune*, 28 May 1927. 90 The quota of Irish emigrants to the US in 1927 was fixed at 28,000, with 9,000 of these originating from West of the Shannon. As passengers were subject to medical examination, a disinfecting chamber was established at the docks, the cost of which, £1,500, was split between the board of health, the harbour board and the urban district council. Woodman, *Safe and commodious*, p. 192. 91 *Connacht Sentinel*, 8 Jan. 1929.

SEPTEMBER 1927 ELECTION

Although Cumann na nGaedheal had been largely successful in restoring stability to the new state, the resources simply did not exist to allow them to create prosperity and improve living standards. Their policies were conservative in nature, and when Fianna Fáil finally entered mainstream politics in 1927 following the June general election, winning forty-four seats, they did so because they were offering the Irish people real change, and the promise of self-sufficiency; Cumann na nGaedheal could only offer more of the same. The loss of Cumann na nGaedheal's working majority ensured that the 5th Dáil would be short-lived once the Fianna Fáil deputies finally took their seats.[92] They did so in August 1927, as a result of the assassination of Kevin O'Higgins on 10 July, an atrocity that appeared to many to signal a reversion to the dark days of the Civil War.

With tensions rising, the government introduced a second Public Safety Act (which provided for the death penalty), and an Electoral Amendment Act that forced elected TDs to take an oath of allegiance. The oath is what led to Fianna Fáil's forced entry to the Dáil, as a result of which, in August 1927, the government only narrowly survived a vote of no confidence. A general election was called for 15 September 1927, and it was widely expected that McDonogh would stand again. Given his age, his businesses and civic commitments,[93] and perhaps also because he had found the first few months of his Dáil career frustrating and physically gruelling, McDonogh was far from enthusiastic about the prospect. But stand he did, and in his first speech in Galway, in September 1927, he explained his reasons, in vintage McDonogh style:

> It is no pleasure to me to be in the Dáil. I would be far better off at home looking after my business. Three months ago I was approached, and it was put up to me that those who had a stake in the country should do their bit and go forward as candidates in the interest of the Cumann na nGaedheal party. I consented, so here I am now, out here to solicit your votes.[94]

92 Only three votes separated the two major parties, Cumann na nGaedheal and Fianna Fáil. 93 Added to his official roles in 1927 was that of president of Corrib Rowing Club. 94 *Connacht Sentinel*, 13 Sept. 1927.

Although his opening comments were hardly the ingratiating rhetoric of an election candidate, McDonogh soon compensated for this in an impassioned defence of Cumann na nGaedheal policies, particularly with regard to the Shannon scheme, then under construction:

> the Shannon scheme, when completed, would be one of the greatest schemes ever promoted in any country ... I know it is, as I speak from experience. I have spent more on electricity than all the eighty Fianna Fáil candidates put together. I am willing any day to bring you through my works and prove to you the value of electricity as a driving power.[95]

McDonogh was not afraid to court controversy either, as he defended the wages paid to the workers on the scheme, which had been criticized as being too low, by stating that had they been any higher, local farmers would not have been able to attract workers to work for them, and that would have 'done a great injustice to the farmers in that district'.[96] But while the Shannon scheme was something about which he felt strongly and spoke with authority, it was the aforementioned Fianna Fáil candidates who elicited his ire and disgust, because of what he considered the party's hypocrisy with regard to the oath:

> It is all very well for those people ... who after five years discovered that the oath was an empty formula, to come out here and promise you a lot of nice things. How can you possibly rely on men who, at the last election, told you that they would never take the oath? If elected all their promises will amount to the same thing. Consider all the lives that have been lost, bridges blown up, burnings of all descriptions, and the millions all those things cost. All over an empty formula. What the Fianna Fáil party did over a month ago they could have done five years ago. It is the same oath today as it was when the Treaty was signed.[97]

During a subsequent election meeting at the Claddagh Hall, McDonogh repeated that 'he was not anxious to stand again', but, significantly, added that 'he would rather drown himself than do what J.J. Walsh did'.[98] McDonogh

95 Ibid. 96 Ibid. 97 Ibid. 98 Walsh was a TD for Cork and minister for posts and telegraphs when he resigned suddenly in 1927. His reason for resigning was a personal belief in the Griffithite policy of protectionism, which he believed preferable to the free trade ethos of others in the Cumann na nGaedheal party, particularly those in the cabinet. Walsh sent an open letter to Cosgrave, claiming that

clearly saw the Cork TD's resignation as an act of betrayal and desertion of his party. He resolved to stand, in spite of his own misgivings, and appealed to the voters to 'support the local men, whom they knew, and leave foreigners alone'.[99]

As we have seen, the targetting of McDonogh as a member of the party, and his subsequent grooming as a prospective election candidate, had been bitterly resented by some members of the party, including Fr Brennan, who, having left the party prior to the June 1927 election, wasted no time in taking aim at McDonogh's political pedigree when he was presented to the electorate for the second time. He observed that 'Mr McDonogh, at Easter 1916, called a meeting of sympathizers in Galway city to demand the arrest of certain Galway professors who were inciting the young men to rebellion, as he called it.'[1] The timing of this statement was designed to damage McDonogh's chances in the election, and McDonogh was understandably furious, and emphatically denied Fr Brennan's claims, declaring during an interview with the *Connacht Tribune*, 'The statement is a lie, as all who know me will testify. Those who are using it for the purpose of the election know that it is a lie.'[2] The *Tribune*, which published McDonogh's rebuttal of Fr Brennan's claims, stated that:

> A leading member of the old IRA, who was with Mr McDonogh during the interview, added that so far from Fr MacBrennan's allegations being true,[3] it was well known in Co. Galway and throughout the West that Mr McDonogh visited the prisoners in England some weeks after the Rising,[4] and then and subsequently did all in his power to secure the release of those imprisoned or interned.[5]

the party had gone 'over to the most reactionary elements of the state'. Bew, P., Hazelkorn, E. and H. Patterson, *The dynamics of Irish politics* (London, 1989), p. 29. 99 *Irish Independent*, 15 Sept. 1927. 1 *Connacht Tribune*, 10 Sept. 1927. The meeting referred to was the public meeting chaired by McDonogh that took place in the town hall on Wednesday 26 Apr. 1916, at which the 'committee of public safety' was established. At that meeting McDonogh had stated that 'it was not the unfortunate fellows who were out lying under the walls that were to blame, but those gentlemen – teachers and professors – and such intellectual gentlemen, those who ought to know better … it was not the young fellows … who were to blame, but the men who had fooled them into it.' *Connacht Tribune*, 29 Apr. 1916. 2 *Connacht Tribune*, 10 Sept. 1927. 3 Fr Brennan is referred to in a number of sources, including a number of BMH witness statements, as 'Fr MacBrennan'. 4 Of the 1,804 men sent to Frongoch in the aftermath of the 1916 Rising, 322 were from Galway, representing a quite significant 17.85%. However, the men who were later to represent Galway in the Dáil did not, by and large, come from that number, with only two of the 30 former Frongoch inmates who later became TDs (6.66%) coming from Galway. Kenny, *Politics and society*, p. 24. 5 *Connacht Tribune*, 10 Sept. 1927.

The identity of the 'old IRA' man is not given, and no evidence has so far emerged to substantiate the claim that McDonogh visited Galway prisoners in England following the Rising.[6] However, if McDonogh did visit and try to secure the release of those involved in the 1916 Rising in Galway, it would have been a truly remarkable volte-face, and may go some way towards explaining why, in spite of his considerable contribution to the war effort, he never received any honour or award (such as the OBE bestowed on Joe Young) in recognition of his services.

While McDonogh did not canvass as vigorously in the September 1927 election as he had the previous June, because of ill health, he nonetheless continued to steer his various businesses, and fulfil his civic commitments, to the best of his ability. He was not a man to express his feelings readily, but at the Municipal Authorities Association conference held in Galway in 1927 he revealed much regarding his own philosophy on the role of the civic man. He paid tribute to the people of Galway and analysed his own relationship with them thus:

> I get on very well with them, because I tell them the truth. I never try to hurt anyone's feelings, or do an unkind or unfair thing, and they can trust me. What we want in this country is trust in each other. Things happen at our urban council meetings sometimes that make us wish we had a commissioner. We have a very excellent urban council, but there are some urban councillors [who are] not very excellent, and the ones that are not very excellent can attend more regularly than the other sort. It is a pity there would not be a better civic spirit among the people in this country. We could do a lot if there was.[7]

Reflecting on the Civil War, he observed:

> You had son against father, and sister against brother – all on account of the celebrated oath. The other day when it was put to them, it was only an empty formula. But the empty formula will not bring back the men who were shot and murdered, and it will not redeem the destruction and ruin.[8]

6 Frank Hardiman confirmed that two Galway MPs – Captain Stephen Gwynn (Galway Borough) and William Duffy (South Galway) – visited the Galway prisoners in Wandsworth Prison shortly after their arrival there in 1916. BMH WS 406. 7 *Connacht Tribune*, 1 Oct. 1927. 8 Ibid.

But he was not prepared to leave it at that, adding: 'of course, if de Valera was an Irishman he would never subject this country to what it has gone through. It is up to us now. We have the country to make what we can of it.' [9]

Perhaps because he was not up to canvassing as vigorously as he had in the past, McDonogh appears to have resorted in the September 1927 election to more underhanded methods to secure votes. He was not averse to using his role as an employer to exert pressure on his workforce to vote for him. In the June election, Labour's Gilbert Lynch noted that of the sixteen polling boxes in Galway city he had 'beaten the local employer Máirtín Mór in fourteen of them'. Mindful of this, McDonogh did not take any chances in the September election of that same year, and Lynch records that:

> on the night before the poll a meeting was called by the manager of the chemical works, in the chemical works, and all the workers were instructed to go down there and they were given a lecture by the manager, who pointed out to them the amount of employment that Mr McDonogh gave and the serious consequences … if he was forced out of the public life and public business.[10]

Lynch was in no doubt that this talk cost him a lot of votes in the election, and he consequently lost his seat.[11] Lynch's suspicions were borne out by newspaper commentators at the time, who noted the high percentage of first preferences for McDonogh, followed by second preferences for the Labour candidate.

McDONOGH IN THE DÁIL

McDonogh was easily re-elected in the September 1927 election, securing 5,007 first preferences, a significant improvement on his first showing in the June 1927 election.[12] A fascinating portrait of him as a TD emerges in a piece written by the anonymous political diarist of the *Sunday Independent*, 'Politicus'. Written in 1929, when McDonogh was 69, it reveals a man with a highly distinctive, not to say, intimidating, personality:

9 *Connacht Sentinel*, 6 Sept. 1927. 10 Lynch, *The life and times of Gilbert Lynch*, pp 62–3. 11 These events were later fictionalized by O'Flaherty in his 1929 novel, *The house of gold*, as was the occasion when McDonogh led his workers across a dockside picket line. 12 Overall, Cumann na nGaedheal regained most of the ground it had lost in the June 1927 election, winning 62 seats and 39% of the vote.

> He never yields to the soporous influence of the legislative chamber. When he fears that the wings of Morpheus are being set a-flutter by the whispered incitements of a colleague, he bestirs himself suddenly and takes a couple of sharp turns in the division lobby. Then he leans across the handrail … and listens – impatiently, I fear – to the remainder of the dirge. The man who has been accustomed to an active life finds the duty of sitting still and silent in the Dáil purgatorial. You will never find Mr McDonogh in the same place for long. Inactivity to him is imprisonment. Mr McDonogh is what the modern lady novelist would describe as 'a masculine man'. He is, indeed, massively and aggressively masculine. His thick, upstanding, wiry hair, just beginning to show an odd snowdrop, is about a foot nearer to the dome of the Dáil chamber than the skimpy and sleek locks of those who sit around and about him. When he takes his seat a deputy of dumpy and diminutive build who sits behind has his vision clouded by an expanse of Galway tweed.[13]

Expanding on McDonogh's 'masculine' traits, the commentator noted that McDonogh was:

> Silent, strong, and – I say it with fear and trembling – gruff. He is that type of man that you find it convenient to agree with – even at the expense of conviction. You know that if you do not agree with him his language, if he speaks at all, will be blunt, emphatic, and rich in volume if lacking in cadence. He has, of course, all the advantage of stature. The man who has to stare heavenwards in a dialogue is handicapped. He cannot afford to be adequately expressive. It is the difference between the big boy and the small boy at school.[14]

Having described McDonogh as 'the silent type', who rarely spoke in the Dáil, the correspondent noted nonetheless that McDonogh:

> spends much time in interviews on behalf of his constituents, and is reputed to be a successful advocate. I suppose in McDonogh's presence, ministers are discreet rather than valorous. To say 'no' to the giant for Galway would be to challenge the fates rashly.[15]

13 *Sunday Independent*, 6 Jan. 1929. 14 Ibid. 15 Ibid.

And it was not just ministers who apparently quailed in the presence of McDonogh. Politicus referred to an incident involving McDonogh's constituency colleague, Fianna Fáil Deputy Dr Séan Tubridy of Carraroe:[16]

> A political opponent of Mr McDonogh was drawing the attention of the western hemisphere, through the medium of the Dáil, to some grievance of the good people who have the Atlantic as their neighbour. He was a mild-mannered man and spoke with apologetic voice. Inadvertently – it could not be otherwise, I am sure – he made an irreverent allusion to Mr McDonogh. That gentleman rose in haste and in wrath. There was thunder in his look. Regarding his puny adversary contemptuously, he enquired in the voice of Stentor: 'You Carraroe whippersnapper, what do you know …' and more to the same effect. The roll of the r's in that fine euphony 'Carraroe whippersnapper' is something to remember. It sounded like a waterfall – or a couple of competing waterfalls. The interrupted deputy was stunned by this avalanche of homely vituperation and said no more.[17]

The altercation with Tubridy took place in June 1928 in a hot-tempered debate relating to Article 47 of the Constitution. In the course of the debate Tubridy referred to the fact that McDonogh had fallen asleep, adding sarcastically 'not realising the terrible danger that he is in from rebellion and revolution'.[18] McDonogh replied that he was 'very much awake' and added 'the sort of revolution you will bring will not make much difference. A half dozen of your sort would not make a man.' Later in the debate McDonogh hammered home his disregard for Tubridy, stating that he 'did not hear Deputy Tubridy's references to me, as he did not speak loud enough', a charge which could never have been levelled at McDonogh. If the lengthy debate had, in fact, prompted McDonogh to sleep, Tubridy's intervention certainly woke him up, and he was soon engaged in a spirited attack on Fianna Fáil policies, and the men, such as Tubridy, who represented them:

16 Describing Carraroe as 'the Cork of Connacht', Politicus observed that 'everybody leaves it as quickly as possible, but everybody keeps a maiden aunt or a rheumatic uncle stationed there for old association sake and in order to uphold the prestige of Carraroe as the place where everything in the West happens, from flooding to "flu and fluke"'. *Sunday Independent*, 6 Jan. 1929. 17 *Sunday Independent*, 6 Jan. 1929. 18 Dáil Debate, Constitution (Amendment No. 10) Bill, 1928 – Declaration under Article 47 of the Constitution, 28 June 1928.

> The people want peace; they want to be allowed to go on with their work, and this hot air and nonsense we hear from the other benches goes for nothing. What good do these men do? I employ more men than the whole lot of them over there, and do more good. Yet we have this little whipper-snapper from Carraroe giving cheek.[19]

While Tubridy, as Politicus correctly observed, appears to have been rendered speechless by McDonogh's verbal assault, others were not, and in the course of the rest of the debate McDonogh went on to spar with his fellow Galwegian, Deputy Killilea, over his actions in 1916. McDonogh had been reprimanded by the cathaoirleach for addressing the deputies on the other side of the house, and politely deferred to the cathaoirleach's ruling, something Killilea swiftly rounded on:

> McDonogh: I bow to your ruling.
> Killilea: He has practised that all his life.
> McDonogh: Practised what? I am pretty well known where I come from.
> Killilea: Faith you are since 1916.
> McDonogh: They know who I am, sonny, what they do not know about some people. I have a pedigree, at any rate.
> Killilea: Some of us have a record, which counts for something more.
> McDonogh: Put up your record. I have never done anything I was ashamed of or that I want to retract.[20]

And there was yet another heated exchange with Deputy James Ryan. When he stated, 'I will not admit what Deputy McDonogh says, but we can have it out some other time,' McDonogh replied, bullishly, 'Any time you like,' and Ryan responded, 'The sooner the better.'[21]

In the Dáil chamber McDonogh frequently denounced the populist and interventionist policies of Fianna Fáil in language that was unequivocal. The press gleefully reported one such occasion, stating that 'A dull debate was enlivened by a passage-at-arms between Mr McEntee and Mr Martin McDonogh, when the Galway deputy charged the Fianna Fáil party with ruining confidence in the country and thereby damaging credit and industry.'[22] At one point in the argument McDonogh suggested to McEntee,

19 Ibid. 20 Dáil Debate, Constitution (Amendment No. 10) Bill, 1928 – Declaration under Article 47 of the Constitution, 28 June 1928. 21 Ibid. 22 *Irish Times*, 3 Dec. 1931.

'Why do you not employ somebody, and not be talking to us over here. You people are a curse in this country.'[23]

McDonogh regularly complained of lengthy debates and unnecessary delays in the passing of legislation, but his bête noir in the Dáil, Deputy Sean McEntee, criticized men like McDonogh for simply turning up at the appropriate moment and voting for legislation in line with the party whip, or, as he put it, 'relying on their feet to pass them through'.[24] McEntee argued that:

> It is the weary feet tramping up these stairs … those weary feet are the things that make the laws for the people of this country, not the brains, not the intellect, not the great business capacity, for example, of Deputy McDonogh … but the weary feet tramping up these division stairs, up to these lobbies through the twenty-four hours of a single day – it was these passed these important Constitution amendments through their most important stages.[25]

Such painstaking constitutional politics did not come easily to McDonogh, his business empire was always in need of his attention, he continued to be an active member of various civic and public bodies in Galway, and he held a number of directorships with companies such as Hibernian Insurance. As a result, his absences from the Dáil were frequent.

Outside of the Dáil, McDonogh continued to attend to his civic duties at local level, to a quite remarkable degree, and his interest in, and knowledge of, the minutiae of the workings of such bodies was impressive. As a member of the city of Galway technical instruction committee, he enquired at a meeting in 1929 as to 'how the recently formed motor engineering classes were progressing', and when informed that the classes were held late at night to accommodate apprentices who were working during the daytime, observed, 'I notice light there some nights about 11 o'clock'.[26] McDonogh also kept his ear to the ground, and was remarkably well informed on local gossip, enquiring at one point, regarding the engineering classes, 'if it were true that the only pupils were ladies, who could well afford to employ people to teach them … talk of that kind was going around the town'.[27] Quite how talk of this kind came to his ears is unclear, but he clearly liked to be kept informed. When it was suggested that with increasing numbers of the more well-heeled members

23 Dáil Debate, Unemployment Relief Bill, 1931 – Second Stage, 2 Dec. 1931. 24 Dáil Debate, Constitution (Amendment No. 13) Bill – Fifth Stage, 5 July 1928. 25 Ibid. 26 *Connacht Tribune*, 2 Feb. 1929. 27 Ibid.

of Galway society attending the classes, 'people with shawls will be afraid to come', McDonogh emphatically declared that such would never be the case, proclaiming, 'The classes are for everyone.'[28]

There were a number of other causes particularly dear to McDonogh for which he also continued to lobby. One was the needs of fishermen, and, as a county councillor representing the Aran Islands, the islanders in particular. It was largely due to his efforts that Galway chamber of commerce had collaborated with the National lifeboat institute in securing a new Galway lifeboat station in Galway Bay, the boat to be based at Kilronan on Inis Mór. In proposing a vote of thanks for his efforts in securing the much-needed lifeboat, Sean Ford (Mac Giollarnáth), district justice, described McDonogh as 'the big spoilt child of Galway', adding 'they were all proud of him, nevertheless'.[29]

Racing continued to be McDonogh's main passion outside of his business and political interests, but his choice of J.J. Parkinson as trainer of his expanding stable of racehorses was based as much on Parkinson's political philosophy as on his reputation as one of the best trainers in the country.[30] Like McDonogh, Parkinson had been on the pro-Treaty side during the Civil War, was a great supporter of Cosgrave, and despised de Valera. Parkinson was elected to the senate as an independent, non-party candidate, but his political affiliations were avowedly Cumann na nGaedhael.[31] Another senator, who was a mutual friend of both McDonogh and Parkinson, was Oliver St John Gogarty, who had similar political affiliations. They shared a detestation of de Valera, Gogarty remarking that he looked 'like a laugh in mourning'.[32]

Gogarty and Stephen Gwynn frequently attended the Galway Races as McDonogh's guests. McDonogh's enjoyment of racing was enhanced by the fact that he had two particularly good horses in his stable, Kyleclare and Irish Fun. While Kyleclare had already scored a number of successes, Kyleclare's half-brother, Irish Fun, was at that point just beginning what would become a glittering career. McDonogh kept a couple of brood mares and had other horses in training with Parkinson. Given his lifelong interest in racing, and the enormous influence he had had on the development of the Galway course, it is hardly surprising that his proudest moment on the turf was winning the Galway Hurdle in 1931 with Kyleclare, a horse he had bred himself. The horse

28 *Connacht Tribune*, 2 Feb. 1929. 29 Ibid., 10 Sept. 1927. 30 Parkinson's record of 2,577 wins stood for over 50 years, when it was finally beaten by Dermot Weld in 2000. *The Kerryman*, 18 Aug. 2000. 31 Hyland, *History of Galway Races*, p. 110. 32 Lyons, J.B., *Oliver St John Gogarty* (Lewisburg, PA, 1976), p. 81.

had looked like an exceptional prospect, having won races at both the Curragh and Leopardstown in 1930, and impressively winning his maiden hurdle race at Naas in early 1931. Kyleclare then appeared to lose some of his momentum, losing at Baldoyle some months later. But the Galway Races loomed, and, as Hyland notes:

> It is probable that Kyleclare only ran in the big Galway race because his owner was the chairman of the racecourse, because he did not appear to be at all fancied. However, Kyleclare rose magnificently to the occasion, winning the Galway Hurdle in some style, beating Gus Mangan on Sahabelle by five lengths.[33] Although the horse had not been backed,[34] the public loudly cheered Martin McDonogh, who had done so much for Galway, as an employer and a politician.[35]

The *Tribune* agreed, noting that:

> the most popular win in the Galway Hurdle race for years was that of Kyleclare ... which cantered home. Mr McDonogh, who was accompanied by Captain Stephen Gwynn, ex-MP for Galway, received many congratulations. There was a rush from the stand to greet him, and loud cheers were raised when he proudly led the winner in.[36]

Kyleclare never won another race, but he had delivered when and where it mattered.

LABOUR ISSUES

In February 1927 a dispute arose between the ITGWU and the Employers' Federation concerning the appointment of stevedores, who essentially operated as subcontractors, managing the loading and unloading of ships. They had control over the selection of those employed to load or unload a particular vessel, and, the union argued, were frequently guilty of favouritism. The union was seeking to dispense with stevedores, and allow the union to

33 The *Connacht Tribune* reported that Kyleclare won by seven lengths. *Connacht Tribune*, 1 Aug. 1931. 34 There was, however, one lucky winner, who had a double on the Galway Plate and the Galway Hurdle, and won £73 2*s*. as a result. *Connacht Tribune*, 1 Aug. 1931. 35 Hyland, *History of Galway Races*, p. 111. 36 *Connacht Tribune*, 1 Aug. 1931.

appoint and manage dock labourers, which would have been anathema to McDonogh and his fellow employers. When no resolution to the conflict was forthcoming, the dockers went on strike, at a time when a ship carrying a much-needed cargo of coal for McDonoghs was due for unloading. Mobilising a group of his employees, McDonogh took matters into his own hands, as the *Connacht Tribune* reported:

> Mr Martin McDonogh appeared on the scene today at 10.15. The dockers who were standing around advanced to meet Mr McDonogh's men who were called upon not to undertake the work. Mr McDonogh brought his men forward and there were several interchanges between him and Mr Lynch and other leaders of the dockers. Things looked unpleasant for a while, and Mr McDonogh was obliged to push back men who stood in his way.[37]

A shouting match between the two sides commenced, in the course of which one of the union men stated that they only wanted fair play, and McDonogh replied that 'they always got that from him'.[38] An incensed McDonogh declared that he would 'close down my whole place rather than put up with this', noting, not without justification, that he had 'increased wages when others did not'. McDonogh eventually sent his men away, some of them still protesting that they 'would do the work if you want us to do it',[39] and the dockers agreed to unload the cargo a few hours later.

The writer and Inis Mór native Máirtín Ó Direáin recalled that when he first encountered him in Galway sometime between 1928 and 1930, McDonogh wore a monocle – or, as Ó Direáin puts it, 'Bhíodh súil ghloine aige' ('He had a glass eye'). Ó Direáin relates that while staying in lodgings in the docks in Galway his landlord took him to the door one day, during a dockers' strike, and, pointing to McDonogh, said, 'Do you see him going down now, do you see him now with his glass eye? Ea! He'll be pushing up daisies in Forthill yet!' Ó Díreáin's description of McDonogh at the time was of a large man carrying a big stick, and he recalls his landlord noting, with some bitterness, that McDonogh 'wouldn't give the poor workers a shilling'.[40] However, Ó Díreáin was another who acknowledged that McDonogh was

37 This was the Gilbert Lynch, who, as we have seen, was subsequently elected as Galway's first Labour TD in the June 1927 election. *Connacht Tribune*, 5 Feb. 1927. 38 Ibid. 39 Ibid. 40 This is a reference to a claim for an increase in wages of 1*s.* which the dockers had demanded and which McDonogh refused to agree to. The result was an all-out strike of dockers, which crippled the port for months.

considered to be a 'big' man, both in terms of his size and his generosity, observing:

> Cinnte, bhí sé mór i dtoirrt. Níl a fhios agam an raibh sé mór ó aon taobh eile! Déarfadh daoine go raibh, daoine a raibh aithne acu air, go ndearna sé cuid mhór garaíochta do dhaoine, mar a dearfá, os íseal. [Certainly he was large in body, I don't know if he was large in any other way! But people said that he was, people who knew him. That he did a lot of good turns for people, as they say, quietly.]

Ó Direáin wrote a poem about his experiences of that time, entitled 'An stailc' or 'The strike', which refers to a Galway expression of the time, 'Ne'er a wing, ne'er a wet', 'wing' being a colloquialism for the word 'penny' (derived from the Irish word for penny, 'pingin'), and 'wet' being the Galway slang for a pint of porter. When the workers in Hynes' mills went on strike for a rise of one shilling, and with only limited strike pay available, one of the workers told Ó Direáin that they had 'ne'er a wing nor a wet'. Ó Direáin's poem is an indictment of employers such as McDonogh, who were considered to be wholly unsympathetic to the great poverty and deprivations of their workforce, referring to them disparagingly as '*toicí*' or 'tycoons'.

Although not naming them directly, Ó Direáin expressed the view that there were merchants in Galway:

> nach dtabharfaidís pingin rua duit dá mbeifeá ag fáil bháis ar an dtáirseach, agus ní raibh aon spéis acu in ealaín ná i litríocht ná in aon rud mar sin. [I'm certain they would not give a penny if you were dying on the threshold, and they had no interest in art or literature or anything of that sort.]

There is some evidence that McDonogh had no real interest in art or literature, but one writer whom he did know well was his cousin, the writer Pádraic Ó Conaire. Ó Direáin records that Criostóir Mac Aonghusa was present when someone was upbraiding Ó Conaire for his lifestyle,[41] which was somewhat dissolute when compared to that of his cousin Máirtín Mór:

41 Born in Bannagher, Co. Offaly, Criostóir Mac Aonghusa (1905–91) was an Irish-language writer and teacher.

> Is é an scéal a bhí ag Criostóir MacAonghusa go raibh duine éigin ag caitheamh síos ar Phádraic i ngeall ar a gcineál saoil a bhí sé a chaitheamh. 'Cén fáth nach mbeifeá mar seo is mar siúd. Féach do dhuine muintreach anois, Máirtín Mór, an chaoi a ndeachaigh seisean ar aghaidh sa saol'. 'Dá dtagadh Tolstoy go Gaillimh', arsa Pádraic, 'ní hé Máirtín Mór a bheadh sé ag iarraidh a fheiceáil ar chor ar bith, ach Pádraic Ó Conaire!' [Criostóir MacAonghusa had the story that someone was denigrating Pádraic on account of the kind of life he was leading. 'Why can't you be like this or that. Look at your relative now, Máirtín Mór, and the way he got on in life'. 'If Tolstoy came to Galway' says Pádraic, 'it wouldn't be Máirtín Mór he'd be looking to see at all, it would be Pádraic Ó Conaire.']

The complex relationship between McDonogh and his talented but somewhat feckless cousin lasted throughout their lives. In spite of Ó Conaire's personal problems and his difficulties with alcohol, McDonogh showed great tolerance and kindness towards him, providing him with money and shelter when he needed them. Ó Conaire's biographer, an tSr Eibhlín Ní Chionnaith, notes that McDonogh was not alone in this, and that another of the extended family, Pádraic Ó Máille, was similarly disposed to extend hospitality to Ó Conaire when it was needed,[42] stating 'bhí gean ag Pádraic Mór Ó Máille ar Ó Conaire fosta, agus ag Máirtín Mór Mac Donncha, fear nár chuir mórán spéise sa litríocht. Bhí lóistín le fáil aige am ar bith sa teach seo acusan' ['Pádraic Mór Ó Máille always had affection for Ó Conaire, as did Máirtín Mór MacDonogh, a man who did not have much interest in literature. There was always a bed available to him in their houses'].[43] While familial ties were clearly important to McDonogh, his cousin, twenty-two years his junior, was a source of both pride and embarrassment to him.

Ó Conaire's literary brilliance, even as a young man, was widely acknowledged, as were his charm, his gentle personality and the sterling work he had done, through his teaching and writing, on the preservation and promotion of the Irish language. However, his desertion of his family in England, his

42 Another who did so was Dr Michael O'Malley, from Kilmilkin, Co. Galway, another cousin and a respected surgeon, and professor of Surgery at UCG. Ó Conaire had introduced O' Malley to his future wife, Christina Ryan, (of the noted republican Ryan family of Tomcoole, Co. Wexford) at a Gaelic League function in London in 1916. Thereafter when Dr O'Malley set up his medical practice in Galway, Ó Conaire was a frequent visitor, soliciting 'loans' from O'Malley, which were never refused, and never repaid. The late Eibhlín Uí Chionna, daughter of Dr O'Malley, is the source for this story.

43 Ní Chionnaith, An tSr Eibhlín, *Pádraic Ó Conaire: scéal a bheatha* (Indreabhán, 1995), p. 435.

problems with alcohol, and the soliciting of financial and other help from friends and family doubtless strained relationships with relatives such as the McDonoghs. And so did behaviour like that McDonogh witnessed when he attended the first public performance of Mac Liammóir's production of *Diarmuid agus Gráinne* at the Taibhdhearc theatre on 27 August 1928. The minister for finance, Ernest Blythe,[44] and Galway's leading civic and artistic figures, including Lady Gregory, were in attendance.[45] The performance was about to commence when Ó Conaire, clearly inebriated, appeared on stage and had to be forcibly removed when he tried to make a speech.[46] While McDonogh may have disapproved of such conduct, he appears never to have fully abandoned Ó Conaire, and was among his chief mourners at his funeral when he died only months later in October 1928.[47]

HORSES AND HOUSES

By the late 1920s, McDonogh was a significant figure in the Irish racing world, both as a breeder and owner of racehorses and in his capacity as chairman of the Galway Race Committee. The regard in which McDonogh was held in the racing world is evidenced by the fact that in 1928 the Irish Provincial Racecourse Executives' Association ended hostilities between the various racing bodies when they nominated McDonogh to be their representative on the new tote board of control.[48] It had, quite literally, been involved in a 'turf war' with the Turf Club and the Irish National Hunt Steeplechase Committee over the question of who would control the tote about to be introduced as a result of the Totalisator Act of 1929.

In September 1928 the Turf Club called a conference of all racing interests

44 Blythe, a keen Gaelgeoir, had granted a subsidy of £600 a year to the fledgling Irish-language theatre. *Irish Times*, 29 Aug. 1928. 45 Stafford, S., 'Taibhdhearc na Gaillimhe: Galway's Gaelic theatre', in *Journal of the Galway Archaeological and Historical Society*, 54 (2002), 183–214. 46 Ní Chionnaith, *Pádraic Ó Conaire*, p. 447. Ó Conaire bitterly regretted his actions on the night, and, as Ní Chionnaith records, having been forced from the stage, 'Thosaigh sé ag caoineadh, agus chonaic Mícheál Ó Droighneáin é in aice le Coill Bhearna agus é ag gol fós.' ('He started crying, and Mícheál Ó Droighneáin saw him beside Barna Woods, and he was still crying.') 47 Ó Conaire died, alone and penniless, in the Richmond Hospital, Dublin, having been taken ill with stomach pains while visiting the offices of the Gaelic League, on 6 Oct. 1928. He was 46. The other chief mourners were Ó Conaire's brother, Isaac Conroy, his nephew P. Ó Conaire, and J.S. Conroy, solicitor and coroner. *Irish Independent*, 9 Oct. 1928. It is unclear whether Ó Conaire's widow attended the funeral, some accounts saying that she did, money having been raised to enable her to travel from England, and others that she did not. 48 Hyland, *History of Galway Races*, p. 84.

to discuss arrangements for the introduction of the tote. As Fergus D'Arcy has noted:

> it was widely expected to be a bloody encounter, but instead turned out to be marked by give and take. The general agreement in principle of all those concerned on the composition of the tote board constituted a major achievement in the circumstances and cleared the way for the government to proceed to the necessary legislation.[49]

By August 1928, McDonoghs had entered the property development business. Having secured a prime site at Presentation Road, four new houses were built and advertised for sale by Thomas McDonogh & Sons.[50] These well-designed, substantial homes were intended to house the families of members of the up-and-coming business and professional classes, of which there were increasing numbers in Galway, thanks largely to the efforts of McDonogh and his fellow members of the Galway chamber of commerce. To his credit, McDonogh was also mindful of the housing needs of Galway's less affluent citizens. His brother Michael, medical officer for Galway, had designated the Claddagh fishing village as 'unhealthy', and recommended the demolition of all of the houses.[51] Martin, then chairman of the urban district council, was adamant that 'no houses will be pulled down until homes are built first. We are not such fools as to waste money pulling down good houses.'[52] In this, Martin McDonogh had the support of a good many of the Claddagh residents – 200 of them – who favoured improving the houses rather than demolishing them. McDonogh noted that there were a good many of the houses 'that could, with a little expense, be made habitable, and it seems a pity to knock these down and build new ones when the people don't want them.'[53] His support of the Claddagh people, however, fell on deaf ears, and demolition of the houses began in 1931, with the last two tenants removed in February 1935.[54]

While housing was one pressing issue, another – which occupied the harbour commissioners – was the prospect of increased numbers of passenger liners calling to the port. The arrival of the *Muenchen* had led to a

49 D'Arcy, *Horses, lords and racing men*, p. 286. 50 *Connacht Tribune*, 28 Aug. 1926. 51 Two hundred fifty-five Claddagh houses had been surveyed, and of these 51 were classed as 'poor', 69 as 'bad' and 106 as 'very bad'. *Galway Advertiser*, 18 Dec. 2008. 52 *Connacht Sentinel*, 23 Oct. 1928. 53 Galway urban district council minutes, arbitration inquiry into Claddagh housing scheme, 30 Sept. 1931. 54 *Connacht Tribune*, 9 Feb. 1935.

number of cruise-ship companies expressing an interest in visting Galway. By 1928 various unsuccessful attempts had been made by the harbour commissioners to secure a suitable tender to facilitate the calling of liners to the port. McDonogh's frustration with the procrastination of the commissioners eventually resulted in him taking matters into his own hands. He went to London and offered £2,600 to shipbrokers Little and Co. for a tender named the *Lancashire,* which was capable of carrying 1,000 passengers.[55] His offer was refused, the asking price being £3,600. McDonogh promptly offered £3,000, which was accepted. He arranged a temporary overdraft to pay for the vessel and have it inspected, and to have repairs totalling £400 carried out. Feted by the commissioners on his return to Galway, who congratulated him on the money he had saved them, McDonogh's response was typical: 'I do not know that I saved you a lot of money,' he replied, 'but I surely saved you some.'[56] The tender was subsequently renamed *Cathair na Gaillimhe* on the orders of the minister for lands and fisheries.[57]

The year 1929 brought extreme highs and lows for McDonogh, which was reflected in the fact that he rarely attended the Dáil, and only made one contribution to a Dáil debate.[58] The fertilizer-manufacturing division of McDonoghs became a limited company with share capital of £15,000, and the continuing success of the flour mill and the fertilizer plant, and the other employment provided by McDonoghs in the sawmills, fertilizer stores, timber stores, offices and coal yards saw to it that McDonoghs was the principal driver of Galway's economic recovery in the difficult first decade of the fledgling Free State. The management of a business empire that was by now employing more than 400 people was a considerable burden, and although Martin was well served by his senior managers such as Frederick Coy and could draw on the services of his brother T.C. when required, it was he who controlled the reins. He could no longer depend on the counsel and company of his friend Fr John Flatley, who died on 8 September 1929.[59] At the funeral, McDonogh heard Flatley described by the archbishop of Tuam

55 The vessel was purchased from the Birkenhead Corporation. *Irish Times,* 11 Nov. 1929. 56 Woodman, K., *Safe and commodious,* p. 194. 57 In 1931 the harbour commissioners were approached by a steamship brokers in England who wanted to know whether the *Cathair na Gaillimhe* might be for sale. McDonogh responded 'Ask them what offer they would make us for her. We might consider a tempting offer.' *Connacht Sentinel,* 17 Feb. 1931. 58 Dáil Debate, Private Deputies' Business – Erasmus Smith Endowment, 29 May 1929. 59 Fr Flatley left his entire (quite considerable) estate to his two sisters, with the proviso that on their deaths, the residue would accrue to the Jubilee Institute for Nurses for the support of a Jubilee nurse to be appointed to his final parish, Aughagower, and thereafter to Jervis Street and St Vincent's hospitals 'for the advantage of poor patients in those institutions from the parish of Aughagower'.

as 'a remarkable man who had a well-defined character. He was a lover of justice and when there was a question of principle with him, there was no compromise. He never tried to take the path of least resistance.'[60] Within five years, similar sentiments would be expressed at McDonogh's own funeral.

AIRMAIL FLIGHT

Galway's development, for which McDonogh was so ambitious, received a major boost with the departure from the city of the first airmail service linking Ireland and the UK. This experimental flight, organized by Col. Charles Russell, a founder member of the Irish Air Corps, left Oranmore Aerodrome for London on 26 August 1929. Russell's arrival was eagerly anticipated in Galway, and McDonogh received a telegram from him, which McDonogh posted in the window of the GPO, stating that Russell was leaving Chester and would 'wire the time of his arrival in Galway from Baldonnel'.[61] Having arrived in Galway at 4.05 p.m., Col. Russell collected the mail. Several thousand items of mail went on the flight, weighing 90 lbs, franked with a special oval lithograph inscribed 'First Airmail Galway-London, 26th August 1929'.[62] Col. Russell then flew to Croydon, and the bulk of the mail destined for London was delivered that evening. The plane returned to Oranmore that evening at 7 p.m. A celebratory banquet, hosted by McDonogh, was attended by over a hundred guests, including T.J. Connell, leader of the Labour Party, and Senator St John Gogarty.[63]

THE HOUSE OF GOLD

The elation McDonogh must have felt as a result of the successful mail flight soon dissipated as a result of the publication of Liam O'Flaherty's book *The house of gold*, which, although nominally a work of fiction, was based 'on the rise to affluence of the MacDonagh [*sic*] family in Galway',[64] and depicted

60 *Mayo News*, 14 Sept. 1929. 61 Ibid. 62 *Irish Independent*, 26 Aug. 1929. 63 President Cosgrave and Eamon de Valera were to have attended the banquet, but had to pull out at the last minute. *Irish Independent*, 26 Aug. 1929. 64 Sheeran, P., quoted in Higgins, M.D., 'Liam O'Flaherty & Peadar O'Donnell – images of rural community' in *The Crane Bag*, 9:1 (1985), 41–8 at 41.

Martin McDonogh as the 'fat-faced sweaty-headed swine' Ramon Mór Costello. As the writer A.J. Cronin has observed:

> Post-independence Ireland was a disappointment to many who had hoped for a true 'revival' of ancient culture for a revolutionary new form of society. Poverty, piety, and political conservatism produced a petty bourgeois state and the writers became increasingly critical of the existing order.[65]

Among these writers was O'Flaherty, a native of Inis Mór in the Aran Islands, whose 'pet hates were oppressors, especially clerical bullies, and those who would grind the poor'.[66] O'Flaherty wasn't alone in his views. As John Zneimer has observed, 'Sean O'Casey thought that all hope for Ireland died when the dream of the republic was abandoned in favour of the Free State supported by a combination of Catholic church and middle-class business interests.'[67]

Set in the fictional town of Barra – easily recognizable as Galway – *The house of gold* charts the way in which, as O'Flaherty saw it, the old order was replaced in the emerging Free State by 'an equally oppressive native gombeen ascendancy, buttressed by the Catholic church',[68] symbolized in the novel by the avaricious Ramon Mór Costello. Ramon Mór is clearly based on Martin McDonogh, from his enormous size, gruff manner and humble origins to his domineering mother, spinster sister (who in the book is clearly a lesbian) and the fact that 'one of his eyes was closed, the other was wide open and fixed', a reference to McDonogh's monocle. Ramon Mór lives in a substantial seaside house, with his mother and sister, and is married to the beautiful Nora, a much younger woman, who despises him. That O'Flaherty names his main female character Nora, the name by which McDonogh's mother Honoria was most commonly known, is no accident, and neither is the fact that the name Ramon is clearly a reference to McDonogh's grandfather of the same name. It was not, however, the similarities with the real-life McDonogh family that caused the most controversy when the book was published in 1929. In the moral climate which existed in Ireland in the 1920s and 1930s, the book was controversial for a great many other reasons, incorporating, as it did,

65 Cronin, A.J., 'The Irish novel', *A question of modernity* (London, 1966). 66 *Irish Independent*, 29 May 1993. 67 Zneimer, J., *The literary vision of Liam O'Flaherty* (Syracuse, 1970), p. 23. 68 Mac Síomóin, T., 'Introduction' in O'Flaherty, *The house of gold*, p. 4.

themes of greed, priestly lust, alcoholism, sexual frustration and ultimately murder. It is hardly surprising, therefore, that it was banned.

O'Flaherty's knowledge of the dynamics of the McDonogh family resulted in a keenly observed portrait of that family, which is in turn cruel, searingly honest and incisive. At one point it is said of the Costello family that 'they were great managers … they denied themselves, and they have the benefit of it',[69] but there was a price to pay for that self-denial, and, as Patrick Sheeran observes, although the character of Ramon Mór is 'assured in the public world of men and affairs, he is pathetic in the private',[70] being under the thumb of his bitter, controlling mother, and unloved by his beautiful trophy wife, with whom he is impotent. Ramon Mór is a terrifying character, but, as Zneimer notes:

> for all his colossal exterior and eccentricities of avarice, Ramon is not a monster or a caricature. He has feelings, fears, doubts, but in keeping with the character of a person who by force of will has raised himself from poverty to wealth and power.[71]

O'Flaherty's portrayal of the McDonoghs as being typical of the ruthlessly ambitious dynastic families who emerged to dominate the business and political worlds of independent Ireland is to a degree justifiable. The family's calculated and tenacious rise to power represented everything O'Flaherty – who had committed to the communist cause briefly in the early 1920s – hated. Political philosophies aside, however, O'Flaherty and his extended family had a much more personal reason to dislike the McDonogh family. The O'Flaherty family had been the subject of an attempted eviction from their home in Gort na gCapall in 1892, and Tom O'Flaherty gives a searing account of the experience in his book *Aranmen all*, remarking, 'I never got over it. The bitterness born within me by this act only grew stronger with the passing of years.'[72] The bailiff who tried to bring about the eviction was Bartly Hernon, brother of Honoria Hernon, and Martin McDonogh's uncle. Traumatic as the eviction was for the O'Flaherty family, Tom O'Flaherty, a lifelong communist and a talented writer, acknowledged that the treatment of his family was far from unique:

69 O'Flaherty, *The house of gold* (Leipzig, 1929), p. 93. 70 Sheeran, P.F., *The novels of Liam O'Flaherty*, p. 171. 71 Zneimer, J., *The literary vision of Liam O'Flaherty* (Syracuse, 1970), p. 106. 72 O'Flaherty, T., *Aranmen all* (Dingle, 1991), p. 69.

> I learned soon enough that this was no isolated act of vengeance vented on us, but the common lot of those who got caught between the iron fangs of the world's misfortune, and that the punishment for poverty was not only visited upon the parents, but even on their little children.[73]

Although Tom O'Flaherty's younger brother, Liam, was not born until 1896, four years after the attempted eviction, the O'Flahertys' bitterness and hatred towards the Hernons and their McDonogh relatives did not escape him, and was rendered even more pronounced by the increasing gap between the well-off McDonoghs and the academically gifted but increasingly impoverished O'Flahertys of Aran.

The animosity between the O'Flahertys and the McDonoghs antecedents went back even further than the attempted eviction in 1892. Liam O'Flaherty's mother, Margaret (Maggie) Ganly, was the sister of the Tomás Ganly, who, as we have seen, had in 1882 fired upon Martin McDonogh's uncle, the bailiff Bartly Hernon, and then fled to America, only confessing his guilt on his deathbed. Maggie Ganly had eloped and married Mike O'Flaherty (Maidhc Ó Flaithearta) of Gort na gCapall, and he had been arrested on a number of occasions in connection with Land League activities, including on a charge of firing on a bailiff – who could only have been Bartly Hernon. The antipathy of the combined O'Flaherty/Ganly families to the Hernons, and by extension their McDonogh cousins, was therefore of long standing, and was certainly not helped by the fact that, by 1920, Martin McDonogh was one of the three councillors elected to represent the Aran Islands on Galway county council (another being Patrick Hernon), in spite of the fact that he did not – and never had – lived there.

The characterization of Ramon Mór as a classic 'gombeen' man was to some degree a fair representation of Martin McDonogh. According to one definition, the 'gombeen man' was:

> the one who grabbed up the derelict sites, the farms denuded of people, the residue of once thriving commerce and local enterprise. He was the big shot of his times. He saw opportunities and seized them. He knew the price of everything, and of every person. In many areas he was the sole grocer, landlord, and canny money lender. It never bothered him that he was known as a gombeen man. It was a derogatory term when

73 Ibid., p. 70.

> used by others, but what did he care? The others in almost all cases were in his debt.[74]

While much of this description could apply to McDonogh, there is no evidence that he was ever involved in moneylending. There is, however, anecdotal evidence to suggest that it was not unusual for him to provide the money for a ticket to America to a would-be emigrant, in exchange for the deeds to property being left behind.[75] Sheeran also observed that 'if one wished to escape from the drudgery of rural life, the paternal firm could place a man or advance the fare to America, provided of course, that he professed the right political beliefs'.[76] Although perceived as exploitatative by some, in reality this was simply a pragmatic answer to a common problem, the sort of barter arrangement that had been the lynchpin of McDonogh's dealings with small farmers, who, short on cash, preferred to exchange goods for feed, seed and other provisions.

O'Flaherty can hardly have been surprised at the reaction to *The house of gold*. Writing to his literary agent, A.D. Peters, in January 1929, O'Flaherty observed, 'My novel is going splendidly but it's becoming rather terrible. It will frighten the life out of people.'[77] And frighten – and antagonize – people it did. The reaction of the McDonogh family was understandably hostile.[78] Still, Martin McDonogh made no public statement regarding the novel, and does not appear to have considered legal action against O'Flaherty, however much he might have been infuriated by the unsavoury caricatures of himself and his family. Perhaps this was because he recognized that 'if a man libels an individual he is called strong names; if he libels a whole people collectively, and does it with literary craftsmanship, of a high order, he is called an intellectual'.[79] In the end, the censorship of publications board decided the matter, the story making the pages of the *New York Times*. *The house of gold* was not subsequently published in Ireland until more than eighty years later, in 2013.

74 *The Canadian Vindicator*, 7:9 (1 Oct. 2009). 75 This was a not-uncommon practice. The Conroys of Gairfean, Rosmuc, cousins of the McDonoghs, who owned a shop from which they also operated a travel agency, frequently sold tickets to America by instalment, or on the basis of credit, the money being repaid when the emigrant secured employment in the US. 76 Sheeran, *The novels of Liam O'Flaherty*, p. 41. 77 Kelly, *The letters of Liam O'Flaherty*, p. 228. 78 The McDonogh family's resentment of O'Flaherty lasted for some time. At a party held by one of Dr Michael McDonogh's daughters, when the guest list was being reviewed, and the name of Bréandán Ó hEithir, a nephew of O'Flaherty's, appeared on the list, it was immediately struck off. 79 *The Kerryman*, 28 Dec. 1929.

A QUESTION OF LEGITIMACY

The depiction of Martin McDonogh's alter ego, Ramon Mór Costello, in *The house of gold*, is one of the few insights we have into McDonogh's character, even though it takes the form of literary fiction. No personal correspondence from him survives, and with virtually no surviving official document pertaining to his life and career, the few documents that do survive must be closely scrutinized for clues as to who Martin McDonogh was. In this regard, the 1901 and 1911 census records prove perplexing. In both, the ages of the McDonogh siblings are wildly understated, with eleven years taken off McDonogh's actual age in both census returns, the first of which was completed by his father, the second completed by himself (see table below).

	1901 Census			1911 Census		
	Stated age	Actual age	Difference	Stated age	Actual age	Difference
Martin	30	41	-11	40	51	-11
T.C.	27	37	-10	38	47	-9
Mary Ann	22	32	-10	36	42	-6
Kate	20	28	-8	32	38	-6
Michael[80]	27	30	-3	34	40	-6

A report from the register general in 1896 stated that the age column was 'the most liable to the suspicion of inaccuracy',[81] in many cases due to genuine confusion as to the atctual date of birth. In Ireland, official birth records date from 1864, when the civil registration system was introduced. Prior to this, the birth of a child was recorded only by baptism or christening. And even when it became compulsory to register all births with a local registrar, some were not recorded, particularly in the early years, for a variety of reasons. This was particularly the case in the West of Ireland, where estimates on non-registration of births are put as high as 15 per cent, largely as a result of the remoteness of vast areas there, which meant that making a trek to an official registration office might take a day or more, in difficult conditions.[82]

Discrepencies could also be related to attempts to cover up an illegitimate

80 Michael was, as we have seen, a medical student in Dublin when the 1901 census was taken, but an age discrepancy is also reflected on the census return completed at the address he lived at in Dublin at that time. 81 Christian, P. and D. Annal, *Census: the family historian's guide* (London, 2014), p. 102. 82 The rate of non-compliance with registration laws is estimated at 10% for the rest of the country, for at least the first fifteen years following their introduction.

birth, a birth that had occurred before the parents had married, or so soon after the marriage that it would have been obvious that conception had taken place prior to the marriage. An illegitimate birth was so shameful that families often went to great lengths to hush it up, even to the point of falsifying official records. Discrepancies of a few years were common particularly following the introduction of the old-age pension in 1909, when changes sought to increase the ages of the respondents to make them eligible for the state pension sooner.

The question then remains: why were such significant discrepancies a feature of the McDonogh census returns, and if, as seems certain, the errors were deliberate, why did the McDonoghs find it necessary to falsify official state documents?

Given that birth certificates exist for all of the McDonogh children from T.C. onwards,[83] the only children whose birth details might be open to question are Martin and Redmond, whose births preceded the introduction of civil registration in 1864. The question must be asked, therefore, whether Martin, and possibly Redmond, were born to Thomas McDonogh and Honoria Hernon before they married. While civil Irish marriage records date back to 1845 in respect of non-Catholic marriages, registration of all marriages, regardless of religion, dates only from the introduction of civil registration in 1864. Prior to this, the only records of marriages are to be found in local parish registers. An examination of parish records has, to date, yielded no record of the marriage of Thomas and Honoria, so we cannot be sure when or where they married. Similarly, the parish register of An Chillín, Carraroe, where, according to the certification provided by Fr Melleth to the University of London in 1878, Martin and Redmond were baptized, does not, in fact, record their baptism.

It is, of course, entirely possible that Martin McDonogh was baptized in a parish other than An Chillín, whose records have since disappeared, or indeed, as result of an error, that his baptism was simply never recorded. However, McDonogh's evasiveness regarding his age raises suspicion – he was the only student of 73 who entered the college that year not to enter his age on the register of Queen's College Galway in 1878. Other clues also give credence to the possibility that Martin McDonogh was born illegitimate, or at the very least born so close to his parents' marriage that his conception outside marriage might have given rise to scandal. Local folklore provides a

83 Thomas Christopher McDonogh is recorded as having been born on 25 Dec. 1864.

possible answer, although it is clearly unverifiable. Anecdotal evidence suggests that the abrupt departure of Martin's father, Thomas McDonogh, from Gorumna was not primarily as a result of his frustration with life on the remote island and his ambition to improve his lot, but rather as a result of the scandal created when he 'made a young girl from Aran pregnant'.[84]

If such were indeed the case, then it would certainly explain a great deal regarding the depiction of the Ramon Mór/Martin McDonogh character in O'Flaherty's *The house of gold*. O'Flaherty, as we have seen, had every reason – including one of a very personal nature – to dislike the McDonoghs, and if his intention was to hurt Martin McDonogh in his depiction of Ramon Mór, then naming Ramon Mór's wife Nora could be interpreted as a very effective means of doing so. Martin McDonogh, as we have seen, was extremely close to his mother, and Nora was the name by which she was commonly known. The fact that the Nora of *The house of gold* is revealed, prior to her marriage to Ramon Mór, to have had a child outside of wedlock when she was only 16 may have been O'Flaherty's way of sticking a barb into Martin McDonogh in a way that he knew would wound him to his very core. If there was a long-buried secret in the McDonogh family, a secret that necessitated a deliberate falsification of census records to convey the impression that the McDonogh children were younger than they actually were, and were all born, respectably, following their parents' marriage, then O'Flaherty may have been letting McDonogh know that, in spite of all his power, money and influence, memories in Connemara and Aran were long, and that Honoria and Thomas McDonogh's indiscretion had not been forgotten.

O'Flaherty's depiction of Ramon Mór as being in thrall to his domineering and paranoid mother may also give credence to the illegitimacy theory. In her choice of husband, Honoria Hernon, the daughter of a bailiff, a man of significant status and power in the community, could be seen to have married somewhat below her social status. That she may have been obliged to do so as a result of an unplanned pregnancy could potentially have had significant consequences for all of Honoria's children, but particularly Martin. Honoria kept a very tight rein on her children, especially Martin. His mother's apparent determination to strictly control his social life and to actively discourage her sons from marrying may have been linked to a fear of allowing into the family outsiders who might have uncovered the truth behind Martin's birth, something she may have been determined to avoid at all cost.

84 John Bhaba Jeaic Ó Confhaola of Ionad Oidhreachta Leitir Mealláin confirmed this aspect of local folklore.

The depiction of Ramon Mór's mother in *The house of gold* certainly infers that this was indeed the case with regard to Ramon Mór Costello. O'Flaherty's observation of the Costelloes, that 'they denied themselves, and they have the benefit of it',[85] is telling in this regard, but, there was a terrible price – the price of isolation and loneliness – to pay for that self-denial. In the absence of hard evidence, we can never know for certain whether Honoria McDonogh, similarly, was prepared to pay that price in order to avoid the loss of face resulting from the scandal of illegitimacy, and was determined that her precious son and heir would not fall prey to an opportunistic woman who might trap him in marriage and threaten or undermine the McDonogh family. O'Flaherty hints at such when he observes of Ramon Mór's mother:

> She idolised her son, with the avaricious love of a peasant woman. She hated Nora for having come between her and her son. For fifty years Ramon had belonged completely to her. The first time he escaped from her he was captured.[86]

All of this is, however, mere conjecture, and cannot be proven. But, were it to be the case that Martin McDonogh was illegitimate, or possibly conceived before his parents were married, it would explain a great deal about the complex, secretive man, who revealed very little of his personal feelings, who never drank, never socialized with women to any great degree and never married.

The other point on which McDonogh was sensitive – and vulnerable to ridicule – was that he never married. The fact that he did not do so, and that he did not have any romantic relationships with women that we know of, raises the question of whether he was romantically attracted to men, but unable or unwilling to pursue such relationships. O'Flaherty's portrayal of Ramon Mór Costello as impotent with his young and attractive wife may resonate with McDonogh's own character. While there is some anecdotal evidence to suggest that McDonogh may have been attracted to men, there is no concrete evidence to support this theory, and the fact that McDonogh did not marry may simply be attributable to personal choice or societal factors, rather than to his own sexual preference. There is a case to be made that McDonogh was a prime example of what was a relatively common social phenomenon in Ireland at the time, particularly amongst men of his class and

85 O'Flaherty, *The house of gold* (Leipzig, 1929), p. 93. 86 Ibid., p. 51.

status: the rich man, who chose, as Cameron has observed, to remain in 'single blessedness'.[87] Late marriage and 'permanent celibacy' were a marked feature of post-Famine Ireland. In the period 1864–70, the annual marriage rate per 1,000 of the population was 5.10; that figure dropped to 4.02 for the period 1881–90, and, as Cosgrave has noted, those born between 1896 and 1910 'displayed the greatest reluctance to marry of any Irish generation'.[88] This trend was much more pronounced in Ireland than was the case with her nearest neighbours, Ferriter noting that in 1907, the marriage rate in Ireland was '40 per cent below that of England and Wales, and 35 per cent below Scotland', the *Farmer's Journal* even going so far as to conclude that men preferred 'the selfish ease of batchelor life'. [89]

It was also the case that, in a practical sense, McDonogh didn't need to marry, as he enjoyed the comfort of having unmarried sisters who were prepared to fulfil the role of unpaid housekeepers – what Guinnane has termed 'marriage substitutes'.[90] Guinnane has noted that 'living with a sibling enabled a household head to share risk and household services without assuming the burden of child rearing'.[91] Noonan, similarly, was moved to observe that by the mid-twentieth century it was frequently the case that:

> it is the man in possession of all the normal comforts of life who emerges into confirmed batchelorhood. He does not require a woman to cook his meals or to keep his home in order. He can pay a maid, or he may have a loyal unmarried sister. In his eyes marriage is more a disability than a blessing.[92]

In addition, possibly as a result of the shadow of illegitimacy that hung over his family, McDonogh may have had an innate fear of sex, and its consequences, a fear that O'Flaherty implies in *The house of gold* was compounded by McDonogh's mother. It was certainly the case that McDonogh lived in an age when, as Ferriter has observed, 'condemnations and warnings abounded and there were deemed to be sexual traps and temptations around every corner'.[93] He was, then, a man of his time in a culture that was not overtly sexualised, and where the compulsion to marry was infinitely less pressing in

87 Cameron, C.A., *Reminiscences of Sir Charles Cameron CB* (Dublin, 1913), p. 168. 88 Cosgrove, A. (ed.), *Marriage in Ireland* (Dublin, 1985), p. 3. 89 Ferriter, D., *Occasions of sin* (London, 2009), p. 21. 90 Guinnane, T.W., *The vanishing Irish: households, migration and the rural economy in Ireland, 1850–1914*, (Princeton, 1997), p. 230. 91 Ibid., p. 231. 92 Noonan, P., 'Why few Irish marry' in O'Brien, J.A. (ed.), *The vanishing Irish: the enigma of the modern world* (New York, 1953), pp 45–6. 93 Ibid., p. 10.

the case of better-off men, who had unmarried sisters, or domestic servants, to fulfil both their housekeeping and companionship needs.

THE VILLA

In 1930, the same year *The house of gold* was banned, the McDonogh family bought The Villa, a substantial house at Sea Road in Galway, and Dr Michael McDonogh and his family took up residence there. (The Villa had previously been home to the Colohan family, who left following the death of Prof. Nicholas Colohan.)[94] Martin, T.C. and Mary Ann continued to live at Belmore, Salthill. By now in better health, Martin began to attend to his Dáil duties more energetically, so much so that by June 1930 his role in the promotion of an employment initiative in Gaeltacht areas, the kelp scheme, was praised by the minister for lands and fisheries, Fionán Lynch,[95] who acknowledged that 'Mr McDonogh … played a big part in fathering the scheme, and will now have a big part in furthering it.'[96] The minister went so far as to say that the entire scheme:

> had been rendered possible almost solely by the interest and intervention of a deputy of this house [McDonogh] whose reputation is a sufficient guarantee of his ability to carry through successfully any commercial enterprise to which he may set his hand. His sympathy for the people of the Gaeltacht is very well recognised by all who know him.[97]

McDonogh was similarly engaged in suggesting ways in which the milling industry, in which he had considerable experience, should be managed in the Free State.[98]

In July 1930, the 40-acre farm at Monatigue was acquired and divided up by land commission inspectors. The much-contested lands were split into six new holdings, approximately twelve additions were made to the holdings of existing tenants on the estate and divisions were also given 'to four landless

94 Previous residents of The Villa had been the Very Revd James Daly, last warden of Galway, who died in 1864. The following year, 1865, the house was taken by a Captain Lambert. The Colohans took a lease on the house in the late 1880s. Ó Cearbhaill, D., 'The Colohans: a remarkable Galway family', in *Journal of the Galway Archaeological and Historical Society*, 54 (2002), p. 124. 95 A native of Caherciveen, Co. Kerry, Lynch was minister for education (1922–30), minister for fisheries (1922–30) and minister for lands and fisheries (1930–2). 96 *Irish Independent*, 2 June 1930. 97 *Connacht Sentinel*, 3 June 1930. 98 Dáil Debate, Private Deputies' Business – Saorstát Milling Industry, 2 May 1930.

men', the press noting that the people returning to the lands were the descendants of those who had previously been evicted from the lands.[99] McDonogh was well compensated for the loss of the lands at Monatigue, and received 'an exchange holding in Co. Meath from the land commission'.[1]

McDonogh's steam trawler *John Summers,* in addition to its uses as a fishing and cargo boat, also served as a tender to cruise ships visiting the port, and as a replacement for the *Dún Aengus,* which provided the service to the Aran Islands.[2] And in 1931, McDonogh provided the *John Summers* for use as a support vessel when the famous long-distance swimmer Mercedes Gleitze attempted a swim from Kilronan in the Aran Islands to Galway.[3] One by-product of the swim attempt was increased interest in swimming in Galway, and calls for the establishment of a swimming club, and the building of a swimming pool at Salthill. When it was established on 6 June 1933 at Blackrock, McDonogh became one of the vice presidents of Galway Swimming Club, and one of its major sponsors.[4]

JUGGLING BUSINESS AND POLITICS

In spite of his frequent trips to Dublin to attend Dáil sittings during this period, McDonogh remained very much a hands-on employer. In 1931 a man named Tynan took a case for compensation against Thomas McDonogh & Sons, alleging that he had sustained an injury while unloading timber from a boat at the docks.[5] At the hearing, McDonogh stated that he was in his office on the day the alleged incident occurred and saw Tynan, who 'made no complaint and he seemed to be all right then'.[6] McDonogh revealed that he knew the man, who worked infrequently for the company, and stated that had he had his way, 'Tynan would never have been employed.' Tynan, a veteran,[7]

99 *Connacht Tribune,* 6 July 1930. 1 Ibid. 2 This was due to the fact that the *Dún Aengus* needed to conserve her coal supply, and the *John Summers* stepped in to maintain the usual sailings 'as she is much cheaper to run. The available supplies of steam coal for the *Dun Aengus* is about 40 tons, and about 3 1/2 tons of this is required for a single sailing.' *Connacht Tribune,* 30 Oct. 1926. 3 Born in Brighton, England, in 1900, in 1927, on her eighth attempt, she became the first English woman to swim the English Channel. In 1928 she was the first person to swim the Strait of Gibraltar, taking nearly 13 hours. In 1929 she swam Lough Neagh in Ireland in over 20 hours. The attempted swim from Kilronan to Galway took place on 2 Aug. 1931. Gleitze became fatigued after having been in the water for nearly 19 hours, and had to land at Awleen Bay, Spiddal. *Connacht Tribune,* 8 Aug. 1931. 4 The first president of the club was the Very Revd Canon Davis. *Connacht Sentinel,* 6 June 1933. McDonogh sponsored the provision of the McDonogh Cup, a perpetual trophy presented to the winner of the annual Ladies Prom Swim. 5 The alleged incident had occurred on Saturday, 11 Oct. 1930. 6 *Connacht Sentinel,* 16 June 1931. 7 In the course of

had been employed by McDonoghs after the war, when 'there was some sentiment for those coming back',[8] but had proved unreliable and lazy. While the judge agreed that Tynan was 'a thoroughly untrustworthy type', the facts of the case were deemed to be proven, and Tynan was awarded compensation in the amount of £24 7*s*. 6*d*.

Some months later, in August 1931, a strike occurred when a number of dockers were employed to unload three boats with cargoes for McDonoghs, but one docker, Patrick McDonnell, was not employed. The dockers believed he was being victimized because he had given evidence in the compensation case taken by Tynan against McDonoghs.[9] Martin McDonogh headed straight to the docks and dismissed the claim of discrimination, stating that the cargo being unloaded was sulphate of ammonia, so 'only very strong men were suited' for the work. He negotiated with the union representatives, and arranged to give lighter work to McDonnell on one of the other boats. The strikers returned to work, McDonogh continuing to insist that 'he was at liberty to employ the most suitable men'.[10]

Maintaining such a close eye on his business interests and attending to his constituency duties meant that McDonogh's role on various civic boards in Galway suffered.[11] A letter to the *Connacht Tribune* in 1931 posed the question, 'How long more will Mr Martin McDonogh be kept away from the chairmanship of the urban council of Galway because of his work in the Dáil?' The writer bemoaned the fact that the urban district council was 'rapidly degenerating from the dignity and commonsense that for a time it seemed to possess' under McDonogh's stewardship, and had descended to 'graceless discourtesy' and 'individual interference with officials'. With the urban district council floundering, the letter writer begged, 'Come back Máirtín Mór, and give us a touch of your manly vigour and commonsense.'[12]

McDonogh's 'vigour and commonsense' were very much in evidence when he became involved in the establishment of the Saorstát Sea Fisheries Association, the inaugural meeting of which he chaired at the Claddagh hall in August 1931. McDonogh's knowledge of the vagaries and challenges of the fishing industry was considerable, and his frustration at the mismanagement

his testimony, when Tynan was asked by the judge 'You are an old soldier?' he replied, 'Don't be insulting me sir, I am an ex-sailor', and indicated his 'liberally tattooed' hands in evidence. *Connacht Sentinel*, 16 June 1931. 8 *Connacht Sentinel*, 16 June 1931. 9 McDonnell had been considered by the judge as 'a very credible witness'. *Connacht Sentinel*, 18 Aug. 1931. 10 *Connacht Sentinel*, 18 Aug. 1931. 11 McDonogh was a much-sought-after board member of various private companies, and was co-opted onto the board of the Hibernian Fire and General Insurance Company in Feb. 1931. *Irish Times*, 19 Feb. 1931. 12 The letter was signed 'Fides'. *Connacht Tribune*, 18 July 1931.

of the Irish sea fisheries by the government had led to his sharply criticising the department of lands and fisheries in 1928 for overemphasizing administration, and lacking vision when it came to the use of resources, stating that 'he had more boats fishing than the board, although they had four inspectors between Galway and Cleggan. They have perfectly good boats there … and a storeful of gear, and why not give them to the fishermen and let them pay by result?'[13] McDonogh's recommendations were taken on board, and the SFA was established with the objective of providing fishermen with boats, engines and gear, and marketing the fish on their behalf. The association had four directors appointed by the government, and four other directors elected by the fishermen themselves. The government invested an initial £65,000 on boats and gear, and fishermen who joined the SFA purchased £1 shares in it, giving them a say in the election of their representatives, the chairman noting that 'nothing like that has ever been seen in Ireland before'.[14] At the inaugural meeting, the secretary to the department of lands and fisheries declared that 'opportunity is hammering on the gates of Galway, and if Galway will open its gates to that opportunity it will find many hands stretched out to help it … Galway is the city which in this country in the future should lead the race'.[15]

The SFA was a major boon to the fishing industry in Galway, because, largely at McDonogh's insistence, it had fixed prices for its fish. Price regulation had increased demand, and the landing of fish from the association's steam trawlers provided much-needed employment.[16] The *Connacht Tribune,* in praising the work of the association, noted that 'last year there was no Irish market for this quality of fish, and they were all sent to London' but observed that one Irish fish merchant 'who in August last ordered one box of fish has sent in an order this morning for thirty-five boxes'.[17] The founding of the SFA in 1930 prompted a revival in the fishing industry, but lack of development funds and private investment hindered progress.[18] McDonogh had set the ball rolling by ensuring that his steam trawlers, including the *John Summers,* sold their catches to the association, and he encouraged other fishermen to do likewise, with varying degrees of success.[19]

13 *Connacht Tribune,* 21 Apr. 1928. 14 *Connacht Sentinel,* 18 Aug. 1931. 15 Ibid. The man concerned was a Mr Bradley. 16 Men were employed in coaling the boats, taking off the cargo and packing and grading the fish, and women were employed in filleting and packing fish. 17 *Connacht Tribune,* 4 Mar. 1933. 18 His cousin, Joseph Mongan TD, of Carna, was elected to replace McDonogh on the Committee of the SFA when McDonogh died in 1934. 19 A crew members of another McDonogh-owned trawler, the *Successful,* Patrick Walsh (45), was tragically killed when he was hit on the head by a crankshaft in the course of a fishing trip. *Irish Press,* 17 May 1933.

In a subsequent Dáil debate McDonogh clashed with de Valera on the question of fishery patrol vessels protecting Irish waters. De Valera felt that the one vessel currently being used by the navy, the *Muirchú,* was inadequate. McDonogh was his usual blunt self:

> This idea of getting a new protection vessel is all humbug. If you had fifty of them you could not prevent poaching. The man who wants to poach will poach in the dark. It is rather a lovely idea to get a sea-plane to go out on dark and blustery nights. It is ridiculous and nonsensical.[20]

OPPOSITION TO PROTECTIONISM

Gwynn observed of McDonogh that 'he could talk, and shrewd talk it was, but on his feet in the Dáil he was only an inarticulate explosion'.[21] McDonogh's most memorable contributions in the Dáil related to two topics: labour issues, and Fianna Fáil's policy of protectionism, to which McDonogh was vehemently opposed. While Arthur Griffith had observed in 1910 that 'if Irishmen studied economics as the people of other countries do in the right of their own interests, all Ireland would be vehemently protectionist',[22] as James Meenan notes, 'that theory collided with reality when it came to the practical administration of the new state. The government did not have a doctrinaire attitude on free trade and protection, rather circumstances dictated policy.'[23] As a successful businessman, McDonogh did not see the logic of protectionist policies when applied to the fledgling Saorstát economy, the success of which was inextricably tied to that of Britain. In 1930 he clashed with the Fianna Fáil Deputy Thomas Derrig, over the imposition of safeguards to protect the milling industry, and control the price of flour.[24] McDonogh was adamant that the millers 'did not want any protection. All the millers want is to be let alone to do their own work in their own way.' When Derrig – rather naively – asked McDonogh 'what do you know about it?' McDonogh replied, 'Considering I am in the business I ought to know,' and proceeded to give an articulate account of the circumstances facing the milling industry at that time:

20 Dáil Debate, Vol. 5, No. 19, Committee on Finance, Fishing Industry, 18 June 1930. 21 Gwynn, obituary of Martin McDonogh, the *Observer*, 31 Dec. 1934. 22 *Sinn Féin*, 12 Mar. 1910. 23 Meenan, J., 'From free trade to self-sufficiency' in F. Mc Manus (ed.), *The years of the great test, 1926–39* (Dublin, 1967), p. 69. 24 Dáil Éireann, Private Deputies' Business – Saorstát Milling Industry, 2 May 1930.

> For the last two years prices have come down all over the world ... One of the biggest millers in England, Spiller and Baker, quite as big as Rank or very near it, last year made a loss of £350,000. That is the figure, as far as my memory serves me, that was given in their balance-sheet ... If deputies opposite succeeded in their policy of putting a duty on flour they would close down every small mill in this country. Capitalists would then come along and start big, efficient mills at the seaports, and the small mills in Ireland would be finished.[25]

Here was a subject on which McDonogh was well informed, and even Derrig acknowledged as much, noting that:

> if Deputy McDonogh thinks that any people in this house have a grievance against him because he is an important business man he is making the greatest mistake. On the contrary, some of us have the very greatest respect for him for that reason.[26]

When Derrig's party colleague, Frank Aiken, however, stated defiantly, 'We are not going to leave the flour millers alone,' McDonogh's reply, 'Nor anybody else either,'[27] revealed his deep-seated frustration at what he perceived as the folly of protectionism, and the lack of business acumen among members of the Fianna Fáil party.

McDonogh's considerable commitment to promoting the needs of Galway in the Dáil, and elsewhere, was fully recognized. Monsignor McAlpine, the controversial parish priest of Clifden, campaigning for McDonogh in the run-up to the 1932 general election, characterized him in the following terms:

> a man whose name is a synonym for all that is noble, generous and good; one who is simply unpurchaseable; money could not buy him; titles could not change him. He is a man of few words, but splendid deeds. He says what he means, and he means what he says; and when he speaks many words from him are not required to make the pigmies, McEntee and company, sink into their boots.[28]

McDonogh's achievements, inside and outside of politics, were also recognized by his old school, by now subsumed into Clongowes Wood college. The *Clongownian* described the Tullabeg alumnus thus:

25 Ibid. 26 Ibid. 27 Ibid. 28 *Connacht Sentinel*, 19 Jan. 1931.

> Martin McDonagh [*sic*] represents a Galway constituency in the Dáil. Seldom can there have been so representative a representative, for he seems to carry Galway on his shoulders. He is an important coal merchant; he runs the biggest timber works in the city; he has an enormous factory for chemical manure, that towers above the rest of the city; he has decisive influence in the counsels of the Steam Packet Company; he is the corner-stone of the Galway woollen trade; and he controls a large grocery. This is a veritable Atlas of commerce, yet his friends know him for the most simple and most hospitable of men.[29]

Although he could not have known it, McDonogh's last contribution in the Dáil occurred on 11 November 1931, in a debate on government securities. Deputy Ben Briscoe had queried the amount of the state's liability to foreign investors, arising out of the second national loan, and had received a vague reply from the minister for finance. McDonogh commented that 'foreigners can do what they like in this country'. With that one short, bitter comment, the parliamentary participation of Deputy Martin McDonogh ended.

1932 ELECTION

In January 1929 McDonogh was elected chairman of the Galway branch of Cumann na nGaedheal, following the death of Dr Michael Davitt.[30] McDonogh was expected to play a major part in coordinating the party's campaign to challenge Fianna Fáil in the 1932 general election, but by the time the election was called, his health had once again failed, presenting a very real worry for the party. At a pre-election meeting held in Galway, attended by Cosgrave, the absence of McDonogh was regretted. In proposing a toast in his honour, Prof. Dillon expressed the view that:

> No matter whether the people were opposed to Martin McDonogh or not, he always heard people say he was a great man. When he came to know Martin McDonogh he found that the reason he had such personality was that he was typical of the people of the West of Ireland. He made no difference between the rich and the poor. He had as much respect for the poorest man on the Aran Islands as he had for the richest

29 *The Clongowian*, 1931, pp 65–6.

> man in Galway. His outstanding feature was to employ people in productive work, and he hoped that the day was not far off when Mr McDonogh would be restored to health again and be able to take his place in the Dáil to help on the good work of the government, and to carry on the good work which he himself had been doing for Galway.[31]

Tom Kenny, in his capacity as president of the Irish Tourist Association, added that 'there was not a man in Galway who had not a warm spot in his heart for Martin McDonogh'.[32] McDonogh's friend, the minister for agriculture, Patrick Hogan stated that McDonogh was:

> supposed to be a capitalist, but if the people only knew him as well as he did, they would not think so. He remembered in the middle of last year when they had to find a million pounds to balance the budget, and did not know where the money was to come from, the executive council proposed putting an additional sixpence in the pound on income tax and to get the remainder by imposing a tax on sugar. Martin McDonogh held up the party meeting for an hour, because he said it was not fair to put an additional tax on the sugar, as the poor man could not afford to pay it, and he wanted the full million to be raised by an increased income tax. That was the man who was supposed to be a capitalist and against labour.[33]

At a subsequent meeting, Hogan revealed an even more personal regard for McDonogh when he declared, 'I have more respect for Martin McDonogh of Galway than I have for any man in Ireland.'[34]

Cosgrave echoed the sentiments of the previous speakers, and referred to McDonogh as:

> the great man of Galway.[35] To the city he was an institution not an individual, and his work for Galway would be long remembered, and he hoped he would be spared them many years to help them in the work which they had yet to do.[36]

Interestingly, Cosgrave, in referring to what he called the 'remarkable progress' made in Galway, attributed this to the tenacity of its sitting TDs, including

30 *Connacht Sentinel,* 15 Jan. 1929. 31 *Connacht Tribune,* 6 Feb. 1932. 32 Ibid. 33 Ibid. 34 *Connacht Sentinel,* 16 Feb. 1932. 35 *Connacht Tribune,* 6 Feb. 1932. 36 Ibid.

McDonogh. Cosgrave revealed that the executive council were 'in awe' of Patrick Hogan, noting, to much laughter, that they 'did not want his wrath to descend upon them … if they refused anything that was needed in the West'. He also referred to McDonogh's second cousin, Deputy Mongan, who would 'lash anyone who opposed any scheme for Galway', adding that they had 'another great fighter in Mr Broderick'.[37] Politically speaking, in fighting Galway's corner, McDonogh was in good company.

There was an air of finality in the sentiments expressed at the meeting, and an inference that this time McDonogh might not rally. At an election meeting in Tuam, Sean Broderick TD, referring to McDonogh's contesting the election in spite of his illness, added, to the surprise of many, that McDonogh had 'refused the office of senator in order to do the more important work for the people in the Dáil'.[38] It is unclear when the offer of a senate seat was made to McDonogh, or by whom, but Broderick's reference to it, on a platform that included the minister for agriculture, Patrick Hogan, gives credence to the fact that such an offer was indeed made.

McDonogh lost the 16 February 1932 general election, his first preference votes having dropped from 5,007 in the September 1927 election to 3,384.[39] His increasing age and his health problems may have convinced some of his supporters that the time had come to make way for a younger and more vigorous man. Even the *Irish Times* regretted McDonogh's loss, noting that the departure of older deputies 'severed a link with an age that has gone – an age in which Irish politics was rich in colour and drama and fervent local patriotism'. He would be remembered for 'the silent patience with which [he] endured the performances' of his colleagues.[40] The *Times*' Dáil correspondent noted that even during long, wearisome speeches that left few deputies in the chamber, McDonogh ('a burly, round-faced figure') and Deputy Daniel Buckley of Fianna Fáil, 'two watchdogs', remained in their seats, intervening 'only on the rarest occasions', but 'there was a hint of smouldering fires beneath the placid exterior of the man from Galway, and when fanned by wrath they were apt to blaze out in fiery denunciations, which scorched whomsoever they touched'.[41]

The *Times* was premature in consigning McDonogh to the realm of parliamentary has-beens. He rallied, physically and politically. In May 1932, at a meeting of the Cumann na nGaedheal Galway branch attended by Deputies Hogan and Broderick, a vote of congratulation was passed to McDonogh 'on

37 Ibid. 38 *Connacht Tribune*, 13 Feb. 1932. 39 *Irish Press*, 22 Feb. 1932. 40 *Irish Times*, 9 Mar. 1932. 41 Ibid.

his marvellous recovery from his recent illness'.[42] The vote was doubtless heartfelt, but for the party McDonogh's recovery also seemed to solve the practical problem of who would – or could – replace him on the Cumann na nGaedheal ticket if he was forced to retire owing to ill health. The relief, however, was short-lived, for McDonogh relapsed, and the following month, at a meeting of the harbour commissioners, his long-time colleague Joe Young, in proposing the absent chairman for re-election, noted that he was 'sorry that Mr McDonogh is not now as often with us as we should like but … I hope that he will be back with us in the near future.'[43] Martin McDonogh was re-elected in his absence, T.C. thanking the board on his brother's behalf and stating that, 'when he gets better of his illness, I'm sure he will do all he can for the interests of Galway Harbour'.[44]

In due time McDonogh recovered once again, and it appeared that there was still plenty of fire left in the 73-year-old. At the launch of Muintir na Tíre, he spoke to the objectives of the organization and said that:

> There is a lot wrong with this country … and it is up to every one of us to help towards the ideals put before us by this new organisation. If such ideals were put into action, Ireland would be a wonderful country, for, no matter what people might say, there is no other country in the world like it. We have the climate, the land, and the people. The thing is to make proper use of them. Some have an idea of doing it one way, and others another way, but if we all came together and help one another this would be the number one country in the world.[45]

Much of the anxiety surrounding McDonogh's ill health stemmed from the fact that there was concern in some quarters that the heir apparent to the McDonogh business empire, T.C., might not be up to the job. That T.C. was not of the same calibre as his older brother was evidenced by an episode in 1933. At an urban district council meeting, T.C. complained of what he termed a 'lack of interest in the city' shown by the Irish Tourist Association. It appeared to be an off-the-cuff remark, but his claim is rendered all the more remarkable by the fact that his brother, Martin, then chair of the urban district council, was also vice president of the ITA, and another Galwayman, Tom Kenny, was its president. The general manager of the ITA, J.P. O'Brien, expressed his fury at T.C.'s ill-informed outburst, and stated that the ITA had

42 *Connacht Sentinel*, 10 May 1932. 43 *Connacht Tribune*, 18 June 1932. 44 Ibid. 45 *Connacht Tribune*, 9 Dec. 1933. 46 *Irish Press*, 8 Nov. 1933.

'done more for Galway than to deserve a blow below the belt'.[46] At the next meeting of the urban district council Martin readily agreed that there was no foundation to the claims T.C. had made. T.C., no doubt having been suitably chastened, opted to keep his head low, and did not attend the meeting.

In January 1933, though, the focus was firmly on whether Martin McDonogh would be well enough to stand in the forthcoming general election and retake his seat. Martin's health was once more a cause for concern, and in thanking the Galway cumann for selecting Martin as a candidate in the forthcoming election, T.C. stated that it was with the greatest difficulty that his brother had been persuaded to go forward, and he would not have done so but for the fact that 'he was informed that he would be the means of gaining an extra seat which he hoped would be a benefit to the new government'.[47] Although nationally Cumann na nGaedheal lost eight seats, McDonogh was re-elected in the 24 January 1933 election, the *Sentinel* noting that voting was 'extremely mixed, a number of those voting No. 1 for Mr McDonogh completing the paper on the Labour ticket'.[48] McDonogh polled an impressive 4,328 first-preference votes.

In April 1933 McDonogh was elected president of Galway chamber of commerce for the second time. In welcoming McDonogh's appointment, the *Tribune* observed that 'in these days of depression and keen competition in business it is obvious that towns which desire to survive must put the best brains of the community into the work of survival', and McDonogh, 'as a businessman, and as an industrialist', was just the brains that Galway needed.[49] With the arrival of the transatlantic liners, the Galway docks had been transformed, and 'Galway docks were no longer the Galway docks; they might have been the waterfront of a Continental city or the Boco of a South American port.'[50] The North German Lloyd line was the first to make Galway a port of call for its liners, but others were to follow, including Cunard.[51]

The chamber had also made great strides in promoting Galway as the 'capital of the Gaeltacht', and McDonogh was incensed when Deputy Clery of Mayo, in a Dáil debate on fisheries and Gaeltacht services, observed tartly that in Galway, 'which is boasted as being the chief city of the Gaeltacht, there was a distinct lack of interest amongst shopkeepers to favour Irish-manufactured goods'. McDonogh assured the deputy that, 'if he goes to Galway city he can get Irish-manufactured goods in practically every shop'.[52]

47 *Connacht Sentinel*, 10 Jan. 1933. 48 Ibid., 24 Jan. 1933. 49 *Connacht Tribune*, 1 Apr. 1933. 50 *Connacht Sentinel*, 24 May 1932. 51 Ibid., 9 Oct. 1934. 52 Ibid., 16 June 1931.

Two of the city's best-known shopkeepers, members of the extended McDonogh/Hernon families, died in 1933. McDonogh's aunt, the formidable Monica Mór McDonogh, who was over 80, died in January 1933,[53] and his second cousin, Martin Hernon, died in December of that year, aged 84.[54]

McDonogh's own mortality appeared far from his mind when, in October 1933, he presided at the United Ireland Party Convention that attracted 300 delegates to Galway, with General Mulcahy and McDonogh's fellow TDs Patrick Hogan and Sean Broderick in attendance. A guard of honour of 150 blue-shirted men welcomed the guests, and the convention was distinguished by the fact that it was the first major one following the amalgamation of three parties – Cumann na nGaedheal, the National Guard (the 'Blueshirts') and the National Centre Party – into one organization, the United Ireland Organisation, otherwise known as Fine Gael.[55]

CHARLES LINDBERGH

That same month, McDonogh helped welcome the famous aviator Charles Lindbergh to Galway. While conducting a series of survey flights over Ireland,[56] Lindburgh and his wife Ann landed in Galway Bay on 23 October 1933 in their Lockheed Sirius.[57] Lindbergh's arrival had not been anticipated, and when he landed his seaplane off Nimmo's Pier, Martin McDonogh, Galway's leading civic figure, was otherwise committed. Lindbergh was instead greeted by T.C. McDonogh, the harbour master and the senior pilot. The Lindberghs were entertained at dinner at the Great Southern Hotel by Martin and T.C. McDonogh, Tom Kenny and other civic figures.[58] Subsequently, 'Col. And Mrs Lindbergh were the guests of the chairman of the harbour commissioners during their two-day visit to Galway and Connemara.' It is unclear whether the Lindberghs actually stayed with the McDonoghs at Belmore, the family home in Salthill, but the couple were

53 Ibid., 31 Jan. 1933. 54 Martin Hernon was the son of Tom Hernon, whose father Pat Hernon was Bartly Hernon's eldest son. His obituary noted that Hernon, the owner of several cargo vessels operating between Galway, Belfast and Glasgow, had 'aided many "wanted" men in their escape from crown forces during the Irish war'. *Connacht Tribune*, 2 Dec. 1933. 55 *Connacht Tribune*, 21 Oct. 1933. 56 Lindbergh undertook the survey on behalf of Pan-American Airways to examine the feasibility of establishing a North Atlantic air route. The local press reported that following Lindbergh's visit, 'Galway port had been included very favourably in that survey.' *Connacht Sentinel*, 31 Oct. 1933. 57 Traynor, M., *Iona: Ireland's first commercial airline* (Dublin, 2004). 58 *Irish Press*, 24 Oct. 1933.

certainly chaperoned by T.C. McDonogh, with whom 'they visited the Corrib and Inishambo'. The Lindberghs' visit to Galway occurred 20 months after the abduction and murder of their 20-month-old son Charles Lindbergh Jnr in March 1932, and the surprise nature of the visit to Galway was attributed by Lindbergh to the fact that the events surrounding their son's abduction 'had so unnerved Mrs Lindbergh that, while she was quite content to fly the oceans with her husband, she could not stand the crowds who would meet the couple everywhere if there was extensive publicity as to their movements'. It appears that the Lindberghs 'enjoyed the hospitality of Galway very much', and were full of praise for the assistance they received from all quarters, including from Martin McDonogh, who saw to it that the harbour commissioners decided to 'defray the cost of all labour in connection with the mooring and moving of the seaplane'.[59]

The year ended on something of a high for McDonogh when he took a break from his business and political responsibilities to see his horse Irish Fun win the Irish Cambridgeshire, 'in a storm of blinding wind and rain',[60] at the Curragh in November 1933.

McDonogh appeared to be very much back to his old self, and, when the steamship *Brimm*, loaded with a general cargo bound for Sligo,[61] sprang a leak and was beached by her skipper west of Mutton Island, he soon had his men on board, assessing the damage to the vessel and the condition of the cargo. Two months later the Galway Foundry Company, of which McDonogh was the major shareholder, bought the ship 'lock, stock and barrel'.[62] The cargo was taken off her, and she was towed by two of McDonogh's boats, the *John Summers* and the *Faugh-a-Ballagh*, into Galway docks. The *Brimm* was put into dry dock, repaired and sold.[63]

McDonogh's final political nomination, to contest the Galway county council elections in June 1934, took place at a Fine Gael convention in the National Club at Bishopscourt, Galway, in May 1934.[64] The club had been established in 1922 by members of the Irish Nationalist Party. Money had been subscribed to secure the premises, and as president of the National Club, McDonogh was one of four trustees charged with managing it. After

59 *Connacht Sentinel*, 31 Oct. 1933. 60 *Irish Independent*, 2 Nov. 1933. Describing the win as a 'very popular' one, and McDonogh as 'one of the landmarks of the West', the article went on to say that 'you may speak of Martin McDonogh and find no need to mention Galway; but no one ever speaks about Galway without bringing in Martin McDonogh as a matter of course'. 61 The cargo consisted of galvanised iron, glass, slates, stonework pipes and 480 tons of cement. 62 *Connacht Tribune*, 1 Sept. 1934. 63 Ibid. 64 The convention took place on Saturday 28 April 1934. *Irish Examiner*, 2 May 1934.

the Treaty, it had been decided to re-establish the club on a non-political and non-sectarian basis. Prior to the general election of September 1927, members of Cumann na nGaedheal had approached the committee and asked for the use of one of the club's rooms.[65] The committee had agreed, on the basis that the arrangement would be temporary, but Cumann na nGaedheal had instead 'remained in possession, but never offered any rent'.[66] The matter dragged on until the party offered to buy the premises in its entirety, for a derisory sum. When a notice appeared in the Cumann na nGaedheal newsletter stating that the party intended to start a social club in Galway, the members of the National Club, not unreasonably, assumed that the intended venue would be their premises. Tensions rose considerably when the committee received, en bloc, applications by thirty-six individuals for membership of the National Club, the existing membership at that time amounting to about forty. More ominously, the committee noted that 'they were all Cumann na nGaedheal followers', including Patrick Hogan TD and Sean Broderick TD. It was clear that a coup of sorts was being attempted, and the committee were outraged. At the meeting to consider the applications for membership, which McDonogh did not attend, the members refused to propose or second the names of the thirty-six individuals, and stated that they regarded the submission of the names 'as an attempt by Cumann na nGaedheal to gain control of our club, and we would not agree to that'.[67] At the next meeting, which McDonogh attended, the matter was quietly allowed to drop.[68]

In June 1934 McDonogh, by now standing as a Fine Gael candidate,[69] was comfortably elected in the Galway county council local elections, securing 1,205 first preferences.[70] Strangely, in the urban elections, McDonogh, in an attempt to 'exclude politics' from the council chamber, stood as an independent – even though he was a sitting Fine Gael TD. McDonogh was elected to the urban district council, but his election as chairman of that council was opposed by another independent, M.J Cooke, one of whose supporters stated that McDonogh 'was the principle cause of the Blueshirt movement getting into the town', and referred obliquely to McDonogh as

65 It can probably be assumed that McDonogh was one of those members who broached the subject, although his name is not specifically mentioned. 66 *Connacht Tribune*, 30 June 1934. 67 Ibid. 68 The attempted coup by Cumann na nGaedheal never materialised, and by 1950 (with a membership of 108) the National Club was used 'more as a place for the sale of intoxicating liquor than as a club', and when Gardaí objected to the renewal of its licence, it was not renewed. *Tuam Herald*, 4 Mar. 1950. 69 Fine Gael was founded on 8 Sept. 1933 following the merger of its parent party, Cumann na nGaedheal, with the National Centre Party and the National Guard, the latter of which were popularly known as the 'Blueshirts'.

Figure 8 Martin McDonogh chatting with Patrick Hogan TD, James Dillon TD and T.C. McDonogh at a 'Blueshirt' meeting in March 1934.

having something in common with various unnamed 'dictators' in 'Italy, and all over Europe'.[71] Cooke defeated McDonogh and was elected as chairman on a vote of 13 to 10.

One of the last public events McDonogh attended prior to the onset of his final illness was the Athenry agricultural show, which took place in September 1934. He was one of the judges in the pure-bred bull competition.[72] The cattle driving that had plagued McDonogh for so long continued into the final month of his life; in November 1934, the *Irish Press* recorded that cattle had been driven off his lands, and walls and fences thrown down, in the Ballybane and Kiltulla districts.[73] But he would not be able to take on this fight. He fell seriously ill as a result of a paralytic stroke on 10 November. He was ministered to by his cousin, Dr Thomas McDonogh,[74] at his home in Salthill, but grew gradually weaker, and, having 'rallied, only to relapse',[75] he died on 24 November. In an article headed

70 *Connacht Tribune*, 30 June 1934. 71 Ibid., 10 July 1934. 72 *Connacht Sentinel*, 11 Sept. 1934. 73 The stock of six other landowners were similarly driven off lands. All the animals were later discovered, except for two head of cattle and thirteen sheep, the property of McDonogh. *Connacht Tribune*, 3 Nov. 1924. 74 Dr Thomas Mc Donogh was the Medical Officer for Galway No. 1 dispensary district for over thirty-four years, prior to his resignation in 1938. *Connacht Tribune*, 29 Oct. 1938. 75 *Sunday Independent*, 25 Nov. 1934.

'Galway's great loss' the *Connacht Sentinel* declared, 'Gloom has been cast over Galway and indeed over the West,' and noted that the death of McDonogh marked 'the end of an epoch in Galway – an epoch during which the city recovered in some measure at least some of its former greatness'. It remained to be seen how Galway would fare in the absence of 'the great citizen and great Irishman' Máirtín Mór McDonogh.[76]

76 *Connacht Sentinel*, 27 Nov. 1934.

6. Departing the scene, and legacy

The death of Máirtín Mór McDonogh made national news, the *Sunday Independent* reporting on its front page that it had 'cast a big gloom' on his native city, and adding that McDonogh, 'physically and commercially, was the big man of Galway'.[1] The *Irish Independent* introduced its notification of McDonogh's death *as Gaeilge*: 'Is truagh linn a chraobhscaoileadh go bhfuair Máirtín Mór MacDonnachadha, TD, bás i nGaillimh Dé Sathairn seo caite' ['We regret to announce that Máirtín Mór McDonogh TD died in Galway last Saturday'].[2] The following day the paper headed its more extensive editorial 'Galway city in mourning'.[3] The *Irish Times* noted the death of 'one of the best-known businessmen in the West of Ireland', and observed that he 'employed a greater number of people than any other firm in the Western counties'.[4] But it was in his home city that his loss was most keenly felt, and the shock of his loss most profound. The *Connacht Sentinel*, having declared that 'Máirtín Mór, as he was universally known in the county, was one of the greatest men of the West,'[5] encapsulated perhaps more than any other of the obituaries and tributes written about him, the nature and complexity of McDonogh:

> Martin McDonogh was a great man in the true sense; for he possessed the gift of personality that was in itself great, but in addition to this he combined with a strong personality an unerring sense of citizenship. Perhaps it was because of this strong, intellectual armour that he never suffered fools gladly. He had little use for the shop-window politician, and less for the insincere local representative who sought to hide his Pecksniffian hypocrisy, or his playing for votes, under the guise of spurious patriotism. In days like these it is well that we should have men like Martin McDonogh, for whatever his faults – and all things human suffer from faults – he had the courage of his convictions, and never wavered in expressing them. Apart from all this, he was a great Galwayman, of whom everyone in Galway could be proud.[6]

1 *Sunday Independent*, 25 Nov. 1934. 2 *Irish Independent*, 26 Nov. 1934. 3 Ibid., 27 Nov. 1934. 4 *Irish Times*, 26 Nov. 1934. 5 *Connacht Sentinel*, 27 Nov. 1934. 6 Ibid.

News of McDonogh's death was greeted in the Dáil with expressions of sadness at the passing of a tenacious advocate for his constituency. De Valera, speaking in Irish, moved that the house extend its sympathy to the relatives of the late Deputy McDonogh and stated:

> Bhí sé ar na theachtaí ba shine san Dáil, agus bhí dlúth-bhaint aige le fada le saoghal puiblidhe agus le cúrsaí gnótha na tíre. Is mór an chailleamhaint é, go mór mhór do Chonnachtaibh agus do Chathair na Gaillimhe. Go dtugaidh Dia solas na bhflathas dá anam. [He was one of the oldest members of the Dáil, and had a long-time involvement with public life and with national matters. He is a great loss, especially to Connacht and to Galway City. May God grant the light of heaven to his soul.]

Once news of his death began to circulate in Galway, the *Irish Times* reported that 'all through Saturday evening and yesterday thousands of people visited Belmore, Salthill, where the body of Mr McDonogh lay'.[7] Particularly noticeable among the crowds 'was the constant stream of poor people from the Claddagh, who came to pay a last tribute to one of the greatest industrialists that Ireland has ever known, and to a man who never failed to befriend them in need'.[8] Although the publication of *The house of gold* preceded McDonogh's death by some five years, Liam O'Flaherty's visceral description of the death of McDonogh's alter ego, Ramon Mór Costello, vividly presages the scene at Belmore, as described by the local media, Stephen Gwynn and others, on the evening before McDonogh's funeral:

> The moonlight poured into the hall upon the wailing women, upon the kneeling men, upon the old woman tearing her hair, upon Ramon Mor's enormous corpse, stretched stiff upon the mattress, and upon his eye that stared, unblinking, at eternity.[9]

McDonogh's funeral, on 26 November 1934, was an impressive affair, as befitted his significant stature in the community, and was as close to a state funeral as Galway could manage. After Solemn High Mass in St Joseph's church, the large oak coffin was carried by employees of the various McDonogh firms. The *Irish Times* described it thus:

7 *Irish Times*, 26 Nov. 1934. 8 *Connacht Tribune*, 1 Dec. 1934. 9 O'Flaherty, L., *The house of gold*, p. 348. 10 *Irish Press*, 27 Nov. 1934.

> Headed by twenty eight clergy and followed by 110 motor cars, the enormous cortege proceeded to the Forthill Cemetery. All the business houses along the route were closed and shuttered. The vessels in the dock, including two British boats, the Hon. E. Guinness's yacht, and other merchant trading boats, flew their flags at half-mast. Over 700 workers, drawn from the firm of Thomas Mc Donogh and Sons, marched three-deep in the funeral procession.

Twenty-three sporting fixtures were suspended on the day, and players in a rugby match between Galwegians and UCG wore mourning armlets and observed two minutes of silence. The tricolour over the sports ground was flown at half mast, and at Galway Golf Club, which McDonogh had played such an essential role in establishing on a firm footing, golfers stopped play.[10] The list of dignataries who attended included: W.T. Cosgrave, the former president; Frank Fahy TD, the ceann comhairle;[11] Senator Oliver St John Gogarty; Patrick Hogan TD, the former minister for agriculture; General Séan MacEoin; a host of other local TDs; and the leaders of Galway's political, civic and commercial life. The funeral cortege proceeded to Forthill cemetery via Mill Street, Mainguard Street, Shop Street, Eyre Square, and, fittingly, the docks. Among the thousands of ordinary Galwegians who came to pay their respects and follow Máirtín Mór to his final resting place were the union men and dockers with whom he had frequently clashed. As Seán Spellissey has observed, 'many were his fights with organized labour over questions about the harbour, and he fought hard; but at his funeral organized labour in Galway dropped work and wages for a day to pay him their parting tribute.'[12]

In an obituary of McDonogh written by his old friend Stephen Gwynn for *The Observer*, the affection and regard Gwynn had for the gruff, abrasive Galwayman, 'whose very words were rough-spoken', is obvious:

> Galway is the most Irish city in Ireland, and nothing in Galway was more Irish than the big man who was buried there last Monday – Martin McDonogh, Maurteen Mór, as the whole county and its islands called

11 The ceann comhairle was involved in a motoring incident on the morning of McDonogh's funeral. A car carrying two representatives of the department of fisheries skidded on a greasy road outside Kinnegad and overturned. Miraculously, neither of the men was hurt, and the press reported that Frank Fahy 'came along soon after the accident, and picked up the two passengers, whom he drove on to Galway.' *Connacht Sentinel*, 27 Nov. 1934. 12 Spellissey, *The history of Galway*, p. 115.

> him. He was a member of the Dáil, he had held every civic post in Galway itself; but office did not give importance to this Galway merchant. It was the man that mattered. Much of his work will stand, but Galway will feel the loss of him for many a long year.[13]

In his will, dated 15 June 1932, McDonogh named his brothers T.C. and Michael as his executors.[14] In keeping with his lifelong reticence about revealing anything of his true self, McDonogh's will yields precious few clues as to who or what was important to him, aside from his immediate family. To his sister Mary Anne he left a house on Presentation Road and an annuity of £200 a year for life; to his brother Michael he left the The Villa and two-fifths of his shares in the three companies Thomas McDonogh & Sons, McDonogh Milling and Trading Company and McDonogh's Fertilizers. Almost everything else went to T.C., including the house at Belmore and Martin's remaining cash assets, which amounted to £89,763. Martin left charitable bequests, including £100 to each parish priest of the three parishes of Galway at the time of his death for Masses to be said 'for the repose of his soul'.[15] He also left £200 to his doctor and cousin Thomas McDonogh.

Interestingly, in light of his own ambivalence – indeed hostility, on occasion – towards the Irish language, as writer Breandán Ó hEithir noted, McDonogh was 'one of the few TDs to have been commemorated by a lament in Irish'.[16] The lament is a song entitled 'Amhrán Máirtín Mór' or 'The song of Máirtín Mór',[17] a version of which was collected, as part of the Schools Folklore Collection, from Brighidh Ní Flaithbhearthaigh, of Ard Mhór School, Carna, Co. Galway, in 1937/8 (see appendix). Martin McDonogh's passing also prompted the publication of a poem entitled 'Fragments by a graveside' by an anonymous writer, which likened him to a great general marshalling the people of Galway as his troops:

> Elsewhere yours might have been a great command
> A power to sway mankind as it passed on;
> For nature and the gods had truly planned
> An eagle worthy to depend upon.[18]

13 Gwynn, obituary of Martin McDonogh, the *Observer*, 31 Dec. 1934. 14 Probate was granted on 25 Jan. 1937, *Irish Independent*, 17 May 1937. 15 *Irish Independent*, 17 May 1937. 16 *Irish Times*, 4 Feb. 1984. 17 UCD School of Irish, Celtic Studies, Irish Folklore and Linguistics. National Folklore Collection UCD. Schools' Manuscript Collection – Carna. SMS 11:163. 18 *Connacht Sentinel*, 27 Nov. 1934.

Figure 9 T.C. McDonogh (centre) with cousins.

While such eulogising would not have sat comfortably with the famously straight-talking McDonogh, his memorial card, which he designed himself, is notable for the fact that it outlines a comprehensive and quantified list of the indulgences granted to those who recited the prayers listed. Even in death, as historian Peadar O'Dowd has noted, 'Máirtín Mór was still giving to the needy.'[19]

Following the death of his older brother, it fell to T.C. (figure 9) to assume responsibility for the family businesses, with the help, when he could give it, of his brother Michael, who continued to serve as the medical officer for Galway. T.C. became the senior partner in the McDonogh Milling and Trading Company, McDonogh Chemical Works and the extensive sawmills, and he assumed responsibility for the lands the family owned in Galway, as well as farms in Meath, Dublin and Limerick. In spite of his long apprenticeship in the various family businesses, and his own considerable experience of serving on civic and public bodies, it was soon clear that T.C. was not made of the same stuff as Máirtín Mór. Always more of a social animal than his workhorse brother, T.C. was a keen golfer, racegoer and angler. He enjoyed entertaining his wide circle of friends at parties at his substantial fishing lodge on the island of Inishambo in Lough Corrib, where he had entertained

19 O'Dowd, P., *In from the West*, p. 134.

the Lindberghs during their visit to Galway in 1933. The *Irish Times* noted that 'the hospitality of the McDonogh family is well known not only in Galway, but throughout Ireland',[20] but it appears that T.C. McDonogh took such hospitality to new levels when the sober influence of his older brother was no longer there to be exerted.

With Martin McDonogh's Dáil seat vacant, attention focused on finding a replacement for him, and at its meeting of 6 December 1934, the standing committee of Fine Gael were informed that 'Col. Ryan had gone to Galway to find out how the position stood'.[21] By the following May 'Dr O'Higgins and Senator Blythe were deputed to interview Messrs Mongan and MacDonagh [*sic*]', and a convention was to be held in Galway on 25 May to agree a candidate. General Mac Eoin was to be director of elections in Galway.[22] T.C. McDonogh was selected by a unanimous vote to contest the by-election to fill the vacancy created by the death of his brother.[23] Despite a vigorous campaign and strong support from the Fine Gael hierarchy, T.C. was defeated, polling 24,088 votes, failing to meet the quota of 30,752.[24] Eamonn Corbett of Fianna Fáil[25] took the seat.[26] Conceding defeat, McDonogh stated, 'I am not very keen on politics; I have never before sought the electors' votes;[27] it is my first time seeking election to the Dáil, but I am just as good an Irishman as Mr Corbett.'[28]

Politics aside, with only one of the six McDonogh siblings having married – and he married rather late in life – the question of who would inherit the McDonogh empire doubtless weighed on the minds of the surviving members of the family. Happily, fears were allayed when on 4 June 1935, in an article headed 'Heir for McDonoghs', the *Connacht Sentinel* announced 'the birth of a son and heir to Dr Michael McDonogh at Seamount Hydro, Salthill'.[29]

With the future of Thomas McDonogh & Sons secured, T.C. continued to ably steward the various McDonogh businesses, while at the same time enjoying the fruits of his significant wealth. And then, with profound shock, Galway learned of his sudden death. He had been enjoying a two-week vacation in Europe, and had been in good health. According to the press, he

20 *Irish Times*, 18 June 1935. 21 Minutes of meeting of standing committee, 6 Dec. 1934, Fine Gael archive, UCD. 22 Ibid., 15 May 1935, Fine Gael archive, UCD. 23 *Irish Times*, 1 June 1935. 24 *Connacht Tribune*, 29 June 1935. 25 Others who offered themselves as Fianna Fáil candidates were Dr T. Powell and Dr Sean Tubridy. Corbett, however, was selected by a big majority. 26 Corbett polled 37,415 votes. *Irish Times*, 27 This was not strictly true, as T.C. McDonogh had stood for election as an urban district councillor. 28 *Connacht Tribune*, 29 June 1935. 29 Ibid., 4 June 1935.

had 'travelled through Belgium and was on his way home when death occurred'.[30] T.C. died on Wednesday, 9 September 1936 at the American Hospital in Paris,[31] and, like his father, who had also died abroad, some thirty-four years earlier, his remains were carried on the evening mailboat to Dún Laoghaire and thence by train to Galway.[32] News of T.C. McDonogh's death was greeted with 'profound sorrow' in Galway, where, according to the local press, this 'devout Catholic' and possessor of a nature that was 'kindliness itself when a good deed could be done' had, in what was acknowledged as a McDonogh trait, 'always exhibited great charity'.[33] Interestingly, in view of Martin McDonogh's comment that T.C. was the 'gentleman' of the family, the *Connacht Tribune* described him as 'the possessor of all those noble characteristics which go to make a true Irish Catholic gentleman'.[34]

At the time of his death T.C. McDonogh was a member of the county council, urban district council and harbour board, as well as senior partner in the various McDonogh trading and industrial interests. The *Irish Times* noted that 'both brothers had taken active parts in all that tended to promote the welfare of Galway city and county,' and acknowledged McDonogh as 'a well known figure in the sporting life of the country'.[35]

A crowd of three thousand greeted the train carrying T.C. McDonogh's remains at Galway, and the coffin was taken by hearse to St Joseph's church, flanked by a guard of honour on each side made up of 'workmen in the mills and factories of Messrs T. McDonogh and Sons. Burial took place in the McDonogh family vault at Forthill Cemetery.'[36] Cosgrave and General Richard Mulcahy attended the funeral, as did all the local TDs, Senator J.J. Parkinson, and the artist Charles Lambe RHA, as well as virtually every civic figure in Galway. The number who turned out to pay their last respects to T.C.'s funeral was almost as impressive as the number who had turned out only two years previously at Martin's. Close on three thousand people and about 160 motor cars followed the hearse through the streets to Forthill,[37] and once again it was noted that 'there was a very big attendance in the cortege of Claddagh people, to whom Mr McDonogh had always been a kind friend', and there were about 700 employees of the firm of Thomas McDonogh & Sons.[38]

30 *Irish Press,* 10 Sept. 1936. 31 Founded in 1906 and located in Neuilly-sur-Seine, in the western suburbs of Paris, the American Hospital is a private, not-for-profit hospital. 32 *Irish Examiner,* 12 Sept. 1936. 33 *Connacht Tribune,* 12 Sept. 1936. This McDonogh trait was also referred to with regard to McDonogh's aunt, Monica Mór McDonogh, who, upon her death, was described as having been 'exceedingly charitable, and never refused help to those whom she thought needed it.' *Connacht Sentinel,* 31 Jan. 1933. 34 *Connacht Tribune,* 12 Sept. 1936. 35 *Irish Times,* 19 Sept. 1936. 36 Ibid. 37 *Irish Press,* 14 Sept. 1936. 38 Ibid.

'Mr Tom McDonogh', as the *Irish Times* described him, was 'an old Clongownian', who 'nearly all his life [had] concentrated on building up the commercial structures of his native city. No matter what the stage of political unrest or economic depression his country was in, he saw to it that employment was provided for the people of Galway to the limit of his capacity.'[39] Those who knew him best, his fellow Galwegians, spoke of McDonogh in much the same terms as they had done his late brother, one councillor commenting, 'although I could not always see eye to eye with him, I always found him a straight-going man. If he had a thing in view, he saw it to the end. He was also a kind man to the poor; he never let down a poor person when he could assist.'[40]

The initial shock at T.C.'s sudden death soon gave way to controversy of a type the McDonogh family had never experienced before, and which undoubtedly would have horrified Máirtín Mór. The first whiff of scandal came when the press announced that T.C. McDonogh had left an estate of somewhere between £100,000 and £200,000, and that 'he had bequeathed to his cousin, Maire O'Malley, Belmore, Galway, £20,000 free of all duty'.[41] A probate suit ensued, which was heard in the high court,[42] between the surviving McDonogh siblings, in which Michael was the plaintiff and Mary Ann the defendant. Michael, as T.C.'s executor, sought to have the will – dated 9 September 1936, the day of his brother's death – admitted to probate.[43] Mary Ann objected on the grounds that 'the alleged will was not duly executed; that the deceased did not know and approve of the contents of the alleged will at the time of the making of it; and that at the time of the making of it, he was not of sound mind, memory and understanding'.[44]

In the course of the proceedings it was noted that T.C. had 'very considerable assets, the bulk of which had come to him under the will of his brother, Martin',[45] and that these assets were estimated at over £100,000. The fact that T.C. made the contested will on the day he became ill, and later died in hospital, would have been remarkable but perhaps not controversial were it not for the fact that on the holiday in question, and on the day he made his

39 *Irish Times*, 19 Sept. 1936. 40 Cllr Cooke, at a Galway county council finance committee meeting. *Connacht Sentinel*, 15 Sept. 1936. 41 *Irish Times*, 1 Aug. 1939. 42 The proceedings took place in the high court, Dublin in April 1937, before Mr Justice O'Byrne and a jury. 43 Dr Michael McDonogh employed the services of two senior counsel, Mr J.M. Fitzgerald and Mr Vincent Rice, and Mary Ann McDonogh was represented by John A. Costello SC, TD (attorney general 1926–32, taoiseach 1948–51 and 1954–57), and Mr A.E. Wood KC. Mrs Maire Wall (née O'Malley), as an intervenient, was represented separately by Cecil Lavery SC, TD and Brerton Barry SC. 44 *Connacht Sentinel*, 20 Apr. 1937. 45 *Irish Times*, 20 Apr. 1937.

will, 'he had with him a young cousin, Miss Maire [Maura] O'Malley – now Mrs Wall – who had always been a protégée of his, and to whom he left a considerable sum'.[46] It was noted that, 'unfortunately he forgot to leave anything to his sister',[47] an oversight Martin had not made in his substantial provision for Mary Ann, who had assumed the role of unpaid housekeeper for the brothers since their mother had died fifty-three years previously.[48]

The beneficiary of T.C. McDonogh's generosity, Maura O'Malley, was the daughter of Peter Joseph and Kate O'Malley of Kilmilkin, Co. Galway.[49] Born in Kilmilkin in October 1906, her father was a member of the well-known and prosperous O'Malley family of Maum. Her mother, Kate, was the daughter of Pádraic (Páidí) Réamonn Mór and Sabina McDonogh, of the Hotel of the Isles, Lettermullan. Maura O'Malley, therefore, was T.C.'s second cousin. The O'Malleys of Kilmilkin had much in common with the McDonoghs of Lettermullan. Both families were industrious and ambitious, and by the latter part of the 1870s Maura O'Malley's grandfather, Peter O'Malley, owned 594 acres in Kilmilkin, Maum, Co. Galway. The O'Malleys were also climbing the social ladder by becoming members of the professional classes, and two of Maura O'Malley's uncles were eminent doctors in Galway. In addition, her aunt, Kathleen O'Malley, was secretary of the local branch of the Gaelic League.[50] It is unclear when, or why, Maura O'Malley came to live with the McDonogh family in Galway, but it appears that T.C., in particular, became quite attached to her, and she regularly fulfilled the role of hostess at the parties which he organized for his friends on Inishambo. Following T.C.'s death, she married Mr Arthur Wall of Dublin. She died on 21 January 1964 at the Mater Hospital in Dublin, and was buried in Kilmilkin.[51] The couple had one daughter.

The events that occurred in the hospital room of T.C. McDonogh on 9 September 1934 revealed just how different a man he was from his older

46 *Connacht Sentinel*, 20 Apr. 1937. 47 Ibid. 48 Mary Ann was 14 when her mother died in 1883, and although the family employed domestic servants, Mary Ann appears to have assumed the role of mistress of the house, while her sister Kate (aged 10 at the time of her mother's death) assumed a more active role in the family business. 49 Peter Joseph O'Malley was a son of Peter O'Malley, a shopkeeper and farmer, of Kilmilkin, Co. Galway. His brother, Dr Michael O'Malley, became professor of surgery at University College Galway, and another son, Dr Connor O'Malley, became professor of opthalmology at the same university. 50 MacPherson, D.A.J., *Women and the Irish nation: gender, culture and Irish identity, 1890–1914* (London, 2012), p. 90. 51 An obituary in the *Connacht Tribune* noted that Mrs Maura Wall was 'a member of the well-known Kilmilkin, Co. Galway, family, and was well known in Galway in the 1940s. *Connacht Tribune*, 25 Jan. 1964.

brother. The contested will had been drawn up by an English barrister, Patrick Selby Ormond, a member of the Inner Temple, who practised in Paris as an expert in international law, and who specialized 'in making and witnessing wills for foreign residents in that city'. Selby Ormond stated that he had received a phone call on 9 September 1936, as a result of which he visited the American Hospital and met with McDonogh, who was 'suffering from pneumonia, and had been examined by two very eminent Paris doctors'. McDonogh told Selby Ormond that he wished to leave a legacy of £20,000 to his cousin, Maura, and the rest of his estate to his brother, Michael. In response to Selby Ormond's question as to whether he wished to make any more legacies, McDonogh 'replied that he did not'. When McDonogh was asked the total value of his estate, he put a value of £200,000 on it. Selby Ormond expressed the view that, in his opinion, McDonogh 'was in a proper state to make a will when he executed it, and he fully understood what he had done'. Asked about his next of kin, McDonogh 'had replied that he wished to leave his estate to his brother'. There was no mention of Mary Ann McDonogh. In the event, a very public airing of McDonogh family linen was avoided when an out-of-court settlement was agreed, the terms of which were not read out in court. The will was admitted to probate, with all the parties allowed their costs out of the estate. The estate left by T.C. McDonogh amounted to £116,723, of which £20,000 was bequeathed to Mrs Maura Wall (née O'Malley).[52]

Squabbles over his will aside, the untimely death of T.C. McDonogh barely twenty-two months following the death of his older brother was recognized as a major blow to Galway, one councillor describing it as 'a catastrophe as far as Galway is concerned'.[53] And while others declared that they 'had not always seen eye to eye' with the McDonogh family, it was acknowledged that they were good employers and 'always had Galway's interests at heart'. Cllr Colman McDonogh expressed the views of many when he stated:

> Although I was opposed to Mr McDonogh in politics, I was never opposed to him in spirit. The deaths of Mr McDonogh and his brother have been a severe loss to Galway and to the country that reared them. The credit of the McDonogh family stands high in any country and as self-made men they have accomplished what no other three brothers in Ireland have accomplished.[54]

52 *Irish Times*, 20 Apr. 1937. 53 *Connacht Tribune*, 19 Sept. 1936. 54 Ibid.

Figures 10 and 11 Agnes McDonogh and Michael McDonogh

It was left to the last of the three McDonogh brothers, Michael (figure 10), to take on the role of custodian and director of the McDonogh business empire. Aged 65 at the time of T.C.'s death, Michael had, in July 1935, retired from his position of dispensary medical officer for Galway No. 2 district after thirty years service. Dr McDonogh may have intended spending his retirement enjoying his young family, but this was not to be. Although suffering ill health, he assumed the role of managing director of the McDonogh group of companies with as much energy and enthusiasm as he could muster, aided by his wife, Agnes (figure 11), who also became a director of Thomas McDonogh & Sons.[55]

Michael J. McDonogh died of bronchopneumonia and heart failure on 30 December 1947 at this home, The Villa, in Galway.[56] According to his son Thomas, his clothing had become soaked while attending a patient in bad weather, and he had contracted a chill, which had developed into a serious infection, affecting his spine. For some years prior to his death, he had experienced a degree of paralysis, which had necessitated his using a wheelchair. Still, 'his death was rather unexpected as he had been complaining of only a

55 Agnes McDonogh continued to take an active role as a director of the McDonogh group until her death on 23 May 1975. *Connacht Tribune*, 6 June 1975. 56 His death certificate noted that he had been ill for three days prior to his death, and he was attended by Dr J.M. Kennedy.

slight cold for a few days'.[57] The local press mourned his passing, and noted that 'he was as successful in his business career as he was in his medical career'.[58] He was survived by his wife, Agnes, and three children: Honor, Mafra (Mary Frances) and Thomas. As a mark of respect, on the day of his funeral, New Year's Day 1948, all Fine Gael public meetings in the West Galway constituency were cancelled. McDonogh had been president of Galway Golf Club, and the flag there was flown at half-mast and the club premises closed. Unlike his siblings, Dr McDonogh was not buried in the McDonogh family plot in Forthill. Instead, he was buried in the New Cemetery, Prospect Hill.

Mary Ann McDonogh was now the last surviving McDonogh sibling, and she continued to live at Belmore alone, except for a cook and general domestic, until her death on 22 August 1948.[59] She was 79 years old, and the cause of death was given as 'old age, without dementia, heart failure'.[60] She was buried in the family grave in Forthill Cemetery.[61] When Belmore was finally sold in 1964,[62] the auction of its contents provided a rare window into the lives of the McDonogh siblings there,[63] and revealed a wealth of good-quality antique furniture, including Sheraton mahogany chairs, tables and sideboards, Regency card tables, a Georgian stick stand, a 10-foot dining table, and 'a small but important collection of oil paintings'. Remarkably, the house also contained a grand piano by Beckhardt,[64] and, perhaps unsurprisingly, given McDonogh's lifelong love of racing, a 'set of Punchestown engravings'.[65]

LEGACY

It was said of the McDonoghs that 'they were large employers and good employers, men of the type that build nations'.[66] As, unquestionably, the foremost member of that family, how should we assess the role of Máirtín Mór McDonogh in that dynasty, and what might his legacy be? He has been

57 *Connacht Tribune*, 3 Jan. 1948. 58 Ibid. 59 She placed an advertisement for 'Cook – general; good wages to suitable person' in the *Connacht Tribune* of 26 July 1947. 60 The death certificate incorrectly records her age as 85. 61 *Irish Press*, 23 Aug. 1948. 62 The advertisement of the sale noted that the house and lands were 'held on lease from 1908 for a term of 999 years subject to £18–2–0 per annum'. *Irish Independent*, 25 Apr. 1964. 63 Thomas McDonogh, the current chairman of the McDonogh group, recalls visiting the house and remembers it as a somewhat dark and gloomy place, 'crammed with furniture'. Interview with author, 2014. 64 There is no reference to any of the McDonoghs having been musical, although Kate and/or Mary Ann McDonogh may well have been. Very little is known about them. 65 *Connacht Tribune*, 27 June 1964. 66 Ibid., 12 Sept. 1936.

called everything from an outstanding entrepreneur to a fifth columnist.[67] Writing in 1926, his friend Stephen Gwynn observed that 'Ten Martin McDonoghs would give us a different Ireland.'[68] Michael D. Higgins, on the other hand, has observed that 'To the artist and social theorist … the power of McDonogh and Sons Ltd, Trader and Importer, would seem as monstrous as that of the kulaks who betrayed the Russian Revolution.'[69] The truth, it appears, lies somewhere between these extremes. McDonogh would doubtless have taken a degree of satisfaction from an assessment of his contribution to Galway life and industry that was published two years before his death. Following his re-election as chairman of Galway harbour commissioners, an editorial in the *Connacht Tribune* pointed to the fact that McDonogh:

> long ago learned that the real stimulus to big business lay in seeing far ahead, in laying down policy and depending upon the carrying out of policy rather than upon merely working forward at random. This required not alone a big business brain, but steadfast and unfaltering courage. True, there are many who achieve comparative and even great wealth and some success by the exercise of industry alone. But the really great men operate otherwise, and in so operating they serve not merely their own interests but those of a wide humanity all around them. It has been so with Mr Martin McDonogh; and those who know him best know the almost passionate sincerity with which he desires the welfare and progress of the city to which he has given life-long service. The resurgent nation could well do with many more Martin McDonoghs in these days when reconstruction and sound business instincts are so much needed.[70]

Following his death, the same writer took up the theme that men like McDonogh were 'needed to rebuild the country', and acknowledged the debt Galway owed to McDonogh:

> Aside from the great public services, in which he never wavered once he had made up his mind to the right, he was a king amongst industrialists – in an Alpine village, perhaps, but nonetheless a king. If he had not Midas's gift of making gold, he was endowed with talents and perspi-

67 John Hosty, BMH WS 373, p. 4. 68 Gwynn, *Experiences of a literary man*, p. 294. 69 Higgins, M.D., 'Liam O'Flaherty and Peadar O'Donnell: images of rural community', in *The Crane Bag*, 9:1 (1985), 41–8. 70 *Connacht Tribune*, 18 June 1932.

> cacity that stood him in good stead throughout a business career of half a century. He brought employment to many doors, and the good cheer of a bountiful and good-natured heart when there was none. For beneath that seemingly brusque exterior there was a nature that was kindliness itself when a good deed had to be done, and could be done without ostentation.[71]

Regardless of how his name was spelt – 'Morty Mor' (St John Gogarty), 'Maurteen Mor' (Stephen Gwynn) or 'Martine Mor' (William O'Malley MP) – it is nonetheless significant that this was the name by which McDonogh was most commonly known in business, civic and political circles in Ireland and abroad. As a brand it was a most effective one, encapsulating, as it did, his large size, his dominant personality and civic position and his rootedness in the Connemara Gaeltacht, from which he had come and which always laid claim to him. In 2014 the author, speaking to a group of Connemara men, most of them in their sixties, was told that their shop of choice for all major hardware items was, and always had been, 'Tí Mháirtín Mhór' – and this was eighty years after McDonogh had died, which had been some twenty years before the men had been born. In a similar vein, Aran Islander Tomás Ó Fatharta, from Inis Meáin, recalled that when he was a young man and word reached the islands of the great McDonoghs fire of 1971,[72] the older islanders immediately set to saying decades of the rosary that 'Tí Mháirtín Mhór' would be saved, so integral was the McDonogh enterprise, and the goods it supplied, to the island population. A character as large as Máirtín Mór casts a long shadow, and it is therefore hardly surprising that, in the wake of his demise, the *Connacht Sentinel* exorted the people of Galway to strive 'by every means in our power to make the capital of Connacht worthy of a province that can breed from its iron-bound coastline such great citizens and great Irishmen as Martin McDonogh'.[73]

The fact that the death of Martin McDonogh resulted in a subtle shift in public perception of the McDonogh family is revealing of the degree to which McDonogh, personally, quite aside from his family, was held in such high esteem by the people of Galway. Two indicators of this shift in public perception may be considered. In January 1935, barely two months following

71 *Connacht Tribune*, 1 Dec. 1934. 72 On 16 August 1971, a major fire started in McDonogh's timber yard, which was completely destroyed, and soon engulfed a large block of the city centre. Fire brigades from all over Cos. Galway and Mayo were brought in to try to contain the blaze. 73 *Connacht Sentinel*, 27 Nov. 1934.

McDonogh's death, T.C. and Dr Michael McDonogh, along with Joe Young, Christopher Kerins and Martin Hynes of the Galway Race Committee, claimed compensation at the Galway circuit court for damage done to the racecourse wall as a result of ongoing agrarian troubles. The McDonogh brothers, however, also claimed £5 in respect of damage to cattle owned by them that were driven off the racecourse in the same incident. In making an award of £5,[74] Judge Wyse Power noted that 'the days had gone when people were entitled to compensation for cattle driven off land, just because they had been driven ... damage should be proved in these claims as well as in every other claim.'[75] The judge's comments were a clear rebuke to the McDonoghs, and indicated that for wealthy men such as they, the days when they could have everything their own way, without the need to prove their case, were coming to an end.[76] The second incident occurred in July of that year at a meeting of the Galway county board of health. The board were being asked to consider 'an unusual request'. Dr Michael McDonogh had recently retired from his position of dispensary medical officer for Galway No. 2 district, having completed thirty years of service. It was noted that Dr McDonogh's salary and emoluments as dispensary doctor had amounted to £353 10*s.* 2*d.*, with an additional £5 9*s.* 4*d.* paid to him as medical officer for Galway. Dr McDonogh would have been entitled to a pension of £179 14*s.* 3*d.* per annum, but he had indicated that it was at the discretion of the board 'to add years to his service if they wished'. One member of the board, Harry O'Toole, expressed his surprise 'that a gentleman like Dr McDonogh, who had so much, should ask for anything from the poor people'. Eamon Corbett TD,[77] another board member, added, 'Too much money he has. The ratepayers would not get any years added.'[78] Corbett acknowledged that there were cases where the board might have been justified in adding years to service, but, he pointedly remarked, 'this was not one of them'. Dr McDonogh's superannuation was therefore fixed at the statutory rate.

Both incidents signalled a distinct shift in the manner in which the McDonogh family were going to be handled by both civic bodies and the

74 The judge also awarded the £12 claimed by the race committee in respect of the damage to the racecourse wall. 75 *Irish Independent*, 10 Jan. 1935. 76 A more serious attack took place later that year, in Mar. 1935, when a landmine was used to blow up a stable at the racecourse in which the McDonoghs' brood mares were usually kept. The stable door was blown off, windows broken and the roof damaged, but fortunately no animals were injured, as they were not in the particular stable at the time. On that occasion the McDonoghs were awarded damages of £10. *Connacht Tribune*, 16 Mar. 1935. 77 Corbett, a Fianna Fáil TD, had been elected in the 1935 by-election in Galway to fill the seat vacated by the death of Martin McDonogh. 78 *Connacht Tribune*, 6 July 1935.

general public in the wake of Máirtín Mór's death. There was a perception that throughout his long career McDonogh had never personally benefitted from his involvement in public bodies – indeed, his purchase of the *Cathair na Gaillimhe* had been but one instance in which he had reached into his own pocket in order to supplement civic coffers – and that he had worked single-mindedly and at great personal sacrifice, to fulfil his civic commitments, despite frequent ill health, and a personal disinclination to stand for election. Apart from his love of racehorses, McDonogh had not lived ostentatiously, was a teetotaller all his life and had never been known to socialize widely. His brother Michael, however, was a well-paid public servant, and T.C. was known for dressing well and revelling in the life of a wealthy playboy – which extended to hosting his many friends (including, it was rumoured, a variety of lady friends) at lavish parties on his private island in Lough Corrib. Máirtín Mór had invested his entire life in the furtherance of Galway and its citizens, and the people of Galway acknowledged that, and forgave him his occasional outbursts and flashes of temper. They were not to be as tolerant of his siblings.

It is perhaps well that McDonogh did not live long enough to see his final home, Belmore, purchased, alongside two of the other 'once stately manions near Leisureland' – namely Revagh House and Brinkwater – by Galway corporation for the combined sum of over £100,000. The corporation's intention was that the purchase of the three properties, and the 17 acres of land surrounding them, would prevent the erosion of Salthill's 'green belt'. By 1982, however, the houses had stood empty for over ten years, and general deterioration and vandalism resulted in Belmore and Revagh House having to be demolished. The McDonogh home in Flood Street, however, where Martin McDonogh had lived most of his life, survived.

Somewhat surprisingly for a man who led such a full and varied life, he failed to leave behind an archive of personal correspondence. No private letters or other correspondence survived when Belmont was vacated, and the house cleared out after the death of his sister Mary Ann in 1948, and subsequently demolished.[79] Extensive fires in the McDonogh businesses in 1942 and 1971 destroyed many of the company's records. There are also precious few photographs of McDonogh, and none of him 'off duty' with his family.

79 The house, on three acres, was sold for more than £30,000 in June 1964 (*Irish Independent*, 11 June 1964) to Galway Corporation, who subsequently advertised the property for lease. *Connacht Tribune*, 1 Aug. 1964. The house was eventually leased to the Rehabilitation Institute, and used as a home for the physically disabled until the mid-seventies. *Western People*, 9 Jan. 1971.

The final mark that Máirtín Mór left on Galway was the great Celtic cross that marks his grave in Forthill Cemetery. Gwynn, in his obituary of McDonogh, recorded that this was originally ordered by a wealthy American. However, the Wall Street crash of 1929 bankrupted him, and was about to do the same to the unfortunate Galway stonemason who had completed the commission, and would not now receive payment. Hearing of the plight of the stonemason, McDonogh stepped in, and, 'with a quick "we can take it" he purchased the cross for eventual use by himself'.[80] While many would consider this an act of kindly generosity – tempered with a healthy dose of pragmatism – McDonogh's action was interpreted somewhat differently by some of his contemporaries. In an altercation with a fellow businessman, whom McDonogh derided by claiming, 'You're no businessman, you'll die a pauper and be buried at the side of the road', the man replied, 'Well maybe I will, but at least I won't be buried under a second-hand tombstone!'

Gwynn, whose well-observed descriptions of his long-time friend provide valuable insights into the personality of this complex man, believed that McDonogh would never have chosen such an ostentatious headstone to mark his final resting place, observing, 'I think had he ordered it, there would have been nothing but the rough-hewn stone.'[81] Perhaps.

But, then again, perhaps not. For McDonogh was very much a product of his class and of his upbringing. He could not escape the restrictions that both of these placed on him, even had he wished to do so. Success came at a price, and that price was a significant degree of isolation – self-imposed, to some degree, but also conferred by those both above and below him and his family in the social rankings. Gwynn said of another of McDonogh's friends, Lord Morris, that 'he was a kind of wonder to the country people; half alien in mind, half of their own marrow'.[82] Though not of gentry stock, like Morris, McDonogh was viewed, and viewed himself, in much the same light. On the one hand he was one of them, 'the son of a poor man who got a foothold in business',[83] and who, as a result, had given his sons the chance to make good. And there is no doubt but that the McDonoghs, as a family, assiduously orchestrated their professional success and subsequent rise up the social ladder. But it was something of a double-edged sword, as issues of class and culture impacted upon and ultimately came to define both their private and public lives. For, once ascended, the fear of middle-class slippage was ever-

80 Gwynn, *Memories of enjoyment*, p. 99. 81 The *Observer*, 2 Dec. 1934. 82 Gwynn, *A holiday in Connemara*, p. 64. 83 Ó Faoláin, S., *An Irish journey* (London, 1940).

present in the lives of the McDonoghs. In addition, McDonogh and his siblings found themselves in the difficult position that they had outgrown their humble origins on Gorumna, had become successful and wealthy, and yet, at least in the early years, were not fully accepted in the upper echelons of Galway society because they had made their money in trade. Nor indeed did they wholly wish to be accepted. The extended McDonogh/Hernon clan found both comfort and safety in keeping the circle tight, and they relied on each other to fend off the threat of those who might potentially seek to undermine them. The commercial connections with Connemara and Aran, moreover, were extremely valuable to the McDonoghs from a business perspective, and they were always careful to ensure that those connections were nurtured and protected.

That McDonogh never strayed far from his Connemara roots is evidenced by an exchange he had with Talbot Clifton in 1917, shortly after Clifton had bought Kylemore House and brought his family to live there. Clifton's wife, Violet, recorded that on a visit to the house McDonogh 'entreated him not to fly his heraldic flag – "The people will take it as an insult, they will be certain it's political; they will pull it down, and perhaps raid the house."'[84] Clearly anxious to benefit from some more of the experienced insider's advice, Clifton then asked McDonogh 'If we ask for help of the police to trace theft, will the people forgive us?' McDonogh replied "Yes, yes, you can make known a theft, but not a murder" … and did not understand why the Englishman laughed.'[85]

One significant fact that was known about the McDonoghs, and which undoubtedly blighted their lives, was the presence of tuberculosis in the family. Thomas Snr and Redmond McDonogh both died of the disease, and it is likely that the two Anthonys who died as babies were similarly affected. Because they were such a prominent family, it was impossible for the presence of TB to be hidden, and while all the members of the family would have found their marriage prospects adversely affected by this fact, it was Kate and Mary Ann who perhaps suffered most, and, having found the traditional route of marriage and children blocked to them, lived out their lives caring for their brothers and becoming respectable but socially estranged spinsters.

As for Martin McDonogh himself, we can never know for sure why he did not marry, although, as we have seen, some possible scenarios suggest themselves. But the fact that he wasn't married and didn't have an heir meant

84 Clifton, *The book of Clifton*, p. 329. 85 Ibid.

that Galway, in a sense, became his heir, and he invested it with all the care, attention and ambition that would otherwise have been given to a favoured son. To a large degree his personal ambition became fused with his ambition for Galway. Not having the responsibilities of marriage and the distractions of children meant that McDonogh did not need to trouble himself with the minutiae of ordinary family life – his sisters took care of such matters – and he instead focused his attention on the business, and, in a wider context, the 'bigger picture', as it related to Galway.

If the Kennedys of Boston were the ultimate talented and ambitious Catholic merchant family, who judiciously worked their way to the top of the social and political ladder, then the McDonoghs were their Irish cousins. For both families, there was a price to be paid for that ascent. The McDonoghs paid that price, and, as we have seen, 'had the benefit of it'. But Martin McDonogh perhaps paid a higher price than his siblings, and that price was to live a life that in many regards was not his to live as he wished. His ferocious workload saw to it that he never really had a private life as such. He was, at various times, president of a golf club, a swimming club and a rowing club, and yet he never played golf, swam or, after he had left university, rowed, as he never appears to have had the time. His chairmanship of the Galway Race Committee undoubtedly gave him a great deal of pleasure and satisfaction, but it too added to the workload he carried for most of his life. The elation he experienced when one of his horses won a race was a small but significant reward for the hard work and dedication he brought to every aspect of his life, including his love of racing.

McDonogh's size was commented on frequently throughout his life, often in the context of his physical size matching his predominance in Galway's commercial and civic life. His sheer physical presence in many ways set him apart as a towering and somewhat aloof figure, although his close friends described him as convivial, with a good sense of humour. But, here again, an interesting contradiction arises, for McDonogh was not averse to using his physical size and his gruff manner to intimidate others, including his employees, when the occasion demanded. He was, on occasion, combative, and happy to let his fists do the talking when it suited him, even to the point of threatening his fellow deputies in the Dáil chamber.

By the time McDonogh joined Cumann na nGaedheal, two of the party's founders – Arthur Griffith and Michael Collins – were already dead. However, as a lifelong nationalist and pragmatist, McDonogh found much to support in the philosophy of Collins, the former gunman, who had through his actions, both in the field and at the negotiating table, won freedom for Ireland, albeit 'not the ultimate freedom … but the freedom to achieve it'.[86] Collins had become a leader who wanted to live not die for Ireland, yet was also 'a pragmatist who recognised the work required for progress'.[87] He had recognized that 'true devotion lies not in melodramatic defiance or self-sacrifice … It is the steady, earnest effort in face of actual possibilities, towards the achievement of our hopes and visions, the laying of stone upon stone …'[88]

If nothing else, it could be argued, Martin McDonogh's life represented just such 'steady, earnest effort'. He took the hand that he had been dealt in life, and played it exceptionally well. He worked hard, and he had an entrepreneurial drive, tempered with an all-important pragmatism, which allowed him to adapt to circumstances, and seize opportunities when they presented themselves. And while undoubtedly the McDonogh business empire benefitted not only from his own management skills, but also from his actions in the public and civic arenas, this was not always the case, nor did he solely focus on projects or policies that benefitted him or his business interests. There was, throughout his life, a much broader, and deeply held, sense of civic responsibility behind much of his work, for which he strived, often at great personal cost, even if there was no obvious benefit to him. His vision was defined by his understanding, which was founded on two pillars: what was good for business and economic development, and what was good for Galway. His belief system began as local, but he was intelligent enough to realize that in order for the good of both to be served, the local needed to be extended to the national. He did not – could not – know what was coming next. All he could do was respond – and he consistently did so – in a manner that was informed by the pillars that supported his professional, public and political lives. Few could deny that he succeeded spectacularly, and his native city is still reaping the benefits of his vision.

It is to his credit that, in the face of increasing age and infirmity, when he could have done without the incessant work and travel necessitated by his Dáil career, he doggedly ploughed on, never losing sight of the main prize: a vibrant and successful Galway. It is therefore fitting that the effort McDonogh had expended throughout his long life to achieve his great

86 Michael Collins TD, Treaty Debate, Dáil Éireann, Public Session, Monday 19 Dec. 1921. 87 Simon Coveney TD, MEP, Michael Collins Commemorative Oration, Béal na Bláth, 22 Aug. 2004. 88 Collins, M., *The path to freedom* (Dublin, 1922), pp 22–3.

ambition for Galway was recognized in his home town. An editorial in the wake of his death observed:

> It was not given to him to live to see the fruition of his dream that Galway might become a great industrial distributing emporium with a new outlook on the sea and a permanent trans-oceanic port of call. Nevertheless, as a realist with a big outlook, he helped to lay the foundations of that plan, and he will deserve to be remembered with gratitude when it comes to full fruition.[89]

He did. And he does.

89 *Connacht Tribune*, 1 Dec. 1934.

Appendix A

Amhrán na Jumpers (na Wóthers)
By Maolra Ó Conchubhair

A Mhuire dhílis ní mhionnód choíchin
Nach bhfuil cionn ímpí a'ad ar Mhac na nGrást
Agus a liachtaí oíche fhada 'chaith tú a' caomhacht
I mbuaireamh aolmhar[?] agus i bhfaitíos báis
'gcúrsaí 'n Phretender nó aimsir a dhéanta [í]
Nach feasach díb-se nach mbeidh muid ann
Ach mo mhionna baoithe a thabhairt go cínnte
Gan fuil Íosa ná'n chomaoin 'fháil.

Dá mbeinn chomh gaibhtheach le Coirnéal Máirtín
Is mé 'bheith go státúil 'sa teampall mór
Ag ithe aráin ghil 's ag ól fíon Spáinneach
A' mionnú fállsa 'gus a' tabhairt mo vót'
Ní hé do chóna-sa a choinnigh ansiúd mé
Do bhuaic faoi phúdar 's do bhúclaí bróg
Ach a' trumpa buartha dar liom a chuala
'S ag Críost i gcluaise[?] tá'n bhreith á tabhairt.

Dá dtugainn fhéin mo dhá mionna dhéag
Is beagán éifeacht a bheith agam mar dhuais
San am le séidfeas an trumpa déannach
Beidh saol éitheadh ann ag rith go luath
Beidh 'n chrois chéasta ag na h-aingle 'tíocht
Beidh Críost 's a chneáchaí dá nochtadh dúinn
Ansiúd nach ndéanfaidh siad na mionnaí éithigh
Beidh cláir a n-éadain chomh dubh le gual.

Ná roud níos fearr i maoin ná in árus
Más rud é 'chaillfeas dom féin a' glóir
Is fheabhas an t-arán dom a bheith mar tá mé
Agus a-laigheadh mo chairdeas ar a saol seo beo
'Sé léas a lán dúinn ar phriocaí 'n bháis

Ar na piúnta 'tá ar na bealaí romhainn
'S go mb'fhearr an tÁrd-Rí aon uair amháin
Ná 'bhfuil de Ghallaibh agus de Choirnéil beo.

Amhrán Máirtín Mór
By Báibín an Táilliúra

Bliain an taca seo, déanadh an chreach, ní hé amháin ar Ghaillimh ach ar chuile áit sa tír,
Nuair a sciob an bás uainn an seanfhear álainn, Máirtín Mór, a bhí ina T.D.

Nuair a chuaigh an scéal brónach ar fud na háite, bhí lag agus láidir i ndólás faoi,
Mar bhí a gcaraid caillte acu a chroithfeadh láimh leo, i ngach cruachás a dteidís third.

Tráthnóna Dé Domhnach tógadh amach é, as am bparlús álainn ar chaith sé a shaol.
D'fhág sé a dheirfiúr go brónach cráite, ní inniu ná amárach, ach chuile lá dhá saol.

Bhí a dhearthair Tomás go buartha cráite, Doctúir Mícheál, is beag nár bhris a chroí.
Bhí Máire Ní Mháille ann, an óg-bhean álainn, le cúmha i ndiaidh Mháirtín, ní mhairfeadh sí.

Bhí cáil mhór go raibh de Valera go mór in éad leis, ach mo léan gear, ní mar sin a bhí,
Mar nuair a fuair sé an scéala go raibh sé éagtha, chuir sé a dhólás in iúl dóibh faoi.

Lá arna mhárach bhí Aifreann árd ann, an séipéal lán is ag dul thar maoil.
Bhí íseal is uasal as chuile chéard ann, ó fhear an bháinín go dtí an T.D.

Níl bother ná cosán ná coirnéal sráide, ó shéipeál árd go dtí an tornóg aoil,
Nach raibh mná agus páistí ag gol is ag gárthái, mar gheall ar Mháirtín ag dul sa gcill.

Ba chráidhte an t-amharc a d'feicfeá an lá sin, a cholainn álainn dhá hiompar síos,
Thar a chuid stórtha leasuighthe, a mhuileann adhmaid, a shiopa álainn, 's a stórtha síl.

Bhí a chuid báid mhóra tarraighthe sa dug an lá sin, ón mbáidín pléisiúr go dtí an soitheach seóil.
An brat a bhí orthu i gconaí i n-áirde, ní raibh said an lá sin ach ag leath an chrainn.

Chruinnigh na healaí sa gcuan an lá sin, aniar ó Árainn is ó Sruth na Maoil.
Mháirseáil said isteach ann mar bheadh saighdiúir gárda, agus bhí said roimhe ag an tornóg aoil.

Ansiúd a chloisfeá an cantal grána, iad fhéin le chéile ag déanamh bróin.
Lá arna mhárach a bhí dhá chéad díobh, iad sínte caillte le briseadh croí.

Dá mbeitheá islighthe is an chroch le fail agat, is gan an tsúil agat go dtiocfeá soar,
An trom-chlár tarrnaighe is an tsnaoim le fáisceadh, is dhá mbeadh fabhar Mháirtín agat, thiocfá soar.

Ní íseal ná uasal a thriail ar Mháirtín, nach dtug sé bia dhóibh is lóistín oiche.
Bhí croí mór fairsinge ag a dhream i gconaí, a bpocaí lán is iad go flaithiúil faoi.

Ní file mise, cé nach comhair dhom cliseadh, níl mórán ealaíon istigh i mo cheann,
Ach molaim Máirtín thar aon fhear i n-Éireann, mar thug sé cabhair dhúinn nuair a bhí muid gann.

Cén mhaith bheith ag seanachas náag síor chur síos air, a leath ní inseoinn dá mbeinn dhá scríobh le peann,
Ach tá súil le Muire, 'am is le na haon Mhac Íosa, go bhfuil an chathaoir socraithe i ríocht na nGrást.

The song of Big Martin
By Báibín an Táilliúra[1]

A year ago, we suffered the loss, not alone in Galway, but throughout the country,
When death took the lovely old man, Big Martin, who was a TD.

When the sad news spread through the land, weak and strong were in sorrow for him,
Because their friend was gone who raised a helping hand in every misfortune they had been through.

Sunday afternoon, they took him out of the beautiful parlour where he spent his life.
He left his sister broken-hearted, not today, or tomorrow, but for every day of her life.

His brother Thomas was devastated, Doctor Michael's heart was nearly broken.
Maura O'Malley was there, the beautiful young woman, she would not survive with lonliness after Martin.

It was often said that de Valera was very envious of him, but truly, that was not the case.
Because when he heard that he was dead, he sent his condolences to them.

The following morning, a High Mass was said, the chapel was full and overflowing,
Rich and poor from every corner were there, from the business man to the TD.

There isn't a road or a footpath or street corner, from the high chapel to the lime kiln,
That didn't have women and children crying and wailing because Martin was going underground.

Terrible was the sight seen that day, his beautiful corpse being carried hence.
Past his fertiliser stores, his sawmill, his beautiful shop and his grain stores.

1 Bríghidh Ní Fhlaithbheartaigh of Árd Mór national school, near Carna, collected a version of the song from Máirtín Ó Mogán of Kilkieran, Co. Galway, in 1937/8.

His big boats were anchored in the docks on that day, from pleasure yacht to sailing vessel,
The sails that were always high on them, were at half-mast that day.

The swans gathered in the bay that day, over from Aran and the Sea of Moyle.
They marched in as if they were soldier guards and they were before him at the lime kiln.

There you would hear the harsh racket, they together making sadness.
The following morning, there were two hundred of them, lying dead with broken hearts.

If you were down, and receiving the noose, and no hope of getting free,
The heavy plank pulled and the knot about to be tightened, if you had Martin's favour, you would get free.

Neither low nor high went to Martin that he didn't give them food and a night's lodgings.
His clan had always a big, expansive heart, their pockets full and always generous.

I am not a poet, although I should not flinch, there is not much of the sort inside in my head,
But I praise Martin above any man in Ireland, for he gave us help in times of want.

What's the use of reminiscing or always talking about him, I wouldn't tell half of it were I writing with a pen.
But I hope with Mary and her only son Jesus, that the seat is ready in Heaven.

Appendix B:
Hernon and McDonogh family trees

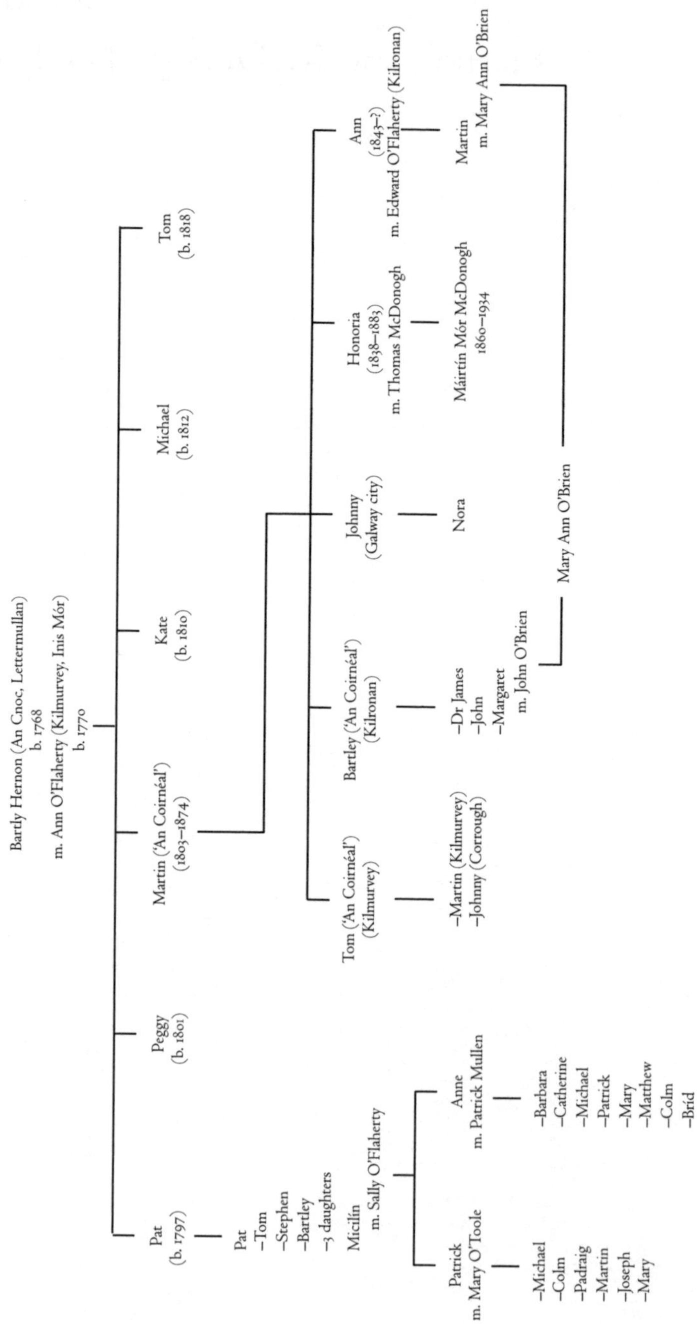
Bartly Hernon (An Cnoc, Lettermullan)
b. 1768
m. Ann O'Flaherty (Kilmurvey, Inis Mór)
b. 1770
Pat (b. 1797)
Peggy (b. 1801)
Martin ('An Coirnéal') (1803–1874)
Kate (b. 1810)
Michael (b. 1812)
Tom (b. 1818)
Pat
–Tom
–Stephen
–Bartley
–3 daughters
Micilín
m. Sally O'Flaherty
Patrick
m. Mary O'Toole
–Michael
–Colm
–Padraig
–Martin
–Joseph
–Mary
Anne
m. Patrick Mullen
–Barbara
–Catherine
–Michael
–Patrick
–Mary
–Matthew
–Colm
–Bríd
Tom ('An Coirnéal') (Kilmurvey)
–Martin (Kilmurvey)
–Johnny (Corrough)
Bartley ('An Coirnéal') (Kilronan)
–Dr James
–John
–Margaret
m. John O'Brien
Johnny (Galway city)
Nora
Honoria (1838–1883)
m. Thomas McDonogh
Máirtín Mór McDonogh
1860–1934
Ann (1843–?)
m. Edward O'Flaherty (Kilronan)
Martin
m. Mary Ann O'Brien
Mary Ann O'Brien

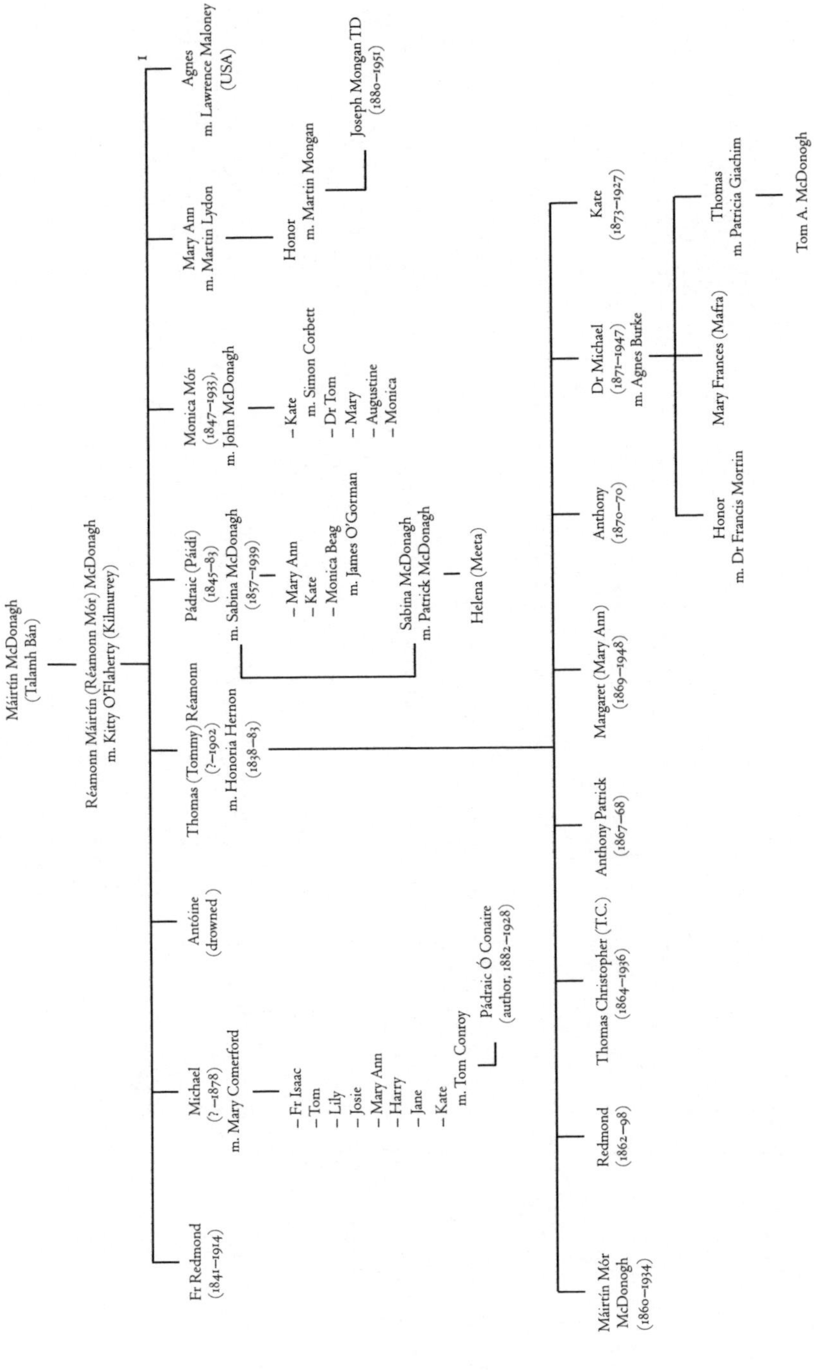

[1] Réamonn McDonagh and Kitty O'Flaherty had a total of 21 children

Index